THE CAPTAIN'S YEAR

HarperSports

An imprint of HarperCollinsPublishers

RICKY PONTING

THE CAPTAIN'S YEAR

Harper*Sports*
An imprint of HarperCollins*Publishers*

First published in Australia in 2010
by HarperCollins*Publishers* Australia Pty Limited
ABN 36 009 913 517
harpercollins.com.au

HarperCollins*Publishers*
25 Ryde Road, Pymble, Sydney, NSW 2073, Australia
31 View Road, Glenfield, Auckland 0627, New Zealand
A 53, Sector 57, Noida, UP, India
77–85 Fulham Palace Road, London, W6 8JB, United Kingdom
2 Bloor Street East, 20th floor, Toronto, Ontario M4W 1A8, Canada
10 East 53rd Street, New York NY 10022, USA

National Library of Australia Cataloguing-in-Publication data:

Ponting, Ricky.
    The Captain's Year / Ricky Ponting and Geoff Armstrong.
    1st ed.
    ISBN: 978 0 7322 8958 4 (pbk.)
    Ponting, Ricky.
    Cricket captains – Australia – Diaries.
    Cricker players – Australia – Diaries.
    Cricket – Australia.
    Cricket.
    Other Authors/Contributors: Armstrong, Geoff.
796.358092

Cover and internal design by Matt Stanton
Front cover image by Marty Melville/Getty Images
Back cover image by Robert Cianflone/Getty Images
Typeset in 11/17pt Sabon by Kirby Jones
Printed and bound in Australia by Griffin Press
70gsm Classic used by HarperCollins*Publishers* is a natural recyclable product made from wood
grown in sustainable forests. The manufacturing processes conform to the environmental
regulations in the country of origin, Finland.

5 4 3 2 1   10 11 12 13

*For everyone who played a part in making the
2009–10 cricket year one of my most enjoyable ever.*

*And especially for Rianna and Emmy,
for their unrelenting support,
love and inspiration.*

GEOFF ARMSTRONG

Ricky Ponting's co-author on *The Captain's Year*, Geoff Armstrong, has worked — as writer, editor or publisher — on more than 80 books on sport, more than 30 of them on cricket. Between 1993 and 2005, he collaborated with Steve Waugh on each of Steve's 12 books, including all of his diaries and his autobiography *Out of My Comfort Zone*, and has worked with Ricky on the current Australian captain's annual cricket book since 2006. Geoff is the author of *A Century of Summers*, the centenary history of the Sheffield Shield (featuring an epilogue by Sir Donald Bradman), *ESPN's Legends of Cricket*, which profiles 25 of the game's greatest players, *The 100 Greatest Cricketers*, and is the co-author, with Mark Gately, of *The People's Game*, a history of Australia in one-day international cricket. He has worked as co-author on books by David Boon, Ian Healy, Mike Whitney, Bob Simpson and Michael Bevan, and with Ian Russell wrote *Top 10s of Australian Test Cricket*, a study of Australian cricket statistics.

Geoff is the co-author, with Peter Thompson, of *Phar Lap*, the definitive biography of the legendary racehorse, and *They Shot Phar Lap, Didn't They?*, the story of the most remarkable of Phar Lap's many big-race victories. He also produced *And the Crowd Went Wild*, written by Ian Heads and Gary Lester to commemorate the 200-year anniversary of organised sport in Australia, and supported Wayne Bennett and Steve Crawley in the making of the great coach's two bestselling books, *Don't Die with the Music in You* and *The Man in the Mirror*.

Contents

INTRODUCTION BY RICKY PONTING XIII

CHAPTER ONE   AUSSIES ON THE RISE   1

CHAPTER TWO   INJURY CRISIS   23

CHAPTER THREE   AS GOOD AS IT GETS   45

CHAPTER FOUR   HOME, SWEET HOME   65

CHAPTER FIVE   GLENN ARCHER WOULD NEVER RETIRE HURT   103

CHAPTER SIX   RIGHT TO PLAY?   121

CHAPTER SEVEN   TOSSED AROUND   143

CHAPTER EIGHT   BACK TO BELLERIVE   163

CHAPTER NINE   THE BEST OF THE BEST   181

CHAPTER TEN   ONE DAY AFTER ANOTHER   191

CHAPTER ELEVEN   NEVER UNDERESTIMATE THE NEW ZEALANDERS   217

CHAPTER TWELVE   ANOTHER ASHES QUEST FOR THE BAGGY GREENS   263

EPILOGUE   SIX WEEKS BEHIND ENEMY LINES   299

STATISTICS   SCORES AND AVERAGES   321

PHOTOGRAPHY CREDITS   363

RUN RICKY RUN   364

CO-AUTHOR'S NOTE

In May 2009, to coincide with the launch of his 'Run Ricky Run' campaign (details of which can be found on the back page of this book), Ricky Ponting launched a page on Facebook where he interacts with his many friends and fans. As his co-author on this book, always keen to discover the background to the latest development in his cricket life, this fan page quickly became an ally, and about midway through 2009–10 it occurred to me that it could only benefit this book if we included some of Ricky's Facebook comments alongside his 'traditional' diary entries.

Consequently, throughout *The Captain's Year*, you will see features like this ...

January 15 Thanks for all the messages after my 209 today. It's an innings I will never forget and to do it in front of my family and all my fellow Tasmanians means so much to me. It's also great to have been able to do this at Bellerive Oval which has been such a part of my career. I am quite moved by some of the messages I have received and I look forward to digesting them all when I get a chance after the Test ends.

That has come straight from the Facebook page. The intention is for these grabs to provide a change of pace and a sense of immediacy to these pages that help set this book apart from our previous efforts.

The other major change we've introduced for this year's book is that, as well as recalling all the major events of the past year, Ricky also looks forward — to an Ashes series that could well shape how ... five, 10, even 50 years from now ... the sporting world measures his reputation as a cricketer and captain. Of course, given all that he has achieved — more than

12,000 Test runs and more than 13,000 ODI runs, more Test victories and ODI wins than any other captain — this is a harsh reality, but such is the magnitude of Ashes cricket, we all know that if the Australians fail to claim the urn this coming summer Ricky will be remembered as much for his Ashes setbacks as for all the remarkable things he has managed over the past 15 years (including a number of tremendous efforts against England). Conversely, if the Aussies do prevail, almost certainly he will be remembered much more as a great batsman and the captain who twice regained the Ashes, rather than the bloke who lost them in 2005 and 2009.

The stakes are high. That Ricky is fully aware of all this comes out in his Ashes Preview that starts on page 263, most notably for me when he writes:

> *In the lead-up to November 25, I want to set an example in everything I do, so that come the toss at the Gabba I will be as well-organised and well-prepared as I can possibly be. I've always tried to do that, but this time I'm pushing the bar even higher. I expect the other guys in the squad to see what I'm doing and join me on the journey. I'm looking at this series as being potentially the biggest series that I'll ever play, so I want to make sure I'm fitter and fresher than I've ever been in the past. That's the commitment I'm making to myself. If things don't work out for me, there will be no excuses ...*

As well as keeping his Facebook page regularly updated, Ricky, as usual, also made notes throughout the year on all the major events and cricket stories that impacted on him and his Australian teams. These jottings and our later conversations — allied to the truckloads of newspaper and internet reports the games he was involved in generated, his columns from the *Australian* and transcripts of interviews and media conferences he was involved in during the year — formed the basis for the book.

The Ashes Preview comes predominantly from conversations we had from mid May to the end of July, as the build-up to the series began to take shape.

In making *The Captain's Year*, Ricky and I have been grateful for the backing of a number of important people. Ricky's manager, James Henderson, and James' team at DSEG have provided constant support, as has everyone at HarperCollins, especially the legendary Graeme Jones, Julian Gray, Mel Cain, Tim Miller, Matt Stanton, Belinda Yuille and Sandy Weir. Once again, the people at Cricket Australia have been extremely helpful, and our thanks go especially to Peter Young, Philip Pope and Lachy Patterson. We also appreciate the help we've received from Alexia Pettenon, Stella Tarakson and Steve Keipert.

A variety of statistics, records, scores and averages are included through the book, and these were derived from a number of sources, including the websites *Cricinfo.com*, *cricketarchive.com* and *Howstat.com*. As with Ricky's previous four books, all the photographs come from Getty Images, and our thanks go to everyone there, especially Philippa Hutson and the posse of superb photographers who never seem to miss a moment throughout the cricket year.

Geoff Armstrong
July 28, 2010

INTRODUCTION
by Ricky Ponting

EVERY CHRISTMAS, WHEN I was a kid, one present that was always on my list was the Channel Nine *Wide World of Sports Cricket Yearbook*. It was a book that looked back on the past 12 months of cricket, and included stories by all the Nine commentators and plenty of photos of my heroes — champions like David Boon and Allan Border. There were a few pages of history in there too, so I learned a little of the game's 'good old days', just enough to realise that guys like 'Boonie' and 'AB' were following in the footsteps of some true legends. But I never really stopped to ponder the achievements of names like Don Bradman and Victor Trumper, Keith Miller and Bill O'Reilly, and while I knew that Richie Benaud had been a successful Australian leg-spinner and captain, he was to me more my favourite commentator than a former great cricketer.

Gradually, though, this thing called 'cricket history' started to grow on me a little. I remember when my uncle Greg Campbell made the Australian team for the 1989 Ashes tour, how I rushed around to his house so I could try on his brand new baggy green. When I thought about the guys who'd worn this cap before, I wasn't thinking only about my latest heroes but about the old names from the *Cricket Yearbook* too. And when I went to the Cricket Academy in Adelaide and got to work with past greats like Rod Marsh, their advice and praise meant plenty to me because they'd 'been there and done that'. One day, I wanted to be like them. So when I made my Test debut as a 20-year-old in 1995–96, one of the things that stuck with me proudly was the realisation that I was now part of a great tradition. In those days, we might not have thought of ourselves by our numbers (in my case No. 366 because I was the 366th Australian Test cricketer) — that innovation was still a couple of years away. But we knew we were members of an exclusive club, one that had at that point been going for nearly 120 years.

Since then, I've been lucky enough to visit many of the most revered sites in international cricket — places like the Long Room at Lord's and the 100,000-capacity Eden Gardens in Kolkata. I've sat in the old part of the dressing room at the SCG, where so many great players of years gone by have prepared for a day's play in a Test match, before they walked past the members and out onto the field. The Hill in Sydney might be gone and most of the grandstands have changed, but when I put myself at second slip I'm standing on the same turf as the Australian slip cordon did during the bodyline series, and I can't help but be proud of that. I might not be able to tell you who was in the slips in 1932–33, I've never looked it up or studied the old black-and-white footage, but it still gives me goosebumps thinking that I'm now doing what legends like Don Bradman and his team-mates did 70-plus years ago.

The remarkable contribution of Sir Donald to our game was really brought home to me after I was asked to give the annual Bradman Oration for 2008. In the weeks before my speech, I read more about his life and the cricket played in the years of his career, 1928 to 1948, than I'd ever done before and it was a process I really enjoyed. The Don's batting average is remarkable — essentially a hundred per innings, proof in itself of his standing as unquestionably the greatest batter of them all — but for me what stands out is the way he invigorated a nation in the years between the wars, in the days of the Great Depression. The wonderful example he set is an inspiration to all cricketers, young and old. I was lucky enough to briefly meet him one day while I was at the Cricket Academy, and it was an experience I will always remember. He was a little shorter than I am, and softly spoken, but everyone in our group was in awe of him and we listened as hard as we could, hanging on his every word.

For just about every Australian cricketer, the time we think most about the history of our game is at times like now, when an Ashes series is just around the corner. I bet most of the old champions think first about their Tests against England when they look back on their careers, and as for us current guys — well, as kids we all dreamed about playing Test matches, and most of those dreams involved the Ashes. Whether it be making a century at Lord's or the MCG or taking the vital catch and scoring the winning run, it was always about beating England. When I came into the Australian team, the first Tests I played in were against Sri Lanka, India and the West Indies and I savoured every minute. But then I was picked for the 1997 Ashes tour, and it was as if the level of importance of Test cricket shifted up a gear. You could see it in the faces and attitudes of the senior players — men like captain Mark Taylor, vice-captain Steve Waugh and wicketkeeper Ian Healy — and also in the way some of the England players struggled under the intense pressure of these contests. Part of this came from the history; that we were fighting for the same national pride that

Sir Donald and his team-mates fought for, and for possession of that precious little urn that has been the winner's prize since 1882. The atmosphere was special and unique, and I loved it. It's never changed; indeed, since England beat us in 2005 it has probably become even more intense. To me, in Australia in 2006–07 and then in England in 2009, the stakes seemed even higher.

SO WHILE I NEVER have and never will consider myself a cricket history buff, in the manner of a couple of my team-mates over the years, I have always been aware of the game's traditions and been grateful for those who forged the path on which we now tread. Similarly, I've never really been one for statistics, unless they can give us a clue as to how we can improve our game. In my view, the time for me to really ponder milestones and landmarks relating to my career will be when my career is over. However, in putting these diaries together, I do sometimes stop to wonder what record might have been set, or how does a particular achievement rank alongside the greats of the past, and in these situations I might ask my co-author, Geoff Armstrong, who is much more into cricket stats than I am, if he can find the answer for me. Or Geoff might throw a set of numbers at me and we might include them in the book. That is why, occasionally but not too often, some statistical achievements or landmarks are included in the diary entries, or in the 'breakouts' that accompany them.

This is what happened tonight when I sat down to work on this introduction to what will be my eighth cricket diary. As you will read, our preparation for England's fast-approaching tour of Australia is a constant underlying theme through these pages, and the primary focus of chapter 12, when I preview the upcoming Ashes Tests. It's Sunday, July 11, 2010, two days before the first match of our two-Test series against Pakistan, which is being played in England. We're in London, with the game that starts on Tuesday to be played at Lord's; the book is due to go to the printers in two-and-a-half weeks time, straight after the second Test at Headingley, and it will be officially launched at Coolum in Queensland on August 23.

The past few days in sport have been unbelievable, pushing our two-day game against Derbyshire that ended last Friday a long way into the background. Last week, in America, LeBron James's decision to join the NBA's Miami Heat was a colossal news story. Yesterday, at Bristol, Bangladesh beat England in an ODI for the first time in their history and then today was amazing — I trained at Lord's with my team-mates this morning and then enjoyed the afternoon with some children and their parents at a special Ponting Foundation net session, while at the same time my good mate Mark Webber raced away with the British Formula One Grand Prix and another Aussie, Cadel Evans, claimed the yellow jersey in the Tour de France. Then tonight in South Africa, football's World Cup reached its climax as Spain defeated Holland 1–0 in the final.

As a sports fan, it was exhilarating trying to keep up with it all. But I have this introduction to write, so I went back to contemplating cricket, and the Ashes and how that urn has meant so much for so long. Then I started thinking about all the great players of the past and it occurred to me, as I sat here in my hotel room, that Don Bradman and his team-mates would have been in the middle of an Ashes tour exactly 80 years ago. Again, I stress that I am not a 'tragic' when it comes to cricket history, but I am aware that 1930 was the year of The Don's extraordinary first trip to England, when he scored nearly 1000 runs in the Test series, including one triple century and two doubles. So I sent a text to Geoff, asking him if he could help with some anniversaries from that famous series. The results were fantastic.

On the night of July 11, 1930, Don Bradman would have been in his hotel room, resting after scoring an incredible 309 on the first day of the third Test at Leeds. Of course, he wouldn't have been sitting in front of a laptop as I am at the moment, but he might have had a pen in hand and paper in front of him, perhaps writing a letter back home or responding to fan mail. He made a century before lunch that day and the following morning went on to 334, which was then the highest innings ever played in Test cricket. If I could be half as lucky on Tuesday ...

August 23 was also a special day on that tour, but more so for the many people back in Australia who were following each day's play with great interest, via newspaper reports and on what was then a very recent innovation: the wireless. The Australians actually won the fifth and deciding Test of the series on August 22 but in Australia, because of the time difference, it would have been very early on August 23 when the final wicket fell. And it was during the morning of August 23 when the news would have reached the eyes and ears of most Australian cricket fans. So, in a way, the book launch will be staged 80 years to the day after Bill Woodfull's team regained the Ashes. Maybe that's an omen for us for this coming summer; it certainly wasn't planned that way when my manager James Henderson and I sat down last month with our publisher, HarperCollins, to work out the right day for the function, but it's a nice coincidence.

This book covers the period of cricket from the 2009 Champions Trophy in South Africa in September 2009 to the end of this current series against Pakistan. For us, it was a time of great success, if tempered slightly by our loss to England in last month's ODI series, and a terrific preparation for the Ashes battles ahead. I feel we've grown as a team since we lost in England in 2009, as so many members of our team became more used to the demands and stresses of big-time cricket. Men like Brad Haddin, Nathan Hauritz, Peter Siddle, Doug Bollinger and Shane Watson now know what it takes to succeed at the top level, while our more experienced players like Simon Katich, Michael Hussey, Michael Clarke and Mitchell Johnson — guys whose Ashes careers began before the 2009 series (Mitch was in our squad throughout the 2006–07 campaign, though never in our final XI) — all had excellent seasons. And while it's not for me to say whether I 'grew' as a captain, I do know that it was one of my most enjoyable years in charge, as I watched guys who've become my good mates become tough and impressive international cricketers.

The challenge now is for us to keep improving, as the great Australian teams of previous eras always did. In the months ahead, I'd love this group of players I lead to make some history of their own, to produce exceptional performances that can sit proudly and appropriately beside some of the game's most famous stories. But it won't be easy — we are definitely a better side than we were in 2009, but I'm pretty sure England will be too. It could be a classic series, fought out by two sides on the rise. As I sit here now it is all of 80 years since the Don scored 300 in a day, and just 137 days to the opening day of the first Ashes Test.

I can hardly wait.

Ricky Ponting
July 11, 2010

CHAPTER ONE
AUSSIES ON THE RISE

ICC CHAMPIONS TROPHY 2009

Friday, September 25

Game 1, Group B, at Centurion (September 22): Sri Lanka 8–319 (50 overs:
TM Dilshan 106, KC Sangakkara 54, DPMD Jayawardene 77; DW Steyn 3–47,
WD Parnell 3–79) defeated **South Africa** 7–206 (37.4 overs: GC Smith 58, JH Kallis
41; BAW Mendis 3–30) by 55 runs (D/L method)

Game 2, Group A, at Johannesburg (September 23): West Indies 133 (34.3 overs:
NO Miller 51; Mohammad Aamer 3–24, Umar Gul 3–28) lost to **Pakistan** 5–134
(30.3 overs: Umar Akmal 41*; GC Tonge 4–25) by five wickets

Game 3, Group B, at Centurion (September 24): New Zealand 214 (47.5 overs:
BB McCullum 44, LRPL Taylor 72; WD Parnell 5–57) lost to **South Africa** 5–217
(41.1 overs: AB de Villiers 70*) by five wickets

NORMALLY, THERE'S A BIT of a gap between the final date
in one of my diaries and the beginning of the next ... but not this
time.

Less than 24 hours ago, four days after the final game of the
NatWest Series in England, I was making the final changes, via
email, phone and text messages, to my '09 book, which will be
released towards the end of next month. Today, I'm in
Johannesburg preparing for the Champion's Trophy — cricket's
second most important one-day competition behind the World
Cup — which actually began three days back at Centurion with
Sri Lanka upsetting South Africa.

Our first game is tomorrow, a potentially awkward match-
up with the West Indies. The cricket train rarely stops; if I

hadn't taken a rest straight after the Ashes Tests and if I hadn't made the call to retire from Twenty20 Internationals, I reckon I would have been mentally fried by now. The stress of playing game after game, often a long way from home and with no prospect of a decent break in sight, can sometimes be a little overwhelming.

Right now, though, I'm fired up for this tournament. The Ashes loss is a vivid memory and will stay with me, I'm sure, throughout the next 18 months until we play England again, but the 6–1 win in the NatWest Series and the fact I batted so well

ANYONE CAN WIN

The Champions Trophy involves the top eight ODI teams in the world, divided into two groups with the top two in each group going through to knockout semi-finals. We're with the West Indies, Pakistan and India in Group A; England, South Africa, New Zealand and Sri Lanka are the other foursome.

It's really a tournament that anyone can win, because one bad result could be the end of you. The South Africans didn't appear to have a lot of luck against Sri Lanka in the rain-shortened game that opened proceedings, which means one more misstep and they're definitely out. Even though they beat New Zealand last night, they could still win their final Group-B game but only finish third and thus miss the semi-finals.

Because the West Indies are weakened through the absence of so many of their top players, who are involved in a pay dispute, and also because they struggled in their opener against Pakistan, everyone is telling us we'll be starting with a win.

However, I know it won't be that simple. They've still got some talent in their ranks, and if we drop our guard for even a moment they could easily embarrass us.

have left me confident about our chances and feeling good about myself.

We're the defending champions, having won the most recent staging of this event in India in 2006, and given that we've also claimed the past two World Cups, we've got a proud record to sustain.

It's not just another tournament for us.

Of course, our squad here is much changed from the group that won three years ago — with Nathan Bracken's withdrawal yesterday because of a knee injury, only Michael Clarke, Mike Hussey, Mitchell Johnson, Brett Lee, Shane Watson and I return — but I sense the desire to succeed is as strong as ever, quite an achievement given all the cricket we've played in the past 18 months.

Part of this, I guess, comes from the Ashes loss; but a larger part comes simply from the reality that there is a real opportunity here and over the next few months for young guys in our squad such as Tim Paine, Peter Siddle, Ben Hilfenfaus, Nathan Hauritz, Cameron White and Callum Ferguson to really make their mark as international cricketers.

Our original squad was: Ricky Ponting (captain), Michael Clarke (vice-captain), Nathan Bracken, Callum Ferguson, Nathan Hauritz, Ben Hilfenhaus, James Hopes, Michael Hussey, Mitchell Johnson, Brett Lee, Tim Paine, Peter Siddle, Adam Voges, Shane Watson and Cameron White.

It was very disappointing to lose Bracks, who was going really well in the games in England until his knee got the better of him. He is our highest ranked bowler in ODI cricket, at No. 6, three ahead of Mitchell Johnson, which underlines how much his absence will hurt us. Doug Bollinger, another 'young gun' with a real chance to make a name for himself, will be called into the squad.

Sunday, September 27

Game 4, Group B, at Johannesburg (September 25): Sri Lanka 212 (47.3 overs: SHT Kandamby 53, AD Mathews 52; JM Anderson 3–20, SCJ Broad 3–49) lost to **England** 4–213 (45 overs: OA Shah 44, PD Collingwood 46, EJG Morgan 62*) by six wickets

Game 5, Group A, at Johannesburg (September 26): Australia 8–275 (50 overs: RT Ponting 79, MG Johnson 73*) defeated **West Indies** 225 (46.5 overs: ADS Fletcher 54, TM Dowling 55) by 50 runs

Game 6, Group A, at Centurion (September 26): Pakistan 9–302 (50 overs: Shoaib Malik 128, Mohammad Yousuf 87; A Nehra 4–55) defeated **India** 248 (44.5 overs: G Gambhir 57, R Dravid 76, SK Raina 46) by 54 runs

THIS WAS NOT OUR finest performance, but it was better than it looks on paper. In the end we did enough to win reasonably comfortably, but there were different stages in the game — when we were 7–171 in the 40th over and then when the West Indies were 1–124 and 3–170 in reply — when an upset seemed to be on the cards.

Mitchell Johnson's effort with the bat was tremendous. He went into the game with a strangely mediocre record as a batter in one-day internationals — he was averaging less than 10 in 56 ODIs before he made a couple of decent scores in the recent NatWest Series — but he set things right in emphatic style, slamming 73 from 47 deliveries to take us to a reasonable total. And then he followed up by breaking the important second-wicket stand between Andre Fletcher and Travis Dowlin with a direct hit from mid-off. The Windies were right in the game until that moment, but from that point we controlled the contest pretty well, with none of our bowlers dominating but none of them going for a stack of runs either.

The pitch for this game wasn't too good, with some real uneven bounce a feature of the early exchanges. I would have bowled if I won the toss; instead, after Shane Watson was bowled by the first ball of the game, both Tim Paine and I copped quite a few deliveries that spat up into our gloves, and I thought we did pretty well to add 85 for the second wicket.

It was amazing how much quieter the wicket was when the Windies batted, and I think that impacted on the way our blokes bowled. They got a little frustrated when the ball didn't bounce as much, which I think explains why we conceded too many wides (16 in all), but they still stuck to their task throughout, and I was happy with that.

One real concern for us is the health of vice-captain Michael Clarke, who has suffered a recurrence of the back injury that has

PARTNERSHIPS

One thing our innings in this match underlined was the reality that it's very hard to make good totals in one-day matches without good partnerships. It's something we regularly talk about during team meetings, and I felt that this game showed that we've taken this lesson on board. It was important after Watto was dismissed so early that Tim Paine and I got things back on track, even though the wicket was playing some tricks. Then Mitch and Brett Lee and then Mitch and Nathan Hauritz worked really well together during the final 10 overs of our innings.

Partnerships were a key when we bowled, too, especially in the latter stages when we closed the game out in efficient fashion. Those last few overs have been a bit of an Achilles heel for us over the years, so I took a lot of satisfaction from the way we took 6–55 from the final 61 deliveries of the game, to clinch the game by 50 runs with 19 balls to spare.

bugged him from time to time in recent years. Pup didn't play in yesterday's game, and right at this moment I'm not too sure if he's going to appear in the Champions Trophy at all. Dougie Bollinger only arrived in South Africa today, so we only had 13 fit guys to choose from when we picked the team to face the Windies.

Tuesday, September 29

Game 7, Group B, at Johannesburg (September 27): New Zealand 7–315 (50 overs: BB McCullum 46, JD Ryder 74, MJ Guptill 66, DL Vettori 48; ST Jayasuriya 3–39) defeated **Sri Lanka** 277 (46.4 overs: TM Dilshan 41, DPMD Jayawardene 77, KMDN Kulasekara 57*; KD Mills 3–69) by 38 runs

Game 8, Group B, at Centurion (September 27): England 8–323 (50 overs: OA Shah 98, PD Collingwood 82, EJG Morgan 67; WD Parnell 3–60) defeated **South Africa** 9–301 (50 overs: GC Smith 141; JM Anderson 3–42, SCJ Broad 3–67) by 22 runs

Game 9, Group A, at Centurion (September 28): Australia 4–234 (42.3 overs: TD Paine 56, RT Ponting 65, MEK Hussey 67) v **India**. No result due to rain.

THE RESULTS OF THE past couple of days have underlined the brutal nature of this competition, in that one slip can mean you're just about gone. South Africa's first-up defeat to Sri Lanka left them in an awkward position, and then England's batters, led by Paul Collingwood, went past 300 against them last Sunday, which proved enough to knock them right out of the tournament. Twenty-four hours later, the rain came in to wash out our match against India, leaving MS Dhoni's team (who had lost their first match against Pakistan) needing results to go their way over the next couple of days if they are going to make it through to the semi-finals. Amazingly, after nine of 12 group games, only two teams — Pakistan and England — have definitely made it through to the last four and only one — West Indies — has been eliminated.

It was a shame our batting effort against the Indians was wasted. Tim Paine, Mike Hussey and I all went past fifty, and we probably would have finished with around 300, maybe a few

SWEPT AWAY

We've seen quite a bit of the Indians during the past couple of years, and we're due to see them some more during our one-day tour there next month, but there was no sense that this familiarity was lessening the competitive edge that is a feature of Australia-India clashes. By the end of 2009, we will have played India in eight Tests and 20 ODIs in a little more than two years.

A couple of moments stood out during our innings. One came when Ishant Sharma was introduced into the attack. Ishant has given me some tough moments in recent times, but on this occasion Tim Paine and I took 16 runs from his first over — two scoreless deliveries, a four and a six to Tim, a single, a wide, and then I cracked a four through the covers.

Later on, our young keeper reached his half-century with a clever reverse sweep off another occasional nemesis of mine, Harbhajan Singh, and I got the strong impression that Harbhajan wasn't overly impressed by the cheekiness of the shot.

> **September 29** I'm feeling let down this morning – by the weather! We were in a commanding position yesterday when the rain washed out our game against India. We must beat Pakistan now to ensure we go into the semis. Nothing wrong with that but it would have been nice to freshen a few of the boys up if we had beaten India. I enjoyed my knock again and am really pleased with my form. I'm feeling really good at the moment.

more, if the thunderstorm hadn't moved in. The only downside of our innings was Shane Watson's third straight ODI duck, going back to game seven of the NatWest Series. The outfield was drenched by the storm and there was no way the game could be restarted, meaning that India have to thrash the West Indies tomorrow and hope that at the same time we are beaten badly by Pakistan. At the moment, their net run-rate is significantly inferior to ours, so we are clearly in the box seat.

However, if we are going to progress to the semi-finals and beyond we'll have to do so without Michael Clarke, who is heading home so he can focus on getting his lower-back injury fixed as quickly as possible. We've still got to get approval from the ICC to make another replacement, but if it's okay most likely it will be David Hussey who comes into the squad. Our depth is being tested, maybe like never before.

Thursday, October 1

Game 10, Group B, at Johannesburg (September 29). England 146 (40.1 overs: PD Collingwood 40; GD Elliott 4–31) lost to **New Zealand** 6–147 (27.0 overs: BB McCullum 48, MJ Guptill 53; SCJ Broad 4–39) by four wickets

Game 11, Group A, at Centurion (September 30): Pakistan 6–205 (50 overs: Kamran Akmal 44, Mohammad Yousuf 45, Misbah-ul-Haq 41) lost to **Australia** 8–206 (50 overs: MEK Hussey 64) by two wickets

Game 12, Group A, at Johannesburg (September 30): West Indies 129 (36 overs: P Kumar 3–22, A Nehra 3–31) lost to **India** 3–130 (32.1 overs: V Kohli 79*)

THERE WERE SO MANY different scenarios going into these final three games. We went into our game against Pakistan needing at least a tie (or a no result) to be *certain* of our place in the semi-finals, but we knew that even if we lost narrowly we'd be okay unless India had a colossal win over the West Indies. As it turned out, our game was a thriller and though the Indians won comfortably a few hours later they needed a lot more than that to sneak into the final four. We'll be playing England at Centurion tomorrow, while Pakistan will face New Zealand in the other semi, at Johannesburg.

I've played in some terrific ODIs over the years that have since been forgotten, because they were just one game in a series or tournament but not a decider or a knockout game, and I guess our match yesterday against Pakistan will fall into this category. Once again, the Centurion pitch was tricky — it was tough to score quickly, the bounce was inconsistent and it spun quite a bit, especially at the end of the game — so 200 was a pretty fair total. At 2–140 in the 32nd over, I felt like we were cruising; at 8–187, it seemed as if we'd be beaten, but Brett Lee and Nathan Hauritz handled the pressure of the last few overs superbly, and we got ourselves in a position where we needed a score off the final delivery of the 50th over to win, and Bing and Horrie achieved that running a desperate bye. Had their keeper Kamran Akmal hit the stumps with his underarm throw the game would have been tied and Pakistan would have topped the group, but now we'll be playing in the semi-final at Centurion, which suits

TIME TO KNUCKLE DOWN

I've already had the travelling English journalists asking me just how much of a psychological advantage we can take from the 6–1 drubbing we inflicted on Andrew Strauss' team on their turf in the recent one-dayers over there. I don't think it's too much – the conditions are different here in South Africa to what we had in England, so for both teams it's a fresh start – but as I said yesterday, 'I'd much rather have won that series 6–1 going into a game like this than lost it 6–1.'

It is true that we know the England players well. Because we've played a lot of cricket against them recently, we are aware of their strengths and weaknesses. We were able to exploit this during the NatWest Series, so now it's a matter of us doing that again. Most certainly, there'll be no excuses from us – our batsmen are in terrific touch at the moment, so we just have to knuckle down and make some big scores in the semi and (if we win that game) in the final, too.

us as we feel like we're coming to grips with the conditions there. And, given what happened in the recent NatWest series, we have to feel good about the fact we're playing England ...

Though please don't ask me — as I'm sure a number of people will — if a win against Strauss' side will be some compensation for the Ashes loss. This is a huge game for us, a semi-final in one of cricket's most important competitions.

But it won't be.

Saturday, October 3

Game 13, First Semi-Final, at Centurion (October 2): England 257 (47.4 overs: LJ Wright 48, TT Bresnan 80; PM Siddle 3–55) lost to **Australia** 1–258 (41.5 overs: SR Watson 136*, RT Ponting 111*) by nine wickets

Game 14, Second Semi-Final, at Johannesburg (October 3): Pakistan 9–233 (50 overs: Mohammad Yousuf 45, Umar Akmal 55; IG Butler 4–44, DL Vettori 3–43) lost to **New Zealand** 5–234 (47.5 overs: GD Elliott 75*, DL Vettori 41) by five wickets

TAKE OUT THE SECOND half of England's innings, and our performance in this semi-final was one of the best I've been a part of in one-day cricket. We lost the toss, but bowled beautifully to reduce them to 6–101 in the 21st over, with the wickets spread between four bowlers — Peter Siddle, Mitchell Johnson, Brett Lee and Shane Watson — and with keeper Tim Paine and James Hopes at square-leg each having taken an excellent catch. The pitch was a new one, quicker and truer than the previous decks we'd played on at Centurion, and all our bowlers were in super form until Luke Wright and Tim Bresnan mounted a surprise counterattack that allowed England to finish with a competitive total.

In reply, Painey was dismissed in the second over, but from there I was involved in one of the most enjoyable partnerships of my career, as Watto and I went all the way to the win, adding 252 in 40.2 overs. This was the highest partnership by a pair of Australians in ODI cricket, beating the old Aussie record of 237 I'd held with Andrew Symonds (versus Sri Lanka in Sydney in 2005–06) and the ninth highest by batters from any team. I also scored my 12,000th ODI run, becoming the third man, after Sachin Tendulkar and Sanath Jayasuriya, to reach this landmark. And I thought I batted really well, miscuing my first drive off Graham Onions but middling pretty much everything else.

But Watto was even better, almost Matthew Hayden-like at times in the way he dominated proceedings. He reached his century with a huge six off Jimmy Anderson and put a fantastic seal on our victory by hitting his fifth, six and seventh sixes in the space of four balls during Paul Collingwood's last over. The closest Shane came to getting out was when he was 41, when he hit Graeme

Swann out towards the long-on boundary, where Wright gallantly tried to make an over-head catch but only succeeded in helping the ball over the boundary for six. The ground at Centurion isn't the biggest in world cricket, but gee it felt small the way Watto was belting them. When he's in this sort of mood there isn't a venue in world cricket big enough to rein in his biggest hits.

There were extended periods when I felt like we had *total* control of the game. There was a stage, though, when I had to work hard with Watto to keep him on track, and I took plenty of satisfaction from the way I went about this task. It's funny with some blokes who bat at the top of the innings, how they can look a million dollars when the ball is new and the field is up, but then in the 'middle overs', when the fielders go back, the run-rate drops a little and the bowling is not as quick, suddenly batting gets a lot harder for them. It's as if they're compelled to keep going at six, seven, eight runs an over, even though the game situation doesn't ask for that. I kept saying to Watto, 'Don't force things, mate, take the singles.' In my view, the way Watto refocused was one of the most impressive aspects of his innings, and from about 100 runs out we were always going to win. It did help that we've played a lot of cricket against England in recent times — there was nothing about the way Onions, Anderson and the rest of them bowled that was going to surprise us.

The game did have its bizarre moment, too, at the beginning of our innings when play had to be delayed because the ground was invaded by what I can best describe as large flying ants. Otherwise, the evening was just about perfect. I was really pleased with the way the boys approached the occasion, a point I made at the post game media conference.

'When we took the field I think we had a different sort of energy and aura about us than we probably have had for a

ICC AWARDS 2009

The night before our semi-final, the ICC's player-of-the-year awards were presented at a function in Jo'burg, and the big winner was our very own Mitchell Johnson, who edged out MS Dhoni, Gautam Gambhir and Andrew Strauss to be named the overall cricketer of the year. Gambhir is the Test player of the year and Dhoni won the ODI award.

It is true that Mitch was below his best at times during the Ashes series, but before that he was outstanding home and away against South Africa, and his form in the other Tests during the 12 months in question, and as a bowler in ODI cricket, was very good. So in a year in which there was no real standout candidate, I felt he was a deserving winner.

Cricketer of the Year: Mitchell Johnson (Australia)

Test Player of the Year: Gautam Gambhir (India)

ODI Player of the Year: MS Dhoni (India)

Captain of the Year: MS Dhoni (India)

Emerging Player of the Year: Peter Siddle (Australia)

T20I Performance of the Year: Tillekeratne Dilshan (Sri Lanka)

Test Team of the Year: Gautam Gambhir (India), Andrew Strauss (England), AB de Villiers (South Africa), Sachin Tendulkar (India), Thilan Samaraweera (Sri Lanka), Michael Clarke (Australia), MS Dhoni (India, captain), Shakib Al Hasan (Bangladesh), Mitchell Johnson (Australia), Stuart Broad (England), Dale Steyn (South Africa); 12th man: Harbhajan Singh (India)

ODI Team of the Year: Virender Sehwag (India), Chris Gayle (West Indies), Kevin Pietersen (England), Tillakaratne Dilshan (Sri Lanka), Yuvraj Singh (India), Martin Guptill (New Zealand), MS Dhoni (India, captain), Andrew Flintoff (England), Nuwan Kulasekara (Sri Lanka), Ajantha Mendis (Sri Lanka), Umar Gul (Pakistan); 12th man: Thilan Thushara (Sri Lanka)

Umpire of the Year: Aleem Dar (Pakistan)

Spirit of Cricket Award: New Zealand

Associate & Affiliate Player of the Year: William Porterfield (Ireland)

Women's Cricketer of the Year: Claire Taylor (England)

while,' I said. 'I pride myself on big games and I think all us experienced players do. It's up to players like myself to set the example and lead from the front. Most of our experienced guys did that for us today, when it mattered.'

The concept of setting a good example really resonates with me. You can't fake it, but if you are up for a game why not let everyone know it? I was one of the first guys down in the hotel foyer waiting for the bus at 12 o'clock, and by the time the game started I was fair dinkum jumping out of my skin. Even after five months on the road, after more than 14 years in the Australian set-up, I still get goosebumps before the big games!

Tonight, we learned that our opponents in the final will be New Zealand, who despite some injury worries have now won three games straight after losing their first game to South Africa. They will be a tough opponent, but before I start thinking too much about them I'm revelling in our achievement in getting to the final despite being without injured guys like Michael Clarke, Nathan Bracken, Shaun Marsh and Brad Haddin. Very few players in our squad had ever appeared in a tournament as big as this before, but as a group we've handled the pressure really well and I can't help but be encouraged by what we've done.

But I won't be totally happy until we've produced an even better performance in the final.

> **October 3** Great win by the boys last night and there's a real buzz around the breakfast room this morning. This group has worked so hard over the past two months and deserves its chance to win the Champions Trophy. I'm very proud of this team but we need to keep a lid on things and have ourselves 100 per cent ready for the game on Monday. We have today off so will be keeping an eye on the other semi to see who we will be playing.

Sunday, October 4

I REALLY LIKE THE CURRENT Champion's Trophy format. The contrast with the World Cup, which has become increasingly drawn out during my career, is huge, and while the World Cup — as our pivotal ODI competition — needs to be a more elaborate event than any other on the cricket calendar, I think there is something to be learned from the way this tournament here in South Africa has been staged. The simple format has meant that every match matters, which has to be a good thing.

'I think it's been an excellent tournament,' I said at a media conference today. 'It's been very rushed for us and England, coming in as late as we did. But this has certainly been the best and most enjoyable Champions Trophy that I've played in. People in this country and all over the world have enjoyed the one-day cricket played over the last couple of weeks. These events are about showcasing the game, and I think the ICC and the players have done a terrific job of making this tournament a spectacle for the 50-over game.'

With the rise of Twenty20 cricket there has been plenty of conjecture about the future of the 50-over game, whether it should be reduced maybe to 40 overs a side, or maybe even eliminated. I remember Shane Warne wrote an article late in the recent Ashes series when he said that it should be phased out, but I don't think that's right. People forget how important the World Cup is, and how popular 50-over cricket has been for the past 30 years. Played right, it's a terrific game and a superb advertisement for our sport.

'The key issues with the 50-over game come down to the way teams want to play it,' I said when the subject was raised today. 'The middle overs have been what the administrators have been worried about. Bringing powerplays into the game has added a

IN CONTROL

I've had a terrific run with the bat over the past month, and it's not hard to attribute at least part of my good form to the break I had straight after the Ashes Tests. Since I've come back I've felt good at the crease and, most importantly, I've felt in control. Whether I'm batting or leading the side, I always want to feel that way; when I look back on my most successful days as a cricketer, one constant has been that sense of authority that comes with being on top of things. There's no clutter, I'm more focused and the game is so much more enjoyable.

The shot against England that got me to 12,000 ODI runs was a pull shot off Graham Onions. At the time, I had no idea I was approaching this landmark – no one had mentioned it prior to the game – and it was a bit weird hearing the crowd applauding and then to look up on the scoreboard to see what I had done. 'It is a nice achievement,' I said afterwards, '(but) I just hit runs for my country. When my career is over I can reflect on the successes.'

different dimension to it. If you want to play the game as best you can, as a batting side, you have to maximise those middle overs. If you do that, you'll make good scores. The more attractive the players can make the game, the more the fans will enjoy it as well.'

Wednesday, October 7

Game 15, Final, at Centurion (October 5): New Zealand 9–200 (50 overs: MJ Guptill 40; NM Hauritz 3–37) lost to Australia 4–206 (45.2 overs: SR Watson 105*, CL White 62; KD Mills 3–27) by six wickets

I WAS VERY CONFIDENT going into the final. The thing I couldn't help thinking was that if we won the Champions Trophy we could actually say that we'd had a pretty good last six months ... except for the Ashes. Of course, that is a mighty big 'except', but we have won a Test series in South Africa, one-day series against Pakistan and England, and now we've played really well here. In the process, a number of young guys have played a fair chunk of international cricket, often in high-pressure situations, and come through with their reputations enhanced. More and more, I'm liking the concept of this current group of players taking the Australian team forward over the next one or two years.

We bowled well in the final to keep New Zealand to 200. There was a slight hiccup at the start of our innings, when we lost two wickets in the first 14 balls (Paine 1, Ponting 1), but Shane Watson and Cameron White were magnificent and in the end we cruised to a big win. To watch Watto and Bear — two blokes who have really developed as international cricketers in the past 12 months — play so professionally to get us across the line was very satisfying. It was one of the great strengths of most Australian cricket teams of the past 15 years that if the bigger names didn't stand up, then someone else always put his hand up to get the job done. In the final here it was Nathan Hauritz and Peter Siddle with the ball, and then Shane and Cameron with the bat who did a great job for us. None of this quartet have been regulars in the Australian ODI team over the past two years, but on this big stage — when it mattered — they were outstanding. In the process, we became the first team to win the Champions Trophy twice.

Australia-New Zealand clashes always have a bit of a special edge — whether they be cricket, netball, rugby league or rugby union — and we expected this one to be no different. We also had the memory of the recent Chappell-Hadlee Trophy series, which ended 2–2 after the Kiwis won the first two games, to remind us that anything less than our best wouldn't be good enough. As it turned out, the key moment probably came when we were 2–41 in the 18th over, when Cameron top-edged an attempted pull off Ian Butler. The ball went high in the air … but keeper Brendon McCullum, who was also captaining the Black Caps because Daniel Vettori had hurt a hamstring, spilled the difficult chance. The next wicket didn't fall until we reached 134 in the 35th over, by which time Watto was in command. With Callum Ferguson having damaged his knee in the field, Mike Hussey and then James Hopes prevented any late-innings drama, and we ended up prevailing with 28 balls to spare.

Unfortunately, Callum's injury looks a serious one. The talk is he'll need a reconstruction, which will keep him out of the game for six to 12 months. It's a terrible blow for him and for the team — he'd played really well in South Africa and in England, and while he didn't get too many chances in this tournament he was still entrenched in the side. One thing that really impressed me was that even though Callum was really worried that he'd done some serious damage — he's had knee problems before, having ruptured an anterior cruciate ligament when he was in the Australian under–19 team — he was still keen to bat if he could. Instead of sitting forlornly in the dressing room letting the joint stiffen up, he was walking around, with his bat and gloves out ready to go, just in case. Our great hope is that he can make it back as good as new and then push hard for a place in our squad for the 2011 World Cup.

At the post-match presentation we each received a white jacket as a memento of our victory, which I guess is cricket's answer to the green jacket they give the winning golfer at the US Masters each year. Recently, I was contacted by some people from the Tasmanian Cricket Museum in Hobart, who intend to create a 'Ricky Ponting Corner' that will feature some memorabilia from my career, and they asked if I had anything I could spare. As soon as I saw the white jackets, I thought of the Hobart Museum and resolved to get the jacket to them in time for the exhibition's opening during the Australian season.

For some of the team, including me, now it's back to Australia for a little break before we head to India for seven ODIs. However, the guys from New South Wales and Victoria (Brett Lee, Doug Bollinger, Nathan Hauritz, Cameron White, Peter Siddle and David Hussey) are off to India early, for the lucrative Twenty20 Champions League, which — especially in the case of Sidds — is not, in my view, ideal. The big Victorian has been charging in for five months now, and at the end of his last spell in the final he was doing it pretty tough, but instead of even a short break he remains on duty. Once again, I couldn't help but think that if we don't pay more attention to some guys' workloads, then careers are going to be cut short, or at least they might not be as productive as they otherwise could have been.

THE REAL WATTO

Shane Watson followed up his man-of-the-match performance in the semi-final with another 'best on ground' effort in the final, scoring an unbeaten 105 to guide us to victory, including successive sixes off the last two balls of the tournament. After the game I found it hard to contain my enthusiasm about the way he played.

'I think in the last couple of months of his cricket life, we've started to really see the real Shane Watson,' I said. 'Getting his opportunity in the Ashes to open the batting – a position he is not really accustomed to – he played beautifully there.'

The thing is, he's not just looking fantastic at the top of the order; he's also doing a good job for us with the ball. It can't be easy, bowling 10 overs and then walking out to open the batting, but right at the moment he's handling the challenge really well. Now Watto is back to full fitness, he's showing everybody just how good a cricketer he can be.

Thursday, October 8

A REMINDER OF JUST how quickly cricket moves these days came only hours after I landed back in Sydney — I hadn't even had time to get on the golf course when the schedule for the 2010–11 Ashes series was announced. As has usually been the case since 1928–29, the first Test will be played in Brisbane, followed by Adelaide, Perth, Melbourne and Sydney.

'Australian cricket fans always love an Ashes series,' Cricket Australia CEO James Sutherland was quoted as saying. 'I know we have only just finished an Ashes series in England but I also know that the Aussie players — and Australian cricket in general — are already thinking about the Ashes series which starts in just over 12 months.'

He was right about that. We all know there is a lot of cricket — Tests, ODIs and Twenty20 — to be played before we get to November 2010, and we are also fully aware that you should never get too far ahead of yourself. But the memories of those scenes at the Oval after we lost the fifth Test a few weeks back are still vivid, and I won't rest until the urn is back in Australian hands. The recent one-dayers in England and the Champions Trophy victory are just the first stages in the process of getting Australian cricket back on top. My strong ambition is that by the time the '10–11 Ashes series and then the 2011 World Cup three months later are over, the revival will be complete.

> **October 8** Thanks to all of you that have left congratulatory messages over the last few days. Yes, it's great to be back as the No.1 ranked ODI team in the world and personally, I've really enjoyed the last month of games. Time to rest now and get ready for a big ODI series in India later this month.

CHAPTER TWO
INJURY CRISIS

THE AUSTRALIANS IN INDIA, OCTOBER 20–NOVEMBER 4, 2009

Friday, October 9

BEFORE THEY COULD PICK the Aussie team to go to India for a series of seven ODIs, the selectors first had to work out who is fit enough for the tour and who is not. In the end, Michael Clarke (back), Brad Haddin (finger), Callum Ferguson (knee) and Nathan Bracken (knee) were not considered, Mike Hussey was officially named vice-captain, and a 22-year-old left-arm finger spinner from Victoria, Jon Holland, was the surprise selection. I must confess to not knowing too much about Jon — the only time I've faced his bowling was in the MCG nets in the lead-up to the Boxing Day Test last season — but the guys from the Victorian Shield team speak highly of him and I like the logic of bringing a talented young slow bowler on tour, to give him a close-up view of how the Australian team set-up works and to gain some experience in Indian conditions. I'm not sure how many games he'll play, but the next few weeks will be valuable for him ... and for us.

Tim Paine has been given a further chance to impress as Hadds' one-day 'shadow', while Shaun Marsh comes back after recovering from a torn hamstring. The full squad, which was announced yesterday, is: Ricky Ponting (captain), Michael Hussey (vice-captain), Doug Bollinger, Nathan Hauritz, Jon Holland, Ben Hilfenhaus, James Hopes, Mitchell Johnson, Brett

Lee, Shaun Marsh, Tim Paine, Peter Siddle, Adam Voges, Shane Watson and Cameron White.

We are scheduled to arrive in Mumbai on October 20, with the first game being five days later in Vadodara, and my intention is to take things as quietly as possible over the next week or so. There was a stage when I found it hard to 'switch off' for just a few days, but I think I manage my time away from cricket better these days, which has made me a more effective player whenever I return to the game after a short break.

> **October 12** Having a good break and looking forward to a few games of golf this week. Rianna and I are also planning a few days in Melbourne and might even get to the Caulfield Cup on Saturday.

Friday, October 16

I DID TRY TO think about cricket as little as possible over the past week, but that's never easy — especially this time of the year, with the tour of India just around the corner and the Australian home season fast approaching. More than once, I've tuned in to watch a little of the Twenty20 Champions League from India, and I can't help but be impressed with how NSW and Victoria have been going. The final is still a week away, but at this stage both Aussie teams appear to have a real chance of taking out the tournament, which might surprise a few people outside Australia who have not rated us too highly as a T20 nation.

Another prominent news story in world cricket has been the settling of the West Indies players' dispute with their board, which clears the way for a full-strength team to tour Australia this season. I'm really glad this has happened, because I'd much rather face a side containing guys like Chris Gayle, Shivnarine Chanderpaul, Ramnaresh Sarwan and Jerome Taylor than the much-weakened outfit that was embarrassed by Bangladesh earlier this year and then lost all three of their matches at the recent Champions Trophy. The competitor in me much prefers a genuine contest; at this stage of my career I want every game I play to be a genuine test, to give me a chance to keep improving as a cricketer and captain.

October 20 Have arrived in Mumbai after a long trip from home. Big tour ahead and we are looking forward to the rest of the squad joining us after the Champions League ends. It's a bit strange only having half our squad with us – there's so many of the guys playing for NSW and Victoria. Their semi will be a beauty and we are looking forward to watching it. Doing my arrival press conference shortly.

Thursday, October 22

WE LEFT AUSTRALIA LAST Tuesday, three days after Rianna and I were lucky enough to be on course to see the master horseman Bart Cummings win his seventh Caulfield Cup with last year's Melbourne Cup winner Viewed. If I could get better with age the way Bart does, then maybe I will be a chance to make it back to England for the 2013 Ashes tour! I didn't back Viewed and none in the group I was with did either; in fact, the only bloke I know who backed it was my dad, and he was on the phone straightaway to tell me what a good judge he is.

Since landing in India, we have been working hard at the Mumbai Cricket Association's training facility, and pondering exactly what to do with our team for the opening game in Vadodara (we leave for there tomorrow). One thing that is making life a little awkward for us is that NSW is still involved in the T20 Champions League, and the Victorian guys only joined up with us today, after they lost to the Blues in a semi-final at Delhi last night. The final is tomorrow — NSW v Trinidad and Tobago — and only after that will we have our full squad together.

One nice selection quandary we have is what to do at the top of the batting order. Shaun Marsh was going pretty well as an opening bat until he was injured earlier in the year, and it would be good to give him more opportunities, but Tim Paine and Shane Watson were terrific in the games in England and at the Champions Trophy, so it would be hard to split them up. With Michael Clarke and Callum Ferguson out, we have the option of tweaking the opening partnership and playing either Tim or Shane in the middle order, or instead playing Adam Voges and Cameron White in the top six, which would give us the luxury of having six front-line bowlers (Watson and five

A NEW T20 CAPTAIN

Just before we left for Mumbai, Michael Clarke was officially named as Australia's new Twenty20 captain. It would have been a great shock if anyone else had been appointed and I certainly feel it is the right call.

Pup has always done a terrific job as Aussie skipper on the occasions I've been absent, be it in T20 or ODI cricket, and his effort in the recent one-dayers in England, when he led the team to three straight victories (after winning the series against Pakistan earlier in 2009) only added to his credentials.

from Hauritz, Hilfenhaus, Hopes, Johnson, Lee and Siddle) with Adam and Cameron also capable of sending down an over or three.

As I said at Sydney Airport before we departed: 'Whichever way we go there we know we've got very good depth in our batting ... hopefully we get it right on the morning of the first game.'

The way most people are talking, given our winning performance in South Africa and the fact we've regained our No. 1 ranking, we'll be going into this series as slight favourites. That's the feel I got from Tuesday's media conference, held straight after we arrived in Mumbai, and then at the media session that was conducted after training yesterday. But I'm not sure about that. Yes, we're in form, but we have got a few blokes out. And India are still No. 2 in the world and they are always particularly hard to beat at home. They definitely play a lot better on their own turf than they do when they travel.

At the same time, I've learned to handle the lifestyle, culture and cricket conditions in India much better than I did when I first toured the subcontinent and this has helped me to play some of my better cricket here over the past four or five years.

The rivalry between the two teams has definitely grown over the past few seasons, which I think is good for international cricket. I'll be astonished if this isn't a very entertaining series.

Saturday, October 24

FRESH FROM THEIR T20 Champions League win last night, the NSW boys joined us at 8.30 tonight and seemed extremely

IT HAS TO MATTER

I think there is a real worry about one-day series like the one we played recently in England and this one we're about to start here, in that there isn't really anything other than pride and prizemoney on the line in terms of the series result. It's all about context. It would be much better if these games mattered for something beyond the series itself. Maybe we need to create a genuine world championship table, with a winner crowned after 12 months or two years, to build interest in all the ODIs played across the planet.

'The way that one-day cricket is played at the moment, with one-off series like this, until there is a points system in place then it might get to the same sort of situation as it did in the UK,' I said a couple of days ago when the subject was raised by a reporter. 'We were 4–0 up after four games (on the way to a 6–1 series victory) and all of a sudden there is talk of teams rotating players in and out and doing all sorts of things. The important thing is we make sure that every game of 50-over cricket has some significant meaning.'

keen to talk about their triumph. I guess they're entitled — it was a great victory, and I was especially taken with the way Simon Katich led the Blues in the final. Kato could have used Stuart Clark, Dougie Bollinger or even Nathan Hauritz to open the bowling with Brett Lee, but instead he threw the ball to the young leg-spinning all-rounder Steve Smith and the move worked pretty well. Smith's first three balls did go for four, four, six, but he took a wicket later in the over to leave Trinidad and Tobago 2–21 chasing 160. They couldn't recover.

It's been a bit hard for us, trying to prepare properly for an ODI series but having some of our key players arriving so late. We have to be up at 7am tomorrow to get to the ground for a morning start, which means the Blues boys will have had precious little time with us before the first game gets underway. That doesn't seem right to me.

I have to say that the Champions League didn't appear to capture the imagination of the locals as I'm sure the organisers would have expected. The cricket was excellent and there was some interest in the games, but there wasn't the same fervour for this competition as there is when the Indian national team is playing. From our perspective, the form of Brett Lee was probably the No. 1 highlight: he was named man of the match in the final and also won the player-of-the-tournament award. Bing's been going really well since he recovered from the injuries that kept him out of the Ashes series, and will most likely be a key man for us in all forms of the game during the upcoming season.

> **October 24** Great win to the NSW boys last night. Binga was sensational and thoroughly deserved his player-of-the-match and player-of-the-series awards. He's in excellent form and I'm looking forward to him continuing to spearhead our attack in this series. Everyone coming together today, which will enable us to round off our preparation for tomorrow night.

Monday, October 26

First ODI, at Vadodara (October 25): Australia 8–292 (50 overs: TD Paine 50, RT Ponting 74, CL White 51, MEK Hussey 73; I Sharma 3–50) defeated **India** 8–288 (50 overs: G Gambhir 68, Harbhajan Singh 49, P Kumar 40) by four runs

IT'S FUNNY HOW AN injury 'crisis' (as the press always like to call it) can sneak up on you. One day, you've got one or two blokes out and it's all about the opportunities that have been created for players who might have been on the fringe of the team for a while. Even with three or four guys out, you still have faith in the replacement players. But then, when the sixth or seventh guy falls over you're suddenly welcoming blokes into the squad who you've never met, men are being asked to take on roles they've never coped with before, and as captain you're wondering who is the right bloke to turn to. In this situation, things often turn bad but they can work in your favour, too — if the more experienced guys can handle more responsibilities and the new players rise to the challenge of being called unexpectedly into the side.

A long career in international cricket can start because of an injury to another player, such as when Jason Gillespie came into

NOT WELL ENOUGH

I would have been desperately disappointed if we didn't win this game after holding the upper hand for so long. In the end, we needed Peter Siddle to bowl a cool last over and it turned out to be a great experience for him. Harbhajan Singh had been threatening to steal the game away from us but Sidds bowled him second ball of the over, then conceded just three runs from the final four balls and we were home.

Afterwards, I was more concerned with the way we performed in the last few overs, rather than thinking too much about how well Harbhajan batted (though he did make things interesting, smashing 49 from 31 balls).

'I think our bowling in the last 10 overs ... I don't think that we can be that bad again,' I said, after being asked whether I was worried he was going to take the game away from us.

'But Harbhajan did play well, didn't he?' someone asked.

'He played well,' I responded with a hint of a grin. 'But not well enough.'

the 1996 World Cup squad when Craig McDermott was hurt, or when Damien Martyn was recalled to the Test XI after I had to pull out of the tour of New Zealand in early 2001. Glenn McGrath's great career really began in the West Indies in 1995, when he was asked to lead our pace attack after McDermott and Damien Fleming were injured, and he handled this new responsibility superbly. Then there was Ben Hilfenhaus in England recently — he wouldn't have played in the first Test if Brett Lee had been fit, but Bing had to withdraw and Hilfy went on to be the Ashes series' leading wicket-taker.

So here I am now, 24 hours after our tight one-day win in Vadodara, wondering if someone might take a similar big leap forward on this tour. The big negative of the win was the leg injury to James Hopes, which looks like it will keep him out for at least the next few games of the series. My understanding is that we'll definitely be calling for a replacement, most likely Moises Henriques from NSW. My worry is that with guys such as James, Michael Clarke, Brad Haddin and Nathan Bracken all unavailable, we're really starting to lack players who have experienced playing ODI cricket in India; some of our young blokes are about to go on a very steep learning curve.

And things could be even worse if Mitchell Johnson's ankle keeps him out for a while or if Brett Lee's elbow doesn't improve. Bing got a little sore towards the end of his second spell; he went

October 27 It worries me a lot that we have a growing number of injuries creeping into our squads. It's to be expected with the amount of cricket we are playing and reinforces the need to have an individual workload management plan in place for the squads in all three forms of the game. Not sure if Mitch will come up for the game either. Not good.

off and had it looked at, came back to field for the rest of the game, but said he wasn't quite right to bowl when I talked to him before the 48th over.

With James unable to give us more than two overs and Bing unable to bowl at the end, I think we did a terrific job to win the game. It was a tough decision not to send them in (I heard that MS Dhoni said he would have bowled if he had won the toss) but we batted really well — the only criticism being that none of the top-order guys who got starts went on to a really big score — and then we bowled and fielded just well enough to hold on. The key moment came when Mitch trapped Gautam Gambhir lbw at the start of their last powerplay, when they were 3–167 in the 35th over. But our best bowler was Nathan Hauritz, who started with a maiden when India were 2–101, conceded just 15 runs from his first seven overs, and finished with 1–34 from nine. We all know there was a lot of controversy about our decision to leave Horrie out of the final Ashes Test, but since then he has been magnificent in ODI cricket and you have to say he is really established in this side.

About the only thing I'm not happy about — other than the injuries — is the way we finished the game. Hopefully, we'll learn from the way we bowled and fielded in the last 10 overs (which went for 87 runs) and especially how we performed from overs 46 to 49 (when we conceded 54 runs). We should have been able to close the game out, rather than give them a chance to steal a win. Shane Watson is usually one of our most dependable bowlers in the final overs, but his last over — the 49th of the innings — went for 20 (a six, three fours and two singles) and almost cost us dearly, as that left them needing just nine from the final six deliveries.

'He's got a bit to work on,' I said when asked about Watto's last over during the post-match interview. I could have been talking about all of us.

Thursday, October 29

Second ODI, at Nagpur (October 28): India 7–354 (50 overs: V Sehwag 40, G Gambhir 76, MS Dhoni 124, SK Raina 62; MG Johnson 3–75) defeated **Australia** 255 (48.3 overs: MEK Hussey 53; RA Jadeja 3–35) by 99 runs

I'M PRETTY SURE THIS is the worst injury run we've had in my time with the Australian team. The most recent victim of this 'curse' is Tim Paine, who busted his left ring finger while trying to glove a Peter Siddle bumper early on during our heavy loss at Nagpur. Painey gallantly kept going for the rest of the game, even taking two catches and being involved in a run out, but he'll be going home as soon as possible. His replacement will be Graham Manou, who went to England for the Ashes Tests as our second keeper but couldn't be considered for the NatWest Series or the Champions Trophy because of a hand he damaged while making his Test debut at Edgbaston.

TWIN PASSPORTS

The initial prognosis on James Hopes' hamstring was correct – he is going to be missing for at least three games – so Moises Henriques has been called back to India as his replacement.

I say 'called back' because Moises, of course, had been part of the Blues' successful Champions League campaign. No sooner had he flown home to Australia and he was being told to repack his bags for a return journey, and he was asked to take not only his own passport with him but Doug Bollinger's as well. Apparently, at the start of the Champions League, Dougie gave his passport to the NSW manager for safe-keeping, and in the buzz of celebrating their win in the final and also rushing to get to Vadodara for the first ODI of our tour he forgot to get it back.

We needed to make the call on Painey's successor as quickly as we could, so we'd have a keeper for game three of this series, which takes place in Delhi on Saturday, Victoria Derby day back home. Because of the time difference between Australia and India, the selector on duty here, David Boon, couldn't immediately get in touch with chairman of selectors Andrew Hilditch, but as soon as he did they opted for Graham over Queensland's Chris Hartley (who played for us, as cover for Brad Haddin and Graham, at Canterbury during the recent England tour). Our new keeper could be on a plane right now; if he's not, he will be very soon.

Painey's bad break was just the worst thing to happen during a game in which we were totally outplayed. I won the toss and bowled, but after a promising start in which we dismissed Sachin Tendulkar for just four, the Indians took to us, racking up their highest ever total in a 50-over game against Australia. MS Dhoni's hundred came in 94 balls, and he finished with 124 from 107. Peter Siddle (1–55 from 10 overs) and Nathan Hauritz (0–54 from 10) were the only two bowlers not to average worse than a run a ball, and we conceded an ugly 108 runs from the last 10 overs. In contrast, India's Praveen Kumar took 2–37 from eight, Ishant Sharma finished with 2–34 from eight and left-arm spinner Ravindra Jadeja claimed 3–35 from 39 deliveries.

October 29 About to fly down to Delhi. Things didn't go to plan last night. We should have batted – I made a mistake in deciding to bowl. Dhoni was awesome and we have to improve all facets of our game in the next match. Big blow to lose Tim Paine but it gives yet another player the chance to step up. These are the conditions that we will confront in the World Cup in 2 years time.

Sunday, November 1

Third ODI, at Delhi (October 31): Australia 5–229 (50 overs: SR Watson 41, RT Ponting 59, MEK Hussey 81*) lost to **India** 4–230 (48.2 overs: Yuvraj Singh 78, MS Dhoni 71*) by six wickets

IT WAS A LONG while since I'd opened the batting in a one-day international. Back in October 1999, in an ODI versus Zimbabwe at Harare, I went in first with Adam Gilchrist and finished with 87 not out. Despite my success that day, it remains the only time I've gone in first in either an ODI or a Test; in fact, for the past few years I've been pretty much exclusively a No. 3. A quick search of *Cricinfo* tells me that of the 318 innings I've played in ODI cricket (including the one just completed, where we lost to India by six wickets) in 287 of them I went in 'first drop'. Before the game in Delhi, 120 of my past 122 ODI innings, going back to May 2004, were made as a No. 3, and 27 of the 28 ODI hundreds I've scored during my career have been made from that position in the batting order.

The reason I opened the batting in the game yesterday was for team balance. We could have brought Shaun Marsh into the side, but that would most likely have been instead of Adam Voges, who for this match we looked upon as our 'sixth bowler'. It would also have been a bit unfair on Adam, who's been with the squad through the NatWest Series and the Champions Trophy but only came into the starting line-up at the start of this series. With our XI for this game decided, I looked at the line-up and realised that I was the most experienced player in our side and to put one of the other specialist batters up to open the innings would have been more of a challenge for them than it would be for me. Maybe we could have gone for a straight keeper-for-keeper swap at the top of the order — Graham

WET AND WILD

Our preparations for this third one-dayer were frustrated by what I now consider to be inadequate facilities at the Feroz Shah Kotla ground in Delhi. When our group, which included newcomers Moises Henriques and Graham Manou, arrived last Friday morning for a hit, we were informed that the practice wickets were wet, and as such unusable.

It was as if everyone in the world except the bloke that mattered – the groundsman – was aware that we'd be there ready to go at 9am. There was only one training day between the second and third games of the series, we had blokes who were very keen for a hit, and I couldn't help thinking: *I bet the wickets will be dry when the Indians get here later in the day.*

Manou for Tim Paine — but while Graham has batted really well in the South Australian middle-order for the past couple of years it would have been a big ask for him to open up so soon after landing in India. So up to the top of the innings I went, and while we did lose the game I did manage a reasonable half-century. If everyone is fit and ready for our next game, at Mohali, there's every chance I'll open again.

This was one of those games that appears one-sided when you first look at the scorecard but it was pretty close for a while. I felt our total was probably only a few less than par, the sort of score where if we bowled and fielded really well we'd just about win. And we started okay, reducing India to 3–53 in the 16th over. But then Yuvraj Singh came out to play the innings of the match, MS Dhoni gave him strong support, and they eventually cruised to victory. About our only alibi during the latter half of

their innings was the extraordinarily heavy conditions at night —
the dampest I've experienced since the 1996 World Cup final at
Lahore — which made it very hard for our slower bowlers to get
a decent grip on the ball.

We went into this game having just learned that James
Hopes' recovery from his hamstring injury was going too slowly,
so he'll be going home, and having known for around 24 hours
that the damage to Brett Lee's elbow is severe enough that he'd
have to leave us too.

Clint McKay, a quick bowler from Victoria, will be joining
us in Hyderabad next week, and Moises Henriques, who would
have been going home if James recovered, will now be staying
for the rest of the tour.

I think deep down we've known for a few days that James
was in trouble, but Bing's departure came as a surprise. He was a
little sore straight after the game in Vadodara, but things got
worse rather than better over the following couple of days and
our medical crew eventually decided it was best that he head
back to Australia to consult an elbow specialist. This way, he
will be best able to manage the injury and it will give him the
best chance of being available, we hope, for at least most of the
Australian summer. He'll be back in Australia before the
weekend is out, and James will leave us after our game in
Mohali.

Our list of unavailable players seemed to be growing by the
day: Bracken, Clarke, Ferguson, Haddin, Paine, Hopes, Lee. But
it's not all doom and gloom for us … the spirit in the squad that
has built up over the past two months is still very strong, we're
giving 100 per cent and we're preparing ourselves the best we
can. I know we've got the ability to bounce back and I really
believe we will.

> **November 1** On our way to Mohali early this afternoon after our disappointing loss last night. Given the conditions, I thought we had done enough with the bat with Huss batting as well as I have seen him bat in India. I was also pleased with my knock although I wasn't happy with myself the way I got out. We should have defended that score but Yuvraj and Dhoni batted extremely well. Mohali is now a must-win game for us.

Tuesday, November 3

Fourth ODI, at Mohali (November 2): Australia 250 (49.2 overs: SR Watson 49, RT Ponting 52, CL White 62, MEK Hussey 40; A Nehra 3–37) defeated **India** 226 (46.4 overs: SR Tendulkar 40; DE Bollinger 3–38, SR Watson 3–29) by 24 runs

WE WON THE GAME, but ridiculously we lost another player, with Peter Siddle suffering a tour-ending injury. At least James Hopes will have some company on his flight home, but I think another replacement will now have to be called for. It's almost as if, no matter how well we battle on, the cricket gods are conspiring to defeat us. Fortunately, I smell a real resilience in the group, which came to the fore in the latter overs of this game in Mohali and enabled us to grind out a narrow but decisive victory. Afterwards, I talked about the team's 'fighting qualities' … we've certainly got plenty of that.

I didn't think 250 would be enough, but then we came out and bowled and fielded quite superbly. There were two run outs, plenty of runs saved in the field, our bowlers never slackened and the pressure kept building and building. I was stoked with the way we really tightened the noose whenever a wicket fell, making it doubly hard for the new batter to settle into a groove. Virender Sehwag and Sachin Tendulkar were the crucial wickets, and it was the Blues boys — Nathan Hauritz and Doug Bollinger — who came up with the answers. Mitchell Johnson did have a difficult night, going for 74 from his nine overs (Sehwag, who scored 30 from 19 balls, really took to him at the start of their innings), but Shane Watson was terrific at both ends of the game, scoring 49 and then taking the last three wickets of the Indian innings, to claim the man-of-the-match award. It might not have been a dominant win, but it was still was one of the best performances by an Australian one-day team in recent times.

The Melbourne Cup was run back home this morning, and it was won by Shocking, a 10–1 chance. Given that we had a late finish the night before, the 9.30am start of the Cup (Mohali time) tested a few of the boys, and there was a mad scramble to get to Adam Voges' room so we could listen to the race on his laptop. A couple of the boys managed to cheer home the winner, and I reckon I was just about the loudest, which might have had

A RUN-OUT TRIFECTA

We actually batted pretty well for most of our innings, but came a little unstuck at the end. I went back to No. 3, with Shaun Marsh opening and Adam Voges left out, and played as well as I have all series, rushing to 52 from 59 balls before I ran myself out going for a second run on Ravindra Jadeja's throw from square-leg. We got to 4–201 after 40 overs and were hoping to reach 280, but then lost 4–27 in our powerplay and limped to just 250 all out. None of our last six batters made it to double figures.

I was dirty on my run out, but I made up for it in the field by first nailing Yuvraj Singh with a direct hit from cover point after MS Dhoni called him for a sharp single, and then dismissing Suresh Raina after the Indian No. 6 called for a quick run to cover but was left stranded when Harbhajan Singh knocked him back.

something to do with the fact that not only did I get top odds, I drew him in the team sweep as well.

Later, on the bus to the airport for our afternoon flight to Hyderabad, as I pondered our chances for this series, I couldn't help thinking that the Indians must be worried about what the reaction to them losing to such an under-strength Australian side might be, while we're really starting to believe we can pull off a stunning win away from home. I know which of these two mindsets I'd rather have — I'll take hope over fear any time.

Wednesday, November 4

YOU'VE GOT TO THINK, the way our injury toll keeps mounting, that there something a little unsustainable about international cricket's crowded schedule. Our latest casualty is Moises Henriques, who tweaked his hamstring during our win at Mohali. Of course, not all the injuries we've suffered can be blamed on the team's workload — things like broken fingers and even Callum Ferguson's ACL rupture could have happened any time — but the hamstrings and the backs and the side strains … surely we'd be seeing less of these if our top cricketers were getting more rest.

It is true that participants in all big professional sports are being asked to do more and more, but top-level cricket is almost unique in that it doesn't have a set off-season. Sure, we sometimes have breaks between tours or two, even three months off, but at other times we are asked to be 'on the road' for ridiculously extended periods. A player who is part of all three Australian teams (Test, ODI and T20) is being asked to keep going pretty

FOR THE FIRST TIME

Moises Henriques' hamstring injury, coming on top of Peter Siddle's departure, is severe enough for us to have to call for further reinforcements and the latest news is that Victoria's Andrew McDonald and NSW's Burt Cockley will be joining us, hopefully before game six at Guwahati.

I'm sure we must have set a record for most replacements on one tour, and I know we've set a new mark for most one-day debuts by Australians in a calendar year, with 12 guys having made their first ODI appearance for us in 2009. The previous highest was 11, set in 1971, the year of the inaugural ODI – Australia v England at the MCG – when, of course, every member of Bill Lawry's Australian side was making his first ODI appearance. Our first-timers this year are Ryan Harris, David Warner, Callum Ferguson, Peter Siddle, Ben Laughlin, Shane Harwood, Doug Bollinger, Marcus North, Dirk Nannes, Tim Paine, Moises Henriques and Graham Manou. Clint McKay will make it 13 if, as we expect, he plays in tomorrow's game at Hyderabad.

much all the time from the end of August 2008 to late July 2010, with never more than a couple of weeks break between the last and the next tour, series or tournament. The body never gets a chance to revitalise itself. Pete Siddle has been charging in pretty much day after day since he made his Australian debut last October, so it's no wonder his body has finally cried enough. But you can see a consequence of this unrelenting schedule not just with the guys like Sidds who are missing games, but also with the blokes who are carrying little niggles but just getting on with it or even with the guys who come into the side at short notice.

Moises isn't a regular in the Australian team at present, but what we asked of him was still a little crazy. He and his Blues team-mates celebrated their win in the T20 Champions League and then he flew home to Sydney. Straightaway, before he even had a chance to unpack his bags, he was called back to India to replace James Hopes. With little chance to settle in, he was making his ODI debut at Delhi and then his hamstring went six days later at Hyderabad.

Steve Karppinen, our trainer, has noticed that a few bowlers have come into our team in the past couple of years and have then got hurt almost straightaway — usually not a major thing as in Moises' case, but a minor injury of some kind. Karps puts it down to the fact that guys making their Aussie debut are really keen to impress but they might not have played in such an atmosphere before, so the adrenalin is flowing and they go really hard, too hard, and they put too much stress on their body. In Moises' case, he was bowling a full six or eight 'ks' quicker than usual right before he was injured. The first reflex when you get a new guy into the team is to assume he's fresh and can do anything, but maybe that's not the right way to think.

We're always trying to learn about how best to manage and prevent injuries. Part of this is about rotating guys shrewdly and part of it, too, surely, is about getting our schedule right. With this in mind, and despite the fact we clearly need to win, we're going to give Mitchell Johnson tomorrow's game off. He has been carrying an ankle throughout this series and we don't want a repeat of what happened to Sidds, especially with the first Test of the Australian summer now just three weeks away. Mitch was as stiff and as sore after the game in Mohali as he's been at any time in the past six months, maybe longer, so it was actually a pretty easy call to give him a break.

November 5 Plenty of press about India attacking us today because we are wounded with all our injuries. That's just the way I like to go into a game with a bunch of guys like we have. India can't afford to be off their game at all as we will be on the attack right from the opening ball.

CHAPTER THREE
AS GOOD AS IT GETS

THE AUSTRALIANS IN INDIA, NOVEMBER 5–12, 2009

Friday, November 6

Fifth ODI, at Hyderabad (November 5): Australia 4–350 (50 overs: SR Watson
93, SE Marsh 112, RT Ponting 45, CL White 57) defeated **India** 347 (49.4 overs:
SR Tendulkar 175, SK Raina 59; CJ McKay 3–59, SR Watson 3–47) by three runs

THIS WAS ONE OF the most exciting games of cricket I have
ever been involved in. It would be easy to say, having scored 350
ourselves, that we nearly threw it away, but I prefer to think
about how well Sachin Tendulkar played and how we kept our
nerve at the end. It was a famous victory.

When Sachin was finally caught by Nathan Hauritz at fine
leg, about halfway to the boundary — a memorable moment for
the bowler, first-gamer Clint McKay — India needed 19 from 17,
with three wickets in hand. In the context of such a high-scoring
game, this was hardly a tough ask. Three balls later, though,
Ravindra Jadeja was run out, and maybe we were back in front.
This was Clint's last over of the innings and it was magnificent,
as he cleverly varied the pace of his deliveries (something you
have to do on such a true wicket), and he conceded just two runs
off the bat. India were 8–335, 16 from victory. Doug Bollinger
dismissed Ashish Nehra with the first ball of the 49th over, but
then Praveen Kumar hit a huge six over long-off. Ten needed
from 10. After two scoreless deliveries, five ones came from five
consecutive deliveries, so with three balls remaining India needed
five to win, one wicket in hand, Shane Watson bowling.

I think this moment will stay locked in my memory. Kumar slashed wide of long-off, where Horrie was guarding the boundary. It was an easy single, not quite two, but the batters took our man on. Had the throw to the keeper's end not been spot-on they might have made it, but Horrie's aim was true, Graham Manou swept off the bails, and after an agonising wait for the video umpire's verdict our victory by three precious runs was confirmed. Funnily, the electronic scoreboard blazed out that we'd won by '4 runs'; in the excitement, who could blame them for getting it wrong.

Sachin played an amazing innings, one of the best knocks I've ever seen. In the fifth over, he pushed a ball from Ben Hilfenhaus that pitched on the off-stump out past square-leg for three, which took him past 17,000 ODI runs. That's more than 3600 runs more than his closest challenger (Sri Lanka's Sanath Jayasiruya). He reached his century — his 45th in ODI cricket and ninth in ODI cricket against Australia — from 81 balls, and just kept going, playing a mixture of glorious and improvised shots. Shane Watson had a superb all-rounder's game, scoring 93 from 89 balls, taking three wickets including Suresh Raina and Harbhajan Singh in one over near the end, and then he kept his nerve at the death. Still, there was no doubt Sachin was man of the match, though you could see by the look on his face straight afterwards that he was terribly disappointed his grand effort didn't lead to a win.

At the same time, I just wanted to share the credit among everyone in our group. The scoreboard might suggest we bowled badly, but the wicket was flat and Sachin was great — I thought we did very well to win the game. We had to experiment late in the innings, with lots of different slower balls and changes of length to try to take some wickets; otherwise I reckon they would have won comfortably. In a situation such as this where the pitch is so good, if you just continue to bowl seam up, aiming at the same spot, they're going to end up belting you back over your head time and again. We'd talked about this before the game, emphasised it during some good discussions on the field, and then the bowlers executed the strategy beautifully.

Clint McKay was especially impressive when it came to this. What I liked most about the way he went about his debut was that I didn't have to give him too many instructions. His read on the game situation was spot on, he had a pretty clear idea of what he wanted to do, and he backed himself to step up and do it. Before the 46th over of India's innings, with the crowd unbelievably excited because their hero Sachin was taking them to a miraculous win, I went up to talk to Clint before he came back on to bowl. But instead of me offering him some advice and support, he told me how he was going to bowl.

'I need fielders there and there,' he said, pointing to specific spots in the field. 'First ball to him (Tendulkar), I'm going to bowl a slower ball ...'

A MAIDEN TON

I was really pleased to see Shaun Marsh score his first ODI hundred. He's been unlucky in 2009, suffering injuries at bad times for him and in the process giving others a chance to grab his spot. He played one of those innings where you never felt he was scoring quickly, but he kept chipping away with ones and twos and the occasional four and eventually he reached his century from just 104 deliveries. His second fifty took just 41 balls.

Shaun and Shane Watson built the stage for our big total, and in the end only five Australian batters made it out to the middle, with all five of us scoring at a run a ball or better. Shaun finished with 112 from 112 balls, Watto made 93 from 89, I was out for 45 from 45, Cameron White for 57 from 33, and Mike Hussey ended up with 31 not out from 22.

That sounds about right, I thought to myself. Clint then did exactly what he said he was going to do. He didn't get a wicket immediately, but it was with the first ball of his next over that he had Sachin caught off another well-disguised slower ball.

As I said to the boys before the game, whether you're experienced or new to the side, when you're under pressure it's important to be tough and to keep doing what you did to get into the side in the first place. Quite often, young blokes come into the side and think that because they're now playing for Australia they have to do a lot more than they've done in the past. But you don't. You just have to do what you can do and play the way that you can play. If you do that for long enough in this game then things will go your way.

But it takes courage and self-belief to do that, which young players don't always have. But our blokes did here.

'It's remarkable considering the number of players we have had injured on this tour and we had a couple of our better players who didn't make the tour,' I said on the ground not long after the final wicket fell. 'When you take all those things into consideration, the way we are continuing to improve our cricket is fantastic. It is a great win for the boys and I am really happy to see some of the young guys doing well. It's a really good sign for the team.'

Later, at the post-match media conference, I continued to talk up the quality of our performance, especially the way we refused to give in when Sachin looked to be taking the game away from us.

'That's what I'm most proud of, (after) everything that has happened over the last couple of weeks,' I said. 'For us to keep finding ways to win games says a lot about the team, a lot about the players and the way we go about it …

'I actually asked the guys for a little bit extra in this game, asked them to be really brave and to play the best form of cricket they possibly could and just back themselves every opportunity.

'I thought in the first half of the game, with our batting, we did that to a T, and I think even in the last half of the game with the bowling we did that really well, so it was a great day for us.

'I can tell you now that the guys were as excited out there and back in the rooms as we have been for any win that we've had.'

> **November 6** Yesterday was a great win by the boys. I'm so proud to be involved with such a tough bunch of players. They have shown so much spirit and pride in representing their country – it's an honour to lead them. Also want to make a special mention of Sachin's knock at Hyderabad. That was just about as good as I have ever seen in a one-day game. What a game of cricket that was and what a series this is turning out to be.

Saturday, November 7

I THINK THE GAME tomorrow is going to be very different to the run-fest we just experienced in Hyderabad. The pitch at Guwahati is notoriously slow, and I think everyone is going to have to fight the urge to try to replicate the better-than-a-run-a-ball pace we saw yesterday.

We won't decide exactly how we're going to approach the game until we see the wicket tomorrow, but with Burt Cockley and Andrew McDonald having arrived yesterday we certainly have more options than we did before game five. I must confess I don't like putting a limit on us as a team, I don't want to say, 'This looks like a 200-run wicket.'

If the deck is going to be slow, though, 'Ronnie' McDonald especially offers us a tempting alternative. He went well for us in the Tests against South Africa last season, and he did a really good job for Victoria in the recent Champions League. The way he goes about things, bowling stump to stump and taking the pace off the ball, is often what you need on slow wickets where

THAT'S MY JOB

With the recent decisions of cricketers like Andrew Flintoff and Andrew Symonds to focus purely on the shorter forms of the game, it is inevitable that from time to time I am going to be asked questions about where the international game is going. It happened again today when I met the press boys to talk about tomorrow's game.

'I've made no secret that I'm a bit worried about some of the attitudes of younger players ... with the amount of money that's around in Champions League and IPL,' I responded.

'I just hope that the next generation of players coming through have the same sort of want and desire to play as much international cricket as I have, because that's what it's all about as far as I'm concerned.

'Hence the reason I retired from international Twenty20 cricket, to play more 50-over cricket and better Test cricket over the next few years.

'One thing we always try to stress, as the more experienced players in this team, is just how much of an honour it is to get a chance to play for Australia. We really ram that home to the young guys coming in and every young bloke I've seen come in has accepted just how big and special it is to play for Australia.

'That's my job and Huss' job and Michael Clarke's job, as the senior players in the side at the moment, is just to keep reinforcing that to those blokes.'

the ball tends to keeps low. He's also in good batting form, having scored 114 for Victoria against South Australia six days ago in the Sheffield Shield and 58 just three days later against the same team in a Ford Ranger Cup 50-over game.

Burt is also in good nick, having just taken 4–39 in a one-dayer against Western Australia at North Sydney Oval. Then again, I feel a sense of loyalty to Adam Voges and Ben Hilfenhaus, who have been with us throughout this Indian adventure. Again, Adam's offies could be very effective on a slow wicket. It's kind of reassuring to suddenly have all these alternatives when just a couple of days ago we only had 12 or 13 fit guys to choose from.

The other thing is, most important of all, as our injury situation has worsened, the belief within the group has stayed strong. That's what got us through. The thing with this Indian team we're playing is that, while they have their superstars like Tendulkar, Sehwag and Dhoni, they really rely on them — if one or more of that trio doesn't do the job for them, or if Harbhajan doesn't get some wickets, the others in their team rarely seem to step up. I've kept saying to our blokes, 'If we play together as a group, our eleven can beat their three or four just about every time.'

This will be only the second ODI to be played at Guwahati in the past six years and the third time Australia has played here (after 1996, when we lost to South Africa in the Titan Cup, and 2003, when we beat New Zealand in the TVS Cup). It is also just the second all-day encounter of this series. Because it gets dark pretty early here — before 5pm this time of year apparently — we've got an 8.30am kick-off, so it could be interesting right at the start.

What I do know is that the locals are very excited about the two teams being in their town. We don't usually get to these parts, the north-east region of India, due north of Bangladesh, when we tour here, and I guess from a cricket perspective at least you could call Guwahati one of the more 'remote' venues in the country, even though it is a city with a population getting up towards one million people. But I've usually found it's good fun to play in these less likely venues in India, because the fans are inevitably very excited and enthusiastic. I bet they'll line the streets all the way from the hotel to the ground, to cheer both teams as our buses drive past. For me, tomorrow can't come quickly enough.

> **November 7** We've just finished our training session in Guwahati and there's a super feeling among our group. Tomorrow is a huge game for us – starts early in the morning so the conditions and the toss are going to be so critical. One more win and we take the series.

Monday, November 9

Sixth ODI, at Guwahati (November 8): India 170 (48 overs: RA Jajeda 57, P Kumar 54*; MG Johnson 3–39, DE Bollinger 5–35) lost to **Australia** 4–172 (41.5 overs: SR Watson 49) by six wickets

I KEEP HEARING THE term 'anti-climax' being used to describe our triumph in this game, but that's only the locals talking … there was nothing anti-climatic about it to me. We went into the game knowing a win would clinch us the series, and from ball one we were right on our game, as the home team collapsed to 5–27 (in the ninth over) and 7–75 (in the 31st) before they recovered slightly to reach 170 all out. In reply, we were pretty clinical — we did fall to 3–90 when I was dismissed by Harbhajan Singh for the first time in the series (and third time ever in an ODI), but Mike Hussey and Cameron White took us to the verge of victory and then Huss and Adam Voges knocked off the last 29 runs we needed in a bit more than five overs.

Straight afterwards, I allowed myself the chance to compare this series win to other ODI successes I've been involved in, and I had to put this one right up near the top of the list. I have been lucky enough to be part of teams that have won the World Cup and the Champions Trophy, but the adversity we've had to overcome this time, and the way we've improved as the series has gone on — even though we were 2–1 down after three games, we've been battling injuries throughout and a number of our players lacked international experience in Indian conditions — makes our triumph extremely satisfying. I thought this Indian team would be a tough one to beat once they get their noses in front, but we've done exactly that. I couldn't be prouder of this group of players I'm fortunate enough to lead.

The ace yesterday was Doug Bollinger, who dismissed Sachin Tendulkar, Yuvraj Singh and MS Dhoni on the way to a five-wicket haul. Dougie only came into our one-day squad this season when Nathan Bracken pulled out of the Champions Trophy and only made the XI for this series after Brett Lee was injured and Ben Hilfenhaus had a rough time in Nagpur, but since then he's got better and better with each game and he fully deserved his five-for. Coincidentally, those figures matched his analysis from the game against Pakistan in Abu Dhabi last May, when again he bowled Australia to a victory that clinched a series win. Both times, he stepped up when we need a bowler to do just that, and in the process he lifted every member of the attack; you should never underrate a cricketer who can do that.

He's only played in four of the six games to date, but I reckon a case can be made that Dougie has been our best bowler during the series, especially if you consider that he is bowling in conditions that he's hardly seen before. The thing I like best about Dougie is that he's going to get better. His attitude is fantastic and he brings a real buzz into our dressing room, but at the same time he's not yet as fit and strong as he needs to be. When he gets himself into prime shape, he's going to be a dangerous bowler.

Our other bowling star here in Guwahati was Mitchell Johnson, whose return to the side after missing the game in Hyderabad was initially welcomed by Virender Sehwag, who slashed the second ball of the game over point for six! The fourth ball of the game was a wide and the crowd was abuzz ... but the next was a beautiful inswinger that spreadeagled Sehwag's stumps. Two balls later, Gautam Gambhir tried to push a fullish delivery to the on-side but the ball held its line and knocked out the off-stump. We were right on top.

I know it's been one series after another for a long time now, so I can understand how we might not be getting as much

WE'VE STARTED SOMETHING

Straight after the game, I was asked if – now that we've won the series – we would take the chance to give some blokes a rest and in the process give an opportunity to guys like Burt Cockley, Jon Holland and Andrew McDonald. Of course, it is tempting to give some blokes, especially guys like Mitchell Johnson, Nathan Hauritz and Shane Watson – who've hardly missed a game in recent weeks – a rest, but my first instinct is not to take the foot off the pedal, not even a little.

'We feel we've started something here with this group, not only here but since the one-day series in England, we've started to get a really good feeling around the group and I don't want to abandon that or let that go,' I commented today.

'It'd be nice to finish off on a winning note. To me, "5–2" sounds a lot better than "4–3".'

attention back home as we did during the Ashes series or even the Champions Trophy. But this series win is special — I just hope that it gets the recognition from the Australian cricket community it deserves.

Tuesday, November 10

DESPITE SHANE WATSON'S good form with the bat in the final three Ashes Tests and in our ODIs since, I sense that many of the people who were upset when Phillip Hughes was controversially omitted from the Test XI are keen for Huey to get back in the side as quickly as possible.

But with Shane just about a certainty for the first Test against the West Indies at the Gabba in a couple of weeks time, these people have come to the conclusion that Mike Hussey will have to give way, with Watto moving into the middle order. So it was that I was asked today if Huss (who scored a century in his most recent Test innings and is averaging more than 100 in the first six matches of this series) is going to struggle to keep his Test place.

'Not if he's playing well enough, no,' I replied. 'If he's playing well, he's one of those blokes who's valuable to any team.

'The thing is, he's been a great player. He probably hasn't scored as many as he would have liked in his last couple of Test series but all that other stuff he brings is pretty vital to the team.'

I've been around long enough to know that most seasons the press get onto one veteran player and almost mount a campaign to get that player dropped. I saw it with David Boon,

TURNING AN INJURY INTO A POSITIVE

No one likes injuries, but while each injury this team has suffered in recent weeks has made it harder for us, it is also true that an injury creates a positive in that it gives a chance for a new man to gain some exposure at international level. We now have a large group of players with quality experience at the top level to choose from – Ben Hilfenhaus and Doug Bollinger have shown they can take five-wicket hauls against the best opposition; Moises Henriques, Graham Manou and Clint McKay have made their ODI debuts on this trip; Nathan Hauritz is really coming of age as a spinner; Shaun Marsh has scored an ODI century; Shane Watson and Cameron White have played a lot of international cricket in the past 12 to 18 months. There's also Tim Paine, Phillip Hughes, Callum Ferguson, Adam Voges …

Not so long ago, we were a very inexperienced outfit, but now the quality in this new generation is really starting to emerge. The fight for spots during the next few months is going to be fierce, which will make for a very competitive Australian team at the 2011 World Cup.

Mark Taylor, Mark Waugh, Steve Waugh and Damien Martyn. Last year, it was Matthew Hayden. But I've really admired the way Huss has kept fighting for his form and the manner in which he has handled his preparation for each match during the past few weeks. Right now, he's batting as well as I've seen him bat for a long time. He's been on a long, hard road for quite a while, playing more cricket than anybody else in our group, but the standards he's set himself have never wavered.

On this trip, Huss has hardly trained, but no one's complained because we all know what a solid pro he is. His aim has been to keep himself as fresh as possible, and the results have been there for all to see.

November 11 It's been raining for a few days here in Mumbai and today's game is in doubt. It will be a real shame to end the tour with a washout or a rain-shortened game but it won't detract at all from what has been an amazing few weeks for us. We are planning a few changes in our team today so I just hope that a few of the younger guys get a chance to play here as it's an amazing place for cricket.

Friday, November 13

Seventh ODI, at Mumbai (November 11): Match abandoned without a ball being bowled; Australia win the series 4–2

THE ABANDONMENT OF the last game of the series was a bummer because, when you're winning, every game of cricket is a good one, yet with the series resolved and so much cricket ahead of us, there was a bit of feeling among us of: *Beauty, now we can forget about cricket for a little while.*

Still, there wasn't much time to waste. We were booked on a 4am flight home — which would have been a real challenge if the game had run its normal course and finished about 10pm — so it wasn't until we were ensconced in the plane that we were really able to switch into neutral, at least for a short while.

For me, at the ground at Mumbai and on the flight back to Australia, as it became apparent there wasn't going to be any play, there was time for reflection. Bar the injuries and the related worry with one or two guys that we don't know exactly when they'll be back, everything seems pretty positive right at the moment. Yet of all the good things that have evolved the one that stands out for me is the rise of Shane Watson as a consistent all-rounder of genuine international class.

I've always maintained that having a high-calibre all-rounder is the key that can turn a reasonable side into a very good one. South Africa have it with Jacques Kallis, England had it with Andrew Flintoff, we had it when Gilly was the best keeper-batsman on the planet.

In this series just gone, straight after scoring consecutive hundreds in the semi-final and final of the Champions Trophy, Watto took 10 wickets at 22 and scored 252 runs at 42, scoring his runs quickly and powerfully at the top of the order and bowling some important overs 'at the death'. When the Indians took their batting powerplays, Shane was the bowler I often turned to. In the process, he's provided plenty of that 'X-factor' that Steve Waugh used to like talking about when trying to explain his Australian team's best performances. For me, it's about balance — until you have a world-class all-rounder in your team, it's hard to have a deep batting order *and* a bowling attack without a weak link. Shane gives us great balance.

Of course, we always knew Shane had the potential. I could find pages in any of my past three or four diaries that have lauded his rare natural talent. Within the group, we knew, too, that he has a fantastic work ethic. However, he's been cruelly hamstrung by injuries, one after the other, including a couple of serious stress fractures that have tested his desire and mental strength. Now, though, it seems he is coming out the other side — his performances over the past few months have been outstanding, and it's no coincidence that the team as a group has been firing at the same time.

We won't be playing any more ODIs until 2010, and we end this year as the No. 1 ranked one-day side in the world, which I'm quite proud of given our struggles earlier in the year. Incredibly, we've played an energy-sapping 39 ODIs in 2009 (40

G'DAY, JIMMY

One unlikely visitor at practice before the final game washout was the superb Geelong footballer, the 2008 Brownlow Medallist Jimmy Bartel. I didn't know Jimmy has been in India for the last week or so, doing charity work for a 'role models' program run by the Red Dust organisation.

Jimmy told me how much he enjoyed trying to show some Aussie football skills to a group of cricket-mad kids from Mumbai. But he's also found it pretty challenging, being with children who come from such impoverished backgrounds. I'm very committed to the Ponting Foundation and I always admire other sports people who devote some of their time to helping those less fortunate, especially kids who are doing it tough.

I like to compare notes with elite sports performers, so it was good to talk to him for that reason, too. Plus, he seems a good bloke. We can't help but benefit from having guys like Jimmy Bartel coming in contact with our team.

if you count this game in Mumbai where we never bowled a ball), winning 23 and losing 14, with two no results. We only won four of our first 14, but from the final game of our seven-match series in South Africa to now, we won 19 of 25, with only five losses and one no result. During those 25 games, we only lost two in a row once — at Nagpur and then Delhi. In a year in which so many guys made their ODI debut, these are impressive numbers.

What I especially like is the consistency we've brought to our one-day cricket.

That hasn't been there in Test matches and it was one thing that was really lacking in our ODI performances in 2008 and the first part of this year.

On a personal level, I'm proud of the fact that throughout this period, with so many new guys in the squad and many days spent travelling from one venue to the next, I've managed to keep my own form going. I've scored 1198 at 42.79 in 2009, with nine fifties and two hundreds, stats that compare pretty well with earlier times — the number of games equals the third-most I've ever played in one calendar year (after 34 in the World Cup year of 2003 and 32 in the World Cup year of 1999); the aggregate is most second-best, after 1424 in 27 games in 2007; and the average is just down on my career ODI average of 43.20. I mention these numbers not to skite, but to underline the fact that we're managing my cricket time very effectively at the moment.

Better than any numbers, I'm really enjoying my cricket; there's not a day or a late night in a hotel room when I wish I was doing something else. We know there will always be cynics who think I should be playing all the time, but these days that simply isn't realistic, at least not with the long term in mind.

Beyond this time management, I think having all the young guys around has freshened me up, too. I've always felt I could handle the pressure of having to lead by example, and I love passing on my knowledge to new blokes in the squad. But one of the greatest challenges of leading an inexperienced group is working out exactly what blokes can and can't do. Sometimes in the past that has led to me asking guys to do things they are just not capable of doing, but I feel now that I'm getting better all the time at knowing what young players can and can't do. Asking Tim Paine to open the batting is one example; maybe an even better one comes from that fantastic game in Hyderabad, when Sachin Tendulkar was in full flight and on the verge of pulling off an amazing victory for India. I sensed that Clint

TIGER TIME

I was really keen to clear my mind of cricket for a few days, and I'm a golf fanatic, so I decided that rather than head straight for Sydney from Mumbai, I'd detour to Melbourne and visit the famous Kingston Heath golf course as part of the gallery following Tiger Woods at the Australian Masters.

I guess it was a bit weird, me trying to 'get away from it all' by getting in among a sea of sports fans and watching close-up the way another sports person goes about his business, but this was a rare opportunity and I wasn't going to miss it. I know Tiger has a long list of commitments while he's here, but on the course he was feisty and professional as ever, showing all the competitive instincts that have made him one of the greatest sporting achievers of our time. As I dashed from one possible vantage point to the next, just hoping for a glimpse, I felt the same as I did when I was a kid rushing around the boundary at Mowbray during grade cricket matches – it was exhilarating and good for me.

Through my connection with Valvoline (who also sponsor the motor-racing team backed by Steve Williams, Tiger's caddy) I had the chance to have dinner with Steve during the Australian Masters. There was talk among the Valvoline guys of them arranging for me to be introduced to Tiger in the practice area, but there were thousands of people there and it was never a chance. The size of the galleries really was astounding. I did have a chat with another Aussie golfer, Richard Green, and he told me he'd never seen so many people at a tournament anywhere in the world. It was awesome, as if the entire city was 'alive'.

Everyone was focused on Tiger, so I was just another face in the crowd. But occasionally, people came up to say g'day and to tell me how much they're enjoying the way the team is going. More than once, I was asked where I ranked Tiger in the list of great sports people and the answer is easy. 'Second best all-time,' I'd say.

Tiger is great, really great. But The Don was better.

McKay was up to the challenge of bowling the 48th over to him, and he came through brilliantly, delivering a terrific over and getting the key wicket that led to us gaining a thrilling victory. There have been times in the past when I've brought the wrong bloke on, but this time I enjoyed the process that led to me making the right call, and I loved the determination on Clint's face when he began that over and the joy he felt when he came through for us.

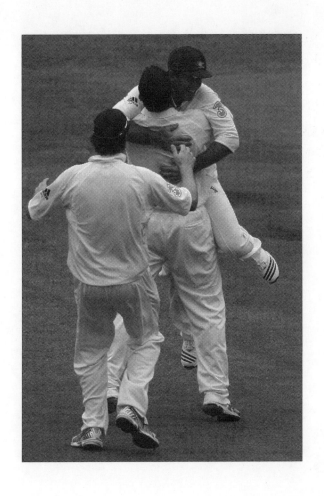

CHAPTER FOUR
HOME, SWEET HOME

THE WEST INDIES IN AUSTRALIA 2009–10

Saturday, November 21

'TODAY IS ONE OF those very rare and unusual days when I wake at home on a Saturday morning and have very little to do …'

That is how my column in the *Australian* begins this morning. And it is very true. As I sit here now, the only noise disturbing my peace and quiet is the occasional clang of my daughter playing in a nearby room. But I have to enjoy this serenity while I can because I'm back to cricket tomorrow, on the road to Brisbane for a camp that precedes the first Test against the West Indies, which begins next Thursday. There might not be another Saturday like this until the end of May 2010, after we've played Tests and one-dayers against the Windies and Pakistan, toured New Zealand and then many of us will be involved in the third edition of the IPL.

It might be quiet right now, but I have had plenty on during the past week. First, I was in Melbourne watching Tiger at the Australian Masters, and since then I've fulfilled a range of media and corporate duties, launching *Captain's Diary 2009* and, of course, I've had to keep myself fit. Most important, Rianna and I have been finalising details of a major initiative the Ponting Foundation will be announcing around the time of the start of the first Test.

Maybe it's a sign of the times, but when someone told me this week that we play 10 Tests between now and the start of the Ashes series next season — three against the Windies, five against Pakistan (three in Australia; two on a neutral venue in England) and two in New Zealand — my first reflex was to ask, 'Is that all?' Perhaps the memory of the recent Tests in England is still raw (and consequently, in my mind, the next Ashes series is still a long way off), or maybe 10 Tests in 12 months just doesn't seem like a lot these days. What I do know is that every moment of each of those 10 Tests is important when it comes to our journey towards regaining the urn in 2010–11.

Even before the selectors announced the team for the first Test two days back, it was my feeling that the Test squad is

HUEY

It seems as if everyone has an opinion on Phillip Hughes, whether he should have been dropped from the Australian XI during the last Ashes tour, and whether he should be back in the team now. As soon as the squad for the first Test was announced that was just about the first thing I was asked.

'We know that he had some technical areas that he had to work on,' I replied. 'It appears with the way he's playing that he's certainly trying to work on those.

'A lot of the beauty about him was that he was a little bit unorthodox. If anyone bowled anything remotely off line and length, he would put it away pretty quickly ... (In England) he was going back to leg-stump probably more than to off-stump. Having spoken to the selectors in Sydney, it seemed he was making a great effort to get in line with the off-stump. That's a good sign. Now he's got to keep working hard and I'm sure the runs will come ...

'He's a young kid who's shown he's got what it takes to be a very good international player, so we'll see where the next couple of Test series go as far as the batting line-up is concerned. He's certainly on the tip of everyone's tongue for the next Ashes series.'

fairly settled right at the moment. With Brett Lee's continued battle with injury (the latest word is that he could be out for quite a while because of his elbow problem), we'll start the season with our Ashes pace attack of Mitchell Johnson, Peter Siddle and Ben Hilfenhaus. Stuart Clark and Doug Bollinger are probably next in line, with Dougie the man preferred as the fourth quick in our squad for the first Test in Brisbane. After his good efforts in the one-dayers in England, in the Champions Trophy and against India, I would have been astonished if Nathan Hauritz wasn't in the squad and the spin-bowling spot is now his to lose. For all the polished work of Graham Manou when he's filled in over the past few months, Brad Haddin is fit again so he's the keeper-batsman. And after Michael Clarke confirmed his fitness with a big first innings in NSW's Shield game against Tasmania that finished today, it was inevitable that the selectors would stick with the same top six that played in the last three Tests in England: Simon Katich, Shane Watson, me, Mike Hussey, Pup and Marcus North. This means Phillip Hughes — who has started the season slowly but apparently did look better in NSW second innings against Tassie this week — will have to wait a little longer to return to Test cricket.

I always like to see consistency in selections, and hopefully the fact our squad is settled will lead to a greater consistency in our cricket. At the same time, we are very aware that the way we manage player workloads will play a key part in how we perform as a group over the next few years, and we have come up with the term 'active rest' to describe what we hope will become an important part of our man management. As I explained in the *Australian*:

> *As captain I have a responsibility to the team to help*
> *each player through certain parts of a game and make*

sure they are as fresh as possible for when they have to perform at their peak. The most obvious of these is bowling rotations but field placements have also become a far more important part of keeping our players fresh.

The old days of having the bowlers field at fine leg in between overs has now given way to a more sophisticated approach to ensuring that each player is able to perform at their optimum when required. Sure, you will still see bowlers fielding at fine leg but you might also see opening batsmen being placed in more restful fielding positions later in an innings to help them get ready to bat. We have also developed a field placement strategy to maximise shifts in momentum when we are in the field.

So you'll see us adapting tactics from time to time to achieve a more consistent performance.

In an unrelated move that should also help make us a more consistent and better side, it was announced last week that a familiar face — Justin Langer — will join our set-up as a mentor and batting coach. Initially, Lang will be with us during this summer's Test matches, a move that can only help us. As a player, he was renowned for his passion and professionalism, and if he can pass on even a little of that to the young blokes in our dressing room then we'll be a better side as a result.

November 22 Today's my last day of a mini-break which has been most enjoyable. Sorry I haven't posted since Monday but have been taking it easy with the family. I'll be back into cricket mode this evening when we arrive in Brisbane to prepare for Thursday's first Test against the West Indies.

Monday, November 23

I'M NOT ONE FOR regularly giving big speeches, but I will talk to the boys as a group before the first Test and one thing I'm going to talk about at length when we have our major team meeting in Brisbane is the fact that we have to win the key moments during the big games this season. The reason this is at the top of my agenda goes back to how we performed during the Ashes series, when on more than one occasion there were periods of cricket when, if we came through, the Test would have swung significantly in our favour. Instead, we played terribly and the games got right away from us.

I can think of the first session on day two at Edgbaston, when Jimmy Anderson and Graham Onions destroyed our first innings — if we'd batted through that session without losing more than one or two wickets and then gone on to make a big total that whole game might have changed. And then there was

BETTER LUCK THIS TIME?

One of the biggest challenges of this series for us will be bowling to Shivnarine Chanderpaul. Last time we faced the Windies, in the Caribbean in 2008, he was awesome. In the three Tests, he scored 118, 11, 107 not out, 77 not out, 79 not out and 50 — 442 runs at 147.33. But I reckon we might have more hope on our pitches. The wickets over there just didn't bounce at all, which suits the way Shiv plays, often on the back foot, waiting for the ball, aiming for the square boundaries.

This time, with Johnson, Siddle and Hilfenhaus in our team and the Gabba likely to be lively, hopefully we can at least look like we're a chance. Because last time we often didn't look like getting him out.

our batting collapse at the Oval, when Stuart Broad shattered our top order, which you can easily argue cost us the Ashes.

In these situations, when batting or bowling isn't easy but you have to fight through, we need to adjust more quickly and be mentally stronger than we did and were in England. It wasn't as if the team had never found itself in these type of situations before. A few years ago, we'd find ourselves in trouble but we'd back ourselves, battle hard, get on top and then go on to what looked like an easy victory. That's what the No. 1 team in the world should be able to do.

> **November 23** In Brisbane and about to head to the season launch tonight. Was great to get together again with the Test squad today. Good session all round and we will follow it up with a sharper session in the morning.

Wednesday, November 25

I'VE ALWAYS LOVED THE Gabba Test match. The facilities are first-class, the sun always seems to be shining, and even the sweat on your forehead as you train in the Brisbane humidity tastes sweet. There's a great sense of expectation for the season ahead, and you feel as if everyone wants you to have a very good series.

Just about best of all, the Gabba deck is invariably a beauty — it has to be one of the finest, most reliable wickets in world cricket. There's pace and bounce for the quicks, but as Shane Warne often demonstrated there is also something there for the spinners, even on the first day. But you can make a score here — since I played my first Gabba Test in 1996, there have been 31

FIRST DROP

From time to time over the past few years I've had people telling me that the 'extra responsibility' that comes with being captain has had a positive effect on my batting. Frankly, I'm not too sure about that – I've always felt the pressure to score runs that comes with being a specialist batter, and I don't think the captaincy heightened that expectation.

The thing that did have a huge impact on my batting was my move up to No. 3, which happened right at the start of my Test career, as I eventually learned to enjoy the responsibility a 'first drop' has to help a team build a big innings. For my first three Tests, I batted at five or six, but then I went in at the fall of the first wicket (with little success, scoring 14 and 13) during our one-off Test at Delhi in October 1996. My first Test as a No. 3 in Australia occurred right here in Brisbane, six weeks later, when I made 88 and 9 against Curtly Ambrose, Courtney Walsh and Ian Bishop. Unfortunately, I was dropped from the team two Tests later and didn't lock up the No. 3 spot until 2001, but right from that first experience in the position I felt it was where I played my best and most consistent cricket.

hundreds scored in 13 Tests: 25 by Australians and six by opposition batters. I've scored four myself, so it's little wonder I like the joint.

About the only downside from my point of view is that in the couple of days before the first Test of the summer, there are inevitably a larger-than-usual number of stories and commitments buzzing around that as captain I have to comment on or be involved in. Some are fun, some are testing, and the occasional one, usually a media beat-up, is just downright ridiculous. This year, there was a little bit of everything ...

FIRST UP THIS MORNING, I looked over, one more time, a media release that will be issued late tonight on behalf of the Ponting Foundation. We are announcing what we see as a major initiative — a three-year project to raise in excess of $500,000 for Tasmanian families who are affected by childhood cancer.

Over the past few months, we've had a number of discussions with key members of the Tasmanian health system and from that a range of essential services, equipment, training and resources have been identified which will now be directly supported by the Foundation. Our ultimate objective is to be able to support each and every Tasmanian family that has a child fighting cancer.

It's not widely known that as many as 20 children are diagnosed with cancer each year in Tasmania. We want to do everything we can to comfort and nurture each of these kids, and on top of that provide emotional and financial support for each kid's family. The first $500,000 will be used to improve the existing MRI scanners at Royal Hobart Hospital and Launceston General Hospital, assist with the training of nurses, provide an additional pool of direct financial assistance, employ and train a psychologist, dietician and additional social workers, purchase new paediatric surgical instruments and to deliver a program of music therapy into Tasmania.

We're also going to help as best we can the Tasmanian families who need to travel to mainland hospitals so their children can get a level of intensive and highly specialised treatment that is not presently available in Tassie. The Hendersons from Lenah Valley are one such family — 12-year-old Francine is currently undergoing treatment for Burkitt's lymphoma at the Children's Hospital at Westmead in Sydney and she, with her parents Peter and Janet, have been in Sydney for the past four weeks and might stay as long as six months. I was lucky enough to meet them recently, and apart from learning that Francine is the school captain at Sacred Heart College in Lenah Valley, I also discovered she is a very brave and confident young lady who was happy to offer me a couple of useful tips on how to get the best out of my players.

The fund-raising program we've got planned will deliver a one-off special event in Tasmania for each of the next three years, an employee/employer corporate giving program for Tasmanian businesses, a wider general community donation scheme and the continuation of the highly successful 'Run Ricky Run' promotion, where Tasmanians will be able to sponsor me for every run I manage to score. I'm really excited about the whole process, especially the fact we'll be distributing 100 per cent of the money raised directly into the essential services we're supporting.

A FEW DAYS AGO, the Marylebone Cricket Club in London published a report that suggests that Test matches are not as popular with the fans as they once were. There was a story about this in the papers this morning, alongside some dire predictions about the size of the first-day crowd for the Test, and not surprisingly, because of my status as Aussie skipper, people want to know my opinion.

My thoughts relate, in a way, to my feelings for the Gabba wicket. I don't think Test cricket is on the way out, provided it remains relevant and interesting, and as part of that we must recognise the importance of the surfaces we play on when it comes to providing good, value-for-money cricket. The state of the pitch often determines the sort of game you get. The sort of game you get will determine if the fans keep watching.

My feeling is that Test cricket is still entrenched in the instincts of sports fans in a number of countries across the world, but I do concede that the challenge provided by Twenty20 could make things harder for the longer form of the game in the seasons to come. All we can do as players is try to play the best cricket we can and make it as entertaining as possible for everyone who's out there watching. Fans crave a genuine contest between bat and ball; make it a bit hostile like they'll most likely get at the Gabba and they like it even more. So if someone really wanted to kill off Test matches, putting on more games like the one just completed at Ahmedabad, where India scored 426 and 4–412 and Sri Lanka compiled 7–760 declared, would be a good way to do it. The faster bowlers never had a chance in that game.

I'm a No. 3 and want my career batting average to be as high as possible, but I don't want to play in a Test like that one. So who'd want to watch it?

A COUPLE OF WEEKS AGO in Mumbai I was talking to Geelong's Jimmy Bartel and yesterday at the Gabba I was rubbing shoulders with two more great footballers — AFL's Jonathan Brown from the Brisbane Lions and Israel Folau, who plays rugby league for the Brisbane Broncos, Queensland and Australia.

The three of us were brought together to promote new cricket supporters' gear that has been produced by Adidas for this summer, and it gave me a chance to tell the other two about how I still dream of getting a game with North Melbourne in the AFL, and at the same time they were quick to talk about how they would have handled themselves as cricketers.

I learned that Jonathan was once a left-arm fast bowler of some ability, who modelled himself on the great Wasim Akram before he gave the game away to concentrate on his life in football. Of course, the photographers had all three of us kicking a footy and then spending some time with a cricket bat and ball.

On September 20, we were in the north of England completing the ODI series that followed the 2009 Ashes Tests; on September 23, I was talking to the media here in Johannesburg before our opening game in the ICC Champions Trophy.

That first match was against the West Indies, and on a lively pitch the welcome was anything but friendly.

With Shane Watson after our big partnership in the ICC Champions Trophy semi-final against England.

Tim Paine stumps New Zealand's Aaron Redmond off Nathan Hauritz's bowling in the ICC Champions Trophy final.

With my wife Rianna at the 2009 Caulfield Cup.

A photo that captures a little of the spirit we built during our tour of India in October-November, as Clint McKay hugs Ben Hilfenhaus after taking his first ODI wicket — Gautam Gambhir, caught by Hilfy at Hyderabad.

Three images
of my run out
of Yuvraj Singh
at Mohali.

Above: With AFL superstar Jimmy Bartel at a training session in Mumbai.

Below: West Indies captain Chris Gayle during his spectacular century in the third Test at Perth.

Above: Paceman Kemar Roach bowled some quick overs, especially at the WACA.

The system that allowed teams to refer an umpire's decision 'upstairs' quickly became a major talking point of the summer. *Above:* I ask for a second opinion after the West Indies' Shivnarine Chanderpaul is given not out at Adelaide. *Below:* Umpire Billy Bowden confirms Kemar Roach is caught behind to end the third Test at Perth.

Above: The moment immediately after I was hit above the left elbow by a short ball from Kemar Roach on the first day of the third Test. Even at this point, so soon after the impact, I was wondering how I got myself in such an awkward position. *Left:* My ill-fated attempt to bat in our second innings ended when I popped up a simple catch to short-leg fielder Travis Dowlin.

Above: The Aussie team with the Frank Worrell Trophy after the Third Test. From left: Nathan Hauritz, Doug Bollinger, Simon Katich, Shane Watson, Mitchell Johnson, me, Clint McKay, Mike Hussey, Michael Clarke (wearing sunglasses at front), Brad Haddin and Marcus North.

Left: Another celebration, this time at the MCG immediately after we clinched the first Test against Pakistan. The focus of our excitement is Nathan Hauritz (with back to camera), who has just taken his first Test 'five-for'. From left: Mike Hussey, me, Brad Haddin, Horrie, Marcus North (obscured) and Peter Siddle.

When we did the latter, Jonathan quickly spun a delivery past my outside edge with an action that suggested he could have been a pretty fair bowler, if he'd really worked at it. 'I really wanted to open the bowling for Australia,' he said at one stage. 'That was my No. 1 sporting dream.'

I'M SURE CHRIS GAYLE often dreamed when he was a kid about opening the batting for the West Indies and he's been lucky enough to live out his dream. For the past few days, though, he's had more important things to worry about, and it seemed for a while that the Windies would have to go into the Test that starts tomorrow without their captain because Chris left Australia last week to go back to Jamaica to be with his mother, who is very ill.

I'm a person who always believes family comes before sport, so I wasn't surprised that he made the call he did and I sympathise with him totally. He arrived back in Brisbane last night, and we believe he will play, though our understanding is that another of their experienced batters, Ramnaresh Sarwan, is going to miss the game because of a back injury he suffered today at practice. The Windies have had a badly disrupted lead-in to this series — first because of the player dispute; then their captain had to go home; then their bowlers were belted all over the park by Queensland last week; now one of their best players is injured. They're not a bad side, but how they'll go here is anyone's guess.

IT'S THE SAME WITH the referral system for umpiring decisions that will be used in the Tests this summer, where each team will have two 'challenges' per innings they can use to have an umpire's verdict reviewed. No one's quite sure if it will be a success or not. Make an unsuccessful challenge, and you've only got one left; get a decision changed and you've still got both challenges; two unsuccessful challenges, and you've got to cop the umpires' decisions for the remainder of the innings. This is the first time the referrals will be used in Tests in Australia and it's been quite a talking point — in the press and in our dressing room, where we have discussed how we're going to use them.

A lot of 'traditionalists' are talking the concept down and I must confess I was once in their camp. However, I now believe these reviews will eventually work out to be a good thing, though I'm sure there will be a fair amount of controversy generated before they are either accepted as a positive or discarded because they cause more trouble than they're worth.

RELAXED AND CONFIDENT

There were times during the Ashes series when I was really worried about Mike Hussey. He was struggling for timing in the middle, but he was still getting just enough runs to justify his place in the side, if only because he had been so prolific during the previous three years. What worried me most was the way he was going in the nets – I remember a couple of times in England when our fast bowlers seemed to be clocking him on the helmet a little too regularly. It was as if he couldn't quite pick up the line and length of some deliveries.

The hundred in the final Test at the Oval was encouraging and his form since then in the one-dayers has been good, but I still wasn't convinced he was back to 100-per-cent right. However, I've kept a close eye on him during the past few days and it's been terrific the way most balls have been striking the middle of his bat. And when I had a one-on-one chat with him yesterday he was relaxed and confident about where his game is right at the moment. A big score is just around the corner.

We did trial the system during the three Tests in South Africa last season and I thought it worked pretty well. I felt we used it better than the South Africans did — they'd call for a review on an each-way bet, get knocked back, and then, because they only had one challenge left, get a bit gun shy and not go for the next one, which probably would have gone their way. It became a bit tactical — we would think harder about making a challenge if, say, it involved a key batter, such as Graeme Smith or Jacques Kallis, or if we needed to break a key partnership. My view is that either one or both of the bowler and keeper, who usually have the best view, have to be certain it's worth challenging before we'll go for it, largely because I don't want to waste a challenge when later in the innings I might really need one, but I haven't got any left.

I'M NOT ONE TO accept a bad umpiring decision easily, but they are definitely easier to cop than some of the more outrageous things that are published in the newspapers these days. The one in today's papers that claimed Michael Clarke is Australia's 'most over-rated player' is a perfect example. Apparently, there is this survey of cricket fans that came to this conclusion, but my problem is that newspaper surveys like this don't reflect the views of all cricket fans, just the few who have the time and inclination to respond to the paper's on-line poll. Other than generating a cheap headline, I really don't know what they prove. Surely, no one can question Pup's cricket ability — he's one of the most gifted players in the game, a bloke who (according to *Cricinfo*'s statsguru) has scored more Test runs in the past two years than anyone except Sri Lanka's Mahela Jayawardene and England's Andrew Strauss.

I guess there are some people out there who have the wrong idea about Pup — they think they know him, but they don't really. But I'm not sure the public know a lot about most of us. They see us out in the middle, usually with our 'game faces' on and sometimes wearing helmets or they see us being interviewed at training or straight after games, and from that they draw conclusions about our personalities and the way we supposedly live our lives. Most often, these judgements are a fair way from reality.

Apparently 73 per cent of the people surveyed want the chairman of selectors Andrew Hilditch sacked, too, which is just ridiculous. I really don't think the selectors have done much wrong in the past couple of years. As I said when I was asked about the survey today, 'Quite often when you're in those sorts of positions you're on a hiding to nothing. You try and do everything right by Australian cricket with the way you look at the team and pick the team and you still have people calling for your head.'

Trying to work out how the Gabba wicket will play ... thinking about how best to use referrals ... mixing with stars of other sports ... conceiving tactics to counter our opponents, whatever line-up that may play ... even talking about the future of Test cricket ... it's all good. But I really don't want to have to worry about stories that should never have seen the light of day. I've got a Test match to play.

Sunday, November 29

First Test, Australia v West Indies, at Brisbane (November 26–28): Australia 8–480 dec (135 overs: SM Katich 92, RT Ponting 55, MEK Hussey 66, MJ North 79, NM Hauritz 50*) defeated **West Indies** 228 (63 overs: TM Dowlin 62, D Ramdin 54) and 187 (52.1 overs: AB Barath 104) by an innings and 65 runs

THE AUSTRALIAN ONE-DAY team's form in the past three months has been tremendous, but of course that doesn't automatically flow on to the Test side. Our previous 17 Tests before this one — dating back to the start of the series in India in October 2008 — had brought six wins, seven losses, four draws, two series wins (home against New Zealand, away against South Africa) and three series losses (in India, at home against South Africa, and the Ashes in England). We've got plenty to prove, and this was just a starting point. Our opponents played like a team short of a gallop, and they were hampered by Jerome Taylor's injury, which forced their most experienced fast bowler out of the match (and most likely the tour). But I'm not sure they deserved the criticism they've been copping since this Test ended, with some knockers even questioning their claims to full Test-match status. I can remember the days when the West Indies ruled the cricket world, and I think it's too early to say those days can't occur again — certainly, they can be much more competitive than they were at the Gabba. Earlier this year they beat England in a series at home, so they can't be all that bad.

For us, it was an encouraging win, with a number of batters getting some time in the middle and the bowlers going about their business in a very professional manner. Ben Hilfenhaus was probably our standout, winning the player-of-the-match award even though he took only five wickets. He was probably even better than he'd been in England, trapped Chris Gayle lbw in both innings, and his effort at the start of their second innings, when he dismissed Gayle, Travis Dowlin and Shivnarine Chanderpaul in his first six overs, was the best bowling spell of the game. I actually challenged him to get Gayle out the way he did, and he duly produced a superb inswinger that had the left-handed Windies captain caught in about three minds before he opted to let the ball go and was struck on the back pad.

It is always good for a captain when his players can deliver on the team's game plan. Unfortunately, though, it looks like

Hilf has a knee injury that could keep him out for a while. It's as if we can't take a trick with injuries — as soon as one bloke returns, another one replaces him on the physio's table …

Day One

WE PUT IN AN even batting effort after I won the toss, getting to 5–322 at stumps even though Shane Watson was out in the first over for a duck and no one was able to cash in and make a big score. Simon Katich, Mike Hussey and I went past 50, Michael Clarke was out for 41 and Marcus North was 42 not out on a nice track for batting, but the Windies were a man down for much of the day because of the injury to Taylor, so it was disappointing that there was no big hundred and thus little likelihood of a colossal first-innings total. However, we felt at stumps that it was

THAT WINNING FEELING

I've said it as much as anyone over the past couple of years: we've been a side in transition. But with the great form of the one-day team in recent months and our clinical effort here, I'm at the stage where I really like the group of players who are wearing the baggy green right now. As I said after the Test, when asked if we could expect to see more young players introduced to the line-up …

'Generally, when a team's having a lot of success there's not a lot of change in the side. That was one thing I said before the game: it would be good to keep a group of players together for a long time, because that generally means the team is performing well and individuals within the team are doing well and performing their roles.

'All going to plan, we won't have too many changes at all over the next 12 months. It would be great to keep this squad together … as I've said with our one-day team, to get that winning feeling back around the team again is really important.'

a typical Gabba wicket that would offer something for our quicks, so it was still a nice position to be in.

Much of the talk afterwards was about the video review system. Watto could have used it after he was given out lbw without offering a shot, but chose not to, which meant that the first time the video referral system was used in Test cricket in Australia occurred during a Ravi Rampaul over during the first session, when I was on 30 and umpire Ian Gould gave me not out on a tight lbw. Chris Gayle quickly challenged the decision.

Out in the middle, I thought the ball had been going over the top but I must confess to feeling pretty apprehensive knowing my immediate future might be in the hands of the 'Hawkeye' technology, which I'm still to be convinced is 100-per-cent right when it comes to judging the bounce of a delivery (and also how much a ball might seam or turn). Fortunately, the video official (and Hawkeye, I guess) agreed with umpire Gould and I survived. A little later, there was another close one when the impressive young quick, Kemar Roach, struck me on the pads but again the on-field verdict was not out. This time there was no challenge, maybe because they'd been knocked back the first time, for which I was very thankful.

Roach did get some revenge two overs later when I was dismissed by a delivery that bounced more than I expected and took the outside edge. He was the quickest bowler in the match and looks to have a real future.

Day Two

Marcus North and Nathan Hauritz took our tally of half-centuries for the match to five, which allowed me to declare half an hour before tea, and by stumps I was contemplating whether I'd be changing our usual policy of not enforcing the follow-on. The Windies were 5–134 at the close, trailing by 346.

Our quicks were in really top form, withstanding an early barrage from the bat of Chris Gayle to take four wickets for 14 runs in five overs, and reduce the visitors to 4–63.

Again, the referrals were a talking point, but while some cynics are trying to create major controversy I think the system is working okay.

Early in the day, Mitchell Johnson was given out caught behind but requested a replay, which didn't offer any firm indication that he hit the ball. But it also didn't offer any evidence that he definitely missed it, so the on-field decision stood.

Later, the Windies wasted their two challenges when Gayle and then Chanderpaul protested lbw decisions that went against them, but both times they were plumb and we couldn't understand why they bothered. Maybe the officials in the grandstand are sometimes taking too long to reach a decision with the replays, but that aside I think it's going all right.

November 27 Today was just about as perfect as I could have hoped for – except perhaps for my dropped catch in slips. The boys batted really well on a wicket that has plenty of runs in it but then our bowlers stamped their immediate authority on the Windies top order to put us in a very strong position tonight. My theme this summer is consistency and the boys have certainly done that in our first six sessions.

Day Three

There was no great significance in our decision to ask the West Indies to follow-on. I've rarely done it in the past, but this time there seemed something to be gained by being as belligerent as we could be, and it was a chance to test us as a unit, too. I guess we could have let the bowlers put their feet up for a while, but I liked the idea of being ruthless, of really 'putting the knife' into an opponent who is a long way off its game. I also thought it would be good for our confidence as a group if we won the game by plenty. As far as this Test is concerned, it was definitely the right call, though I have always been conscious of what might happen in the next game if the bowlers are on the field for a long time — more than once in the past Australia have lost the next Test after enforcing the follow-on (India in 2001, Ashes series in 2002–03, West Indies in 2003). We won't know if we'll pay a price for our aggression here until next week's Test in Adelaide has been played out.

The Windies lost 16 wickets on what proved to be the final day and afterwards Chris Gayle called the result a 'disaster'. But from the wreckage another considerable talent emerged in the shape of Adrian Barath, who scored an impressive second-innings century on his Test debut. Nineteen-year-old Barath is only the third West Indian to make a century on debut in a Test against Australia, and the first to do so in Australia, which is quite an achievement when you think about all the great Windies batsmen of previous generations. Coming on top of Kemar Roach's good bowling display, I thought it offered the Windies some encouragement — they might have been thrashed but they can clearly still produce a good player or two.

Maybe their worst moment came just before tea, when Dwayne Bravo was dismissed, but for us it was a real highlight, as Mike Hussey took his second Test wicket to break the

Windies' last significant partnership. It was all on a hunch — I threw Huss the ball, put two fielders back for the hook shot, and Dwayne Bravo fell for it, caught by Hilf at fine leg. Twelve months ago, I copped plenty after bowling Huss in a Test at Nagpur; this time, everyone thought I was a genius! His previous Test wicket had come in last season's Boxing Day Test, when he was too good for South Africa's Paul Harris. Bravo's batting effort, like that of their other two senior batters, Gayle and Chanderpaul, was unproductive — the trio scored 59 runs between them over the two Windies innings.

Wednesday, December 2

AS WE EXPECTED, Ben Hilfenhaus is definitely out of the second Test, and he could be missing for more than just this game, and even the entire Test-match summer. The diagnosis is knee tendonitis, one of those injuries that might heal quickly, or could linger for a month or three. In his place, the selectors have pulled something of a surprise by bring Clint McKay into the squad instead of Stuart Clark, a move prompted, I think, by the realisation that Dougie Bollinger will come into our starting XI. Rather than bring 'Sarf' back when he wasn't going to play, the selectors have grabbed the chance to give Clint some time with the Test squad.

The need to look after our pacemen and also to encourage our younger quicks was underlined by the news that Brett Lee will be having surgery on his bung elbow this week. At the moment, no one knows when he might be back, and I guess there have to be some doubts about his future as a Test-match cricketer. But I wouldn't bet against him bowling again in the five-day game — he's proved in the past that he's not the sort of bloke you can write off that easily.

I was also disappointed to learn that Brad Hodge has decided to retire from first-class cricket. Hodgey and I are the same age (he was born on December 29, 1974, exactly 14 years after David Boon and 10 days after me), we first met at the Cricket Academy and not long after we were playing against each other in the Sheffield Shield. He was always good enough to play plenty of Test cricket, and everyone knows he was very unlucky to get dropped for our tour of South Africa in 2006, so soon after he made a double century in just his third Test match. The selectors decided to recall Damien Martyn and Michael Clarke for that trip — and Marto responded by playing one of his greatest innings in the third Test, while we all know what Pup has done in the past three years — but Hodgey never really had another chance, which we all thought at the time he'd get for sure.

Of course, he's not the only bloke unlucky not to play more Test cricket for Australia in recent seasons — names like Darren Lehmann, Michael di Venuto, Phil Jaques, Michael Kasprowicz and Nathan Bracken come to mind. Even Stuey MacGill, who took 200 Test wickets but would have taken a lot more if a guy named Shane Warne wasn't around, fits into this category. All these guys were or still are outstanding cricketers, and the fact they haven't played as much Test cricket as they deserve is not a knock on them — it's more a case of the quality of the bloke ahead of them or simply just not getting the right break at the right time. Similarly, guys like Stuart Clark, Marcus North, Shane Watson and Mike Hussey had to wait a long time to get their opportunity, and I can't help but think back to my first Test, when Stuart Law and I made our Test debuts in the same game. Stuart scored an unbeaten 50, but I made 96 and when Steve Waugh came back into the XI for the next Test it was Stuart who gave way. He was never selected for the Test team again, even though he was an exceptional cricketer. That some brilliant players have missed out in this way over the past 15 years just goes to show how strong the Australian team has been during this time.

> **December 2** We have settled into Adelaide and had a good training session today. Lots going on with the redevelopment at Adelaide Oval. It's a special game for me as Rianna and I are hosting some of the wonderful friends of our Ponting Foundation throughout the match. They are all special people who have done so much for us.

Thursday, December 3

I WAS HAPPY WITH the way we went in Brisbane, but I want to go even better here in Adelaide. That's what good teams do — they keep improving. Constantly making yourself better becomes a challenge; our great players of recent times, like Glenn McGrath, Shane Warne, Matthew Hayden and Adam Gilchrist, were always setting themselves new targets in this way.

At the same time, I think our opponents will be more formidable this time. Though it appears to have more grass on it than usual, the wicket here will still be less lively than Brisbane and as such more like the pitches in the Caribbean, and that will suit them. Further, I'm sure they'll get more out of Chris Gayle and Shiv Chanderpaul, we expect Ramnaresh Sarwan to start, and our task will be tougher because of the absence of Ben Hilfenhaus (who bowled so well to Gayle at the Gabba).

DOUGIE

With Ben Hilfenhaus out, Doug Bollinger comes into the team, which – regardless of how many wickets he takes (and he could easily take quite a few) – will be very interesting.

Dougie is a bloke who loves to bowl, and he's a great character too, a case of what you see is what you get. He can get a bit loud in the dressing room, but you can't help but like him because of his terrific sense of humour. He sometimes brings a laugh or two on himself, but he always gives as good as he gets, and he is an extremely generous man. There's always something happening when he's around.

I always want new guys in the dressing room to be themselves, to bring their character with them when they come into the team. I was pretty shy when I first came into the team and I don't think it helped me or the team – you don't want to be seen as cocky, or to upset the existing order but the worst thing you can do is try to be someone other than who you truly are.

I don't want anyone, young or old, to just sit there and wait for people to come to them, we need guys who are confident and able to express themselves on and off the field.

I have no doubt Dougie will be up to this task. It will be interesting to see what the West Indians make of him.

I know Chanderpaul scored next to nothing in two innings during the first Test, but his game seems ideally suited to the Adelaide Oval — he excels on pitches that don't bounce too much and he'll love the short boundaries square of the wicket. As we were in Brisbane, we have to make sure we're spot on with everything we do to him at the start of his innings and not give him any cheap runs early on. That puts the pressure back on him, and might get him to start playing outside his comfort zone.

With Gayle, the key could be for our left-handers, Mitchell Johnson and Doug Bollinger, to 'tuck him up' with the natural angle of their deliveries, in the way Hilfy did with his inswingers during the first Test. Our plan then was to bowl stump to stump at the Windies skipper, which worked like a dream, and we have to do that again this time. If you give Gayle some room to swing his bat he can be lethal, and he's the sort of batter who, once he gets on a roll, can be terribly hard to stop.

We'll continue to keep Mitchell Johnson away from the very new ball, meaning Dougie will open the bowling with Peter Siddle. I quite like the Bollinger-Gayle match-up, and I'm convinced that at this stage of his career Mitch is better suited bowling with a slightly worn ball. I know he bowled well with the new ball in South Africa last season but the reason things went a little bit awry for him at the start of the Ashes series was because he was trying to do too much at the start of an innings.

The result was that sometimes, when he tried to get the new ball to swing but it didn't deviate, his line and length was out by a foot or two. And at this level, if your line and length is out by such a margin, you're going to pay for it. We know Mitch still has ambitions to lead the Australian attack, and I'm sure one day soon he'll be doing exactly that, but for the moment I think we're better off with him bowling first change.

December 3 We are all set to go tomorrow. I was very pleased with our session this morning and the boys have all had a relaxing afternoon. I managed to get 18 holes in at Royal Adelaide which was a lot of fun although it was a bit windy out there. Just having a quiet night tonight and can't wait to get out there tomorrow. Think it's another important toss for me to win.

Wednesday, December 9

Second Test, Australia v West Indies, at Adelaide (December 4–8): West Indies 451 (124.1 overs: S Chanderpaul 62, BP Nash 92, DJ Bravo 104) and 317 (99.5 overs: CH Gayle 165*; MG Johnson 5–103) drew with **Australia** 439 (131.1 overs: SR Watson 96, SM Katich 80, MJ Clarke 71, BJ Haddin 55*; SJ Benn 5–155) and 5–212 (76 overs: MJ Clarke 61*)

THIS TEST WAS controversial from just about the very beginning, when the video review system came under plenty of pressure. One of the umpires, England's Mark Benson, withdrew from the Test after play on day one and rumours flew that he had done so because of either the way the referrals were being managed, the way we players had reacted to it, or a combination of both.

Two decisions caused the most comment in the media. In the first, we were sure Shivnarine Chanderpaul edged a catch to Brad Haddin, but umpire Benson said not out. I must confess I thought the decision would be reversed for sure, but apparently the video evidence wasn't there for this to happen so the on-field ruling stood. I was so surprised, I sought an explanation — and some saw this as me protesting the decision, and then (wrongly) concluded that the ump had quit the Test because of what they tagged my 'dissent'. A few people thought I'd crossed the line in the way I went about this, especially when I approached the fourth umpire during the next drinks break to seek further clarification, but I don't think I did and neither did Chris Broad, the match referee. I believe I was entitled to ask the umps why the final decision had been made, and once they told me I went back to my position in the slip cordon.

Later, an almost identical situation occurred, only this time Chanderpaul was given out. Later, we learned that the video evidence wasn't that strong and most people who saw it were surprised the on-field verdict had been reversed. People wondered if umpire Benson left the Test in protest at this decision, but I don't know about that. I understand that he has been a bit crook lately and we could tell that he wasn't feeling too flash out on the field. He also had an lbw ruling overturned, so maybe the overall impact of the referral system played a part in his departure, but my best guess is that — as was stated officially — ill-health was the main cause. I've always thought Benson is a good umpire and he's always seemed to be a pretty strong-willed sort of guy.

Another situation that really got me thinking came right at the start of the second morning. First ball of the day, Darren Sammy was lbw to Peter Siddle. We thought it was absolutely plumb, umpire Ian Gould gave it out, and Sammy asked for a referral. The video confirmed the original call, but would Gould — who is another good umpire — have had his confidence boosted by that confirmation, or would he start thinking, *maybe that wasn't as close as I thought.* If he starts thinking like that, he's under pressure, and then he might make a mistake.

When they brought in the referral system, I think we players immediately thought every incorrect decision would be fixed. It's hard for us to accept that the reality is there will still be errors, just not as many as there were in the past and the ones that are made will not be the howlers we used to see from time to time. Of course, reducing the number of bad calls is a good thing — what needs to happen now is to find a method that supports the umpire rather than makes it hard for them. We don't want to create a mindset in players where they are not happy to accept what the on-field umpires say; that instead they'll go over the umps' heads every chance they can. Maybe it shouldn't be up to the players to ask for a referral, but for the video umpire to study a replay and then get the message out to the on-field officials that there should be a review. I still think using the available

AB'S LEGACY

Not long after this Adelaide Test, I read a column by the highly respected cricket writer Mike Coward in which he pointed out that December 7, 2009, was the 25th anniversary of Allan Border's first day on the field as Australian cricket captain. I never got to play for Australia with AB – his final appearance, in South Africa in 1994, occurred 10 months before I made my first international tour (to New Zealand in February 1995). But he had a big influence on me, directly through his role as a selector, Cricket Australia board member and commentator and indirectly through the lessons he passed on during his career to cricketers such as Mark Taylor, Ian Healy, David Boon, Shane Warne and Steve and Mark Waugh, which they then shared with me (and many others).

In Mike's article, he revealed that in the period AB was Australian captain (93 consecutive Tests spanning more than nine years) the other Test-playing nations used a total of 40 Test captains. Another revealing statistic: since December 7, 1984, only five men – Border, Mark Taylor, Steve Waugh, me and Adam Gilchrist – have led Australia in a Test match. That's a figure I can turn to whenever I need reminding just how lucky and privileged I am to be the Australian captain.

The other Test-playing nations have used a total of exactly 100 Test captains in the past 25 years, an average of more than 11 per team. As I said, we've used five! People forget just how much the Australian team was struggling a quarter of a century ago, and how AB almost single-handedly restored balance and respectability. As Mike Coward wrote:

'Aside from his enormous contributions as one of the greatest and most courageous batsmen of any era (11,174 runs at 50.56 with 27 hundreds and 63 fifties) his legacy was the provision of certainty, unity and a collective confidence at a time of great uncertainty – a bequest from which Australian cricket in general and Ponting and his men in particular continue to benefit ...'

technology is the way to go, but the lesson from this game is that the officials have to nail exactly what evidence is needed to change an on-field decision. Like everything to do with umpiring, consistency is the key. It won't work if some video umpires want to change things on the slightest evidence while others refuse to over-rule decisions, even when the replays strongly suggest they should.

At one point during the Test, I actually sat down with the umpires to discuss the referrals. I wanted to gauge where they are with the system — and whether they felt they were now under more pressure, which they certainly don't need. The consensus is that it is worth persevering, that this is new to all of us and that, once all the 'teething problems' are sorted out, the innovation will be a good one.

Day One

All those who thought this series would be a walkover were given a shock on the opening day, when Chanderpaul, Brendan Nash, Dwayne Bravo and Darren Sammy steered the Windies to 6–336 at the close. Bravo was the standout, scoring his second Test century against Australia, following on from the 113 he made in Hobart four years ago. He was good back then, but he batted even better this time, restoring his reputation which had been tarnished a little by the way Mike Hussey suckered him out in Brisbane.

We were a fair way from our best, however, dropping three catches and maybe we let the umpire referrals get to us a little in the middle session as Chanderpaul and Bravo built their hundred partnership. However, we fought back well in the final session, dismissing Chanderpaul (albeit in controversial fashion), Denesh Ramdin and Bravo to get the scoreboard back on a more even keel.

If one moment captured the way we were slightly off our game it came when Bravo, on 59, swung a ball from Siddle out towards the backward square-leg boundary, where Shane Watson tried to intercept the ball above his head as he began to over-balance right on the boundary rope. Watto did manage to take the 'catch' but he quickly realised he wasn't going to be able to stay in the field of play … so he tried to throw the ball in the air in the hope he could recover and complete the out like Adam Voges did last year in a Twenty20 International in Sydney. But this time it didn't work; instead both fielder and the ball ended up on the wrong side of the rope and Bravo was credited with a six.

Initially, I was really disappointed with our position at stumps, but then someone told me that it was 13 years since a team had been bowled out on the first day of an Adelaide Test, that only once since 1996–97 has a team taken even seven wickets on the opening day in Adelaide. Maybe we didn't go so badly after all.

> **December 4** Lost the toss and spent the day in the field, which gave us a good chance to have a look at a wicket that has plenty of runs in it. We have some work to do first-up tomorrow to make sure we bowl the Windies out for a respectable score. Then we can go about our business of proving what a great batting strip this is.

Day Two

This day belonged to Shane Watson, who at stumps was 96 not out. He played beautifully, clearly his most assured Test innings to date, as we cruised to 0–174 at stumps, still trailing by 277 but on top all the same. I don't think Shane got enough credit for his batting in the recent Ashes series, when he made three fifties in three Tests, but after this innings I sensed that at least some of the critics now realise that he is good enough to be an accomplished Test opener.

At the other end, Simon Katich was just as comfortable, and we went to bed looking forward to both of them going on to big hundreds and us building a match-winning first-innings lead.

Day Three

I don't know how well Watto slept, but I could tell by the way he was so keen to get out there that he'd spent a fair chunk of his waking hours since stumps on day two thinking about the hundred. Unfortunately, this time it wasn't to be, as he went for an ambitious pull shot off the second ball of the day, missed ... and was bowled. It was a terrible moment for all of us, such an anti-climax, as I think we'd all been thinking about how we'd start the day on such a positive note.

On the other hand, it was a major reward for an enterprising piece of captaincy. I don't think any of us expected to see their tall left-arm spinner Sulieman Benn bowling the first over of the day, and maybe that had something to do with Watto playing such an indiscreet shot.

From that ugly start, we never found our momentum. Kat also fell short of three figures, and after that everyone got a start but no one went on to the big score we needed as the basis for a huge innings total. We finished up 12 runs behind on the first innings and the four overs we bowled before stumps cost us 23 runs. The game was evenly poised, though we were hampered by a hamstring injury to Sidds that prevented him from taking the new ball.

Benn had a very good day, taking five wickets and showing a good mix of skill and perseverance. The young fast bowler, Kemar Roach, was also excellent, taking three wickets and impressing all with his pace and his awkward bouncer, which skids at the batter in a way that can make hooking and pulling a pretty dangerous business. That's how he dismissed me — caught by Bravo at mid-wicket after a short ball got on to me much quicker than I expected.

> **December 6** Today showed Test-match cricket is alive and well. There's also a lot of life left in the West Indies, who so many people were writing off as a Test-playing nation. We weren't able to get on top of them today and they deserve their lead going into day four tomorrow. This Test will go right down to the line.

Day Four

This day belonged largely to Chris Gayle, who batted throughout the day to be 155 not out at stumps and to get his team 296 runs in front, with two wickets in hand. But it was also a good day for Mitchell Johnson, who took four wickets on a pitch that clearly didn't suit him, including a superb spell of 3–16 late in the day. At stumps, we thought we were an outside chance for a win, but the wicket was slowing all the time — more and more it became a wicket that you could defend on reasonably easily, but scoring quickly was risky. Gayle's overall strike rate for this innings was a little less than 58, which is hardly rapid by his standards. If he'd tried to go any quicker, however, I'm sure we would have got him.

For us, it was a bad day with the replays, because we used both our challenges unsuccessfully in the first 45 minutes of play. This meant that later in the day, when we were sure Brendan Nash was lbw to Doug Bollinger but our appeal was turned down, we couldn't take it any further, and Dougie's frustration boiled over to the point that he was reported to the match referee and later fined.

Another area of some concern is our spin bowling. A day after Sulieman Benn took five wickets, Nathan Hauritz and Marcus North bowled 41 overs between them and didn't take one. I liked the way Horrie stuck to his task on a wicket where there wasn't a lot of deviation for him, and the Windies batters didn't take many risks against him, but at the same time I'd like to see him become more of a wicket-taking threat. I had a good yarn with him after the game and he conceded he'd been too conservative, and I left our conversation pretty confident that we'll see a more aggressive bowler when we meet the Windies again in Perth.

December 7 Tomorrow is going to be one of those great Test match days. Chris Gayle has batted his team into a solid position and we are going to have a big job ahead of us once we get in. The wicket is holding up well but the pressure is on us to perform. I have a big job to do myself and am looking forward to the challenge.

Day Five

We went into day five confident we could save the Test but doubting we could win it, because fast-scoring was tricky, and when Chris Gayle batted on for another 6.5 overs that was just about enough to make us forget about going for an unlikely victory. We never totally ruled out having a shot at it until around the 45-over mark, but Watto, Kat and I were all dismissed by the slowness of the pitch as much as any expertise from the bowler, which reflected how hard it had become to force the pace.

In the end, Pup and Hadds batted out the final 21 overs of the Test pretty comfortably, which means we've successfully retained the Frank Worrell Trophy and will head to Perth with a 1–0 series lead. For me, I had the added pleasure of going past Allan Border to become the highest run-scorer in Tests at the Adelaide Oval, a record I achieved when I reached three on this final day. I've always loved batting in Adelaide, and have managed to score five hundreds in 14 Tests here, while averaging a touch less than 60. Forgetting modesty for a second, I reckon that average is very good, but there are more than 20 great batters who've averaged more, including Lindsay Hassett (128.25), Sir Donald Bradman (107.78) and Michael Clarke (102.40), who have averaged or, in the case of Pup, are averaging more than 100.

Afterwards, I wasn't prepared to concede we'd been outplayed, but I was happy to acknowledge the fight our opponents gave us. 'They have bounced back the way you would expect an international team to bounce back,' I said. 'You've got to give the West Indies some credit for the way they have played.'

GOING ON WITH IT

One thing that's been a constant in media reports and in our team meetings has been the inability in recent times for our batters to turn fifties into hundreds. During the recent series in England, we scored eight centuries to our opponents' two, but they won the Ashes; so far in this series, we haven't had a single century-maker while the West Indies have had three, but we're one-up after two Tests.

We have scored 10 half-centuries in the first two Tests (two to Katich, two to Clarke, one each to Ponting, Hussey, North, Hauritz, Watson and Haddin) but no one has pressed on to the big score, which is something we don't want to turn into a habit. But I'm reluctant to talk about it too much, because sometimes these type of things can get almost self-fulfilling – last summer, we started losing wickets either side of the breaks in play and it became almost a constant mantra at team meetings, that we needed to prevent this from happening. Sure enough, the problem only got worse, and it only corrected itself when we stopped harping on about it.

Tuesday, December 15

I'M NOT QUITE SURE what to expect with the pitch at the WACA this season. I used to love coming here to play Test cricket, because I liked the pace and bounce, which was as pronounced as anywhere in world cricket. We had quicks like Glenn McGrath, Jason Gillespie and Brett Lee in our line-up, so a pacy surface suited us just fine, but it was also a nice place to bat — because the bounce was consistent and the ball came on to the bat. Inevitably, the cricket was entertaining.

However, in the past three of four years, the wicket has not been the same, at least not for the Tests. It played lower and slower; like a number of pitches across the world, it was losing its unique character, becoming just another surface. This season, however, there have been good reports about the square, and I was pleased to see that the NSW-Western Australia Shield game was decided inside three days on a lively track, thanks in part to a brilliant performance from Doug Bollinger. At first glance, it looks like the Test pitch might play the same way — it presently has a good cover of grass, and is nice and hard, the way it used to be. I just hope the hot weather they've had over here (the groundsman told us it was up to 45 degrees out in the middle yesterday) won't burn away too much of this grass cover, and that the wicket will stay just the way it is. I got into trouble with the locals last year for bagging their pitch; I don't think that's going to be happening this time.

> **December 10** In Queensland now shooting the next series of Rexona's 'Australia's Greatest Athlete'. Make sure you look out for it next February as it's going to be sensational. Big day of filming ahead today and I'm about to be on 'Sunrise' with Mark Beretta, who is hosting the show with Tom Williams.

It will be interesting to see just how much the pitch suits us, because we're going into the game with another very inexperienced bowling attack: Mitchell Johnson might have played in 28 Test matches, but Nathan Hauritz (nine), Doug Bollinger (two), and Clint McKay (none) have appeared in just 11 Tests between them. Clint will play instead of Peter Siddle, whose hamstring is not quite right, while we've also called up Brett Geeves from Tassie as cover for Shane Watson, who has hardly trained since he arrived in Perth because of a few minor 'niggles'. But Watto will almost certainly be right for tomorrow.

Nathan Hauritz is also under an injury cloud, after hurting a finger during a fielding drill at training today. He should also be right, but the team management has asked for another man to be called up as cover, just in case things worsen overnight. Steve Smith, a 20-year-old leg-spinning all-rounder whom I've never actually met but who has played some dynamic innings of late, is currently flying over from Sydney. My preference is always to have a spinner in our attack, but if Horrie is out, because Brett is here, we have the option of going into the Test with the four-pronged pace unit.

Playing with an inexperienced attack is a challenge we've faced a few times in the past 12 months, ever since Brett Lee was injured during last year's Boxing Day Test. Against South Africa at the SCG in the first week of 2009, our front-line attack of Johnson, Siddle, Bollinger and Hauritz (with Test debutant Andrew McDonald as the fifth bowler) had played in just 23 Tests, while eight weeks later in the Test at Johannesburg, the attack of Johnson, Siddle, Hilfenhaus and McDonald (with Test debutant Marcus North as the fifth bowler) had also appeared in a total of 23 Tests.

This said, the West Indies bowlers are also short on Test appearances, but the talk on their side of the fence is about how

December 12 Stayed in Brisbane last night after finishing the filming of Rexona's 'Australia's Greatest Athlete'. This series was great fun and I'd expect it to come up really well compared to the first series. About to head to Brisbane Airport to fly over to Perth. All the boys fly in from their home ports this afternoon so will be good to get everyone back together.

Kemar Roach is going to bowl if the WACA bounces as much as is expected. Apparently Chris Gayle has said that while he thinks my hook and pull shots are a positive part of my batting, they can also, in his view, be a weakness, so Roach will be out to 'get me'. That sounds more wild west than international cricket, but I can't say I'm that concerned. I've been around long enough and faced plenty of quicks bigger and better than Roach, so I'm not going to spend too much time worrying about him. Sure, he is a good young bowler, but at this stage of his life he's no Curtly Ambrose.

The Windies have been dealt a couple of injury blows, with Adrian Barath and Shiv Chanderpaul ruled out. These days, it seems, it's almost impossible to report on Test cricket without providing a daily injury update.

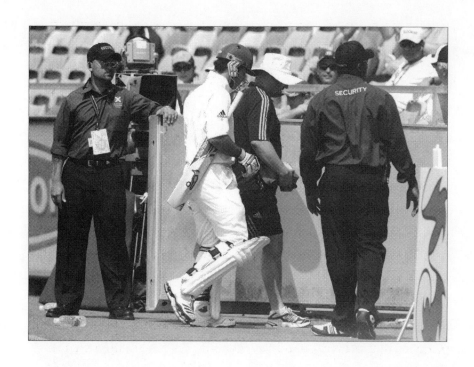

CHAPTER FIVE

GLENN ARCHER WOULD NEVER RETIRE HURT

THIRD TEST, AUSTRALIA v WEST INDIES AT PERTH, DECEMBER 16–20, 2009

Monday, December 21

Third Test, Australia v West Indies, at Perth (December 16–20): **Australia** 7–520 dec (130.4 overs: SR Watson 89, SM Katich 99, MEK Hussey 82, MJ North 68, BJ Haddin 88) and 150 (51.3 overs: DJ Bravo 4–42) defeated **West Indies** 312 (88 overs: CH Gayle 102, TM Dowlin 55; DE Bollinger 5–70) and 323 (94.3 overs: N Deonarine 82, BP Nash 65) by 35 runs

THIS WAS THE seventh time Australia played the West Indies at the WACA, and only the second home-town victory. Back in the days when the Windies had the quicks, from Andy Roberts and Michael Holding to Curtly Ambrose and Courtney Walsh, they were pretty much unbeatable in Perth, winning three times by an innings (1975–76, 1984–85 and 1992–93), once by 10 wickets (1996–97) and once by a mere 169 runs (1988–89). Our first victory over them came in 2000–01, when Glenn McGrath took a hat-trick, and then we won again this time, but only after quite a battle.

It looked like we were sweet after we went past 500 in our first innings, but there was plenty to like about the West Indies' fightback. It's a game I'm not likely to forget in a hurry, and not just because of the constant ache emanating from just above my left elbow, the product of the fearful blow I took there when I couldn't avoid a Kemar Roach bouncer. I had to retire hurt — something I hated — for only the second time in my international career (the first was because of a leg strain in an ODI against

Pakistan at Nairobi, Kenya, in 2002), and then I was only able to bat nine in our second dig. I think I'll be okay for the Boxing Day Test, but to tell you the truth I'm no certainty. Certainly, if that game started tomorrow, I'd be out for sure.

Day One

There was a real sense of expectation in the air when Roach ran in to bowl his first delivery to me. It was only the second ball I faced, after Shane Watson and Simon Katich had put together a 132-run opening stand. Sure enough, the ball was fairly short and quick. Part instinctively, part because I'd convinced myself I was going to get a first-up bouncer, I went for the pull shot, but I was probably a combination of over-anxious and a little rusty — it's true what they say about having to 'get your eye in' — and I totally mistimed it. The next ball pitched in about the same place, maybe a bit shorter, and my first reaction was to duck underneath it. But then I realised it wasn't getting up as much as I expected … so I stopped ducking … but in doing so, I created a 'blind spot', where my front shoulder momentarily blocked my view … though I still sensed the ball zeroing in on me and that I was about to get hit, probably on my arm or upper body; maybe, hopefully, on the helmet. Whack! The ball crashed into the area just above my left elbow …

It's funny, my first thought was not about whether I was hurt, or how much I was hurt; it was simply, *How on earth did I do that?* I've faced so many short balls in my career, and I've probably got myself into this sort of tangle maybe two or three times. Then the pain kicked in. I put on a brief charade that I was okay, but that didn't last long, and all too quickly Alex Kountouris, our physio, was running out to the middle. I kept thinking, *Why did you play him like that?* That question kept buzzing through my mind, even as I waited for Alex to arrive, to check if there was any serious damage.

By the time he joined us, I knew that Roach had got me in a bad spot. I still had some feeling in my fingers, wrist and forearm, but a lump had started to emerge and as it kept growing, the arm grew weaker. If you hold you forearm parallel to the ground, the ball had hit me right next to the pointy bone you can feel on the lower part of your elbow. Alex was pretty confident no bones had been broken, but the nerves and muscles and tendons in that area around my left elbow had taken a hammering. My hope was that after a few minutes all the feeling would come back and the only long-term consequence would be an ugly bruise, but I couldn't get a decent grip on the bat. It was as if every time I flexed my fingers or clenched my fist, I lost more feeling in my arm, to the point that within an over or two, I knew I was on borrowed time.

In the time immediately after I was hit, it never occurred to me that I should retire hurt. I guess you could argue that the most sensible thing for me to do for the team would have been to walk off, get the right treatment, and then I could bat pain-free later in the innings. But a much bigger part of my brain, the competitor in me, I guess, was saying that would be giving in, a terrible example. That Roach would win. Frankly, I didn't want to give the West Indies the satisfaction — to them, me walking off with the physio would have been the same as if Roach had got me out. Only easybeats retire hurt. The least I could do was bat on for an over or two, to give my arm a few more minutes to settle down.

The two remaining balls of the over were short and quick. The first crashed into my ribs, as I made an awkward attempt to get out of the way. That hurt, too, but no way was I rubbing it. The last was on the line of off-stump, and I parried it into the ground. The pain that shot up my arm when ball hit bat was excruciating, and I knew at that moment that the damage was severe. *I don't think I'm going to be out here too long*, I winced to myself.

Still, we've all suffered knocks where the initial pain was horrible, but it eventually calms down. You see it with footballers who are involved in a sickening collision in the early moments of a tough encounter but come back to be named 'best on-ground'. As Alex had another look at my arm, I did consider retiring hurt, but still not seriously; I was up for this fight, even if I couldn't hit the ball, especially on the front foot. No way was some young fast bowler going to get the better of me.

Kat straightened the mood somewhat by hitting two fours off Dwayne Bravo, and then I handled the first four balls of Roach's next over reasonably well: a two, two dot balls and a single. Their slips cordon was chirpy, and Bravo tried to bounce me, but he wasn't quick enough. By the start of Roach's next over, I was fired up in a way I've rarely been on a cricket field. I

MORE FOR EVERYBODY

I suppose there would have been a few locals having a bit of a chuckle at my expense, after I was hit by a fast riser, given that I've been critical of recent WACA Test pitches because of their lack of bounce. But after the game, I was happy to praise the curator.

'It was a good wicket,' I said. 'I'm not sure if it had the searing pace and bounce that we are all used to, but if you look at this wicket compared to the ones of the last couple of years you have to say it was better.

'This one has offered a bit more for everybody. There's been something there for the quicks if they were willing to bend their backs.

'All I have ever been disappointed with coming here is that you hear one thing and you turn up for the Test and it seems a lot different to what you have been hearing about. This one was closer to what we have been hearing about.'

wanted him to bowl short at me, to try to hit me again, so I could retaliate.

Strangely, of the four balls I faced in his next over, none were really short. But as the over went on, my arm really started to ache, to the point that I had to call for the physio a third time. The umpires decided they'd take drinks at that point, while I told Alex flatly it wasn't getting any better.

'Maybe you should come off then,' he said.

'No way, mate, not yet,' I replied. 'Let's see how it goes.'

I faced only one ball in Bravo's next over, a bouncer that I helped to fine leg. He isn't quick enough to bother me, but the pain that shot from my upper arm to my fingers as I played the shot was acute. Next over, second ball, Roach went for the bouncer, but I was waiting for it and got four to fine leg. The next one was quicker, aimed at my eyebrows, and I swung away and nailed it, straight over the fielder's head for six! The change in mood was palpable, and to rub it in, I went back and turned the fifth ball fine for four more.

With back-foot shots, I could get away with just using my bottom hand, and it was almost exhilarating hitting those fours and that six, but not quite because the ache in my arm was almost intolerable. It was impossible to hide the fact I was struggling, but I did my best. From the slips, Chris Gayle signalled to the Test debutant, Gavin Tonge, to warm up — clearly, he was coming on to replace Roach. Last ball of the next over, I went to hook Bravo but couldn't keep my top hand on the bat and it was close to agony as I ran through for a single. I couldn't have driven the ball off the square. When Tonge went to hand his hat to the umpire I signalled to the dressing room: the battle was over, it was time for me to go. As I walked off, I had a pretty good idea I wouldn't be coming back, at least not for a while.

BY STUMPS, X-RAYS HAD confirmed there was no break and we were 3–339, a terrific score but frustrating in a way because once again no one had gone on to that big innings we craved. Watto made 89 and at times was quite magnificent, while it looked like Kat was going to bat forever until he seemed to get distracted in the nineties and was caught at backward square for 99. Mike Hussey was 81 not out at stumps, and seemed to be playing himself into some real form, while Marcus North looked very comfortable throughout the last hour and a quarter of the day.

Meanwhile, I had my arm wrapped in ice, trying to minimise the internal bleeding in and around the joint. Fielding wasn't going to be a problem, but holding a bat tightly with two hands was just about beyond me.

EVERYONE IN THE AUSTRALIAN dressing room knows I pride myself on being able to get through most situations, that I wear, almost like a badge of honour, the ability to play through knocks and bruises. So they were pretty surprised when I retired hurt. Of them all, I think Justin Langer was the most stunned. I hadn't been back in the rooms long when I looked up at a whiteboard and saw a simple message written in big black capital letters …

'GLENN ARCHER'

Langer had written that. Glenn Archer is one of the greats of the AFL, a giant of the North Melbourne club. The insinuation was plain: Glenn Archer would never have retired hurt. He probably wouldn't have either, but this was a bit rich coming from Lang, a bloke who was a tough a cricketer as there ever was, but a batter who did retire hurt two or three times in his career. I'm sure he's still bitter about the way I sledged him during a Test against

Pakistan in the New Year's Test at the SCG in 2004–05, when a medium-pacer named Naved-ul-Hasan bowled a short one to him. Lang went to pull, missed and the ball hit him in the solar plexus ... and down he went. 'Winded,' he explained later. I was into him, asking politely and often about how quick Naved-ul-Hasan was, and how much that 'blow' must have stung because it knocked him over. For five years, Lang has been waiting for an opportunity to get even.

Day Two

The century curse continued on day two, when Mike Hussey started slowly and then was dismissed after adding one only run to his overnight total. Northy went on to 68 and Brad Haddin smashed a run-a-ball 88, but no one could crack three figures. I declared when Mitchell Johnson was dismissed in the 131st over, not knowing we were only four runs short of the highest innings total achieved in Tests not to include an individual hundred (India 9–524 declared against New Zealand at Kanpur in November 1976). I didn't bat, and when we fielded I had my arm pretty scientifically strapped, to take the load off specific areas around the elbow joint.

When I called our batters in, I really thought I was being aggressive, but Chris Gayle took this concept to a new level when he batted. For a little while, we thought Viv Richards' record for the fastest ever Test century might be in doubt, but we managed to slow him up a little and he reached his hundred in 70 balls, the fifth quickest ever (in terms of deliveries faced). One of his six sixes, which cleared the Lillee-Marsh Stand, was one the cleanest hits I've ever seen.

So powerful and spectacular was the Windies captain's display, he managed to direct some of the attention away from the on-field argument involving Mitch, Hadds and Sulieman Benn that occurred during the middle session. I think this was one of those incidents that looked worse than it was, but there was fault on both sides as first Benn and Johnson bumped near the pitch after Hadds called for a quick single, which prompted Hadds to point his bat angrily at the bowler after the run was completed.

'Don't point your bat at me,' Benn shouted.

'Get back and bowl,' Hadds replied.

More words were exchanged at the end of an over, as Benn shaped to throw the ball at the stumps at the striker's end, and Hadds stepped back and invited him to do his best. Seconds later, there was a bit of push and shove as Benn seemed very keen to get as close as he could to the batters' mid-pitch conversation, and umpire Billy Bowden got involved as the chat continued. Afterwards, the match referee fined our two blokes for bringing the game into disrepute and suspended Benn for two ODIs.

'Conduct contrary to the spirit of the game is completely unacceptable,' Chris Broad said when he announced these penalties, a sentiment I completely agree with. Of course, the critics were quickly on the front foot, slamming our behaviour as if it was a continuing trend, but the truth is we've been on our best behaviour for a while now — if you look at the ICC's list of players found guilty of offences you won't see many Australian names over the past year or two. However, this wasn't good, we need to acknowledge our part in it, and do our best to make sure it doesn't happen again. An incident two days later involving Shane Watson, when he over-celebrated dismissing Gayle in the West Indies' second innings, would give the knockers another chance to get into us.

When Gayle was out in the first innings, two balls after he reached his century, the Windies were 1–137 in the 25th over, still trailing by nearly 400 and with our bowlers reasonably fresh, if a little shellshocked. Mitchell Johnson dismissed Travis

Dowlin before stumps, and though Ramnaresh Sarwan was looking comfortable it seemed we were in the box seat.

ON THE FIRST DAY, AFTER I was struck on the arm, I organised with Kookaburra to send me some armguards and they arrived not long before stumps on this second day, while we were in the field. They were left on top of my kit in the dressing room, and when we came in at stumps I saw them there and I went to put them in my bag. But then I noticed someone had written 'GLENN ARCHER' on the back of them, again in big, black print.

Langer! There was no getting away from him.

FOUR INTO THREE DOESN'T GO

There's no doubt Doug Bollinger was our best bowler in this Test. He was persistent and aggressive throughout, swung the new and the old ball, and fully deserved his first Test five-for, which he achieved in the West Indies' first innings. In doing so, he's created a future conundrum for the selectors, one of those you hate in one sense but love in other: too many good players means someone who is definitely capable of playing is going to miss out, but it also means we should be able to put a good team out on the park.

'Once Siddle and Hilfenhaus come back there's going to be a major decision to be made there from the selectors about which way they go,' I commented after the Test. 'Doug has done everything within his powers to keep himself in the side, there's no doubt about that. He's certainly bowling really well at the moment.

'Hilfenhaus played a club game yesterday and that's a good sign. Siddle, I know, is pretty confident. He's feeling good about himself and is hoping to be picked in the one-day game for Victoria (against NSW on December 23) ...'

> **December 17** What an amazing day of Test cricket today was. Our boys did a great job getting us up to 520 when I was more than happy to declare. Then Chris Gayle put on a show belting us all over the WACA in what was obviously very entertaining for everyone except the 11 of us out in the field. We need early wickets tomorrow to keep ourselves on top. Thanks for all your concerns about my elbow. It's certainly not as bad as yesterday and not needing to bat today can only help my recovery. Was okay in the field but we are going to have it looked at again now as a precaution and to help with treatment. Will keep you updated on how it improves.

Day Three

This day didn't go anything like how we expected. At the start of the day, we primed ourselves to try to gain a significant first-innings lead, but we were on top from the second ball of the day, when Sarwan sliced Doug Bollinger to Mike Hussey in the gully. From there, we gradually chiselled out the rest of the line-up, taking the last eight wickets for 98 runs in 35 overs. Our lead was 208, but this time I didn't even consider the follow-on; instead, the plan was to set them an impossible target on a wearing pitch. But it didn't work out that way.

I was hoping I wouldn't have to bat. That would have been the ideal scenario. Before the start of play, with the expectation we'd most likely be batting in the afternoon, I went into the nets with my elbow strapped in a way that would take as much pressure as possible off the damaged tendon. Initially, I was very tentative, but slowly, as I kept patting throwdowns back to Tim Nielsen, I began to think, *Hey, this isn't too bad ...*

But then I went for a drive outside off stump and as soon as I began to extend my arms in my follow through I lost all the strength in my fingers and forearm, my grip was useless, and the bat flew over my left shoulder to where backward square-leg would have been if I'd been out in the middle. I knew then that as a batter I simply couldn't function properly.

Even trying to play that cover drive was going against the physio's instructions. Alex had explained to me that if I tried to grip and swing the bat too hard I'd worsen the injury, because the muscle fibres in the damaged area would keep tearing, a little at a time. But late in the day Aussie wickets kept falling, and I had to come out at No. 9, when our score was 7–125. I knew the Windies would bowl short at me, and from the first ball I realised I was useless on the front foot and I just couldn't control my back-foot shots either. Roach came back on and third ball I popped up a weak catch to short leg. A few minutes later, the players were coming off at stumps. Our overall advantage was 345 runs, with two wickets in hand.

December 18 As you probably have heard and seen now, my elbow is not too good. I had to bat tonight but didn't last too long and the boys have a big job to do in the morning to push our lead up towards 400. I'll be right to field tomorrow and am having more treatment tonight. I'm anxious to get it right as soon as possible.

Day Four

We eventually scrambled to 150 all out, a lead of 358, still a difficult ask for them, but not impossible. After all, South Africa had made 4–414 to beat us in Perth just 12 months ago. Throughout the day, though, even with a couple of our bowlers struggling with stomach upsets on a hot Perth day, we kept our noses in front and it seemed we'd complete our 2–0 series win just

UGLY AUSSIES?

I haven't seen the term 'Ugly Aussies' applied to my Australian team for quite a while, but it's happening now in the wake of a Test in which we had three guys – Mitchell Johnson, Brad Haddin and Shane Watson – fined for inappropriate behaviour. Our record has actually been pretty good over the past three or four years, so I'm not overly concerned with what went on, though I will be if it is the beginning of a trend.

Of course, I want our blokes to be passionate and aggressive out in the middle, to never let the opposition think they can out-muscle us. But there are ways of doing that without resorting to the antics that got us in trouble at the WACA. We will address the matter at our first team meeting before the Boxing Day Test, and I think that should be the end of the matter. I'm not proud of the fact we've had three guys reported in the same game, and I know the guys involved are embarrassed by what occurred. It's up to me, as the captain, and everyone in our group to do our best to ensure it doesn't happen again.

before stumps. However, their last pair of Roach and Tonge saw out the last five overs of the day, leaving them needing 51 on the final day to achieve an unlikely victory.

It was a memorable day for Clint McKay, who took his first Test wicket ... twice! Clint had gone wicketless in the first innings, despite bowling pretty well, and was still at none-for in the second when Denesh Ramdin came out to join Brendan Nash, with the Windies at 5–197. We were fired up after getting two wickets: Narsingh Deonarine, bowled by Watson for a brave 82, and Bravo, caught Hussey bowled Johnson for 1. Clint came on and Ramdin immediately hit him away for four, but the next ball was much better, Ramdin was struck on the pad and umpire Gould gave him out lbw.

A first Test wicket is always exciting, not just for the bowler but for all his team-mates and we dashed in to share Clint's joy. But then we had to check ourselves, because Ramdin had challenged the verdict. So we waited, reasonably confident the decision would hold, but it wasn't to be. All poor Clint could do was take a deep breath and try again.

It took another 15 balls. Ramdin had just got him away to third man for four, but the next one was a beauty, an off-cutter, and all the Windies keeper could do was chop it back onto his stumps. They couldn't take this one away from our new man, and our celebrations were doubly enthusiastic.

Another guy who experienced different emotions on this day was Theo Doropoulos, a WA player who was filling in as 12th man for us (Brett Geeves and Steve Smith having gone back to play state cricket). As we strove to finish off the Windies before stumps, Theo was called on as a substitute fielder and, poor bloke, promptly made a meal of reasonably easy catch at mid-on. The fact it was Sulieman Benn who benefited only made it worse. I can only imagine how the young bloke must have been feeling, and the way his stomach must have been churning when soon after Benn hit another catch out to where he was now fielding, on the deep square-leg boundary. In the circumstances, any catch would have difficult, but Theo made it look easy. His Test-match experience wasn't so bad after all.

> **December 19** Thanks everyone for the birthday wishes this morning. The messages have really given me a bounce after my embarrassing batting effort last night. I hope we can take full advantage of the pitch and conditions today to win this Test within four days. The way the wickets fell yesterday, I'll be looking to our bowlers to continue the trend.

Day Five

The game went for another three-and-a-half overs and 15 runs before Roach was caught behind. To us, it was a clear if faint edge, but a debate still ensued. Umpire Bowden gave him out, Roach challenged the decision and the original ruling was upheld, which upset many people because there was no visible deflection and the 'hot spot' technology also couldn't find an edge.

I felt this was a contrived controversy. Although there was no blatant video evidence to support the verdict, at the same time I don't think there was clear evidence that the decision was wrong, so in those circumstances I'm sure the right call was to support the umpire on the field. In my view, the same philosophy should be applied to close lbw rulings and also to catches taken at ground-level — only overturn the decision made by the umpire on the field if the video evidence *proves* it is wrong. Instead, in this case, today's newspaper reports are highly critical of what went on, with one experienced journalist describing the last out of the Test as 'a bizarre ruling'. It wasn't even close to that.

Just because Roach challenged the decision doesn't mean he didn't hit it. I never asked him and maybe he genuinely believes he missed the ball, but at that stage of the game, nine wickets down and with a challenge up his sleeve, he had absolutely nothing to lose by 'going upstairs'. Of course, there's no point wasting everybody's time if all three stumps have been knocked out of the ground but if there is a semblance of doubt or, as we believed was the case this time, the edge was very faint, why not extend the game a little?

Our final winning margin was 35 runs, which gave us a 2–0 series victory. Certainly, the visitors had given us a much bigger fight than many had expected after our big win in Brisbane, and they could take plenty of satisfaction from the efforts of their

DOING EVERYTHING I CAN

I turned 35 on the Saturday of this Test, and marked the occasion by spending a couple of hours that night in a hyperbaric chamber, as I set about trying to fix my damaged arm for the Boxing Day Test. My brief knock late that day showed me that the arm is a long way from right, and I am prepared to do anything to get the blood flowing and accelerate the healing process.

During the day, I thought the game was going to end before stumps and I'd be able to have a few drinks to celebrate my birthday, but the Windies tail wagged and then Alex explained how some time in the chamber might help.

We were actually hoping to keep this unusual and not-very-pleasant treatment quiet, but Justin Langer is combining his job as our batting coach with some commentary work for the ABC and he talked about it on air.

There was no harm done by him doing so, by I still decided to have a dig back at him. 'I'll probably have a few more of those treatments over the next couple of days,' I said at the post-game media conference. 'If you want to know if I am, just ring Lang and I'm sure he'll tell you.'

As well as doing all I could to regain my fitness, we also had to start thinking about what to do if I can't play.

To me, the most logical solution is to bring Phillip Hughes (who scored a hundred for New South Wales against Victoria last Friday) back into the XI and move Simon Katich to No. 3, and when I had a chat with vice-captain Michael Clarke and Merv Hughes, the selector on duty, about what could happen I found that their view mirrors mine.

What we must not do, in my opinion, is disrupt the entire batting order, especially if I'm only going to be missing for just the one Test match.

younger brigade — guys like Barath and Roach — and also the all-round resurgence of Dwayne Bravo. But it was their captain who really stood out. I was very impressed by the way Chris revitalised his side, as a batter and as a tactician, especially in Adelaide when he batted throughout their second innings and gave them a chance to win the Test. He fully deserved to be named player of this Test, for his whirlwind first-innings hundred, and player of the series. If the Windies are going to get back to anything like their glory days, he is going to have to lead the way.

December 20 Really good feeling among the boys after this morning's win and I am pleased with the progress we have made throughout the West Indies series. My focus now turns to getting myself fit for Boxing Day. I'll go straight into a hyperbaric chamber tomorrow in Melbourne. Boxing Day is my favourite cricket day of the year and I can't imagine not playing! Whatever it takes, I'm prepared to do it to get right.

CHAPTER SIX
RIGHT TO PLAY?

FIRST TEST, AUSTRALIA v PAKISTAN AT MELBOURNE, DECEMBER 26–30, 2009

Wednesday, December 23

IDEALLY, DURING AN Australian season, there'd be more than a week between the end of one Test series and the beginning of the next. Of course, that sort of schedule would have given me extra time to get my arm right, but that's really not my point — I think the fans would appreciate a longer break and I know the players would. It would also give the media more of a chance to build a sense of expectation before the start of the second series. Instead, we finished up against the Windies in Perth last Sunday; we were on a plane on Monday; we'll celebrate Christmas in Melbourne two days from now; and then on Saturday the first Test against Pakistan commences.

Right at the moment, my arm is improving, but I honestly don't know if I'll be playing. I did get involved in some fielding drills at training today, and I kicked a footy around, but that was it. What my time out of the nets has allowed me to do is focus on a Pakistani team that I really don't know much about — at least from a Test-match perspective. Pakistan are the World Twenty20 champions, a title they won in England last June, and before that we beat them 3–2 in a five-game one-day contest in Abu Dhabi and Dubai in April-May. But we haven't played Pakistan in a Test since our 3–nil clean sweep in Australia in 2004–05.

Earlier this year, including when they won the World T20, they were captained by Younis Khan, but he missed their recently

INS AND OUTS

As expected, Phillip Hughes was called into our squad as cover for me, if the elbow isn't right. Our most likely move if I'm out remains having Simon Katich move to No. 3, but I know Tim Nielsen had a chat with Shane Watson, to see how he'd react if he was first drop, or No. 5 with Michael Clarke at three. Not surprisingly, Watto says he's happy to do whatever is best for the team, but I must confess that I'd be very hesitant to move him out of the opening spot, given how well he's gone over the past few months. Maybe he could bat in the middle-order in the future so he can bowl more overs, but that's not the plan at the moment so I wouldn't be mucking him around for just one game. Pete Siddle has also been recalled to the squad, and he's a certain starter, which means – with Ben Hilfenhaus still on the injured list – Clint McKay will be 12th man.

Hilfy was able to bowl a few overs in Hobart last Saturday, but when I spoke to him afterwards to see how he went he told me that while his crook knee felt okay during the game, it wasn't too happy about the experience afterwards. It might not be until late in this season before he's back playing for Australia again.

completed three-Test series in New Zealand (which ended in a one-all draw) and is unlikely to play against us either. Mohammad Yousuf, an exceptional batter, will continue to lead the team in his absence. Their line-up features a number of young players who did some good things against the Kiwis, including Umar Akmal, younger brother of their wicketkeeper Kamran Akmal, who scored a hundred on debut in the first Test of that series, and a 17-year-old left-arm quick, Mohammad Aamer, who regularly bowled the first over of the innings ahead of the more experienced Mohammad Asif and Umar Gul. Also important to them will be their experienced leggie Danish Kaneria, one of only six Pakistani bowlers in Test history to take more than 200 wickets (the other five were all very handy: three champion pacemen in Wasim Akram, Waqar Younis and Imran Khan, and two outstanding slow bowlers in Abdul Qadir and Saqlain Mushtaq). Their other spinner, the offie Saeed Ajmal, is also world-class, and as a duo I expect them to be effective in Melbourne and Sydney.

I sense many in the press have already written Pakistan off, but I think it's way too early for that. Overall, I think they have more skill than the West Indies, but they are also a bit mysterious and unpredictable. One day they can be brilliant; the next, they're ordinary. We've just got to make sure they have more ordinary days than brilliant ones over the next few weeks.

> **December 22** Not sure if you've ever been in a hyperbaric chamber, but I've had enough of it already! I always feel light headed after it. Another session today. Seems to be helping but won't know until I have a bat later in the week. To tell the truth, I've been tempted to pick the bat up in my hotel room just to see how it feels but I haven't. Am a bit impatient with it all.

Thursday, December 24

AN ARTICLE THAT appeared in the News Limited papers yesterday caught my eye, where our physio Alex Kountouris was quoted as suggesting that — because of the ongoing stress of playing a number of matches one after the other — we might have reached the stage where we will have to rest key players from some Test matches, to make sure we get the most out of them over the long haul. It's a concept I've thought about from time to time — more with our quicks than with the batters. In Major League

Baseball, starting pitchers only pitch every fourth or fifth day; even relief pitchers take a break if they work two or three days in a row. In the major European football leagues, rich clubs such as Manchester United, Barcelona and AC Milan rotate their players to the point that 'second-string' combinations usually start in Cup matches. Is it better for guys to be fresh and lively for, say, four Tests in a series, rather than being exhausted and susceptible to injury after appearing in all five? Personally, if I believed I was okay, I'd hate to miss a Test because our medical team thought it was in my best long-term interests, but maybe I should at least listen to them.

'Anything is possible only because of the way the game is changing,' Alex said about the idea of resting players. 'It could get to that. At the moment we look at one Test match as the equivalent of a World Cup final, (so) we have never considered resting players. Every player wants to play every Test. But that could be subject to change … maybe if you were 2–0 up in a Test series you would look at resting a player.'

He continued: 'Things are changing very quickly as we try to manage players through Test cricket, one-day cricket and Twenty20 cricket. You can't rule anything out.'

One good thing to come out of all our recent injuries is that we now have real depth of talent almost right across the board. Without such strength, I don't think I'd be comfortable with a selection strategy that involves rotation, but with it I can see how we could develop a real advantage over most other teams in the world. I'm not saying I definitely want it to happen, but I do agree it is a concept worthy of further consideration.

Speaking of injuries, the first real test on my elbow came this morning at the MCG nets when I picked up a bat for the first time since Perth. I had the elbow strapped up the same way I'd had it done before the ill-fated hit I had on the morning of

MAKE NO MISTAKE

As a follow-up to the controversy from the Perth Test over player behaviour, the Fox Sports website conducted a survey that had more than 70 per cent of respondents saying our guys' actions were 'over the top and embarrassing'.

'You have to take notice,' I said yesterday, when I was asked what I thought of the survey. 'We try and do the right thing by the game and by the public all the time and we're also trying to win games of cricket ...

'Make no mistake, the guys are very aware that they did the wrong thing and have all come out and admitted it ...

'We've had a chat about how we want to play and how we want to be perceived and how we want the fans to look at us ... I want us to play aggressive cricket but that doesn't mean opening your mouth aggressively or with aggressive actions. It's about our body language and how we are as a group.

'We spent a fair bit of time on it today and Tim Nielsen also addressed us. I'm sure we'll see the boys back to their best behaviour this week.'

day three at the WACA, and first-up I soft-batted some throwdowns from Tim Nielsen for about 10 minutes. That went okay, but then I moved on to facing a few deliveries from Shane Watson. All was going well until Watto pitched one right up outside off stump and I decided to test out my cover drive. It was just like Perth — I missed the ball and couldn't hang on to the bat, which went flying away behind square. *That's it*, I thought, *I'm gone.*

In the rooms straight afterwards I had to concede to Alex that it didn't feel perfect, but it didn't feel terrible either, so we've decided to give it another 24 hours. I really hope I'll be all right, not least because my parents have arrived in Melbourne to spend

Christmas with us and to watch me play in the Boxing Day Test —
something they've never done live before. I've often told Dad about
what it's like to play in front of a big crowd at the MCG, how this
is an Aussie cricketers' equivalent of running out to play in an AFL
Grand Final. I'd really like him to experience it first-hand with his
son out in the middle, rather than with me sitting next to him, my
run of 60 consecutive Test matches having been broken.

Friday, December 25

I USUALLY HAVE TOO many other things to do on Christmas
Day to keep my diary up to date, but today was an important
one in my battle to be fit for tomorrow's Test match. When I
went to bed last night I was resigned to missing the game, but
this morning I had another net, to see if my grip had improved.
Initially, it didn't feel any different, but I decided to focus solely
on controlling my backswing … if I could do that, and play
more off the back foot, maybe I'll be okay. It's really now a case
of me being mentally tough to restrict my batting to the things I
can do. All the sessions in the hyperbaric chamber and the few
fridges' worth of ice I've gone through have done their job.

There is certainly nothing heroic about my decision to play.
I've always hated it when blokes say they're fit but when the
game begins it's clear they're not — that's letting your mates
down. In my case, there is a bit of pain, sure, but nothing to stop
me leading the team and doing enough to justify my place in the
side. I'm fit, so I'll play.

Still, it's been a while since I've been this close to missing a
Test.

> **December 25** Felt so much better when I batted today that I'm confident of being right for tomorrow. We will still wait till the morning before we finalise the team and I hope that my elbow feels better again. Have had a great afternoon with the family. Hope you have had a memorable Christmas Day as well.

Thursday, December 31

First Test, Australia v Pakistan, at Melbourne (December 26–30): Australia 5–454 dec (128 overs: SR Watson 93, SM Katich 98, RT Ponting 57, MEK Hussey 82, NM Hauritz 75) and 8–225 dec (73.1 overs: SR Watson 120*; Mohammad Aamer 5–79) defeated **Pakistan** 258 (99 overs: Umar Akmal 51, Misbah-ul-Haq 65*) and 251 (72 overs: Mohammad Yousuf 61; NM Hauritz 5–101) by 170 runs

I MANAGED QUITE WELL in the first innings of this Test, until eventually I tried to play the shot I'd been fearing. I got a full-pitch delivery from Mohammad Asif and my first instinct was to go for the drive. Mentally, I tried to check and physically my left arm didn't react quite as it was supposed to, and the result was a limp half drive/half push and an edge to second slip. As I walked off, I couldn't help thinking, *You're kidding yourself … the arm's not right, you're not going to be able to play in the next Test.* In the back of my mind, too, were a couple of yorkers that I had jammed down on. It might not have been obvious to those watching, but both times the bat nearly came out of my hands. Today, five days later, I'm not thinking about having a rest — in fact, I'm almost certain to play in Sydney — but it is tough batting while having to resist the urge to launch into big drives when an over-pitched delivery comes along, given that I've been playing that shot instinctively since I was a little kid. But that is what I have to do until the elbow gets better.

My second innings ended when I hooked Mohammad Aamer straight to Salman Butt at deep square-leg. The young quick surprised me with his pace, which made my hook shot look a little awkward, but I think it's a little laughable for critics to be suggesting — after one blow on my arm and one dismissal — that I now have a problem with the short ball. If only they knew that right at the moment it is the pitched-up ball that I'm most worried about.

In the meantime, this injury thing was becoming contagious. Nathan Hauritz has been battling a groin strain for a while now, and it got to the stage that the selectors called Steve Smith down to Melbourne late on Christmas Eve, just in case Horrie couldn't play. And then we heard a whisper that Danish Kaneria was battling a hand injury, and that Umar Gul might be struggling as well. As it turned out, Horrie was not only able to play, he produced his best performance in Test cricket, and an all-round one at that. But Umar and Danish had to drop out, and Pakistan missed them badly.

Day One

We won the toss, batted, and for the first two sessions the day went brilliantly. Shane Watson and Simon Katich were travelling nicely, taking the score to 0–73 at lunch and 0–177 at tea, with Watto looking tremendous, a lock for his maiden Test century. But first ball of the second over after tea, Kato pushed a delivery from Mohammad Aamer to backward point, there seemed to be an easy single, and Watto ran through. But Kato kept his eyes locked on the fielder and then moved back into his crease, so both batters were at the striker's end. The ball was relayed back to the Pakistanis at bowler's end, and the only question was which batter was out — a very tricky one because it seemed as if they had claimed the striker's end at pretty much the same time.

NO FEAR

When, on the eve of the Boxing Day Test, Mohammad Yousuf was questioned about Steve Smith, he had to ask, without any malice, who Smith was. Strictly on figures it was hard to justify Steve's call-up as Nathan Hauritz's potential replacement, as he has a first-class bowling average of 75. But I liked the selection – a few people (including his state captain, Simon Katich, and Shane Warne, who had a good look at him in the nets during this Test) have been impressed by the way his leggies come out of his hand, and he's also got plenty of batting talent, so down the track he could become an important all-rounder for us.

Smithy's performances in T20 and 50-over cricket have been terrific, and like Phillip Hughes he represents something that we haven't had a lot of in recent seasons: guys with genuine talent who get into the Test set-up before they turn 21 or 22. Maybe I'm biased because I played international cricket before my 21st, but I've always believed that it can be a good thing for younger guys to be part of the squad, so they can learn about the game and themselves in the company of the country's best players.

I knew that if Steve was asked to play that the challenge wouldn't scare him; indeed, he'd relish the opportunity. Anything I can do to help him, I'm more than happy to do.

A replay was needed to prove that Watto was the one who had to go.

You couldn't help but feel sorry for the bloke. He was just starting to get a reputation as a batter who can't convert starts into Test hundreds (his previous scores, since he came back into the Test XI last July in England, being 62, 53, 51, 34, 40, 0, 96, 48, 89 and 30), and then this happened to him. The fact he was hitting the ball beautifully and is now established in the side —

THEN AND NOW

Another indicator of the big turnover that has occurred within the Australian cricket team in the past few seasons comes with this series. The last time Australia played Pakistan in a Boxing Day Test match was in 2004–05, when the Australian starting XI was Hayden, Langer, Ponting, Martyn, Lehmann, Clarke, Gilchrist, Warne, Gillespie, Kasprowicz and McGrath. Five years later, Pup and I are the only 'survivors'.

In contrast, seven members of this season's Pakistan touring squad – Salman Butt, Imran Farhat, Mohammad Yousuf, Shoaib Malik, Kamran Akmal, Mohammad Sami and Danish Kaneria – played in that 2004–05 Test. A lot has been made of the Pakistanis' inexperience coming into this series, but you can certainly mount an argument that we're in the same boat.

no mean achievement in itself given the injury setbacks he's had — was of little consolation to him.

It was a bad miscommunication between a pair who have gelled magnificently in recent months, and afterwards Kato put his hand up as the man primarily at fault. It wasn't for me or anyone else in the dressing room to start assigning blame, but I wondered how much the noise of the crowd was a factor. It did seem that Kato just didn't hear Watto's call, but was that a concentration lapse on his part or did Watto not call loudly enough? The pair went into this Test averaging 66 as an opening partnership, and they'd put on another 182 here, so clearly they work well together, but this was an ugly one-off. When I got out to the middle, Kato was a little unsettled by what had occurred and I think he was feeling guilty at having played such a part in Watto missing out on a ton. But whether that played a part in his dismissal, caught at backward point for 98, I'm not sure. We'd added another 51 by that stage, and

I felt things were back on track. It was Kato's third ninety of the summer.

The pitch was playing a bit slowly, but I was determined to be aggressive — partly because the state of the game demanded it; partly because, after what happened between me and Kemar Roach in Perth, I assumed the Pakistani quicks would bump me and I was determined to meet fire with fire. I reached 50 in 55 deliveries and while I sometimes felt pain in the elbow I was able to get by, but then Mohammad Asif pitched the second new ball right up to me and I edged that catch to second slip.

This was the 18th time this summer an Australian batter had reached 50 but failed to go on to a hundred, a statistic I thought more weird than worrying. The way I saw it, we're obviously in pretty fair nick if we're all scoring fifties, so sooner or later someone was going to get to a hundred and that might be the start of a run of three-figure scores.

Day Two

It wasn't until right on stumps that we finally took a grip on the Test, when Mohammad Yousuf was given out by the video umpire, caught off the glove down the legside. We'd been good and aggressive all day, declaring earlier than most expected at 5–454 (with nightwatchman Hauritz making his highest Test score of 75) and then getting three wickets: Imran Farhat before tea; Faisal Iqbal and Salman Butt just after the day's final drinks break. But the Pakistan captain was the crucial wicket, and as the shadows from the grandstands started to encroach onto the playing field we nailed him as he tried to avoid a riser from Peter Siddle.

Umpire Billy Doctrove gave the batter the benefit of the doubt, but I was fielding at mid-on and from that vantage point it sure looked out to me. Of course, being the bowler, Sidds was adamant it was out but behind the stumps Brad Haddin, while he did say there were two noises, wasn't sure if bat or glove was involved. I was confident, though, and quickly sought a referral and the evidence was conclusive, which left Pakistan 4–109 at stumps. For me, it was just about the best example so far of how the referral system can help the game, rather than hurt it. It was a tight decision, but everyone agreed that the correct call had been made.

> **December 27** Couldn't be happier with where we are at after the first two days of our first Test against Pakistan. We have put ourselves in a winning position and I reckon our bowlers will keep the momentum building right through tomorrow. Enjoyed my knock yesterday but wasn't 100 per cent with my arm. Also took a bit of time to get used to the arm guard but I think it helped.

Days Three and Four

By stumps on day three, the fact that Shane Watson had never made a Test century was the biggest talking point in town. We were 3–111, an overall lead of 307, and Watto was 64 not out. The next morning, while wickets fell at the other end, he moved confidently towards the nineties, but once there he slowed dramatically, scoring only nine runs in 12 overs to be 98 not out at lunch.

With the memory of the near misses from Adelaide and Perth and also in the first innings here, I doubt Watto would have eaten too much during lunch and it was a little bit agonising for all of us to watch him try to find those two precious runs after play resumed. A push to the on-side off Saeed Ajmal got him to 99, but next over from Mohammad Aamer he sliced a ball firmly but applishly in the direction of Abdur Rauf at point. Off the bat, we were elated but immediately our hearts were in our mouths as it seemed he was going to be dismissed ... but then Rauf spilt a catch he really should have taken, Watto sprinted through for the single ... and all the talk about he and his fellow Australian batters being unable to convert fifties into hundreds was put to bed. It was a superb innings; it was just intriguing how unlucky he was to get out the way he did in the nineties in the first innings and then how lucky he was to escape being dismissed for 99 in the second dig. Those mugs who say luck evens out in the long run might actually be on to something.

Another batter to impress was Umar Akmal, who smashed a dynamic 51 in Pakistan's first innings, including 19 runs from one Peter Siddle over. There's no doubt the young bloke has enormous talent, but we quickly started wondering if at the moment he might be a little too impulsive for his own good. He was right on top after reaching his half-century, but then he went

I DECLARE

I know my first-innings declaration on day two surprised a few people, but for me it wasn't a tricky call. I've never been one to declare when you reach a certain number – every situation is different and you have to weigh up the way the pitch and outfield are playing, the mindset of both teams, how many overs you need to bowl a team out twice, sometimes the weather becomes a factor.

In this instance, the pitch was slower than your typical MCG wicket and the outfield wasn't all that rapid either. In my view, a total of 450 here was the equivalent of 500 or more from seasons past, and I sensed the game could become a war of attrition unless we were proactive. Further, I liked the idea of saying to our pace bowlers: go out there and show that there's more in the deck than the Pakistani quicks could find. Sidds, Mitch and Dougie responded in a very positive fashion, Horrie bowled as well as he's ever done in a Test, and by stumps we were well on the way to taking a 1–0 lead in the series.

THE LEADER OF OUR ATTACK

In the main, Mitchell Johnson has had a terrific past 12 months (63 Test wickets in a calendar year for the second year in a row, and precisely 500 Test runs in 2009 to go with them), and right at the moment he's doing just about everything right, a point I really wanted to emphasise after the game.

'I said to him after our first-innings bowling, I think that's the best he's probably bowled for us,' I explained in the post-game media conference. 'He's continuing to get better, and to start the way he did this morning with those two very good deliveries to get those wickets early on ... it set the trend for us.

'He's going from strength to strength. I honestly feel one of the big things for Mitch is the fact he's not bowling with the new ball. We've seen at different times how dangerous and damaging he can be with the new ball, but I think we've seen here in conditions where the old ball does a little bit as well that that's when he's at his most effective ...'

for one slash too many against Mitchell Johnson and was caught at second slip. Still, next to Mohammad Yousuf, he's probably their best batter, and we knew at stumps on the fourth day, when Pakistan were 3–170 chasing 422 with those two at the crease, that if we got them out early the following morning that the match was as good as won.

> **December 28** Had a lot of trouble with my arm today. No excuse for the way I got out but I am having difficulty getting the full range of movement. We did well in the field today and the bowlers eventually closed out their innings. Watto and Pup have got us back into a solid position at stumps and tomorrow we need to build a match-winning lead.

Day Five

I'm sure Nathan Hauritz enjoyed his time as a No. 5 batter on day two, and the ripping off-break he delivered that knocked over Faisal Iqbal on the fourth afternoon might have been the best ball he's bowled in Test cricket. However, I think he enjoyed the final day of this Test best of all, as he spun us to victory and completed his first five-for in first-class cricket.

Since the Ashes series, Horrie has been terrific in one-dayers and T20 games in England, South Africa and India, and while he's never run through a Test batting line-up, he's bowled some pretty useful overs. In this game, he was excellent, especially the way he persisted with his bowling plans even if the Pakistani batters hit him for a boundary or two.

They clearly had a game plan to attack him and thus destroy his confidence — on day two, Mohammad Yousuf smashed the third ball he faced from him for six — but Horrie stood his ground and comes out of this game established, for the first time, as Australia's No. 1 spinner. I especially liked the way he responded in their second innings when Kamran Akmal slammed a well-flighted delivery over the long-off boundary, the way he took his time and then tossed up another tempting delivery … the batter took the bait, missed, and was metres down the pitch when Brad Haddin completed the stumping.

It's easy for a legend like Shane Warne to keep tossing the ball up when he's under attack, but not so easy for a younger bowler trying to establish himself, who fears being taken off and then dropped from the side if he goes for too many runs. This was Horrie's first Test stumping, in his 11th Test. It won't be his last.

I'm genuinely thrilled with the way our bowlers performed in this game. As was reflected by my two declarations, it wasn't an easy track for bowlers to get wickets, but our blokes stuck to their plans resolutely and showed a little class in the way they worked the Pakistani batters out. This was especially true in the first innings, when as a group I thought our bowlers performed as well as anything we've produced over the past couple of years, and also on this final day, when I spoke to the guys before the resumption of play about the importance of staying disciplined and starving the batters — especially Mohammad Yousuf and Umar Akmal — for runs. Build the pressure, I demanded, and the wickets will come. As it turned out, Mitchell Johnson snared a couple of wickets with consecutive balls in the first over of the day and we got on a roll from there. It was a great game for us, in my view one of our best Test wins in quite a while.

WINS NO. 42 AND 93

This was my 42nd win as a Test-match captain, a new record, one more than my predecessor Steve Waugh. For me, more than any wrap for my leadership skills, I see this landmark as a tribute to all the guys I've had the good fortune to lead over the past six years.

I try to take criticism and praise of my captaincy in the same way. For example, I was amazed how much acclaim my first declaration in this Test received, as if it was one of the shrewdest things a captain has ever done. Similarly, I'm sure next time I make a decision that doesn't work out, I'll get roundly slaughtered. Each reaction is over the top, but you just have to live with it and hope that over the long run you make more good calls than bad.

This was also the 93rd Test win I've been involved in, the most by a cricketer from any team, one more than Shane Warne achieved during his legendary career. Again, this record is more a reflection of my longevity at the top level and the fact I've played in some great Australian sides. In fact, the top eight 'winningest' Test players are all Aussies from the 'modern' era: me, Warney, Steve Waugh, Glenn McGrath, Adam Gilchrist, Mark Waugh, Matthew Hayden and Justin Langer.

It was our seventh Test win of the year, in 13 Tests, and while we haven't been dominant in this time, I couldn't help thinking after the game: *We're building a squad of players here who — in a couple of years time, maybe even as soon as next season — could go close to being as dominant as the great Australian teams of the recent past.*

One of the best things about finishing a Test early on the final day (this one ended two overs after lunch) is that you have plenty of time to celebrate — we could take our time and savour the progress we've made. 'There's a great feeling around the team,' I said proudly after the game, 'and wins like this one make the feeling around the place a whole lot better.' After their 'breakthrough' performances in this game, Horrie and Watto probably enjoyed the beers most of all, along with Mitch, who was tremendous throughout (3–36 from 22 overs in the first innings; 3–46 from 18 in the second), and Dougie Bollinger, who is bowling so well I'd hate to be one of the selectors who have to decide what to do when Ben Hilfenhaus is available again.

The mood in our dressing room post-game was so different to last year, when we suffered one of our worst defeats ever in the Boxing Day Test against South Africa, so it was little wonder both Tim Nielsen and I were also struggling to keep grins off our faces. Someone asked me how my arm was and I had to confess that, just for a little while, I'd forgotten all about it.

It's not a bad team Tim and I are in charge of here.

IN THE MIDDLE OF your own Test match, it's usually hard to keep track of what's happening elsewhere in the cricket world, but it's been impossible over the past few days to miss the scoreline from South Africa, where England were absolutely dominating the second Test in Durban. It was amazing the number of times someone would say to me, 'Have you seen what the Poms are doing to South Africa?'

I think there is a perception in some circles here in Australia that we lost the Ashes to a pretty run-of-the-mill English outfit, and that consequently we'll regain the Ashes in 2010–11 as easily as we did in 2006–07, but the efforts of guys like Graeme Swann, Matt Prior, Alastair Cook, Ian Bell and Stuart Broad against Graeme Smith's South Africans are going a long way to proving that their victory over us was not a fluke.

I know they're a tough side and that we'll have to play well to beat them next summer. Beating South Africa anywhere is a good trick; thrashing them by an innings on their turf doesn't happen very often, and in this instance they did it without a major contribution from their most dynamic player, Kevin Pietersen.

The final score when the Test ended last night our time was 9–574 declared to 343 and 133. I can feel the sense of anticipation for the next Ashes battle growing, within our set-up and across the wider Australian cricket community. If England keep producing performances like this one, by next November the buzz will be the same as it was last time the two teams met in Australia, which was phenomenal.

December 31 About to head back to Sydney with Rianna and Emmy and I have a big grin on my face after yesterday's win. As I said in the media, it's one of the best wins we have had for a long time and the boys have really savoured the moment. We need to repeat it at the SCG as we are expecting the Pakistanis to improve a lot from this Test.

Saturday, January 2

I'VE ALWAYS REALLY enjoyed New Year's Eve in Sydney, though times have changed since I first saw the fireworks as a member of the Australian cricket team, back in 1995–96. I was then a 'veteran' of just two Test matches, Launceston was my home base, and everything about my cricket life was new and exciting. A peculiar aspect of that season was that there was no New Year's Test in Sydney — not long after the midnight fireworks were finished we were in bed at our city hotel because we had a day/night ODI against the West Indies to play at the SCG later that day. This was the game made famous by Michael Bevan, who hit the final ball of our last possible over for four to win the game nine wickets down; in contrast, my innings was miserable — bowled first ball by Curtly Ambrose for a duck.

I never grew tired of having a good feed and a couple of quiet drinks with my team-mates and then watching the fireworks. From 1997–98 to 2007–08, the Test always started on January 2, so it wasn't as if we had to get out of bed early the next morning; we could stay up a little late and see in the new year (it's only been the past couple of years, with the authorities wisely ensuring that there are three full days between the end of one Test and the start of the next, that this match now commences on January 3). But now that I'm married, based in southern Sydney and with a beautiful young daughter at home, I much prefer to just stay away from Sydney Harbour, take it easy, and maybe I'll make it to midnight before crashing into my own bed. These days, I look forward to this brief time out of the spotlight; it's different to the old days, and better.

I went out to the ground yesterday, but didn't pick up a bat, just worked with the boys and then did a few media interviews.

ONE ELBOW AFTER ANOTHER

One thing that slipped the attention of most observers during our second innings in Melbourne was that Simon Katich copped a nasty blow on the elbow when he was facing Pakistan's impressive young quick Mohammad Aamer. Apparently, it's a similar injury to mine, only worse, and after struggling to complete a net session this morning Kato is very unlikely to play tomorrow. Phillip Hughes is once again on standby.

Ironically, Mohammad Aamer is also unlikely to play because of a groin strain, but softening that blow for the tourists is that Danish Kaneria will return. Five years ago, Kaneria took seven wickets in an innings in a Sydney Test and his record over the past few years stacks up against just about any other spinner in the game. Even though the wicket might suit the seamers if it's damp because of the rain that's been falling, he still shapes as a key man for them. Two experienced quicks, Umar Gul and Mohammad Sami, will also come into their starting line-up.

Today, players, partners and families from both teams were invited to the Prime Minister's Sydney residence, Kirribilli House, for lunch. We were forced inside because there were plenty of showers about, and we learned it is Kevin Rudd's hope that a prime ministerial reception in Sydney for the visiting team in the New Year's Test will become an annual event. 'It's part of our desire as the Government of the country to make you feel genuinely and officially welcome,' Mr Rudd explained to the Pakistani players and officials. I was invited up onto the small stage, where the PM asked me if I could give him any inside information on the upcoming Test.

As the rain continued to fall, I quickly looked through the big doors that open out onto some pretty handy real estate and quipped, 'If this weather keeps up, the SCG wicket might look like the lush, green lawns of Kirribilli House.'

CHAPTER SEVEN
TOSSED AROUND

SECOND TEST, AUSTRALIA v PAKISTAN AT SYDNEY, JANUARY 3-6, 2010

Thursday, January 7

Second Test, Australia v Pakistan, at Sydney (January 3-6): Australia 127 (44.2 overs: Mohammad Asif 6-41) and 381 (125.4 overs: SR Watson 97, MEK Hussey 134*; Danish Kaneria 5-151) defeated **Pakistan** 333 (96.5 overs: Imran Farhat 53, Salman Butt 71; DE Bollinger 4-72) and 139 (38 overs: NM Hauritz 5-53) by 36 runs

FOR THREE DAYS, it was all about the toss — or, to be more precise, what I did after I won the toss. On the last day, though, because of a fantastic late-order partnership between Mike Hussey and Peter Siddle and then a brilliant team bowling and fielding effort, everything changed. We won a game everyone outside our group thought lost and suddenly my decision was the right one.

Or was it?

The thing about being a cricket captain is that you're really only as good as your team. I guess that is true of all team sports, all team ventures. I always thought it was true of Mark Taylor and Steve Waugh when they were Australian captain; I know it's true of me. When Tubby batted first on a bowler's deck at Old Trafford in 1997, everyone thought he was a genius, but the main reason we won that game was because Steve Waugh defied the conditions to score a hundred in each innings and Shane Warne took 6-48 in England's first knock. I'm not saying 'Tubby' was necessarily wrong to bat first, but it sure helped having great players to back his judgment. Steve made a habit of sending teams in, and it always seemed to work for him even though that meant that Shane wasn't bowling on the last day; with an attack featuring Glenn McGrath, Jason Gillespie and Brett Lee (and Warney, who was the best first-day spinner I've ever seen) we usually knocked the opposition over for a manageable total anyway. I guess my most publicised 'gaffe' as captain was to send England in at Edgbaston in 2005, a Test we lost by two runs, but I'll always maintain our biggest problem in that game was that we just bowled badly on the first day. I also remember the Test in Johannesburg 10 months ago, when I backed our top-order batters to survive on a pitch that was clearly going to be difficult at the start and we ended up winning by plenty. We did lose a couple of early wickets then, but got to lunch only three wickets down and then Marcus North (who scored a hundred in his first Test) and Mitchell Johnson (who finished unbeaten on 96) built on that good work superbly.

This time, we didn't have a good first day, but it was an awkward pitch to bat on and we knew that Pakistan had bowlers capable of exploiting the conditions. Mohammad Asif, who is a very good and smart bowler, was excellent, and Mohammad Sami also went well, especially in his opening spell. What I did when I decided to bat first was back our ability to score more in our first innings than they would score in their second innings, and that's just about how it turned out, so maybe I was proved right.

I'm very proud of the fact we were good enough to fight back and win. I'm not sure we could have done that 12 months ago, and I think this victory could become a landmark for us. Winning is contagious, and now we are really starting to believe we can win from anywhere. This happened to Tubby's team in 1995 when we beat the West Indies on their turf, something that hadn't been done for more than 20 years. For Steve's team, it was the Hobart Test in 1999, when Adam Gilchrist and Justin Langer came together at 5–126 chasing

369 against Pakistan and weren't dismissed until we were just five runs short of what everyone agreed was an epic victory. Time will tell if this win here has the same effect, but it could have.

Our aim this summer has been to be more consistent and you can't get that without belief in yourself and your team-mates. We honestly never stopped believing we could win this Test, even when so many people outside our dressing room were doubting us, so you can imagine how positive we're feeling at the moment. Now, we have to remember all the good things we are doing to get these good results and to keep trying to do the same things over and over. Stick to the game plan, work together, keep doing what you're good at, stay confident — do all that and eventually the opposition will be struggling under the pressure you're applying.

When Steve Waugh was captain and when I first started as skipper, the Australian team got itself in as much trouble as any team in world cricket, but we always had the confidence in each other to get ourselves back in front and then we went on and won the game. That's where I want this team to be, and I think we're getting there.

Day One

Had it been a sunny day, there would have been no doubt: bat first. We knew when we arrived at the ground that there was little chance that play would start on time. It was overcast, often drizzling and it seemed like one of those days when we might never get started, when every time it seemed that play could begin it would rain again. We'd do our warm-ups and then we'd go back into the dressing room ... then the umpires decided on an early lunch ... then we stretched a bit more ... another short delay ... then, finally, they settled on a 2pm start.

Even before the toss, people were saying it'd be a 'good one to lose'. I've never believed in that — and as a captain who has lost more Test-match tosses than I've won, I should know. I'd always rather make the difficult call and make a mistake than let the other guy have the chance to do the right thing. I'd always prefer to bat first, on the basis that, one, if you get through the opening session, the first afternoon and into the second day is usually a good time to bat; and, two, batting last is almost always the toughest time to bat in a five-day game. The pitch

A BIT OF HISTORY

A strong part of my decision to bat first was the recent history of Tests at the SCG. There have been 20 instances of a captain inviting the opposition to bat first after winning the toss in a Sydney Test match, but none since 1991–92, Shane Warne's debut Test, when India's Mohammad Azharuddin did so at the start of a high-scoring draw. The last Australian captain to do so was Allan Border in 1989–90, but he was trying to force a result after the first two days of a Test against Pakistan were washed out.

The team that sent the opposition in won just five of those 20 Tests, with five drawn and 10 lost. Four of those five wins came between 1975–76 and 1985–86. I know that in recent times, it has become very unlikely for a captain to do anything but bat at the SCG, such is the great ground's reputation as a spinner's paradise that turns more and more as the game goes on. It was also true, according to those who've seen plenty of cricket in Sydney, that this was the most lively first-day SCG wicket since the Australia-England Test here in 1979–80, but the difference was that the pitch then was so under-prepared it stayed difficult for most of the game. Greg Chappell sent the Englishmen in on that occasion and the match totals were England 123 and 237 versus Australia 145 and 4–219.

here was firm, though with more grass than a typical SCG deck, and initially it was only the overcast sky that had me even thinking about fielding first. However, it seemed like every time the covers came off the pitch was a tinge greener, so that by the time we were about to toss the idea of gambling on sending them in was definitely on my mind.

I went in and donned my blazer and then, before meeting up with Mohammad Yousuf and match referee Ranjan Madugalle in the middle, I spoke to both Michael Clarke and Tim Nielsen while they were continuing with the team warm-up. Suddenly, as is always the way when the umpires finally decide on a starting time after a long delay, it was a bit rushed, but nothing Pup or Tim said swayed my thinking: *If we bat first and get through the first 20-odd overs unscathed, we'll be in front.*

About three-and-a-half hours later, 40 overs into the game, we were 9–117 and I was contemplating a rare first-day declaration. The pitch seamed more than we expected, Mohammad Asif, Mohammad Sami and Umar Gul bowled very well, we played a number of loose shots, and I was wondering if it would be better to get the Pakistani opening bats in to face a few difficult overs before stumps rather than let Doug Bollinger and Peter Siddle take up a few minutes with their last-wicket partnership. In the end, I decided the innings could run its course, Dougie and Sidds added eight runs, and Imran Farhat and Salman Butt then survived 25 balls before bad light brought this testing day to an end. All I could do was remind the boys that the game still had a long way to go.

We had played some poor shots, but in this sort of situation it's often not just the 'out ball' that is responsible for your dismissal. If a wicket is turning or seaming or the ball is swinging — the pressure is on in a way it isn't usually, and that can lead to some ordinary shots. One of the great skills in big-time cricket is to not be distracted by the conditions, but to play to your strengths. I guess life can be like that, too. But it's a lot easier to be clever when the questions are simple. You get a sequence of deliveries that all could have knocked you over and then you see one that looks loose but quickly you realise that it's not that bad a ball. Too late. You can go through with the shot, or try to hold back, but either way the damage is done.

Mind you, this was not the case with my dismissal. In at 1–2 in the fourth over after Phillip Hughes' return to Test cricket was cut short, I was determined to be assertive, to prove my decision to bat first was the right one. Straight away, Mohammad Sami dropped a bit short and my instinct was to go for the pull shot … but I'd slightly misread the length, it wasn't *that* short, and maybe there was a bit of my brain (the logical bit, given the conditions and the fact I hadn't played myself in) saying, *Don't do this!* The result was an ugly lob out to the fielder at deep backward square, and for the second year in a row in Sydney (and third time in 16 Tests) I was out for a first-ball duck. I've probably played a dumber shot at some stage in my career, but as I walked off the SCG I couldn't think of one.

It wasn't a wicket on which we should have been bowled out for such a small total, but we knew the grass on it wasn't going to suddenly disappear overnight. If the weather stayed overcast, and we bowled in the right areas, there was plenty for us to look forward to. Meanwhile, I braced myself for the next morning's press coverage, which I knew wasn't going to be kind.

Day Two

'MUG PUNTER!' shouted the back page of the *Daily Telegraph*, and immediately I thought: *They're not going to miss me*. One reporter described my decision at the toss as 'bizarre' and another said it was 'embarrassing'. The *Tele* ran a poll asking readers if it was my worst ever decision and something like 68 per cent of respondents said it was. But when I cut below the surface, beyond the headlines and the sensationalism, a lot of the criticism in the papers was pretty reasonable, especially that from former players such as Steve Waugh, Shane Warne and Michael Slater.

What we needed at the start of the second day was a continuation of the cloud cover, and to a degree we did get that, though the sun did make an appearance from time to time. In fact, I'm not sure the conditions were much different for the first half of day two to what they were on day one. Our main problem was that Pakistan's openers, Salman Butt and Imran Farhat, fought hard and we struggled to get the early breakthrough we required. I admired their patience and craved their luck, and the first wicket didn't fall until well after lunch, by which time they'd almost reached our meagre total. The good news for us was the way our bowlers persisted — in Melbourne we played some excellent cricket and earned a decisive victory; on this day, we weren't as sharp but we never chucked it in, never stopped working. Often, I felt that if we could follow up a wicket with another their innings might disintegrate, but we just couldn't get that double or triple breakthrough. By stumps, the tourists' lead was 204, with one wicket still in hand, and I was thinking we'd need to score at least 400 in our second dig to have a chance. Get that many, I reasoned, and we might be able to put them under pressure.

There was a time in Test cricket history when a 250-run target was nearly impossible to get in the fourth innings. Wickets over the past 20 years have become more durable, but there's still a certain stress involved in reaching a total on a pitch showing any sign of wear, and all cricketers are aware of that.

> **January 4** Yesterday's conditions clearly beat us and while I'm disappointed with where we are at after day one, I have great confidence in this team. Today is the most crucial day of the Test match and we will be doing everything possible to put the maximum pressure on Pakistan.

Day Three

This was a disappointing day for us. We set ourselves to make a big total, and Shane Watson and Phillip Hughes did the right thing with an opening stand of 105, but after that we never had another really substantial partnership and at stumps our total was 8–286, a lead of just 80. Mike Hussey was 73 not out, with Peter Siddle on 10.

Watto was dismissed in the nineties again, but there was little he could do this time as he copped a brute of a delivery from Umar

JANE MCGRATH DAY

For the second year in a row, the third day of the Sydney Test was designated as 'Jane McGrath Day'. In fact, there was a lot of pink about for the entire Test, but day three was special, as the old Ladies Stand was renamed 'The Jane McGrath Stand' and the fans wore a bold assortment of pink shirts, bandanas, shorts, zinc, anything goes really, to get into the spirit of things.

On day one, during warm-ups, the Pakistani players wore special pink caps that Glenn presented to them, and two days later, up in the commentary box, Michael Slater donned a fetching pink suit and looked the part. Prime Minister Kevin Rudd was among a group cooking sausages with Glenn at a barbecue before play on day three. All the while, money was being collected for the McGrath Foundation (I understand more than $200,000 was raised), and Jane's courage, fight and constant cheerfulness were being remembered.

Gul and could only edge a sharp catch to second slip. The pity here was that instead of everyone talking about how well he played — I thought it was just about his best innings in Test cricket so far — it was all about him being knocked over in the 'nervous nineties' again. There was always the possibility of a lethal ball spitting out of the wicket, though mostly it played really well and we should have done much better. Had we lost this Test, this is where the game would have slipped away from us. If you don't make as many as you need in the first innings, there's always the second dig — Test cricket has been like that forever — but for a while here it looked like we'd wasted that opportunity.

What was needed was an ability to really knuckle down, be patient, and wait for the right delivery to score from. Watto and Huss proved that run-making was far from impossible; the rest of us should have followed their lead. We were lucky, too, in that Pakistan's keeper Kamran Akmal dropped three catches but at stumps we were still, in the words of one senior correspondent up in the press box, 'facing certain defeat'.

> **January 5** Just about to head to the ground and it's a sensational day here in Sydney so perfect conditions for batting. Our top order, me in particular, have a big job to do today and we will be looking to bat for two days to give ourselves a chance of turning this game around. We're confident we can do that.

Day Four

Sydney has made a habit lately of memorable Test-match finishes. In 2006, we won a Test from nowhere on the back of some great batting and a generous declaration from South Africa's Graeme Smith. In 2007, we sealed a 5–0 Ashes clean sweep in what proved to be the final Test for Shane Warne, Glenn McGrath, Justin

Langer and coach John Buchanan. In 2008, Michael Clarke took three wickets in five balls to win a controversial, acrimonious match against India. In 2009, South African captain Graeme Smith defied a broken hand to try to save the game, but Mitchell Johnson got him with 10 balls to spare. And now this one … which is right up there with any of them!

I've played cricket long enough to know just about anything is possible. But I'm also old enough not to believe in Santa Claus. In this case, I knew batting last wasn't going to be easy and if we could just get them under pressure chasing a target it could get interesting.

Before play, I reminded the guys that there were very few people outside our dressing room who truly believed we could

RIGHTS AND WRONGS

It was a strange Test for the referral system. Many people thought that a couple of decisions that were reversed should have stayed the way they were – I'm not sure we should be relying on the hawkeye technology to determine whether the ball is going over the stumps or not – but there were a couple of times when incorrect calls were quickly and correctly changed, not least the one on the final day when Faisal Iqbal was given out lbw but it took just a single replay to demonstrate that this verdict was wrong. The ball obviously hit the inside edge before it struck the pad. It's hard to argue against the system when that sort of thing happens.

The on-field umpire was shown to be in error on that occasion, but there have been other times, in this Test and earlier in the summer, when players have asked for replays when quite clearly they shouldn't have. As Greg Baum wrote in the *Age* after the third day's play: 'One moral of the referral system is that it makes fools of players at least as often as umpires.'

win. I certainly hadn't given the game away. I had a long talk to Huss, reminding him that he is in good form, has been all summer. Sidds, I said more than once, is a good late-order batter who wouldn't let him down, a batter not unlike Jason Gillespie in that he's sensible and has a tidy defensive technique. Jason, of course, once scored 200 in a Test as a nightwatchman, and he was always one of those lower-order batters who can be a pain in the butt — real hard to dismiss, while the more accomplished bloke at the other end is taking the game away from you. Every time a captain pushes the field back to give the better player an easy single, so they can attack the tailender, you can hear the critics moaning but I reckon this is often a perfectly logical tactic; it depends on who the batters are, especially who the 'inferior' bloke is. Where the strategy falls down is if the tailender has a good defence, and is hard to chisel out, and that was the case here. Once Sidds was entrenched, Pakistan should have attacked Huss more, but they kept giving away singles and our blokes were happy to take them.

I also told Huss to keep encouraging Sidds to keep going. I've always found with Sidds that if you give him a task he takes great pride in giving it his best shot. And I told both guys that there have been a number of instances of games being won from these sort of situations, including a few in Sydney. 'It's never easy to bat last here,' I said. 'Every run we get will make it harder for them.'

I was a bit surprised that Mohammad Yousuf went on the defensive pretty much straightaway, seemingly waiting for the wicket to fall. The mood changed remarkably quickly, as it often seems to with late-order partnerships — first, the 100 lead was an important landmark; then Huss hit two fours in one Umar Gul over to reach his hundred. At that point, Sidds had added just a single to his overnight score. Four overs later, our No. 10 managed his first boundary of the morning, an educated edge to third man, to take the lead out to 127, our first-innings total.

If they could bowl us out for such a low score, I thought to myself, *surely we can do the same to them.*

The Pakistanis' body language showed they were deeply worried. Kamran Akmal, who was having a shocker, dropped Sidds down the legside off Mohammad Sami. Then, for the second time in the morning, they referred a decision upstairs but the final decision went our way. Two balls after that setback for them, Sidds cracked a Kaneria full toss for four to take our lead past 150. The mood in our rooms was now ultra-positive, but weird in a way: we knew every run was valuable so we didn't want the innings to end just yet; but we couldn't wait to get out there and try to turn the impossible into a win.

At lunch, we were 8–373, with Huss on 127, Sidds 37, the stand worth 116, the lead 167. The two of them had remained together for more than three hours in all, a remarkable partnership built on pride, skill, tenacity and commonsense. I'm not sure I can remember a more rousing reception for two batters coming into the rooms at a break in play. After the interval, the fun continued for another five overs and seven runs before Sidds was finally out for 38, and then a single later Dougie Bollinger was bowled. Pakistan needed 176 to win.

WE WERE PROBABLY A bit too eager at the start of their second innings, and Imran Farhat and Salman Butt got them off to a flyer: 0–29 after six overs. But last delivery of over No. 7, bowled by Bollinger, Farhat started to go for one big drive too many, checked his shot, but only succeeded in spooning a soft catch to Mitchell Johnson at mid-off. After 10 overs, they were 1–46, but then the Test swung again when in the space of three Johnson deliveries Brad Haddin took two catches — the second, to dismiss Butt, being an absolute classic as he dived miles down the legside to intercept an edge that seemed destined for the fine-leg boundary. Suddenly, we were one wicket away from being on top.

It's been obvious for a while that Mohammad Yousuf and Umar Akmal are their best two batters, and just as clearly Pakistan have adopted a policy of trying to attack Nathan

ARMED WITH A DIFFERENT PERSPECTIVE

I'd be kidding if I said my elbow isn't bothering me. It's a weird injury, unlike anything I've ever endured before, in that it only affects me when I'm doing certain things. I can play some shots and it doesn't matter, but then I'll try a different shot and it's there big-time. I keep telling myself to forget about it, but when I do that I'm concentrating on something other than just watching the ball.

In the days between Melbourne and Sydney, I kept working hard on the injury and I was able to convince myself that it was okay to play, that I could get away with staying on the back foot. This sounds okay in theory, but I have found that because I am not doing what comes naturally, my footwork is less decisive. My usual 'trigger' when I'm batting is to go forward, and then, if the ball is short, I rock back onto my back foot. Now, because of the physical restrictions placed on me by the arm injury, I am stopping myself from doing that and in the process I've found that I am getting a slightly different perspective of the length of each delivery. My shot selection was poor in Sydney — in the first innings I misread the length of the first ball I received and played a dreadful half pull, half scoop out to deep backward square; in the second, same as the first innings in Melbourne, I instinctively went for a drive I knew I shouldn't have attempted, didn't go through with the shot, and was caught in the slips.

In terms of my batting, maybe I've done myself a disservice by playing in the past two Tests. But I still think I did the right thing as captain and by the team, by getting out there and setting a good example.

Haurtiz every chance they get. Maybe they still don't rate him, or maybe they thought or had been told that his psyche is fragile and they can inflict some mental damage if they get after him, but straightaway they were on the front foot when Horrie came on to bowl. Three times in the first over he faced him, Yousuf smashed him for four — through point, backward square-leg and cover. I kept him on, kept the field up, and third ball of Horrie's next over, Yousuf was down the wicket and absolutely creamed a straight drive. But it was uppish, and on a collision course with the bowler, and all our man could do was try to hold on, which with the help of his chest he brilliantly did.

It was a key moment, but as we rushed in to congratulate Horrie it seemed he might have done some very serious damage to his hand, a finger or thumb. Or maybe his ribcage had been crushed. I quickly had visions of Lord's last July when he dropped Andrew Strauss and dislocated a finger, but this one was uglier, though not as bad. It looked like the thumb nail on his left hand had been ripped off and there was plenty of blood, and Alex Kountouris rushed out to the middle. There was a brief delay while the thumb was treated and then Horrie said through gritted teeth, 'I'm going to have to go off.'

'No you're not,' I snapped back. 'You've got to bowl. Put a bit of tape on it and fix it up later.'

And that, pretty much, was the end of the conversation. Later, back in the dressing rooms, the boys kept reminding Horrie how tough he'd been, and I think it was Pup who was the first one to start calling him 'Hard as Nails'. That nickname won't stick forever, but I can certainly see the boys calling him 'Nails' for at least a day or two.

He bowled us to victory, finishing with his second Test five-for, achieved in successive matches. 'Keep backing yourself,' I've kept saying to him, and I know Tim Nielsen has hammered that point with him too. Of course, it's a cheap line saying that if you don't really believe your man can come through, but Tim and I have been confident for a while now that Horrie has it in him. We've been working with him for so long about trying to bowl a really aggressive line and length in Test matches, but in the past, when things have got awkward, he's reverted to his one-day method and become too negative. We needed him to throw the ball up, give it a chance to grip and turn; if batters want to take him on, that's good. If he goes for a couple of fours in the same area, we can plug that gap and make them hit to other parts of the ground, where they're less comfortable. If you get hit back over your head for six, that's okay … you still get the ball back, you get another chance.

The way Horrie bowled made for a great afternoon for me as captain, in that we were able to build pressure, build pressure, until we suffocated the life out of them. I know some of their shots looked a little outlandish, a little too over-the-top, but I think we worked so well as a group that the stress of the situation got too much for them. I know as captain I was really excited, putting fielders back at times to try to block their favourite shots, then bringing fielders up at other times, as if to say, *If you want to try to loft the ball into the outfield, do your best.* The Pakistanis weren't sure how to win, and then they panicked, hit us a few catches, and we hung on to every one of them.

Umar Akmal was the biggest danger, and he batted beautifully to reach 49, but then we brought the field up in the middle of a Doug Bollinger over. Go over the top if you want to, we dared, and he tried almost immediately, only to sky a catch to extra cover, where Mitchell Johnson made a difficult chance look easy.

That made it 8–133 in the 35th over. Nineteen balls later, two more wickets to Horrie, and the game was over. We're 2–0 up in the series.

THE FIGHTBACK CLUB

In January 1950, at Durban, Lindsay Hassett's Australians were dismissed for 75 in their first innings, giving South Africa a lead of 236. The home team didn't enforce the follow on and they were promptly bowled out for 99, and Neil Harvey then scored one of his greatest centuries to lead Australia to an improbable five-wicket win.

In August 1992, at Colombo, Sri Lanka made 547 in their first innings in reply to Australia's 256. No Aussie scored a century in the second innings, but everyone reached double figures and they set the Sri Lankans 181 to win. At 2–127, Arjuna Ranatunga's team looked home, but they then lost their last eight wickets for just 37 runs.

Before this match, these were the only two examples of Australia trailing by 200 runs on the first innings of a Test but recovering to win. We are thus the first Aussie team to achieve this feat on home soil. It's only the sixth time it's happened across all Test cricket – the other three times occurred when Australia lost after enforcing the follow on (against England at Sydney in 1894–95 and at Leeds in 1981, and against India at Kolkata in 2001).

USUALLY AFTER A BIG win, I'd much rather stay in the rooms with the boys and celebrate, but this time a part of me was very keen to get to the media conference, so I could have a quick chat with some of the press boys who'd been into me after the first day's play. I wondered how quickly they'd get to the point. It didn't take long ...

'Ricky, do you feel vindicated for batting first?' was the first question.

'You're putting your own hand up, are you?' I answered the question with a question. 'Can everyone (who thought I was wrong to bat first) put their hands up, please?'

Almost to a man and woman they put their hands up, and there were plenty of laughs to go with them. It was good to have some fun in there, so different to some of the more tense media conferences I've had to live through at different times over the past two or three years. As it always is, it was good to win. The irony, of course, is that you can easily argue that I was wrong not to send them in, but this is such a results-based business.

'I feel better now,' I said with a grin. And then I got on with answering the question.

> 'At the end of the day, I'm trying to do the right thing all the time by the team. Being a top-order batter, the easiest thing for me to do the other day would have been to bowl first. If the top order hadn't failed, then I think we could have posted a decent total, and then a lot of the talk about the toss would have been irrelevant. The reason I think I copped as much criticism as I did was because of the way we performed.
>
> 'What I'm trying to do is give us the best chance of winning games of cricket.'

Later, after the fans had gone home and most of the lights outside the dressing room had been extinguished and before some of us headed off to continue our celebrations with our partners in the city, I sought out Peter Siddle, such a wholehearted cricketer, good bloke and proud Australian. I just wanted to make sure he knew how grateful the team was for what he had done, how much I respected his effort.

'Mate, your batting won us this Test match,' I said. 'What you and Huss did today, it takes a lot of courage and a lot of discipline to do that.'

> **January 7** I'm just so proud of the team and what we achieved in Sydney. The boys showed all their fighting spirit in an amazing win. Huss and Sidds did an amazing job with the bat yesterday and then our bowling and fielding was exceptional. There's a great feeling in this team and it was a special celebration last night.

Friday, January 8

A DAY AFTER OUR thriller at the SCG, over in South Africa, in the third Test at Cape Town, Andrew Strauss' England team were producing their own heroics to protect their 1–0 series lead. For me, as I looked at the scorecard of their game this morning, I couldn't help but think back to last July's first Ashes Test, when their last pair, Jimmy Anderson and Monty Panesar, batted out the final overs to save the game. As things turned out, that draw won England the Ashes. If we'd snared that final wicket, I really think we would have gone on to win the series; instead, England got off to a flyer on the opening day of the next Test, at Lord's, and the mood changed.

This time the last-wicket heroics were performed by Graham Onions and Graeme Swann, who came together with 17 balls remaining and survived some tense moments against the excellent pace duo of Dale Steyn and Morne Morkel. Three weeks ago, Onions and Paul Collingwood saw out the final 19 balls of the first Test to force a draw at Centurion and then the Englishmen had their big win at Durban. If England can retain their series lead, and with India seemingly reluctant to play too much five-day cricket these days, it could be that next year's Ashes series won't just be a battle for the famous urn, it could also be a clash between the top two Test-playing teams in the world.

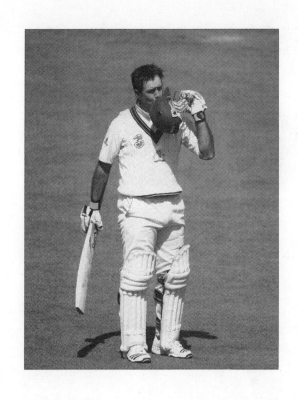

CHAPTER EIGHT

BACK TO BELLERIVE

THIRD TEST, AUSTRALIA v PAKISTAN AT HOBART, JANUARY 14–18, 2010

Sunday, January 10

IT SEEMED THAT MANY of the cricket stories in the weekend papers were focused on my recent form, or lack thereof. It's been pointed out that I haven't scored a Test century since our first innings of the last Ashes series, that my career Test batting average has dropped by more than four runs per innings since the end of 2006, that this season I am averaging 27, that since Kemar Roach hit my elbow my scores have been 2, 57, 12, 0 and 11. I've seen suggestions that with Kato coming back I should move down the batting order, Phillip Hughes stays in the side, Watto goes to No. 3 and Marcus North drops out. Others are theorising that my recent problems with the hook and pull shots are not a consequence of my injury, but evidence that my reflexes are slowing.

First up, I have to say I'll be very disappointed if Northy is omitted. I know he is struggling a little at the moment, but the memories of his hundreds in South Africa and England are still strong. Into the future, though, if the day comes when I believe there is someone who can do a better job at three than me, then by all means I'll consider moving down the order. But at the moment I'm convinced I'm still the best-equipped batter to be at first drop.

As for my batting form, this was what I said during an interview late yesterday, conducted just a few hours before Rianna, Emmy and I jumped on a plane bound for Hobart:

'Wait until I get fit again and we'll see if everyone is still saying the same thing about it then. They (hooks and pulls) are such reactive shots, they are instinctive ...

'I think I have been out twice this summer pulling, but it is a shot that keeps bringing me runs so we'll see how we go with that.

'But, as I said, if I get my elbow right then I think you'll see me playing with a lot more freedom. And not only those shots, but a lot of other shots around the ground as well.

'I know within myself I haven't scored the runs that I felt I should have scored this summer. Coming into this summer off the one-dayers in India I felt I was batting as well as ever. It is time for me to start turning things around again ...'

EVEN WITH THE COMMENTS about my form, I have to say that in the wake of our comeback win the overall media coverage for the team has been very positive. I saw that Ian Healy was quoted as saying that we are 'better placed than any other country' in terms of our depth and quality of young talent, and I have to agree with Heals on that. At the same time, Tim

DROPPED

The fallout from the Sydney Test hasn't been good for Pakistan, and especially for their keeper Kamran Akmal, who has copped a lot of flak following his four missed chances in our second innings. You'd think he'd lost the Test all on his own. Now it appears he won't be playing in the upcoming third Test, because the tourists are flying in a replacement keeper.

Nielsen has been stressing the need for us to keep things in perspective.

'The difference between our performances in Melbourne and Sydney was quite stark, and we will rarely get away with being so far behind in a game like we were in Sydney,' Tim wrote on his blog at the Cricket Australia website. 'Training this week in Hobart is definitely about doing our best to prepare as well as we can to finish our Test season with as good a performance as we can provide. We have five Tests to be played before the Ashes start in Australia next year, so we must aim to eradicate these fluctuations if we are to win the urn back on home soil.'

Wednesday, January 13

THERE WAS A TIME when I put way too much pressure on myself during a Hobart Test match. I so desperately wanted to succeed in front of my home fans that it became almost stifling, and this is reflected in my early scores in Tests at Bellerive: against New Zealand in 1997–98 I scored just four; then in 1999–2000 against Pakistan I made a pair. Since then, I've learned to take things more as they come, and I've managed to score a Test and one-day hundred at the ground, but having the chance to represent my country in front of my fellow Tasmanians remains one of the great privileges of my cricket career.

I may live in Sydney now, but I'm still very much a Tasmanian. It's not hard to stay true to yourself when you're proud of who you are and where you've come from. I have so many wonderful memories of my time learning about the game and myself while playing down here and for the Tassie team in the Sheffield Shield and in the various domestic one-day competitions. Every time I come down for a Test or ODI I always enjoy running into familiar faces and catching up with old friends. Practising at Bellerive yesterday had me feeling genuinely nostalgic, as I started to recall net sessions from years gone by.

Making the return this summer even more memorable was a function I attended last Monday, at the Royal Hobart Hospital paediatric oncology unit, where the Tasmanian Government gave the Ponting Foundation a cheque for $100,000 to support the 'Hitting Childhood Cancer for Six' program we launched last November. Our objective is to raise $500,000 over the next three years to improve the services and support provided to Tasmanian children living with cancer and their families, and this money is a fantastic step in that direction.

After the cheque presentation, Rianna and I met up with some of the kids at the hospital and as always I came away amazed and hugely impressed by their bravery, cheerfulness and optimism. Not all of them were cricket fans, but I hope I was able to win one or two of them over, and that they'll be checking out the scores over the next few days. Whatever they do, I know they'll keep fighting and because of that I'm a huge fan of them all.

Tuesday, January 19

Third Test, Australia v Pakistan, at Hobart (January 14–18): Australia 8–519 dec (142.5 overs: RT Ponting 209, MJ Clarke 100) and 5–219 dec (48.4 overs: SM Katich 100, RT Ponting 89) defeated Pakistan 301 (105.4 overs: Salman Butt 102, Shoaib Malik 58) and 206 (86.2 overs: Khurram Manzoor 77) by 231 runs

I SAID MANY TIMES in the aftermath of the Sydney Test, when people asked me about the toss, that we're playing a results-driven business. I won the toss, we batted, we won the game, so I'm okay. We lose, I'm a mug. Between Sydney and Hobart, there was also plenty of talk about me and the short ball. Am I losing it? Should I move down the order? Should I retire? So here I was facing my fourth ball, still to break my duck, Mohammad Asif bowls a bouncer ... and I tried to hook it.

Maybe it was on to me quicker than I thought, or maybe ... just for instant ... I tried to hold back. I went through with the shot, didn't get it right, and the ball sailed in what seemed like a gentle loop down to Mohammad Aamer at deep fine leg. It was, as they like to say, 'straight down his throat'. The proverbial sitter ...

I'm not sure how it would have worked out if Aamer had caught it. It went so slowly — they always do when you lob an easy catch to the outfield — I guess I would have had to concede that the hook shot was a problem. My batting average for the season would have dropped some more and there would have been more talk about my future. But he didn't catch it. Instead of thinking about what might have been, I was now at the non-striker's end reminding myself as strongly as I could that the 'lucky' batters are the ones who take advantage of a let off, who make their opponents pay for their mistakes.

I was very, very lucky.

Day One

I was in at 1–28, after Simon Katich had been given out lbw by the video umpire after the Pakistanis' original appeal had been knocked back. That was the last ball of the sixth over of the game, Shane Watson faced every ball of the next over from Mohammad Aamer, and then it was my turn. Mohammad Asif is a crafty customer, so I knew it wasn't as simple as him inevitably bowling a short one straight away, but he might ... no, the first two were well pitched up and then the third was well wide of the off stump. The fourth was the short one, the chance went down, and you could sense the exasperation and despair among the fielding team. Next over, from Mohammad Aamer, I got four short ones in a row, one of which I pulled away cautiously for a couple of runs. Watto played out a maiden from Mohammad Asif, and then my battle with Mohammad Aamer continued ...

First ball: I get well forward to let it go outside the off stump.

Second ball: A full delivery, but I was a little on the back foot, expecting a short one, so my drive is slightly mistimed and runs slowly along the ground to mid-off.

Third ball: The short one I was waiting for ... but I'm through my shot too quickly and the ball hits the toe of the bat and dribbles out on the off side. The crowd is hushed, and I feel slightly embarrassed, because this was a very poor bit of cricket on my part. I wouldn't say I'm rattled, but I must concentrate ...

Fourth ball: I get some respite, as the ball is well outside off stump.

FAMILY TIES

This is my sixth Hobart Test, which makes it the ninth Test my Mum and Dad have attended to watch me in action. They'll make the trip down from Launceston for the first two days of the game, but return on Friday night so Dad can play golf on Saturday. He loves his golf so much not even the possibility of seeing his son scoring a Test hundred can drag him off the course, and as a golf addict myself I fully understand that.

Mum and Dad were there when I made my Test debut in Perth in 1995–96, and they travelled to Sydney in 2005–06 for my 100th Test appearance. This year's Boxing Day Test was just the third time they've travelled interstate to see me play.

Fifth ball: Again I can let it go, which I do while exaggerating my forward stretch.

Sixth ball: It's got to be short; I know it, everyone knows it. Sure enough, the young left-armer bangs it in, I'm waiting for it, and my shot, half hook, half pull, is perfect — hit hard and true to the square-leg boundary.

Only now can I breathe a little easier. *Of course you can still play the hook shot*, I think to myself …

Now watch the ball …

There were some more hairy moments — at one point, for example, Mohammad Asif got through me and hit me on the chest, while one attempted pull shot went badly wrong when Umar Gul clunked me on the helmet — but eventually I got into my groove. It helped that the ball stopped darting around off the seam after the lunch break. Watto was out at 2–52 and Mike Hussey at 3–71 (giving the new keeper Sarfraz Ahmed's his first Test catch), but for the Pakistanis that was it, as Michael Clarke and I survived to lunch and then batted together for the rest of the day. It was a long time since Pup and I had enjoyed a substantial partnership in a Test match; in fact, this was only our third century stand in Tests (we put on 210 against India at Adelaide in January 2008 and 113 against South Africa at Johannesburg in February 2009) and only the seventh time we'd put on 50 or more together. Considering we've played 55 Tests together as top-order batters, it's a little surprising we haven't had more success as a pair.

We made up for it here. My first 50 took 111 deliveries, Pup's came up from 88 and the four that took him to his half-century also gave him 4000 runs in Test cricket. By the time he reached this landmark our stand was past 100 and I could tell by the look on his face that he had the same determination as me to make the most of this opportunity. He's a fantastic runner

PLAYER OF THE DECADE

I am honoured to be named *Cricinfo*'s 'Player of the Decade', an award that was announced on the first day of this Test match, but also genuinely thrilled — not least because *Cricinfo* has become such a high-quality website, which means that the award carries much 'street cred'. It's remarkable how quickly it has become a prime source for news, information and stats; I know compiling this diary would be a lot harder if *Cricinfo* wasn't there.

'I have played in an era where there's been a lot of great players,' I said to the website's Brydon Coverdale after he told me about the award. 'Some of the leading run-scorers of all time have played in my time and a lot of the leading wicket-takers of all time have played in my time as well. When you stack that up, to be recognised as the leading player in the decade against some of those other guys makes it a little bit more special …

'The thing that I'm proudest of over my whole career is the amount that I've played and how long I've played. I said that when I played my 100th Test, that the one thing I'm most proud of in my career has been my longevity and the fact that I've been able to play at a pretty high level for a long period of time.'

between the wickets and I love batting with him, because we never miss a run, whether it's a short single or a two turned into a three. When I reached my hundred I kissed my helmet — as Michael Slater used to do and as Pup always does — for the first time in my career. I'm not quite sure where this came from — maybe it was partly because I was batting with Pup and partly because I got the ton in Hobart, in front of my fellow Tasmanians.

There was a slightly funny moment just before I reached my hundred …

The great Glenn McGrath hands out 'baggy pinks' before a special Aussie
team photo in Sydney. Nathan Hauritz is in the back row trying on his
cap; to his left are Clint McKay, Doug Bollinger and Peter Siddle. Michael
Clarke is to my right in the front row; to my left are Tracy Bevan (from the
McGrath Foundation) and Mitchell Johnson.

With Pakistan captain Mohammad Yousuf (left) and coach Intikhab Alam
during the Prime Minister's reception for the two teams at Kirribilli House
on the eve of the second Test.

Above: I've just been caught at deep backward square for a first-ball duck not long after winning the toss at the SCG.

Mike Hussey reaches his magnificent second-innings ton in Sydney.

Huss (left) with Peter Siddle at lunch on day four, after they batted right through the first session.

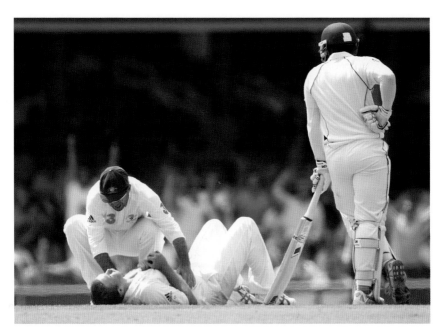

Nathan Hauritz has just taken a red-hot return catch to dismiss Mohammad Yousuf and suddenly we're in sight of a famous victory at the SCG.

Mitchell Johnson (serving) and India's Sania Mirza take on Shane Watson and Australia's Alicia Molik at the Domain Tennis Centre in Hobart a couple of days before the third Test against Pakistan. Note how Mitch, one of the world's best left-arm bowlers, is right-handed on the tennis court.

Below: The moment I thought I'd hooked once too often. Fortunately, Mohammad Aamer spilt the chance and my innings on the first day of the third Test continued.

Right: It was a joy to be able to play front-foot shots with confidence.

Of all the walks off the field after a decent innings I've experienced, this one — chiefly because it was in Tassie — was one of my most enjoyable.

I've just been given out caught behind off the helmet in the fifth Chappell–Hadlee game, at Wellington.

Some Aussie fans try to hold their ground in the face of the unbelievable gale that tore through Wellington on day four of the first Trans-Tasman Test.

Left: New Zealand captain Daniel Vettori on day one of his 100th Test.

Right: With Rianna and Socceroos skipper Lucas Neill at the Australian Captains' Dinner at Star City in Sydney.

At Croke Park in Dublin with hurling legend DJ Carey, three days before the ODI against Ireland that opened our winter tour.

Left: With England captain Andrew Strauss before the start of the NatWest series.

Below: With an Ashes series just around the corner, it was no surprise that our games against the Englishmen were 'full on', such as at Lord's when Stuart Broad surprised me with this sharp, well-directed short ball.

Above: Celebrations at Lord's after Marcus North (centre) took his fifth wicket during Pakistan's second innings of the first Test. Others in the photo are (from left) Tim Paine, Steve Smith, Michael Clarke (obscured behind Smith), Simon Katich (in helmet), Ben Hilfenhaus (wearing sunglasses) and Shane Watson (behind Hilfenhaus). The ball at bottom left had been caught by Mike Hussey at deep mid-wicket to dismiss Mohammad Aamer.

Right: A hook shot during my second-innings 66 against Pakistan at Headingley. Ten months after our opening game at the Champions Trophy, this was my final knock of the 2009–10 cricket year.

I was on 94 and facing Danish Kaneria when I hit him over long-off for four. The ball bounced just before the boundary, but umpire Asoka de Silva signalled 'six' and the crowd duly celebrated. However, I knew it had bounced maybe a metre in front of the rope, and that the 'hundred' would be taken away from me on review. It was a little weird to be standing there, leaning on my bat, seeing what the crowd's celebration for my ton would look like … if I got there. Three balls later, I swept a ball to deep fine leg for two and quickly I was waving my bat to all corners of the ground. Most of all, I enjoyed being able to send a heartfelt wave in the direction of Rianna and Emmy, Mum and Dad and my sister Renee, to acknowledge their unwavering support. It had become a very special day.

The arm never bothered me. I was sure it was right going into the game, though maybe in the back of my mind was a nagging doubt. But during this day I hardly gave it a thought, and on those rare occasions when I did, it was always the same: *It's not bugging me anymore.* By stumps, we'd taken the score to 3–302. I was 137 not out, Pup was unbeaten on 111. I was full of admiration for the way my mate and vice-captain had performed, and I was proud of the way I'd fought through the morning and then kept going all the way to the close of play.

Day Two

A beautiful batting wicket, a somewhat disillusioned bowling attack, two batters who've been struggling a little lately but who were now set and determined to 'cash in'. It was the perfect recipe for Pup and I to go on and record a really big partnership, and we didn't disappoint — going all the way to 352, establishing a number of records along the way. As I've said and written many times, I'm not a cricket stats man, but it was nice to learn that we had compiled the equal 29th highest partnership in Test history,

HOOKED

Having been dropped on nought and then hit on the head as the result of poorly executed hook shots, at stumps on day one the press corps wanted to know why I couldn't just put the shot in my locker for a while, for my own good.

'The bottom line with me is if I can't stop playing it, I'm just going to play it better,' I replied. 'I've played it well throughout my career, and it has brought me a lot of runs. Once I feel I'm in really good touch again, I'll be hitting more of those in the middle than not ...

'Pup asked me if I had thought about not playing it, and I can't. It's an instinctive sort of thing. I don't look at it as being a statement. It's one of those shots that comes more natural to me than it does to most. It has a lot to do with the way I pick the bat up and my foot movements. That's the reason why I play the shot as much and as often as I do.'

the highest in Tests at Hobart, the third highest in Tests in Australia, the second highest by an Australian pair for the fourth wicket in Tests, and the highest by an Australian pair in Tests against Pakistan. I guess there were other landmarks we passed along the way, but that, I think, will do.

However, it is worth noting that Pup also reached 4000 Test-match runs during his innings, and he took his Test batting average back over 50. Of the other 21 Australians to reach this aggregate, only seven — Sir Donald Bradman, Matthew Hayden, Greg Chappell, Neil Harvey, Adam Gilchrist, Damien Martyn and Doug Walters — had a higher career batting average than Pup's when they scored their 4000th run. Our vice-captain is building an imposing record, and I reckon it will only get better.

The stand ended with a strange dismissal, when Pup padded up to a ball from Danish Kaneria, bowled from around the wicket and pitching just outside leg stump. He assumed that it was going to spin away to the offside or that if it held its line it would hit his front leg, but the ball missed the pad and clipped the top of off stump, so he was bowled without offering a shot. He was out for 166, his highest Test score.

I went on to 209, and during the latter stages of the innings I felt as much in control as I've been at any stage over the past couple of years. The problems with the hook shot, my form and my elbow were all a fading memory, and I only got myself out as we chased quick runs before a declaration. This time, we batted on further than we did in Melbourne, partly because run-scoring was a little easier here, but mostly because I could tell the Pakistanis were a very dispirited team, and I sensed we might be able to dismiss them so quickly that the follow-on might be an option. There was some rain forecast too, so that was another factor I had to consider.

As it turned out, they batted pretty well at the start of their innings. However, Peter Siddle was in top form and then two late run outs — a result, I believe, of the pressure we put them under — really swung the match our way. The contrast between my good fortune in making a double hundred after being dropped on nought, compared to Mohammad Yousuf, who was desperately unlucky to be run out for seven after Salman Butt inexplicably declined to take an easy third run, was massive.

> **January 15** Thanks for all the messages after my 209 today. It's an innings I will never forget and to do it in front of my family and all my fellow Tasmanians means so much to me. It's also great to have been able to do this at Bellerive Oval which has been such a part of my career. I am quite moved by some of the messages I have received and I look forward to digesting them all when I get a chance after the Test ends.

Day Three

The follow-on remained an option for much of this day, until a last-wicket stand of 53 between Umar Gul and Mohammad Asif, which occupied 14.2 overs and cut our first-innings lead to 218, forced me to reassess things. In all, their innings lasted 105.4 overs and I felt it best to give our blokes a break. We might not have another Test match to play until the New Zealand tour, but all our bowlers are likely to play in the upcoming ODIs against Pakistan and the West Indies, so it's not as if they're on the verge of an extended holiday.

There were a few other little signs that suggested I would have been wrong to push the accelerator too hard. Mitchell Johnson went wicketless in an innings for the first since Lord's last July, and we needed the part-time spin of Simon Katich to break down their middle order.

I might still have sent Pakistan back in if the weather forecast had been dire, but in fact the chance of extended rain

SECURITY CHECKS

An issue that re-emerged during this Test is the question of security for players competing in this year's IPL in India. Cricket Australia was briefed about the matter during the first day's play by the Australian Government's Department of Foreign Affairs and Trade, and I was later asked if I had been given any inside information. I hadn't.

'The IPL is a couple of months away yet and I'm sure Cricket Australia and all the players and the players' association will do everything they have done for every tour we have been on for the last 10 years to check out some of these threats and most importantly keep the players up to date with everything they are finding out,' I said.

'That happens on every tour we go on and we will be expecting and demanding that happens again.'

periods has declined. So we batted again, and at stumps, we were 1–59 in our second innings.

> **January 17** It's raining here in Hobart tonight but should clear tomorrow. We've put ourselves in a winning position and will be going our hardest in the morning to get an early result. A special credit to our bowlers for knocking over 4 wickets this afternoon. Kato batted brilliantly today and thoroughly deserved his 100 while I was pleased with my own knock. This has been a really solid overall team performance by the boys.

Day Four

It was great to see Kato get a hundred, after so many near misses for him earlier in the season. Before this match, he had scored at least one 50 in his past five Tests without once going on to three figures, so it was nice he was able to go the extra yard. Since he came back into the Aussie team in the middle of 2008 he has been a superbly consistent opening bat, a 'rock' on which much of the team's recent success has been built.

Our declaration just after lunch set Pakistan 438 to win, which I guess some might have seen as a little charitable but I was more concerned with how long we might need to bowl them out as to how many runs they might be able to make. The weather was a little bit of a concern, and we did lose some time after tea, but I felt that they would have to bat better than they have at any time during the summer, and we'd have to bowl worse, for us to lose.

As has been the case from the start of this series, Mohammad Yousuf and Umar Akmal were the big wickets and this time it was Shane Watson who came through for us. The great all-rounders in world cricket — blokes like Jacques Kallis and Andrew Flintoff — often manage to take wickets when they fail with the bat, or get a big score after they've missed out with the ball, and that is what Watto did here, getting the two big wickets with successful lbw shouts. Both times, the batters appealed to the video umpire, but the on-field decisions stood and by the close of play we were only six wickets away from a series clean sweep.

Day Five

Pakistan's new No. 3, Khurram Manzoor, held us for a while on the final day of the series, but the win finally came around halfway through the lunch-to-tea session, when Peter Siddle knocked over Danish Kaneria. That gave Sidds 3–25 for the innings, from 15.2 overs — a good return on a tough wicket for quicks, and an encouraging end to the Test season for him. Given that he also got the two key breakthroughs on the second afternoon, a strong case can be made that Sidds was our leading bowler in this game. Nathan Hauritz also had a good game, taking another six wickets, which gave him 29 for the season. Horrie's consistent form and rising confidence has been one of the stories of the summer.

There was a bit of a 'thank God it's over' feeling in the dressing room after the game, but also a genuine sense of satisfaction. It's been a tough period of Test cricket — six Tests in a bit less than eight weeks — but we've won five out of six, which by any measure is a terrific result. What I like best is that we've got better as the season has gone on, but we have to see this progress as a stepping stone, a point I made after the game.

'We have to keep improving every day,' I said. 'I've never known a player to get better when they are happy with what they've achieved, and I've never known a team to keep improving if they're happy with what they've done either …

'Someone has continually got to put their hand up and make sure the game is going forward. That's the way I will keep challenging the team.'

SEIZE THE MOMENT

During a practice session before this Test, the squad divided into batting and bowling groups, where we talked about specific things relating to the way we go about our cricket business. Justin Langer and I co-chaired the batters' meeting, and much of the discussion focused on the need for us to be more consistent in our run-making. One of the things I said was that we need to keep backing the way we've been preparing recently, to not move away from the methods that have been working for us. The guys have been working as a unit really well at training this summer and I don't want to lose that, but in the inevitable rush between the Melbourne and Sydney Tests maybe we lost that a fraction. I feel like we got it back in this game.

Relating to that need for consistency, we also talked about the fact that we've had a couple of poor second innings with the bat this season, most notably in Perth and Melbourne. It's easy to get complacent when you bat first, make 500, and then go into the second innings with a 200-run lead, but great teams shouldn't make such a mistake. We've got to seize those moments, go for the jugular if you like, which is why I was so happy with the way Kat and I batted in our second dig here.

Of course, critics are always looking for weak links in our line-up, and the focus now is on Marcus North, but as I pointed out it wasn't all that long ago, after his tremendous Test debut and excellent series in England, that some commentators were saying he was our most in-form player. I always like the idea of the selectors sticking with guys who've done it for us in the past, and it was only a few days (and nearly 300 runs) ago that people were saying I was over the hill. 'Hopefully everything turns out the way we want it for Marcus and he can go to New Zealand and have a good series there and then there won't be any speculation about anyone in our line-up,' I said.

YESTERDAY, ALL THE FOCUS was on our five-out-of-six Test summer, but by this afternoon attention had turned to the announcement that the Kolkata Knight Riders are buying out my contract and I won't be playing in this year's Indian Premier League. It seems people are trying to read more into this development than is actually the case — my schedule means I wouldn't have been able to play more than five or six IPL games in this, the last year of my three-year deal, and under those circumstances the Knight Riders don't see the value in me going over there for such a short period of time.

I understand their position, as they appreciate that I was never going to put the IPL in front of my commitments with the Australian team. Now I can be totally focused on the upcoming tours to New Zealand and England, the Ashes next summer and then the 2011 World Cup. It was just a matter of us coming to an appropriate settlement, which we did reasonably quickly, and then about timing the announcement to come after the third Test and before the IPL player auction which will he held this evening, Australian time.

> **January 18** About to head out for a dinner celebration with the boys. Great result to clean sweep Pakistan and it's been a very successful summer winning 5 out of 6 Test matches and drawing the Adelaide game against the West Indies. We'll enjoy tonight before turning our attention to the one-day series against Pakistan that starts in Brisbane on Friday afternoon. I'm a very proud member of this team!

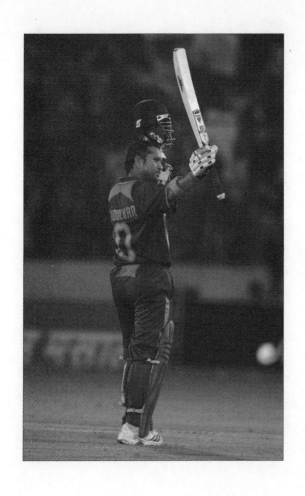

CHAPTER NINE
THE BEST OF THE BEST

A TEAM OF THE DECADE, 2000–2009

BEING NAMED *Cricinfo*'s player of the decade started me thinking about all the great cricketers I've shared a field with over the past 10 years. It's been a decade rich with talent, and for Australia one that has seen plenty of success. In Test cricket, from January 1, 2000 to December 31, 2009, we played a grand total of 115 matches, for 79 wins, 18 losses and 18 draws — a terrific record by any standard.

We lost only five Test matches at home in Australia out of 59 (one against England in 2002–03, one against India in 2003–04, one against India in 2007–08 and two against South Africa last summer). We were involved in 35 series home and away (not including the incomplete series at the start and end of the decade against India and Pakistan respectively or the one-off Test against the ICC World XI in October 2005) and won 27 of them, losing only in India in 2001 and 2008, in England in 2005 and 2009, and at home against South Africa in 2008–09.

I thought about trying to come up with a best Australian Test team of the decade, but I'd end up having to choose between close mates and I don't want to do that. However, I am prepared to stick my neck out and name a team from all the champion opponents I've faced in the past 10 years. The point to emphasise is that just because someone doesn't make this elite XI doesn't mean I don't rate them. It's a bit like the Australian team right at the moment — whenever you've got more than 11 high-class players to choose from, some quality people are going to miss out.

THE TOP OF THE ORDER

Virender Sehwag (India), Graeme Smith (South Africa) and Jacques Kallis (South Africa)

As a selector, I like the fact that I've picked a right-hand/left-hand combination for my opening partnership. I've always thought it is harder for bowlers and captains when there is a left-hander and right-hander batting together, which is why we haven't to date been seriously tempted to change our batting order from No. 3 to No. 7 — me, Huss, Pup, Northy and Hadds — over the past 12 months. Of course, this doesn't guarantee that there will always be a righty and a lefty batting at the same time, but when that does happen, the bowlers are constantly being asked to change their line and the field is always changing, which has to be to the batting side's advantage.

And what a contrast my two opening bats offer. Virender Sehwag, the right-hander, has an almost unique ability to be able to take an attack down and change the course of a Test in an hour, even half an hour. When he is on top of his game he is as good as anyone who has ever picked up a cricket bat, but it is also true that when he is out of touch he looks like he has never batted before in his life. Indian conditions suit him because the ball doesn't swing much over there, so he can get away with not using his feet much. He's scored two triple centuries in Tests, both on the sub-continent, but he's also reached three figures in Tests at Melbourne, Adelaide, Bloemfontein, St Lucia and Nottingham, so he is certainly capable of making runs anywhere in the world.

Maybe it's because we've both been captains for a while, but I've built up a great deal of admiration for my other opener, the left-handed Graeme Smith. I know what it's like to bat in the top order and also be leading the team; that it's often not an easy thing to do. Yet Graeme's Test record is excellent, averaging more than 50 over more than 150 innings, almost all of them as an opener. His style is a little unorthodox, and he is one of those guys who is pretty hard to bowl to because he is so strong through the legside and can be ruthless on anything even remotely short. Initially, we thought he had a weakness on or outside off stump, but he's developed his offside game significantly in the past couple of years.

I've always thought of myself, as a No. 3, as being part of the top order, so I've included Jacques Kallis here, with the openers. When you look at what Jacques has been able to do with the bat, averaging more than 55 in 140-odd Tests over the past 14 years, making something like 35 hundreds *and* taking more than 250 wickets, that is simply amazing. What I like most about his batting is the consistency he's achieved over such a long period of time; maybe he is not quite as dominant a batter as, say, Sachin Tendulkar or Brian Lara, but he is a guy who knows his own game and has the mental strength to stick with what he believes is best for him and his team.

THE MIDDLE ORDER

Sachin Tendulkar (India), Brian Lara (West Indies) and Kumar Sangakkara (Sri Lanka)

I guess it's fair to say the Sachin Tendulkar of the 21st century hasn't been quite as good as the Sachin of the 1990s, but he's still been a fantastic player who remains the wicket every bowler in world cricket would most like in their résumé. The way he batted against us in Hyderabad a couple of months ago is proof he's still a genius.

I guess many people will think of Sachin and Brian Lara together, because they emerged at roughly the same time and then were considered by most experts to be the best two batters in the game for the best part of a decade, from about 1994 to 2003. When Sachin was at his best, we often felt like he was never going to get out, whereas with Brian we always thought we had a chance, especially in his first few overs because he might just go for a shot that wasn't really on. But if you didn't get him out before he faced 60 balls, then look out! After that, he played the way *he* wanted to play, and there was nothing we could do to change that. He was a master at manipulating fields, in the process putting bowlers, fielders and captains under pressure.

I know a lot has been made of the burden Sachin has had to carry during his career, from being the most popular Indian cricketer in history, but Brian had his own stress to deal with which in a way was just as confronting. Sachin was usually part of a batting order that also included gifted batters such as Rahul Dravid, Virender Sehwag, Sourav Ganguly, VVS Laxman and, lately, Gautam Gambhir; in contrast, Brian always batted with the pressure of knowing that the only way the West Indies could possibly win was off his bat. It's amazing looking at his record to see how many of his centuries were scored while the Windies had their backs against the wall.

Kumar Sangakkara is this team's wicketkeeper, but he deserves to make the line-up for his batting alone. There have been few finer knocks played against Australia in the past decade than the 192 he made in Hobart in November 2007, when he was in the middle of an unbelievable run of form. When Adam Gilchrist was at his best, averaging 60 with the bat in Tests and wicketkeeping to a high standard, too, I wasn't sure we'd ever see another keeper/all-rounder capable of influencing a game in the same way, but Kumar at his best is not far behind.

If I was picking the keeper for this team purely on the quality of his glovework I'd go for South Africa's Mark Boucher, but that is not to say that Kumar is not efficient behind the stumps. A good way to measure the quality of a keeper is how many errors they *don't* make, and I can't recall seeing Kumar making too many, which is not a bad trick given he is often working with Muttiah Muralitharan. And as Murali will be my spinner in this team, picking Kumar as the keeper makes a lot of sense, because from what I have seen the two work well together.

THE ALL-ROUNDER
Andrew Flintoff (England)

I am tempted to pick Jacques Kallis as my all-rounder, which is actually very logical given that his Test statistics measure up even against Sir Garfield Sobers, or maybe I could have called Kumar Sangakkara my all-rounder, in the way we used to think of Gilly as an extra frontline batter even though he went in at No. 7. This would have given me the opportunity to include another batter — probably one of India's Rahul Dravid, Pakistan's Mohammad Yousuf or England's Kevin Pietersen — or perhaps a second spinner, most likely Anil Kumble, who was always a handful for us when bowling at home in India.

At the same time, Freddie Flintoff was one of the most talented cricketers I saw during the past 10 years. However, I can't help thinking he should have achieved more than what he did. He was superb against us in 2005, when he had a large influence on just about every game of that famous series bar the first Test at Lord's. His hitting was often prodigious and as a bowler, when he was firing, he was one of those blokes where you never felt like you were truly on top. Freddie also had that rare ability to change the mood of the game through his presence as well as his cricket ability. In recent Ashes Tests in England, the crowd was invariably more involved if he was playing — the difference between the vibe at the Headingley Test in 2009, when he was out injured, and the other Tests of the series was remarkable.

THE PACE BOWLERS

Curtly Ambrose (West Indies), Wasim Akram (Pakistan) and Shaun Pollock (South Africa)

I can hear you saying, 'You can't pick Curtly Ambrose and Wasim Akram, they hardly played in the 2000s!' And in one sense, you're right: Curtly only played 10 of his 98 Tests after January 1, 2000, and made his farewell to Test cricket in early September 2000, while Wasim's final Test appearance came in January 2002. But they are clearly the best two fast bowlers I have faced during my career and they both played in the decade, so that's good enough for me.

Wasim's ability to swing the ball, whether it be old or new, was second to none. And he could do it at high speed. He had that short run-up and a rapid-fire arm action, which meant I always felt under great pressure when I was trying to survive against him. It didn't matter whether I was on zero, fifty or even 150, it always felt like he could get me out at any time.

The pressure Curtly exerted was different, but just as unrelenting. With him, it was more a case that I just didn't know where my next run was coming from. There were times when it was simply a case of waiting for his spell to end, or taking an undue risk to try to get the scoreboard moving. To me, he was Glenn McGrath, only taller and a few ks quicker. I always took some satisfaction from surviving a spell from either Curtly or Wasim; if I ever made a decent score against them, the feeling afterwards was that if I could survive that, I could make runs against just about anyone.

My choice for the third quick was the trickiest call in this whole process. I thought about South Africa's Dale Steyn and New Zealand's Shane Bond, but in the end I've decided to reward longevity at the top level through the decade. To be able to combine excellence and durability is an achievement I will always rate highly, so my decision came down to one of Shaun Pollock or Sri Lanka's Chaminda Vaas. To me, though they are different styles of bowlers, there is little between the two. In the end Shaun got the nod because he was a fractionally better all-round player — as well as taking 421 Test wickets (Chaminda took 355) he averaged more than 30 with the bat in Tests, and he was probably a slightly more effective bowler in ODI cricket (I know that shouldn't be a factor when picking a Test XI, but as I said it is very hard to split the two). But please don't think I am underrating Chaminda at all; to open the bowling for Sri Lanka in more than 100 Tests, often in conditions that are unsuitable for pace bowlers, and to be as successful as he was is in my view an amazing effort.

THE SPINNER
Muttiah Muralitharan (Sri Lanka)

What sets Murali apart is that he spins it both ways, and I, like many other batters across the planet, have rarely been able to pick the difference out of his hand. If he was a traditional off-spinner, with the ability to spin the ball into the right-hander and with a well-disguised arm-ball, then he'd be a totally different kettle of fish. He'd still be a really good bowler, but not the lethal wicket-taker he's been for more than a decade. His figures are quite astonishing really: as I pick this team, nearly 800 Test wickets at less than 22, plus more than 500 ODI wickets.

Knowing that an off spinner can turn the ball the 'other way', away from the outside edge of my bat, means I can't use my

AN ODI TEAM OF THE DECADE

Of course, 50-over cricket is a different game to Test cricket, but I wouldn't make too many changes to my Test XI if I was asked to nominate a one-day international team made up of men who played against Australia in ODIs between 2000 and 2009. My side would be, in batting order:

Sachin Tendulkar (India), Herschelle Gibbs (South Africa), Brian Lara (West Indies), Jacques Kallis (South Africa), Kevin Pietersen (England), MS Dhoni (India), Lance Klusener (South Africa), Shaun Pollock (South Africa), Wasim Akram (Pakistan), Curtly Ambrose (West Indies) and Muttiah Muralitharan (Sri Lanka).

feet against him in the way I would against a normal offie. Thus, if I don't get right to the pitch of the ball, then it might spin away from me and I'm gone. Murali has only got me out stumped once in Test matches — at the Gabba a couple of years ago — but that's more a reflection of the way I have to play him, the way he's pinned me to the crease, rather than evidence that I've been able to handle him effectively. His method is to build pressure and bring his bat-pad fielders into play, and he's been the best in that business for 15 years, superior to others of a similar style, like Pakistan's Saqlain Mushtaq and India's Harbhajan Singh.

So there is my team, and I'll put them in the following batting order so I've got a right-hander followed by a left-hander followed by a right-hander (and so on) all the way from the openers to No. 11: Sehwag, Smith, Kallis, Lara, Tendulkar, Sangakkara, Flintoff, Wasim Akram, Pollock, Ambrose and Muralitharan. Imagine a clash between this XI and Australia's finest from the same period, I'm confident we'd come out on top, but only after a fantastic battle. What a promoter's dream such a game would be.

CHAPTER TEN
ONE DAY AFTER ANOTHER

ONE-DAY INTERNATIONALS IN AUSTRALIA 2009–10

Monday, February 1

First ODI, Australia v Pakistan, at Brisbane (January 22): Pakistan 274 (49.4 overs: Salman Butt 72, Younis Khan 46, Shahid Afridi 48; SR Watson 4–36, CJ McKay 3–61) lost to **Australia** 5–275 (48.3 overs: MJ Clarke 58, CL White 105) by five wickets

Second ODI, Australia v Pakistan, at Sydney (January 24): Australia 6–267 (50 overs: SR Watson 69, SE Marsh 41, CL White 55; Mohammad Aamer 3–53) defeated **Pakistan** 127 (37.3 overs: Mohammad Yousuf 58; CJ McKay 3–15) by 140 runs

Third ODI, Australia v Pakistan, at Adelaide (January 26): Australia 5–286 (50 overs: SE Marsh 83, MJ Clarke 80, MEK Hussey 49) defeated **Pakistan** 246 (47.4 overs: Umar Akmal 59, Shahid Afridi 40; RJ Harris 5–43, CJ McKay 3–48) by 40 runs

Fourth ODI, Australia v Pakistan, at Perth (January 29): Australia 8–277 (50 overs: CL White 44, MEK Hussey 67, NM Hauritz 53; Mohammad Asif 3–42) defeated **Pakistan** 142 (37.5 overs: RJ Harris 5–19) by 135 runs

Fifth ODI, Australia v Pakistan, at Perth (January 31): Pakistan 212 (49.3 overs: Umar Akmal 67, Fawad Alam 63; RJ Harris 3–44, CJ McKay 4–35) lost to **Australia** 8–213 (49.2 overs: RT Ponting 55, MEK Hussey 40*) by two wickets

IN ENGLAND LAST SEPTEMBER, straight after the Ashes, we won six ODIs in a seven-match series. As a group, we thoroughly enjoyed our dominance and the fact that we improved as a unit the longer the series went on, but at the same time a debate was building as to the value and relevance of the one-day game in 21st-century cricket. In part, this was inspired by a column in the

Times by Shane Warne before the final Ashes Test, when he wrote that 'cricket evolves and the 50-over game has passed its sell-by date'. In Warney's view, there should be two forms of international cricket: Tests and T20 games, and as England kept losing ODIs to us and local interest began to wane, there were a number of observers happy to agree with him.

Over the next two months, we went on to win the Champions Trophy and a seven-game ODI series in India, playing some outstanding cricket in the process. However, when we returned home, I found that some people were keener to debate the possible demise of the one-day game than celebrate our success. This was unfortunate on two levels — one, it's

SWAMP JUNIOR

On the eve of the ODI series against Pakistan, I was asked what I expected from Shaun Marsh. This was my reply:

'He has had a bit of an interrupted run with some of those nasty hamstring injuries that kept him out for six or eight months at once. That was where he was just starting to find his feet as an international player at the top of the order for us.

'He's a player who, when he's at his best, can win a lot of games for you at the top of the order.

'We did a lot of one-on-one work in India through the one-day series over there. He is an ultra-talented player that has just started to have those breakout performances at international level that everyone needs to start really believing in themselves.'

The stats back this contention. I wonder how many people knew that Shaun went into this series with a career ODI batting average of more than 40, from 19 matches, with a strike rate of nearly 77. But I'm not surprised at all, because he's a really good player with a terrific future ahead of him.

always nice to receive full credit for your wins and I'm not sure we were getting that; and two, it seemed to me that in the rush to anoint T20 as the future of our sport people were forgetting that one-day cricket is still a really good game, with much to offer, not least the fact that arguably the sport's most important tournament, the World Cup, is an ODI competition.

The problem with one-day international cricket, in my view, is not the game itself, but the scheduling and the lack of context some games seem to suffer from. Asking the public to stay interested in a seven-game series when there is no time-honoured trophy at stake, as was the case in England in September and India in October-November, can be a tough business when there is so much other cricket and so much other top-class sport being played around the world. Straight after the Ashes, we were playing a seven-game series against one team; straight after the Champion's Trophy, we were playing a seven-game series against another team. The cricket being played was still good, in the case of the India series extremely good, but I concede it can be hard to keep the fans' and the players' interest at a peak when there's always another game on tomorrow, maybe the day after that, never more than two or three days away.

In contrast, T20 cricket is still new, and at this point there are relatively few T20 internationals being scheduled for an international tour so every game is an adventure. I wasn't surprised when more than 40,000 went to the MCG during the Christmas holidays for a Big Bash game involving Victoria and Tasmania. There is a buzz about T20 at the moment that is bringing the fans through the gate, while many ODIs are being played before half-full stadiums. So now the argument is that ODI cricket has to change or die — I've seen suggestions that we reduce the game to 40 overs-a-side, introduce bonus points, divide the 50 overs into two innings, and so on.

But I don't think the game is flawed. Rather than damn the 50-over game, we need to protect it. Some of the greatest cricket played in the past 30 years has been in ODIs. Some of my best innings have been in one-dayers, and a number of my most treasured memories revolve around one-day cricket.

As I said, I do believe administrators need to look at the scheduling, yet I also know that the game relies on one-day cricket for a large slice of its revenue. Like many of cricket's problems, the answer, I think, lies in balance. As a player, I find that a sense of sameness develops during a seven-game series; unless the rubber is tied three-all, by the time of the final toss you almost feel like saying, 'Oh no, not you again,' to the opposing captain. If you play too many ODIs in a row, too many of any one form of the game in a row, that same sense of staleness can set in — we've seen that happen when the Tri-Series in Australia has involved too many games and we definitely saw it at the 2007 World Cup in the West Indies. In contrast, the recent Champions Trophy was a beauty because of its two-week format. My guess is that by the time our five-game ODI series against the West Indies is played out next month we'll be feeling a bit of that, coming as it does so soon after these five games we've just won against Pakistan ...

Game 1 (Brisbane)

Given our recent ODI form, the selectors didn't spring any surprises when they picked our squad for the start of this series. Michael Clarke and Brad Haddin came back after missing the matches in India because of injuries, and Mitchell Johnson was rested. James Hopes, who came home early from that India tour, was chosen for this encounter, with Adam Voges coming into the team for game two.

Crucial for Pakistan was the inclusion of Younis Khan and

Shahid Afridi, two men with impressive records in one-day cricket, and they quickly showed their batting ability by scoring 46 and 48 respectively, Afridi's runs coming from just 26 balls. Their total of 274 was competitive, and would have been more but for Shane Watson's excellent bowling through the middle overs and especially at the end of the innings. In the end, though a superb century from Cameron White, suitably backed by Michael Clarke's 58, got us home with nine balls to spare.

Cameron's innings lasted 88 balls and having come to the wicket at 3–84 after 18 overs, he wasn't dismissed until when we needed another 15 runs from 22 balls. I was so impressed by the way he and Pup planned their innings — they kept the powerplay until near the end and when they did put the foot down the Pakistani bowlers had no answer. Overall, the thing that pleased me most was the positive manner in which we handled the transition from Tests to one-dayers. In past seasons, we've had some trouble with this switch.

> **January 21** Had a full day in Brisbane today starting with a BBQ breakfast in the city. Was a lot of fun and we were rapt with all the people who came out to see us. Had a lot of meetings and media commitments throughout the day and of course, we had a 3-hour training session. I'm pretty tired tonight but can't wait for the start of the Commonwealth Bank ODI series tomorrow.

Game 2 (Sydney)

The crowd for that first game at the Gabba was disappointing: just less than 20,000. But those who were there got value for money, so my gut feel was that we'd get a good gate for this second match in Sydney. However, in the days between these two

DOUGIE'S APPEALING

Doug Bollinger had a very productive day/night out in game two. He wasn't required to bat in our innings, but did spend time carrying a bucket among the fans at the SCG, collecting money for World Vision's Haiti Earthquake Appeal. Then he opened the bowling and quickly had Salman Butt and then Younis Khan caught by Cameron White at second slip. Pakistan were 2–7 in the fifth over and never recovered.

games all the press was about how much ODI cricket is struggling, and I think that contributed to what proved to be a reasonable attendance only at the SCG (30,774). We went out and won easily, on the back of a good all-round batting display (Watto's run-a-ball 69 at the top of the order being a highlight) and then some really high-class bowling, and I could only wonder whether the fans in Adelaide would respond to our admirable form by coming to game three or if the one-sided nature of this win, coming on top of our Test clean sweep, would give them a reason to stay away.

Not that I could worry too much about that. It might not have been much of a contest, but there was plenty of entertainment out there and I tried to keep things interesting by constantly pressing for wickets.

'The next game we play is on Australia Day,' I said after this match. 'I'll be disappointed if the boys don't turn up to play in an even better frame of mind than they did today.'

Game 3 (Adelaide)

Queensland pace bowler Ryan Harris was called into our team for game three, in place of Peter Siddle, who had a crook back, and he responded by taking five wickets in just his second ODI.

On paper, his performance was impressive, but it was actually even better than that, as I asked him to bowl during some difficult times in Pakistan's innings and he came through for us brilliantly. What I loved most was the way he responded to the challenge I set him; I can think of one or two guys who've bowled for us in the past few years who wouldn't have relished this opportunity the way Ryan did.

He started with a wicket in his first over, but he really came into his own late in the evening, when I called him back into the attack just as Shahid Afridi was preparing one last assault. Afridi got him fine for four, but the next ball was the perfect yorker and the bails went flying, and then two balls later Umar Gul lobbed a catch to Brad Haddin and the game was as good as ours.

It was clear to us there were problems in the Pakistan camp. There was no buzz about them on the field and a story was about that Mohammad Yousuf was to be sacked as captain at the end of the series. I could only feel sorry for him. He's an outstanding cricketer and a good bloke, and I have great respect for his cricket brain, but he's been under pressure on this tour ever since the final day of the Sydney Test match. Being Pakistan's captain can be an unforgiving job, especially at the moment as their young side tries to compete effectively without being able to play international matches at home.

January 25 Been a hectic time as we get ready for our 3rd game in 5 days tomorrow. Couldn't be happier with the way the boys are playing and we are set for a big Australia Day effort tomorrow. I love playing in Adelaide and will be looking for another win and big score for myself to celebrate what has become a very special day for the whole team.

CHANGES OF PACE

The feeling in the home dressing room after game three was so much brighter than it had been exactly 12 months ago, when our Australia Day was ruined by an eight-wicket loss to South Africa. Even the fact I'd been trapped lbw for 0 earlier in the day this year couldn't dampen my pleasure at claiming this series in three straight games.

Our one-day record over the past 12 months has been excellent despite our quick-bowling stocks being tested perhaps as never before. The list of pacemen we've used in the 38 ODIs we've played in the past 12 months is a long one: 17 different guys in all if you include the all-rounders Shane Watson, James Hopes and Moises Henriques. Can you name them?

(Doug Bollinger, Nathan Bracken, Stuart Clark, Brett Geeves, Ryan Harris, Shane Harwood, Moises Henriques, Ben Hilfenhaus, James Hopes, Mitchell Johnson, Ben Laughlin, Brett Lee, Clint McKay, Dirk Nannes, Peter Siddle, Shaun Tait and Shane Watson.)

Games 4 & 5 (Perth)

We headed to the WACA for the final two games of the series with an unassailable lead but without Shane Watson and Doug Bollinger, who were given the two games off. What they missed was an extension of the 'Ryan Harris Show', as Ryno took a second straight five-for and then three more as we completed a 5–nil sweep. Clint McKay also continued his exceptional form — his career bowling figures at the end of the series were unbelievable: seven games; 17 wickets; average of 16.35; strike rate of 22.24. To give that average and strike rate a little bit of context, Brett Lee took his 324 ODI wickets (eighth best all-time) at an average of 23, with a strike rate of 29.27 (third best career strike rate of all those with more than 50 wickets).

In game four, Ryan dismissed Salman Butt with his fourth ball courtesy of a sensational diving catch at second slip by Cameron White, and then with the first ball of his third over he had Younis Khan caught behind. At this point, he was still to concede a run, and then, during his second spell, he dismissed Umar Akmal and Naved-ul-Hasan with successive balls. Soon after, Shahid Afridi's exhilarating cameo — 29 from 10 balls, including consecutive sixes off Nathan Hauritz — came to an end, and all that was left was to see whether Ryan would get his fifth wicket of the innings and Brad Haddin would get five catches. They both did.

In the afternoon, Horrie was our unlikely batting star, cracking a fifty at way better than a run a ball. I couldn't blame him for hitting out, as it was pretty hot out there. Earlier, I'd been dismissed in slightly bizarre circumstances: I tried to cut a toppie from Afridi, got an edge, and keeper Kamran Akmal spilt it … but the ball got caught between his legs and he held on.

Two days later, we successfully completed a clean sweep with a scrappy victory in which Harris, man of the match McKay and the returning Mitchell Johnson all bowled well, and Mike Hussey was smart and cool as he steered us to victory, eight down, with four balls to spare. However, all the talk afterwards was about two specific incidents.

The first was Afridi's rather comical act near the end of the game, when it looked like he was trying to take a big bite out of the ball as he stood next to the bowler, Mohammad Asif, around the 43-over mark. I'm really not sure what he was trying to achieve, but he's been suspended for two games for an act ('changing the conditions of the ball') that I think was probably more silly than sinister. It did, though, look bad on TV. The game was getting tight at this stage and Afridi, who was captaining the team in the absence of Mohammad Yousuf, might have had too many things going through his head at once.

The second controversy to come out of the final overs involved a moron who ran onto the field and rugby tackled Pakistan's Khalid Latif. This was much more serious than Afridi's breach, and I'm disappointed about the apparent lack of security that allowed it to happen. It wasn't the first time on the night someone had run out onto the ground, but the bloke I'm filthiest on is that mug who was so selfish and stupid to think that jumping the fence, running onto the field and crashing into a player from behind was a good idea.

Straight after the game I was a bit nonplussed. 'We've seen a few replays of it ... I don't know what to say,' was all I offered. 'I've never seen that before. I'm sure that will be dealt with ...'

The more I think about it, though, the worse it gets. I think of Terry Alderman getting hurt during the first Ashes Test in Perth in 1982–83 when some hooligans invaded the field, how he suffered a dislocated shoulder that cost him the rest of that series. Or of Monica Seles being stabbed on a tennis court in 1993 ... what have we learned from such incidents? I can tell you this much — if it ever happens when we're fielding and I'm captain then I'll take my team off the field. At the very least, I'll bring all my players together in the middle and ask them, 'Do you want to put up with this?'

MOST ODI WINS

Earlier in the year, I broke Shane Warne's record for participating in the most Test wins, and during this series I went past Sri Lanka's Sanath Jayasuriya to become the 'winningest' player in ODI cricket. Our victory in game three was the 234th win of my career.

At the time I broke the record, the other cricketers with more than 200 wins were Sachin Tendulkar (220), Inzaman-ul-Haq (215) and Adam Gilchrist (202).

I know it's just a very small minority who think it's okay to behave in this way. But I just hope the authorities are able to make an example of this character — fine him plenty and ban him for life would be an appropriate penalty in my opinion — and at the same time do everything they can think of to make it clear that this sort of behaviour is unacceptable.

> **January 27** Another great win last night and we are moving on to Perth this afternoon. I'm just so rapt in the progress of this team and the fact that we are building such depth in our ranks. Ryan Harris did a super job last night and when you consider we had the likes of Johnson, Lee, Bracken, Hilfenhaus and Siddle not playing – our bowling stocks are in great shape.

ONE INTERESTING DEBATE THAT emerged during this series concerned the future of the Sheffield Shield. There were suggestions that games could be played under floodlights using pink balls from as early as next season, and also that matches might be played in Australia's north, at venues such as Cairns, Alice Springs, Townsville and Darwin, in August-September to clear some room in the summer schedule for more T20 cricket.

The playing of Shield games as day/night matches doesn't seem like a bad move — if they can get the ball right and it doesn't impinge on the natural, traditional way four-day cricket is played. That is, we need the balls (whatever colour they are) and the pitches to behave as they do now, as they've always done. I'd rather not see Tests played under lights; that, the traditionalist in me says, is a step too far.

As for extending the season, I read reports that claimed I'd 'slammed' the concept, but that's not totally true because I understand the reality that cricket has got to pay its way.

THE PINNACLE

On the eve of game four of this series, the *Sydney Morning Herald*'s Will Swanton asked me if it felt a bit weird, ditching T20 international cricket just as it seemed to be usurping ODI cricket in some people's eyes. My answer was simple: 'World Cup.'

'I'd be lying if I said we weren't already looking towards the World Cup,' I said. 'It's important that you start planning a long way out. The standards we've set in our last few tournaments have been very, very high, and it's important you get some experience into some players you might need in a tournament like that. We're definitely on the right track. I have some of my fondest memories out of the game from winning World Cups – and I want to get some more …

'I'm proud of what Australia has achieved (at the World Cup) and, outside of Tests, that's what I'm really looking towards. Fifty-over cricket is a wonderful game, and the pinnacle of the shorter game is the World Cup, which I have been lucky enough to play a few of. I'm looking forward to playing another one and seeing if we can be successful again.'

However, I'd like to think there is a way of achieving this without taking the Shield away from the traditional Test venues. Maybe a few games can be moved, as has been done in the past when some Shield matches have been played in the bush, but playing on a green Gabba deck, for example, or an SCG turner forms part of the education process for potential stars of the future. We have to give our young guys the chance to develop the skills to be able to handle those types of conditions, so I'd be really disappointed if the bulk of Shield games were moved to less familiar places.

What I most definitely don't want to see is any cut in the number of first-class matches played in Australia, so if stretching the season is the only way to manage that, then maybe I could live with it. I'm not against the Big Bash (Australia's domestic T20 competition) — I know the players have enjoyed it this season and the crowds have really taken to it — but the Shield is the rock on which the quality of the Australian Test team is built. I'd hate to think that pathway could be compromised for the sake of fitting an expanded T20 competition into the domestic cricket calendar.

Sunday, February 21

First ODI, Australia v West Indies, at Melbourne (February 7): Australia 8–256 (50 overs: SR Watson 59, RT Ponting 49; KA Pollard 3–45) defeated **West Indies** 143 (34.2 overs: RJ Harris 3–24, NM Hauritz 3–28) by 113 runs

Second ODI, Australia v West Indies, at Adelaide (February 9): West Indies 170 (39.4 overs: DR Smith 43; DE Bollinger 4–28) lost to **Australia** 2–171 (26.3 overs: SR Watson 53, RT Ponting 57*) by eight wickets

Third ODI, Australia v West Indies, at Sydney (February 12): Australia 225 (49.5 overs: MJ Clarke 46, MEK Hussey 44; R Rampaul 4–61, DR Smith 3–45) versus **West Indies** 0–6 (one over). No result due to rain

Fourth ODI, Australia v West Indies, at Brisbane (February 14): Australia 7–324 (50 overs: RT Ponting 106, CL White 63, JR Hopes 42) defeated **West Indies** 8–274 (50 overs: N Deonarine 53, KA Pollard 62, DR Smith 59) by 50 runs

Fifth ODI, Australia v West Indies, at Melbourne (February 19): Australia 5–324 (50 overs: SR Watson 51, RT Ponting 61, MJ Clarke 47, AC Voges 45*, JR Hopes 57*) defeated **West Indies** 199 (36.5 overs: KA Pollard 45, DJG Sammy 47; DE Bollinger 3–33) by 125 runs

MY WORST FEARS FOR this summer's ODI series came to fruition, as our five games against the West Indies failed to capture the public's imagination. The Windies returned to

> **February 2** I rushed back to Sydney early yesterday for a week off with the family. I don't play again until Sunday's first ODI against the West Indies. Great feeling to win the Pakistan series 5–0 and I am just so proud of every player who represented us during the series. We managed our workload well and gave a number of guys a chance to show what they can do and they delivered!

Australia saying they were going to give us a game — captain Chris Gayle predicted a 4–1 win for the tourists — but their cricket was uninspired, Doug Bollinger dismissed Gayle for a low score every time they met, and though we surged through the five games undefeated (four wins and a washout in Sydney) by the time we reached the MCG for the final encounter there were only 15,538 spectators there to greet us. That, I imagine, is one of the lowest crowds ever for an ODI involving Australia at the great arena.

TIME OUT FOR SIDDS

We learned before the West Indies series that we'd have to do without Peter Siddle for the next few months, due to a lower-back stress fracture. This season has demonstrated that we have plenty of depth in the pace-bowling department, but also that we need it.

As well as Sidds, Ben Hilfenhaus, Brett Lee and Brett Geeves will be unavailable for the upcoming New Zealand tour, which is very unfortunate. But it's not the disaster it might have been a few months ago, because of the number of excellent bowlers we now have to choose from. I wasn't kidding when, before the first game against the Windies, I described our quicks as 'the best group of fast bowlers anywhere in the world at the moment'.

Afterwards, the people at Cricket Australia tried to blame the lopsided nature of the contest for the fading interest, but I don't think that's exactly right. It was just too much of the same thing — that 'thing' not being us winning too often, just too many of the same form of the game against the same teams. I tried to make the point forcibly after game five.

'People in Melbourne have paid a lot of money all year to come and watch games of cricket,' I said. 'You can't expect them just to keep coming out day after day. As players, we'll keep doing the best we can to promote the game in the right way and that's by playing good entertaining cricket …

'I just think we've played a whole lot. You look at all the days of cricket that the public have had to pay and go and watch through the summer, I think that's probably the reason why the numbers have dwindled off in the last week.'

Then one of the journalists asked me if this declining interest was a reason for reducing the number of ODIs staged each summer. My reply was succinct: 'Absolutely.'

Game 1 (Melbourne)

A frustrating thing for us was that we were playing some of our best cricket of the season, but not everyone seemed to be noticing.

February 6 Just back to the hotel after a really enjoyable dinner with Rianna. Trained well today and it's great to be back around the team after the week off. It was really good to see the boys win the KFC T20 game last night and tomorrow we are hoping to continue our undefeated form of the summer. The West Indies are always tough to beat in the shorter forms of the game but we have the squad to get the job done.

NINE STRAIGHT

Between the two ODI series, Michael Clarke's Australian team played a T20 international against Pakistan at the MCG, and it evolved into a thriller. An explosive 64 from 33 balls from Kamran Akmal had the tourists in the box seat at 4–98 after 14 overs, chasing just 128 to win, but Pup and the boys held their nerve superbly to get home by two runs. That gives us nine straight wins against the Pakistanis this summer, across three forms of the game.

One feature of the game I really enjoyed was the return of Shaun Tait, who took 3–13 from his four overs. The third ball of his opening over clocked in at 160.7ks per hour, which was described in the press as the fastest recorded delivery ever bowled in Australia.

T20 International, Australia v Pakistan, at Melbourne (February 5): Australia 127 (18.4 overs: MJ Clarke 32, DJ Hussey 40*; Umar Gul 3–26) defeated Pakistan 9–125 (Kamran Akmal 64; SWW Tait 3–13) by two runs.

The series started with the West Indies guys talking a good game — Kemar Roach, for example, was happy to let everyone know how he was going to exploit my 'problems' with the short ball — but they were without some of their best players (Dwayne Bravo, Ramnaresh Sarwan, Shivnarine Chanderpaul and Jerome Taylor were all out because of injury) and after 10 overs of the first game we were 0–50 and in control. The pitch wasn't that easy to score on, and we were confident our eventual total of 8–256 would be very competitive. Then Dougie and Ryno ripped through the top of their order, reducing them to 3–12 in the fifth over, and after that there was no way we were going to lose.

The crowd for this game was a bit more than 25,000, which didn't look too flash compared to the 60,000 who'd come to the MCG for the T20 International two days earlier. It was a big ask expecting people to come out to both games, and obviously in this case a clear majority chose the first T20I Australia has played since the start of the NatWest series in England last September, rather than the 24th ODI.

> **February 8** Another impressive win by the boys last night. Perfect start to the series against the West Indies and we are going to be giving it our all to continue our form in Adelaide tomorrow. I enjoyed my own knock although I'm disappointed I didn't go on with it. Having most of last week off certainly freshened me up. Damn hot in the middle though – even got rid of my helmet to bat in a one-day cap.

Game Two (Adelaide)

Adelaide was the one place we didn't get a Test win this summer (drawing with the Windies), so it was nice to get a little revenge here. It was also here that we really started talking up the idea of going through the entire summer undefeated.

Our opponents had the worst possible start to this match, losing their captain to the first ball of the opening over and crashing from there to 4–16. They did pretty well to make it to 170, but on a beautiful Adelaide Oval track that was never going to be enough and we got home with eight wickets and 23-and-a-half overs in hand.

What I liked most about our performance was the way we maintained out intensity throughout their innings. There was no slowing down. At 8–170 in their innings, I managed a direct hit from backward point to run out Ravi Rampaul and next ball Mike Hussey took a brilliant diving catch out in the open country between long-on and deep mid-wicket to dismiss Dwayne Smith and end the innings.

TEAM CHANGES

There were a few personnel changes in both sides before game three of the West Indies series. The Windies were without my mate Kemar Roach, who is battling an ankle injury, while we lost Shaun Marsh when he felt a twinge in his back during pre-game warm-ups. Before that, our selectors had made the decision to rest two of the stars of this summer, Brad Haddin and Shane Watson. I noticed a few critics questioned this move, arguing that we should be playing our strongest team every time we walk on the field, but I'd like to think we've moved beyond that.

Tim Paine came in for Brad while Shane's replacement was Adam Voges. The original intention was for Hadds and Watto to have a two-match break, but when Shaun was ruled out of game four at the Gabba we brought Watto back early, which he didn't seem to mind. When you're in the sort of fantastic form he's in at present, you really want take advantage of every minute. Then, after game four, the selectors decided to give Mike Hussey and Nathan Hauritz a break, which meant Vogesy stayed in the side and Steve Smith made his ODI debut at the MCG.

February 10 I'm at Adelaide airport on my way back to Sydney after our win last night. Great night again for our bowlers who set up our win. Good to see Dougie Bollinger win the man-of-the-match. His form this summer just keeps getting better.

Game 3 (Sydney)

On paper, I guess this looks like a game we could have lost, given that we were dismissed for 225 when we batted first, and then the game was washed away by a series of storms. You usually need more than 250 to win a 50-over game in this modern era of boundary ropes and excellent batting pitches. However, we found it a somewhat spicy wicket to bat on, and then the rain got into it. Judging by the way Doug Bollinger got a couple of balls to fly in the only over he bowled, I'm not sure the Windies would have enjoyed chasing any sort of target.

That one over from Dougie actually took him more than two hours to complete. There was a bank of dark clouds coming over the SCG when he bowled his first ball, at around 7pm, and he started with a wide, two dot balls, then another wide, then Chris Gayle defended a rising ball to square-leg. The fifth legal ball of the over just took off, flying past Gayle's helmet and over the head of keeper Tim Paine for four byes, and then the rain started coming down and we had to leave the field. Having signed autographs and posed for photos with the fans who'd congregated outside our dressing room, we got back on the field at 9.20pm and Dougie finally finished his over.

The Windies' amended target was 151 in 24 overs but they never got a chance to pursue them. Ryan Harris had just finished marking out his run and was doing a couple of final stretches when it started pouring again, we were off the field once more, and all I could do was run over to Ryno and congratulate him on the high quality of his warm-up.

Game 4 (Brisbane)

I went into this game having scored a Test and ODI hundred at every major Australian venue, except for a one-day hundred at the Gabba. Fortunately, I was able to complete the set in this game, and I did so by batting as well as I have at any time since I hurt my arm back in December.

The only way we could have lost this game after we scored a ground-record 7–324 from our 50 overs would have been if Chris Gayle had smashed something like 150 at better than a run a ball. Of course, he's capable of that and he looked to be in rare form at the start. But Dougie got him in the end, caught behind for 34 (from 21 balls), and after that it was just a matter of whether we'd bowl them out or they'd finish 50 or 60 short at the end of their 50 overs.

All the talk afterwards was about whether we could go unbeaten through the Australian summer. We had one more ODI and two T20 Internationals to go.

> **February 15** Been a bit slack getting updates done over the past week or two. It's been pretty chaotic travelling from city to city for the one-day games. In Melbourne now and about to get ready for tonight's Border Medal. Should be a fun night as we celebrate a really successful summer. Still three games to go but I am very satisfied with what we have achieved over the past three months.

Game 5 (Melbourne)

I was hoping the ODI season might finish with a bang, but sadly it went more with a whimper — though that was hardly our fault, as we produced another polished, professional batting effort that put the game pretty much out of the West Indies' reach even before their innings began. For the second game straight we finished with a total of 324 from our 50 overs, this time five wickets down and despite the fact no individual scored more than 61. Our two standouts with the bat were Adam Voges and James Hopes, who clobbered 82 runs from the final seven overs of our innings, 60 of them from the final four. James reached his fifty in just 24 balls.

I imagine there would have been at least a few people planning to come out to the ground for the evening session, but when the Windies collapsed to 4–39 in the first 10 overs any latecomers would surely have put their entry money back in their pockets. They might instead have headed over to Etihad Stadium

THE BORDER MEDAL

The 11th Allan Border Medal was presented on February 15, a day after our win at the Gabba. Like most people, I went to the night believing it was race between Shane Watson and Mitchell Johnson, and I wondered whether the fact Watto didn't force his way into the Test XI until July would count against him. Mitch is, after all, the reigning ICC Cricketer of the Year, so he's not the sort of bloke you want to be giving a head start.

In the end, though, the judges went for Shane (125 votes), who was also named our ODI player of the year. Michael Clarke actually pipped Mitch for second place (90 votes to 87). The list of award winners for 2010 reads as follows:

Allan Border Medal: Shane Watson

Test cricketer of the year: Simon Katich

ODI cricketer of the year: Shane Watson

State cricketer of the year: Michael Klinger

Women's international cricketer of the year: Shelley Nitschke

Bradman young cricketer of the year: John Hastings

to watch the AFL pre-season game between Collingwood and St Kilda, or decided to stay home that night and then gone off to yesterday's big Blue Diamond race meeting at Caulfield. Typical Melbourne, there's always plenty of sport on. Our win was our 24th in our last 27 ODIs, an impressive sequence by any measure. For the Australian summer, we'd won five Tests out of six (with one draw), nine ODIs out of 10 (with one washout) and, so far, the only T20I the boys had played.

MOST OF THE QUESTIONS afterwards were about the poor attendance, T20 v ODI, and the crowded schedule, but there was still time for me to be asked about the season, and how we'd played and how we've progressed. It's hard for me not to be confident about the future, as we prepare for 12 months of cricket that will include an Ashes series and a World Cup. 'We're heading in the right direction in all forms of the game and with the exposure that we've been able to give a lot of the younger guys as well, a lot of them aren't so young any more in terms of having games of cricket under their belts,' I said.

I'm not sure if it was just before or just after midnight when I got out of the ground. For Rianna and me, our next stop was Launceston, to catch up with family and also to go to Invermay Park — where I played plenty of my junior cricket — to spend some time with a group of promising young cricketers and to participate in the presentation of a $200,000 cheque from the Ponting Foundation to the Premier of Tasmania, David Bartlett. This money has been raised through the Foundation's 'Hitting Childhood Cancer for Six' campaign that we launched last year.

'Rianna and I are thrilled to be able to hand over $200,000 to the people of Tasmania today to assist with the care of children who are diagnosed with cancer,' I said. 'It's only 11 weeks since we launched our Tasmania–specific fundraising program and we have been overwhelmed by the generosity of Tasmanians from all walks of life. We were planning to hand over our first distribution in July this year, but the response has been so fantastic we have been able to bring this donation forward.'

We knew where the money was going. As I explained in a media release, the funds will be used to immediately upgrade the MRI scanners at Launceston General Hospital and Royal Hobart Hospital, to provide additional training for medical staff treating children with cancer in Tasmania and to employ a part-time psychologist and dietician to provide dedicated support to those children and their families. From a personal perspective, I am very excited that we are already well on the way to reaching our initial target of $500,000 across three years. Yesterday's donation is such a great start.

That I was able to hand the cheque over on a sports ground where I spent plenty of childhood hours was a moving, even humbling experience for me. When I was a kid I had plenty of dreams about playing cricket for Australia and kicking a footy for North Melbourne, but I never dreamed I'd be back at Invermay 20 or 25 years later as part of an initiative that will hopefully prove vital to the lives of some Tasmanian children.

That was Saturday, yesterday, a very proud day for me. Tonight, the boys have a T20 game against the West Indies at

THE END OF AN UNBEATABLE SUMMER

The final international games of this Australian summer were two Twenty20 games against the West Indies, first at Bellerive and then at the SCG. They ended this way:

Game 1, at Hobart (February 21): Australia 8–179 (20 overs: SR Watson 37, DA Warner 49, BJ Haddin 37*) defeated West Indies 8–141 (20 overs: RS Morton 40, D Ramdin 44; DP Nannes 3–21, SW Tait 3–30) by 38 runs

Game 2, at Sydney (February 23): West Indies 7–138 (20 overs: TM Dowlin 31, N Deonarine 36*) lost to Australia 2–142 (11.4 overs: SR Watson 62*, DA Warner 67) by eight wickets

Bellerive, then they head to Sydney for another game on Tuesday. Wednesday, they're due at the airport at nine in the morning for a flight to Wellington, where they'll face the Kiwis in the first of two T20 games on Friday. I'll be flying across the Tasman next Sunday and right at this moment that feels more like ages than a week away. But I know it will be on me in a minute; it's always like that.

> **February 24** Pup and the boys did a superb job last night in the final game of our summer - a summer that saw us go through the whole season unbeaten. The team continues to develop and we have multiple selection options for all three teams. I'm relaxing for the rest of the week while the T20 boys left for New Zealand this morning.

CHAPTER ELEVEN
NEVER UNDERESTIMATE THE NEW ZEALANDERS

THE AUSTRALIANS IN NEW ZEALAND 2009–10

Monday, March 1

IT WAS GOOD TO catch up with the boys again today, though a part of me would have loved just a few more days away from cricket, to stay with my family. The five of us in the ODI team but not in the Twenty20 squad flew into New Zealand yesterday and we caught up with the T20 guys here in Napier (where the opening one-dayer will be played) this morning.

One thing I am quickly discovering now that I'm out of the Aussie T20 set-up is that the attention shifts so fully onto the T20 games that I, as a non-participant, am out of the spotlight just about completely, unless a major cricket issue confronting either or both of the Test and ODI teams comes up. What this means is that I can get maximum value from my time off, so in the week before I crossed the Tasman I was free to focus on being a parent, enjoying a cappuccino or two, and fine-tuning my golf swing. It's no coincidence that I usually start series well.

However, there were two occasions during the week when I had to put my 'cricket face' back on …

THE FIRST CAME ON February 23, the day of the last Twenty20 international of the home season — a thumping win that meant no Australian team (Test, ODI or T20) had lost a game all summer — when I attended a meeting in Sydney with a

MORE SACHIN MAGIC

It's more than 20 years since Sachin Tendulkar first played international cricket, but he continues to produce feats that just take your breath away. The latest occurred last week against South Africa in Gwalior, in central India, when he became the first batter to score an ODI double century.

We're coming up towards the 3000th ODI ever played, so it's quite a landmark, especially as it was achieved against one of cricket's heavyweight teams. Apparently late in the historic dig he was struggling with cramp, but he reached 200 off the third ball of the 50th over, facing 147 balls in all as he finished on 200 not out – his 93rd international century (47 in Tests, 46 in one-dayers). India's total was a colossal 3–401, and that proved way too many for the South Africans, who were all out for 248 in the 43rd over. Of course, I wasn't there, but the fact they were dismissed for less than 250 suggests the wicket wasn't *too* flat; even if it was, making 200 is a phenomenal effort, something I can only dream about.

number of Australian cricketers, past and present internationals, where we discussed the latest report on security for players in India. The next edition of the Indian Premier League is just a couple of weeks away, and Reg Dickason, a man with enormous experience in protecting cricketers and a long-time friend of the Australian team, had prepared a detailed, often negative but still interim analysis of the situation on the sub-continent. It was important that we all got together to discover exactly what he had written.

Reg had been commissioned by the Federation of International Cricketers Associations (FICA), which represents players from Australia, Bangladesh, England, New Zealand, South Africa, Sri Lanka and the West Indies, to do this analysis, and though contents of his report have been kept confidential, it was no secret he was extremely concerned by recent threats from terrorist groups and by the IPL's response to those threats. As Australian Cricketers Association chief Paul Marsh told Peter Lalor from the *Australian*, after he was asked if his players still wanted to go to India, 'All the money in the world is not going to help you if you are not around to spend it.'

Unfortunately, for me our meeting became a somewhat bruising one, as I learned that the environment in which we have grown up as Australian cricketers has changed somewhat with the emergence of the IPL. Formerly, it was always 'one in, all in' but now not all of us play for the same team, and that created a situation where I, representing those still playing international cricket, argued that we should all respect the warnings in Reg's report, but a few of the guys who are involved solely in the IPL put it pretty bluntly they don't believe things are so bad and consequently they want to go their own way. I was disappointed with the way some guys tried to downplay the significance of Reg's work. When he was the Aussie team's security expert we did exactly what he said, trusted him completely, but now, apparently, his assessment is not as important as the views of the security analysts working for the IPL. Personally, I'll take Reg's opinion every time.

I'm not playing in the IPL this year, and there were suggestions made that because of this it is easy for me to suggest a boycott, if it came to that (Reg's report was, it needs to be stressed, an interim one and obviously we wouldn't be reaching any conclusion until he signed off on a final report). In fact, as Australian captain, I have a responsibility to find out all I can for the guys in the Test and ODI squads, and to do the right thing by all Aussie cricketers. It's not about me; it shouldn't be about any one bloke — rather, it has to be about all players being confident they'll be safe wherever they go to play big-time cricket. That's why Reg was employed by the association that represents us to make his security assessment in the first place.

The outcome from the meeting was that the ACA would go back to the IPL detailing our concerns with the status and implementation of the IPL's security plans, though some players advised that they had flights booked for India in the coming days and would likely be leaving regardless of the IPL's response to our concerns. I left the meeting annoyed that we wouldn't be confronting this security situation with as close to a single voice as possible, and hoping that next time we face a major issue we can confront it as one, like we did in days gone by (such as when the ACA was formed back in the 1990s), rather than be split by competing interests. As soon as it was leaked that the meeting had been a rough one, IPL boss Lalit Modi had a dig at me via his Twitter account, suggesting I was only arguing the way I was because I'd left the Kolkata Knight Riders, but like I said it was never about that. I want the players to go. It's a great opportunity, I think the IPL can be great for the game and the money is fantastic. Reg is the same — he wants the players to enjoy the IPL and to be able to play cricket safely all over the world.

As it turned out, within a few days of this meeting the IPL and its franchises had toughened their security arrangements and our Department of Foreign Affairs and Trade issued advice that the latest terrorist threats were not as dangerous as first thought. My understanding is these developments will allow Reg, the ACA and FICA to recommend that it's okay for Australian players to go, if they want to.

This is a good result for everyone, but I just wish it could have been reached without the angst that preceded it.

THE SECOND TIME I needed to refocus on cricket came 24 hours after that IPL security meeting, five days ago, when I sat next to Brett Lee at the SCG as he announced he was retiring from Test cricket. I realised such a decision was on the cards, given all the injury troubles Bing has had over the past couple of years, but a part of me still wanted him to keep going, in the hope that he'd return to Test greatness at least one more time. Fortunately for us, he leaves the team at a time when there is plenty of depth in our pace-bowling stocks, though the fact he is retiring essentially because of injury underlined the fact that quick bowling can be a precarious business.

'Doing what he does, running 35 metres every ball that he bowls, bowling every ball at close to 150kph and putting his heart on the line every ball he bowls, this guy deserves a massive pat on the back,' I said after Bing had made his announcement. 'I will cherish every opportunity I have to play with Brett in the shortened (50-over) form of the game from here on in.'

Sitting on Brett's other side was Cricket Australia chief executive James Sutherland, who recalled Bing's debut on Boxing Day 1999, when he took 5–47 against India. 'He bowled a very

ONE SHORT

Unfortunately, Shaun Marsh is still struggling with his back injury, and is out of the Chappell-Hadlee series, but after some serious thinking we've decided to stick with just 13 players, on the basis that an extra man is just a few hours away and can get here pretty quickly if we need him.

Our full squad for the ODI series is: Ricky Ponting, Michael Clarke, Doug Bollinger, Brad Haddin, Ryan Harris, Nathan Hauritz, James Hopes, Mike Hussey, Mitchell Johnson, Clint McKay, Adam Voges, Shane Watson, Cameron White.

quick spell that had the Indian batsmen ducking for cover,' James said. 'I think we all knew then that we were watching the birth of a great fast bowler.'

That comment immediately had me thinking, *Gee, that doesn't seem so long ago.* The game moves so fast these days, we don't always get a chance to draw breath and contemplate just how exceptional the best of the current players are. Bing leaves Test cricket as Australia's fourth-highest wicket-taker, behind only Shane Warne, Glenn McGrath and Dennis Lillee, and he's taken more than 300 wickets in ODIs as well, and while I know many people wouldn't rate him right up there with the absolute greatest bowlers of all time, it's very hard to argue with those numbers. Perhaps my best memories of Brett as a Test bowler are from the 2007–08 home season, when he was consistently superb. I'm sure he was the best fast man in the world at that time; it's such a pity that because of injuries he wasn't able to sustain that form in the two years that followed.

TIE-BROKEN

After Australia won the first T20 international last Friday by six wickets, the Kiwis came back two evenings later to level the series in a thriller.

Game 1, at Wellington (February 26): New Zealand 118 (20 overs: MJ Guptill 30, JEC Franklin 43; MJ Johnson 3–19) lost to Australia 4–119 (16 overs: DJ Hussey 46) by six wickets

Game 2, at Christchurch (February 28): New Zealand 6–223 (20.3 overs: BB McCullum 116*, GJ Hopkins 36) defeated Australia 5–220 (21 overs: BJ Haddin 47, MJ Clarke 67, CL White 64*) in an extra-over 'eliminator'. The teams were tied – New Zealand 6–214, Australia 4–214 – after 20 overs.

BING'S RETIREMENT ANNOUNCEMENT CAME as the Australian T20 team was on its way to New Zealand. First up, the boys were in Wellington on Friday, where they achieved a clear-cut victory, but the winning streak came to an end at Christchurch last night, in a game that was only decided after each team had to bowl an additional six deliveries.

I followed the game from either my hotel room or a café near the hotel here in Napier (where the Chappell-Hadlee series starts on Wednesday), so I was able to appreciate all the big hits from the likes of Brendon McCullum (a resounding undefeated 116 with eight sixes and 12 fours from just 56 balls) and Cameron White (64 from 26 balls).

McCullum's spectacular knock has been a major talking point. He created shots you don't see in 'traditional' cricket, including his party-piece — where he half ducks and puts his bat out in front of him, so he can sort of 'paddle' the ball over his head, help it on its way, if you like. If he gets it right the ball flies away over the keeper's head for four or, off a rapid-fire bowler like Shaun Tait, even for six. It looks fantastic and the crowd loves it, but except in very rare circumstances, you won't see the shot in a Test or 50-over game because the risk of losing your wicket is too great.

However, with 10 wickets to fall in just 20 overs in a T20 game and often no fielder at fine leg it's a piece of improvisation that's worth the gamble on a good batting track, if you're good enough, same as the big hoick over mid-wicket that results in some colossal sixes.

That point about being good enough to pull the shot off is important — if it was easy, everyone would be doing it — so you have to give credit to Brendon, my old IPL team-mate, who is undoubtedly one of the smartest and cleanest hitters in the game.

> **March 1** Have joined the team in Napier after a week off. I'm actually looking forward to getting a hard training session under my belt this afternoon. Great to see that Tasmania won the Ford Ranger Cup final last night. There was a bit of speculation I was going to play but it was never a possibility – I thought the group that got Tassie to the final deserved to be the group that won it. Fantastic result boys!!!

Tuesday, March 2

THE PAST 24 HOURS have been a bit weird. Normally, at the start of a series, all the talk is about cricket — what's going to happen, the players to watch, who's under pressure to perform — but it feels as if most of what the public is concerned about is the state of Michael Clarke's relationship with his fiancée Lara and how Pup is reacting to a spate of stories concerning Lara that have been appearing in the media back home. Pup's doing it a bit tough at the moment, trying to deal with a personal matter while sections of the media keep scratching for any inside information they can find, and all we can do is offer our friend and team-mate our total support.

There's been some bizarre moments, such as when a television cameraman broke an order to stay off the ground today during our practice, and followed Pup wherever he went. Eventually, we had to call security to boot this bloke back behind the fence, where he could read one local newspaper that is offering advice to the New Zealand players as to what sort of sledges they should use to try to unsettle our embattled vice-captain.

TASSIE TIGERS!

I was having a bit of trouble keeping up with all the cricket last Sunday. As well as having a close eye on the T20 game from Christchurch, I was also receiving regular text messages from Melbourne, where Tasmania was beating Victoria in the Ford Ranger Cup final.

It was looking pretty good after the first 50 overs, with Tim Paine making a hundred and the good guys amassing an imposing 6–304. And the text updates during the evening kept getting better, as the Victorians fell to 194 all out in reply. This is Tassie's third domestic trophy in the past six seasons, after the ING Cup (now Ford Ranger Cup) win in 2004–05 and the Sheffield Shield triumph two years later, victories that reflect the quality and depth of talent we have nowadays in Tasmanian cricket. I love the blend of experienced guys and young blokes in the squad, and there's no doubt coach Tim Coyle and captain George Bailey are doing a fantastic job.

THESE PROBLEMS ASIDE, THERE'S still plenty of hype about the cricket — always is when we play over here — and the locals always like building up possible confrontations when they can. This time, in part to get their minds off other things, I'm happy to accommodate them. First, following up Brendon McCullum's hundred in the T20 game in Christchurch, they've been asking me how we're going to prevent an encore, especially given some of the boundaries on the grounds in New Zealand are ridiculously short. This is especially true of McLean Park here in Napier, a ground I have fond memories of because of the unbeaten 141 I hit in 2005. Judging by some of the questions I've been getting and the comments I've been hearing, some Kiwis have visions of McCullum smashing Nathan Hauritz from the North Island to the South. Horrie will be okay, I assured them.

'I'll be surprised if he plays the way he did in the T20,' I countered when asked again about the man of the moment. 'He'll probably feel a bit more responsibility going into a 50-over game. He's one of their most experienced players and probably their batter in the best form at the moment so I think he'll put it on himself to bat for longer periods of time.'

McCullum's batting record in ODI cricket is okay, but actually not too flash. He's only hit two ODI hundreds, neither of them at home, and he averages less than 30 against us. We've talked at team meetings since Sunday about that paddle shot, what is now being called a 'ramp' shot, and the key, I reckon, is to get a handle on when he's going to try it. If we can get him attempting it at the wrong time to the wrong delivery, he might end up looking a bit silly.

Personally, I'd love him to bat like it's a T20 game. That sort of approach might come off once or twice, but the 50-over game is a different creation that needs more than just blind aggression. We're ready and waiting for him

Then it was on to Shane Bond, who I have to admit has a pretty fair record against me. In fact, he knocked me over in each of the first six ODIs I played against him, which gave the impression that I didn't like his bowling very much. I've had better luck against him recently, but now I'm hearing that a few people in or near the New Zealand camp think that Bond 'has my number'. I don't think that's right, but I do know he's a tremendous talent, as his overall ODI record proves. His strike rate of a wicket every 30-odd deliveries is exceptional, one of the best of all time, and without him their attack does lack that 'X factor' that the best bowling line-ups always have.

Funny thing is, Bond has never dismissed me in a Test match. However, before I talk this fact up too much I have to reveal that we've only opposed each other in a five-day game twice, in 2001–02, when I made 157 not out in the second Test of that series and 31 and 26 in the third.

Friday, March 5

Chappell-Hadlee Trophy Game 1, at Napier (March 3): Australia 8–275
(50 overs: SR Watson 45, RT Ponting 44, MEK Hussey 59; DR Tuffey 3–58) lost to
New Zealand 8–281 (49.2 overs: BB McCullum 45, PJ Ingram 40, LRPL Taylor 70,
SB Styris 49*) by two wickets

IT WAS A GOOD game, bit fiery at times, wrong result. Afterwards, the chat was about the clash near the end between Mitchell Johnson and Scott Styris, which I'm sure Styris is a bit dirty on because it has taken a bit of attention away from his match-winning 49 from 34 balls that included a last-over six off Dougie Bollinger that ended the contest. To tell you the truth, I didn't really mind the mid-pitch face off — it showed how much both teams are into this series and while the Kiwis might be crowing now, my gut feeling is that Mitch will have the last word. I'm still not sure what started it, but when I saw the two of them walk up to each other I ran in as quickly as I could to try to get them apart. I know the replays show that their heads came together and some people are suggesting that Mitch might have head butted him, but I don't think that's right — even in the heat of battle there's not much logic in head butting a bloke wearing a helmet. The banter continued all the way to the winning hit, but there were handshakes all round afterwards; it wasn't the first Chappell-Hadlee game I've played where emotions got involved and I sure hope it won't be the last. The key, as always, is to be aggressive, play hard, but don't lose control.

Both players were later charged by the match referee, with Mitch copping the harsher penalty, a level-two infringement which means he missed out on 60 per cent of his match fee. That seemed fair to me, though I don't think it's quite right for Mitch to now be cast as public enemy No. 1, which seems to be happening.

It's already reached the stage where our management have talked to the local officials here in Auckland, to make sure there's enough security in place for tomorrow's game two. It could be a bit like England last year, only this time they'll be getting into Mitch rather than me.

We played okay in parts, but I never felt comfortable defending a score of 275 on such a small ground. Too many of our batters got a start but didn't go on to a big score, and in this regard I was as guilty as anyone, getting to 44 but then James Franklin did me with a slower ball that I hit high up on the bat out to Martin Guptill in the covers. Maybe we relaxed a little after a good start (we were 1–50 after six overs), which was disappointing because we'd spoken about how, with the boundaries so close, there's always that chance for the game to change quickly. We should have relished the pressure, rather than get distracted by it. It was almost like we invited them back into the contest and in the end, the hitting of Ross Taylor (who went from 13 to 51 in just 26 balls) and Styris was the difference.

We went into this game having won our previous 12 ODIs, but we've now lost five straight in New Zealand — this one, three in February 2007, one in December 2005.

I've said to the guys that I want them to play every game like it's their last, but we didn't have enough of that attitude on Wednesday. We've got some work to do to get things back on track.

Sunday, March 7

Chappell-Hadlee Trophy Game 2, at Auckland (March 6): Australia 7–273 (50 overs: SR Watson 47, BJ Haddin 53, CL White 54, MEK Hussey 56) defeated **New Zealand** 253 (43.2 overs: SB Styris 46, DL Vettori 70; RJ Harris 3–34, MG Johnson 4–51) by 12 runs (DL method)

SOMETIMES, IT'S NOT enough just to win. This was a game we should have won more comfortably than we did, and if we possessed the killer instinct I'm after we would have. Maybe it's because we're coming to the end of a long, long season, though I hate using that excuse — it's the 21st century and we should be able to rise above tough schedules. Perhaps all the negativity towards Mitch meant we relaxed before the job was done, which allowed New Zealand to get within 13 runs of an unlikely win, but that doesn't explain how for the second game in a row our batters failed to nail that big score that would have given us a truly unassailable total. It just wasn't a great effort, but we won and for that I'm grateful.

Mitch was booed by the crowd every chance they could. He had two security guys for company when he entered and left the ground during his quick knock of 16 not out, and whenever he touched the ball during the Kiwis' innings, they were into him. His response was to play up to the crowd from time to time and take 4–51 from nine overs; but for Daniel Vettori's double of 70 and 2–43 he might have been man of the match.

'If his byplay with the crowd affected the way he played, then I'd be worried,' I said afterwards when asked about what went on. 'It looks like it actually spurred him on tonight if anything. Sometimes you've just got to try to have a bit of fun with the crowd. As much as they're giving it to you, you're the worst person in the world to them, but you've got to try to have a bit of fun with it otherwise it's going to be a long four or five weeks over here.

'There were chants going around the ground but Mitch came back with wickets for us. That was a good result for him and the team.'

There was a bit of drama when Scott Styris came out to bat with the score at 4–46. Mitch had just had James Franklin caught behind and immediately he fired in a real quick bouncer that sailed over Styris' helmet and Brad Haddin's head for five wides.

'We might have talked about it being a bouncer, mightn't we?' I quipped when I was asked if that delivery was a disappointment. 'I'm not that unhappy if he bowls a bouncer when I've told him to. He was trying to make a statement and that's fine.'

The other bloke who impressed me last night was Ryan Harris. He didn't have the best of games in Napier, couldn't get his yorkers right, but worked hard at training in the time between games one and two and we saw the fruits of that labour when it mattered. The way he bowled to Vettori at the end, when there was a chance the home team might pull off an unlikely victory, was brilliant — nine down, they needed 26 from 24 balls, but Ryno conceded just three runs from his last eight balls and knocked the Kiwi captain over to seal our win.

> **March 7** Just about to arrive into Hamilton. Good to win yesterday but we still have plenty of work to do – we all seem to be a bit below what we know we can do.

Friday, March 12

Chappell-Hadlee Trophy Game 3, at Hamilton (March 9): **New Zealand** 245 (46.2 overs: LRPL Taylor 62, SB Styris 41, GJ Hopkins 45; RJ Harris 3–48, MG Johnson 3–41) lost to **Australia** 4–248 (47.2 overs: BJ Haddin 110, RT Ponting 69) by six wickets
Chappell-Hadlee Trophy Game 4, at Auckland (March 11): **New Zealand** 238 (44.1 overs: BB McCullum 61; NM Hauritz 3–46) lost to **Australia** 4–202 (31.1 overs: RT Ponting 50, CL White 50*) by four wickets with 17 balls to spare (DL method)

HAVING GOT THE SERIES back on level terms after game two, we decided to ease off on our training, because we were facing three games in five days: Tuesday, Thursday and Saturday. First though, the Michael Clarke story took a final turn when he decided to return home. My view is that he has handled an extremely awkward situation in a very sensible way and I've also admired the mature manner in which the team got on with things in his absence. It was disappointing, though, to hear a few cynics questioning Pup's commitment, seemingly on the basis that 'we didn't do it like that in our day'. He'll return to the team with his mind 100-per-cent locked in to us winning the Test series, and that's what we're all after.

It was about 7pm last Monday when Pup told me, Tim Nielsen and Steve Bernard he needed some time back in Sydney. Tim drove him up to Auckland very early on Tuesday morning and I made my first public comment on the matter at a media conference later that day, after we went 2–1 up in the series. Really, there wasn't much for me to say — I did confirm that some of the boys didn't know he'd left until that morning and we weren't sure exactly when he was going to rejoin us, but that was about it …

'I can't tell you anything,' I said when the questions kept coming. 'He is home sorting out some personal stuff.

'I haven't heard from him and I don't really expect to … he knows from all of us within the team that he has all the support that he needs. The last thing I said to him was for him to take as much time as he needed and hopefully we can do the right thing over here and win the series without him.'

BRAD HADDIN WAS FANTASTIC at Hamilton, scoring his second ODI century, after Ryan Harris and Mitchell Johnson had restricted New Zealand to 245, and then at Eden Park we produced a second straight commanding performance to win the series with nearly three overs up our sleeve. Because of heavy rain during the break between innings, our run chase in game four was revised to 200 from 34 overs and then Hadds was dismissed first ball, but we never really looked like losing, even though batting wasn't easy on the damp wicket. A bit like we did in the Test at Headingley last year, Shane Watson and I attacked the bowling and again this strategy worked beautifully, as they bowled too short and we were able to score at seven runs an over for the first 12 overs. After that, Cameron White, Mike Hussey and Adam Voges all batted really well as we cruised to victory and claimed our seventh straight ODI series win (Pakistan in Dubai and Abu Dhabi, England away, the Champions Trophy in South Africa, India away, Pakistan at home, West Indies at home, New Zealand away).

One thing I liked about these two wins was the way we recovered after New Zealand got off to good starts in their innings. It can be hard to turn momentum around in a 50-over

WHO'S THAT 13TH MAN?

When we decided to go into this series with just 13 players, we didn't expect to be without our vice-captain for the final three matches. For game three, we pushed Mike Hussey up from six to No. 4, brought Adam Voges into the side, and at the same time the selectors decided to call George Bailey over from Tassie to link up with the squad for games four and five.

Clint McKay, the one player left outside our starting XI was listed as our 12th man at Hamilton, with fitness coach Stuart Karpinnen, who played some first-class cricket for Western Australia in 2001 and 2002, acting as '13th man'.

game, but we managed to do that, chiefly because we fielded really well and our bowlers stuck to the game plan. Their batters continued to attempt the big shots, but our blokes kept hitting the right areas, building pressure and getting important wickets when we needed them. The way Nathan Hauritz and James Hopes frustrated them into error in game four, as they slumped from 1–120 after 19.4 overs to 7–177 after 38.3 overs, was particularly impressive.

In between games three and four, I was at Ellerslie racecourse for the running of one of New Zealand's most important horse races, the Auckland Cup. I spent a fair bit of time this day with some of the New Zealand players, including Daniel Vettori and Brendon McCullum, and though there weren't too many punters there, it was a terrific experience. The main race — which has been won in the past by some horses well known to Aussie punters, such as Jezabeel (1998) and Castletown (1992) — was claimed this year by an Australian horse, Zavite, which carried my cash, and was ridden by our champion jockey Damien Oliver and trained by Anthony Cummings.

> **March 12** We've arrived in Wellington after flying down
> from Auckland this morning. Great win by the boys last
> night and it's a great feeling to have the Chappell-Hadlee trophy
> safely in our keeping. Our one-day squad has been absolutely
> fantastic over the past 18 months. We're in pretty good shape for
> the 2011 World Cup that will be well and truly under way this time
> next year.

Sunday, March 14

Chappell-Hadlee Trophy Game 5, at Wellington (March 13): New Zealand 9–241 (50 overs: SB Styris 55) defeated Australia 190 (46.1 overs: SR Watson 53, MEK Hussey 46, JR Hopes 40; SE Bond 4–26, TG Southee 4–36) by 51 runs

THE ONE-DAY SERIES ended on a disappointing note for us, as we bowled okay but batted indifferently to suffer our first loss by a clear margin in an ODI since India beat us by six wickets in Delhi last October. We started reasonably, with Clint McKay nailing Brendon McCullum for just a single from 13 balls and their score then stumbling to 3–32 after eight overs, but Scott Styris and Daniel Vettori got their innings back on track and the last four wickets added 86. We then collapsed to 5–96 in the 27th over and couldn't recover.

My contribution was negligible, but I was unlucky — given out caught behind first ball when a short ball from Shane Bond missed my bat but clipped my helmet. This was the only time Bond got me out during the series.

I wasn't happy and stood with my hand on my hip and a bemused look on my face for a few seconds before walking off, but it was hard not to think back only a couple of days, to game

TEST SQUAD

There's been plenty of conjecture about the make-up of our starting XI for the upcoming Test series, most of it focusing on Marcus North's future. Steve Smith has been in sensational touch for NSW in all forms of the game, not least in the Blues' most recent Shield game, when he took 7–64 in South Australia's second innings after scoring 100 in NSW's first dig, and some commentators are pushing for him to make his Test debut. But I've got to admit I'll be happy if we stick with the team that did so well in Australia this summer. I've got a lot of faith in Northy.

Michael Clarke has sent me a text saying he will definitely be back for the two Tests, and I understand he'll be flying in tomorrow with the other Test guys from Sydney – Steve Smith, Simon Katich and Phillip Hughes. The guys from our ODI squad for the last three Chappell-Hadlee games who will be staying for the Tests are Doug Bollinger, Brad Haddin, Ryan Harris, Nathan Hauritz, Mike Hussey, Mitchell Johnson, Clint McKay, Shane Watson and me.

four, when I could have been given out lbw early on but received the benefit of the doubt (rightly in my view) and went on to make 50 from 35 balls.

If the video referral system was being used for these one-day games I would have been saved, but it wasn't to be.

> **March 14** Nice to have a day off today after the hectic ODI schedule. We now have a changeover of squads with the Test guys arriving tomorrow and a few of the boys now heading home. Looking forward to the two upcoming Tests. Seems like more than two months since we played our last Test in Hobart and the two Tests against New Zealand are an important part of our Ashes build up.

Thursday, March 18

I WAS THINKING THE same thing last October when we played them in the Champions Trophy final — there's something about playing cricket for Australia against New Zealand. Part of it is because we're neighbours, with Australia cast as the 'big brother', but there's always a chance that the Kiwis will knock us off so there's a genuine respect between the two teams. We can't intimidate them easily because they've known us too long to fall for that.

Similarly, though, we'll never take them for granted, because often enough in the past they've played above their ranking against us. It is true they haven't beaten us in a Test since I made my international debut back in 1995, but in the 10 years before that they won as many Trans-Tasman Tests as they lost (five wins, five losses, seven draws), and I'll never forget old pros like Mark Taylor, Steve Waugh and Ian Healy constantly reminding us that we should never underestimate the New Zealanders.

This time, with the two Tests coming at the end of an 18-month period in which we've already played 23 Tests (four in India in October-November 2008, five in Australia in 2008–09, three in South Africa in February-March 2009, five in England in July-August 2009, six in the just-completed Australian season) and with the Kiwis weakened by the absence of Shane Bond, who like Brett Lee has announced he's retired from Tests to focus on ODI and T20 cricket, maybe we'd have an alibi if we wanted to ease off a little.

But that's not how we want to play, it's not the Australian way, and there is also a real vibe over here about this series, about how they'd really like to show that we're not as good as our recent record suggests and that they are better than some critics would have you believe.

Inevitably, a lot of the talk in the lead-up to the Test has been about Michael Clarke, but to tell you the truth it's been much less of a discussion point within the squad than it has been outside.

It's been a bit bizarre to see flocks of TV cameramen and news photographers stationed at the front entrance and fire escapes of our hotel here in Wellington, and to see the way they buzz around the team bus and our dressing room at the ground. At one point, management did ask for the hotel foyer to be cleared of them, because it was getting a bit crowded and was

QUESTION TIME

Last Monday night we found ourselves at a reception at Parliament House in Wellington, which was hosted by the New Zealand Prime Minister John Key. Players from both teams were there, though Michael Clarke, who had arrived from Sydney the previous night, stayed back at the hotel to get some peace and quiet after what had been a difficult few days for him.

During the function, Mr Key told us a funny yarn about how one night last week, between working on government business, he tried to help his son with some maths homework. However, there was also an ODI being played, and as the cricket grew more and more exciting the two of them agreed that they'd much rather be watching the finish of the cricket than continuing with the long division.

Both Mr Key and the New Zealand opposition leader Phil Goff said some nice things about the Australian team, and during my response I had to concede that while a few of us have copped some stick from the crowd during the one-dayers, we realise that most Kiwi fans don't think we're all *that* bad.

unfair for all the guests, not just us, but other than that we've really just put up with it. We've had to deal with this type of scrutiny before, when other players have become the focus of specific media attention, and we know that all we can do is get on with it.

Sure, we've asked Pup if he's okay and told him he has our full support, but that's what mates do — it's no more complicated than that and there's no need to overdo it. And, without trying to downplay the stress he has gone through, he is not the first player to have gone through some tough personal issues while on a tour.

By going back to Australia, he was able to resolve things, put a bit of certainty in his life and I sense now he is really looking forward to getting out onto the cricket ground. When you're feeling pressure from non-cricket matters, the field of play amid the buzz of competition can actually be a great place to escape to, so it wouldn't surprise me if he has a good time during the first Test and makes a really big score.

We've talked quite a bit since he came back into the group, but one short exchange has stayed with me. 'Are you right to play?' I asked him straight.

'Yeah mate, I am,' he shot back with plenty of conviction.

I've known the bloke since 2004; I know him well. If he wasn't ready to go, he wouldn't be here. He'd never let anyone down. I'm convinced of that.

There's been some talk that the New Zealanders will sledge him, but I doubt that. Sure, there'll be plenty coming from beyond the boundary, but on the field the Kiwis know Pup's a tough customer who is not going to be put off by a wisecrack, no matter how funny or crass it might be. More likely, such a remark would have the opposite effect.

Wednesday, March 24

First Test, New Zealand v Australia, at Wellington (March 19–23): Australia 5–459 dec (131 overs: SM Katich 79, MJ Clarke 168, MJ North 112) and 0–106 (23 overs: PJ Hughes 86*) defeated **New Zealand** 157 (59.1 overs: DE Bollinger 5–28) and 407 (134.5 overs: TG McIntosh 83, DL Vettori 77, BB McCullum 104; RJ Harris 4–77) by 10 wickets

BACK IN DECEMBER, in the Boxing Day Test against Pakistan, we made 5–454 declared in our first innings from 128 overs. This time, we made 5–459 from 131 overs before we closed and it wasn't just the total, wickets lost and overs faced that were the same or similar. There was also some surprise that I'd declared so 'early', but once again I felt that making this call gave us the best chance to win the game. There was nothing to be gained by grinding New Zealand into the dust; better to be aggressive, keep the game moving and give our bowlers a chance to do some damage on a second-day wicket that we knew, despite our score, still had some life in it.

Reflecting the depth in our line-up at present, the batters who made the bulk of the runs this time were not the men who contributed significantly in Melbourne. The one constant was Simon Katich, who made 98 on the first day against Pakistan and 79 here. This time, Michael Clarke and Marcus North, the two members of the top six to miss out at the MCG, both made big hundreds — which was so impressive given the pressure they've been under. Also gratifying was the fact that the declaration worked a treat, because by stumps on day two the Kiwis had been reduced to 4–108, after at one point being 4–43. I went to bed that night wondering whether this might be a time when I should enforce the follow-on and the next day Dougie Bollinger basically forced my hand by cleaning them up even quicker than I expected. After that, we had to grind them out but we got the win so I guess I made the right call … unless the 200-odd overs we spent in the field has flattened us for the second Test, which starts next Saturday at Hamilton. Only time will tell on that one.

Day One

I know the selectors discussed replacing Northy with Steve Smith, on the basis that Smithy's form in the last couple of months has been great while Marcus has been struggling for runs, but I don't know how close they came to making a change. While I don't agree with the idea that you should *never* change a winning team, I am a big fan of loyalty and I also know you can't always measure a bloke's overall contribution simply by runs and wickets. And while I know that Northy has been down on form of late, the

ONE QUICK AFTER ANOTHER

We've gone though a few pace bowlers over the past few months – of the five quicks who were in our Ashes squad, all of Brett Lee, Ben Hilfenhaus, Stuart Clark and Peter Siddle are missing here. This hasn't been good, but at least it has given a chance to guys like Doug Bollinger, Ryan Harris and Clint McKay, who have all showed they have the skills to succeed at the top level.

In the lead-up to this Test, the injury jinx struck again. First, Ryan suffered a minor side strain that for a while looked like it would prevent him making his Test debut, and South Australian paceman Peter George was called into the squad. Then Shane Watson, better known these days as a batting all-rounder but still quite capable of bowling the odd quick delivery, had to pull out of the Test because of a hip injury, and Phillip Hughes got another chance to show the world just what a special talent he is.

memory of his hundreds against South Africa and England last year is still strong with us.

Furthermore, while I knew that he was struggling with the pressure of being out of form — he told me exactly that when we talked one on one before the Test — after I watched him in the nets, working with Justin Langer and a bowling machine, it seemed to me that the more they worked, the more his feet were moving into the right positions, and more and more the ball was hitting the middle of his bat. You can't always take net form into a game, but my gut feel was that Northy would do just that. Steve Smith's time will come, there's no doubt about that, but I'm glad the selectors made the call they did, and I write that not just because Northy helped Michael Clarke take us from 4–176 to 4–316 by stumps on the opening day.

Pup reached his hundred in the last over of the day, having gone from 50 to 100 in just 39 deliveries, and I think it was good for him that he had Northy out there with him for much of his innings. They've had some good partnerships in the past, such as at Cardiff and Leeds during last year's Ashes series, and they gelled beautifully again here. Later, I heard Pup talking about a mid-pitch conversation they had when he was in the 80s but it looked like he'd run out of time before stumps to make three figures.

Pup: 'I can't stop thinking about my hundred.'

Northy: 'Mate, if you see it, just hit it.'

That seems like a very sensible piece of advice. Pup was on a roll and I'm sure he slept much better having made his century than he would have if he'd finished the day a few runs short.

The thing about Pup is he's only 28 years old; he's probably got his best times as a cricketer ahead of him. Sure, he's been consistently good over the past two or three years, but nowadays it's not until you reach your early 30s that you really blossom as a Test batter. I know he's going to get even better.

There was plenty of emotion in the rooms afterwards, and his body language reminded me a little of how Mark Taylor reacted after he scored a hundred at Edgbaston in 1997, to end a shocking run of outs. Not much has gone right for Pup in the past couple of weeks, and he needed this ton to restore a little faith in himself. He's back doing what he does best, and doing it brilliantly. I'm sure he also relished the way the rest of the team let him know how much they enjoyed his performance.

The spirit in this group has been a feature of the team this summer, and the buzz in the room after this first day's play might have been the best example of it we've seen so far.

Day Two

Pup went on his highest Test score, Northy to his fourth Test hundred and then, halfway through the middle session, Ryan Harris got to bowl his first over in a Test match. Ryno needed to pass a fitness test to make his debut, but if his side strain was nagging him at all it didn't show as he took to five-day cricket like a canny veteran. First, he saw Doug Bollinger take a wicket in the first over of the innings, then — with the score on 1–14 after 12 overs — Mitchell Johnson ran out Tim McIntosh with a nifty piece of footwork, kicking the ball onto the stumps as McIntosh and Peter Ingram attempted a quick single. And then, when I brought Ryan back after a short break for a second spell, he got one to move away off the seam at good pace and McIntosh sliced a catch to Mike Hussey in the gully. It's always an exciting moment when a bloke gets his first Test wicket, and this one, coming when we were right on top, was as good as any.

Ross Taylor is their most dangerous hitter, and we all knew if we could get him quickly we really had control of the game. Back came Bollinger for a second spell and immediately he produced a pearler that Taylor could only edge to Northy at third slip, who snared it like a bloke who was back in love with the game. Not for the first time, Dougie had surprised a batter with that extra bounce he can generate; he's done that consistently for NSW at the SCG (traditionally a spinner's wicket) over the past couple of years and there's no reason why he can't do it all over the world.

Day Three

There were a few reasons why I made them follow on. One, most influential of all, the weather forecast wasn't too flash so I was keen to end the game as quickly as we could. Two, New Zealand's first innings was over in only 59.1 overs, so our bowlers were

VERY BOLLINGER

You've got to love Dougie Bollinger. Of course he was excited to take his fifth wicket of the New Zealand innings, and to show just how much it meant to him – and also, maybe, to stick it up the All Black fans who'd been into him during the innings – he decided to kiss the crest on his cricket shirt. If a batter can kiss the badge on the front of their helmets when they reach three figures, why can't a proud Aussie bowler do something similar when he completes a Test five-for?

Only trouble was, Dougie went for the right breast of his shirt, not the left, and that meant he puckered up to the VB logo, not the Australian coat of arms. To highlight his mistake he then quickly tried again, this time successfully kissing the kangaroo and the emu, and later, he tried to tell us he'd done it deliberately to get in good with our chief sponsor. But we all knew better.

Dougie's sometimes a bit crazy, at other times a real pest, but always good for a laugh. He's also a very, very good bowler, but I'm not sure all our opponents realise that yet. I just hope they keep under-rating him; that's certainly one thing we will never do.

hardly spent. Doug Bollinger, for example, had taken his second Test five-for of the summer, and bowled brilliantly, but he'd only sent down 13 overs. He was keen to have another go at them. Three, after all the success we've had this season I liked the idea of presenting our bowlers with something different, a new challenge to get them out of their comfort zone. And four, I felt the Kiwis were down for the count.

Sometimes in these situations you sense that, after a poor first-innings batting effort, the opposition have steeled themselves for a better performance second time around, that this time they'll really have to be chiselled out. But I didn't see that in the Kiwis here. I really thought we could run through them again and complete an emphatic victory, and on this third day, except for Tim McIntosh, who resisted stoutly for 83, that's pretty much how it worked out. At stumps, they were 5–187, still 115 runs behind, and my only real worry was the threat of rain.

Day Four

This was one of the most bizarre days of cricket I've ever played in. Only one wicket fell all day, as New Zealand gradually built a lead of 67 runs, but what I'll remember more than any scores are some of the scenes created by the wild weather. These included a member of the ground staff being thrown over the boundary rope as he clung to the covers while they ballooned up like a broken spinnaker, a cricket helmet blowing and bouncing across the field like an errant paper bag, spectators being knocked off their feet by the gale, and TV camera operators clinging on to scaffolding for dear life as they gallantly tried to film the action. The ground-staff remembered to turn off the engine on their heavy roller and put the brake on, but that wasn't enough to stop it moving. We were on and off the field more than once because of the weather, and lost 30 overs in all for the day.

The winds blew up to 130kmh and more, which made it hard for everyone — players, fans, umpires and even the TV coverage, which led to a weird situation after we asked for an lbw appeal against Brendon McCullum to be referred. McCullum hadn't played a shot to a Nathan Hauritz off-break, the ball had spun back and struck him on the pad, and we thought we were a big chance ... but then word came back that the technology wasn't working because they couldn't keep the cameras still. The side-on cameras had already been shut down for fear they'd blow away and all the umpires could do was eventually tell me that we could keep the referral for a later time, whenever that might be.

What bugged me at the time was that we didn't know the system wasn't working until we asked for that referral. After a delay, they told us it was no good, which was also the first the on-field umpires knew of the problem. It was Dan Vettori who spoke up loudest when I started arguing that at the very least we shouldn't lose a referral in these circumstances.

You almost couldn't bowl into the gale, and for all but three overs from Ryno early in the day, it was Horrie who drew the short straw. Not long before we finally went off for the day, McCullum hit a six downwind off Mitchell Johnson that went so far it looked like the ball would never be seen again. The Kiwi keeper finished the day 94 not out, and even though conditions were tough for the bowling team it was difficult for him too, and the quality of his effort shouldn't be questioned. It wasn't as spectacular as some of his Twenty20 cameos, but it was better. He scored 90 runs during the day, from 171 balls, while Vettori was the only wicket to fall, bowled by Horrie for 77. By stumps, some locals were even talking about winning, which had been unthinkable 24 hours earlier.

March 22 Sorry I haven't posted lately but have been having some problems with my laptop. All good again now so thanks for your patience. Just about the toughest conditions you could play in today in Wellington. Incredible winds, rain, gloomy skies – not the day we would have all liked. The New Zealand batters did a very good job today and we need to be absolutely on our game tomorrow to close out the Test.

Day Five

The wind was nothing like what it had been on the fourth day (you couldn't have two days like that in the same lifetime!), and after McCullum went to his hundred we cleaned up their tail, getting the last four wickets in seven overs for 19 runs, which left us a very

WINDY WELLINGTON

It was nothing like the cyclone that blew us all away on day four, but 'windy Wellington' was still able to give us one more reminder of what it can do as we flew out of the city today, bound for Hamilton. We could feel and hear the gusts of gale as they buffeted our little plane on the tarmac, and we were bouncing all over the place as we nervously flew out of the city.

I hate to think how many frequent-flyer points I've earned over the past 15 years, but of course it would be plenty. Fortunately, I've never been that nervous about flying, because it can be a tough business if you are. But of all the miles I've clocked up, these ones out of Wellington would be just about the most precarious – as my stomach churned over and over and I wondered whether we'd ever see our loved ones again, being an international cricketer hardly felt as glamorous and exciting as many people believe it to be.

manageable 106 to win. In normal circumstances on a fifth day pitch, we would have battled our way to a win sometime during the middle session, but Phillip Hughes was having nothing of that, as he smashed and crashed his way to 86 not out. The winning run was hit off the last scheduled ball before the lunch break.

This was a terrific win, one of my favourites. I'll never forget the way Pup and Northy responded to the adversity they faced before the game, the character they displayed, and I'll also remember fondly the way our bowlers persisted and kept going after we enforced the follow on. Ryan Harris was feeling his side and carrying a bung toe by the end of the game, but he kept going throughout, even when I asked him to bowl into that cyclone on day four, and he was rewarded with six wickets in the game, four of them in their second innings. Doug Bollinger is battling some soreness, too, but he was just as tough; in its own way his 2–80 in their second dig was just as impressive as his first-innings five-for. We'll have to manage these blokes carefully over the next couple of days so they can back up effectively in Hamilton.

Even though Huey was electric on the final day, Shane Watson will come back into the team for the second Test if he's fit. The reasons why come through in my comments about the two guys after the Test:

> On Watto: *'He gives us so much better balance in our side, the fact that you can throw the ball to him and he can get his 10 or 15 overs out per innings. Every team in the world is after someone who bats in the top six and can bowl like he does. He's shown how important he is. Hopefully we'll get him back.'*

> On Huey: *'He can take a lot out of that (his unbeaten 86 from 75 balls). Every opportunity and every bit of*

exposure he gets is going to be good for him in the long run. He's just such an exciting player. When he gets in that frame of mind, when the ball is in his area, it's going to go. If he keeps getting off to starts like that in Test cricket, it really sets up games. I'll encourage him to keep playing that way. He knows he has got work to do on a few little technique things but he'll continue to work hard on that and down the track he'll be a good player for Australia.'

Later, I boldly compared Huey to India's Virender Sehwag and I'll stand by that even though it's a big wrap given all that Sehwag has achieved in Test cricket (more than 6500 runs in 76 Tests, average 53.53, with two triple centuries, six double tons and a strike rate of nearly 81 runs per 100 balls).

'Being that sort of player, you will have your ups and downs but when you're up, you win games,' I said. 'Phil only got 20-odd in the first innings here but it got the momentum going in our favour. He's had a good Test, as most of our players have. It's a good sign for us.'

Friday, March 26

ONE MORE TEST TO GO ... and then I'll be on my first extended break since July 2008. First up, I'll be going to Augusta, Georgia, for the US Masters, something I can't wait to experience — one, because, of course, I'm a golf nut, and, two, because over there I'll be just one more face in the crowd. Sometimes, that sort of obscurity can be very alluring.

For Mike Hussey and Simon Katich, 'one more Test to go' means they are both about to play in their 50th Test match. It's not a bad trick, two blokes who played cricket against each other as nine-year-olds in Perth now reaching this landmark as teammates in the same game, and I'm very proud of both of them. Neither has had it easy — Huss, who is now approaching his 35th birthday, didn't make his Test debut until after he turned 30, while Kato has fought back after being dropped, seemingly for good, after the 2005 Ashes loss, to become one of the most reliable opening bats in Australian cricket history. Ryan Harris became Australia's 413th Test cricketer in Wellington; that's a pretty small group, but the 50-Test club is much more exclusive. Huss and Kat will become the 43rd and 44th Australians to hit this half-century, and they sit 23rd and 24th respectively on the list of Australia's highest run-makers in Tests. Huss has scored 11 Test hundreds, Kat nine.

The way Watto batted against Clint McKay and a posse of local net bowlers confirmed that he'll be right to go in first with

IN THE DARK

I said straight after the first Test that I expected our quicks would take it easy between games, given how hard they worked in windy Wellington, and they have certainly taken that order to heart. I've hardly seen Mitch, Ryno and Dougie since we landed here in Hamilton.

As fast bowlers are prone to do, they have basically hidden themselves in their hotel room, and most likely won't reappear until tomorrow morning, just a few hours before the toss. I have heard from Alex, our physio, that they're pretty exhausted but other than that they've pulled up pretty well. I'm glad that Watto will be available to share the load, and at this point it's looking as if my decision to enforce the follow on is not going to do us any long-term damage.

> **March 26** I see that Carlton thrashed Richmond in the opening AFL game last night. North Melbourne play Port Adelaide in Adelaide on Sunday and I'm confident the boys can get off to a winning start. We always match up really well against them and I really like what Brad Scott has already instilled into the team. Can't wait for the footy.

Kat when the Test starts on Saturday. He, like all of us, will be looking to build still further on a terrific season, a point I was quick to make when I was asked this morning if I was confident about achieving a 2–0 series win.

'I think it's important that we make statements every game,' I said. 'Inconsistency was something that plagued us 12 to 18 months ago. I think with the Australian summer and certainly with this tour we've played some very consistent cricket and that's a good sign for us.

'But we all know how quickly that can change. If you just take your eye off things that you need to be concentrating on every day, then the game can turn on you really quickly.

'We're always looking at ways to improve and for individuals to find ways to improve themselves. If that happens the results usually look after themselves.'

Friday, April 2

Second Test, New Zealand v Australia, at Hamilton (March 27–31): Australia 231 (74.3 overs: SM Katich 88; TG Southee 4–61, DL Vettori 4–36) and 8–511 dec (153 overs: SR Watson 65, SM Katich 106, MEK Hussey 67, MJ Clarke 63, MJ North 90) defeated **New Zealand** 264 (63.3 overs: LRPL Taylor 138; MG Johnson 4–59) and 302 (91.1 overs: MJ Guptill 58, BB McCullum 51; MG Johnson 6–73) by 176 runs

AT THE SAME TIME as this Test was being played out, the ICC organised a match in Abu Dhabi that was played under lights using a pink ball. The game was a trial, to see whether the ball would behave in a way that might make day-night Tests a realistic possibility in future seasons, and I have been kept up to date on the development of the ball by Rob Elliot and his team at Kookaburra. They have invested a significant amount of time and money into the project and have been working closely with most of the major stakeholders in the trial.

I can see why the ICC is doing this, and knowing how professional the guys are at Kookaburra there's every chance the experiment will succeed, but to tell you the truth part of me hopes it doesn't work out. You see, as I've written before in this book, I'm a bit of a traditionalist when it comes to Test matches — I'd much rather leave Test cricket as it is and use ODIs and T20 matches as the 'entertainment packages'. In my view, this game here in Hamilton proved my point. It wasn't a classic and it lacked a big finish, but there was plenty of high quality cricket produced, by a group of elite cricketers that included Daniel Vettori, Simon Katich, Ross Taylor and Mitchell Johnson. At the end of it, we could look back on one of the most successful southern-hemisphere seasons ever completed by an Australian team, and for me one of the most satisfying. Like the team, I feel I'm in a really good place at the moment.

Day One

This was Daniel Vettori's day, as his feat of reaching 100 Test matches was acknowledged before the start of play and then he came out and took four cheap wickets as we were bowled out for 231. At stumps, New Zealand were 1–19 in reply.

We didn't bat well, playing too many over-ambitious shots on a slow wicket, and the captain running himself out didn't help things either. This apparently makes me the most run out cricketer in Test history, with 13 such dismissals in 216 completed innings, but I'm not too concerned as the list of players with the most run outs (as at the completion of this Test) shows I'm in pretty fair company. The two guys who were run out 12 times during their Test career are Allan Border and Matthew Hayden, while the other blokes in double figures are India's Rahul Dravid (11) and the West Indies' Garry Sobers and Carl Hooper (both with 10).

Still, there's always a real sense of waste about being run out — the 'what might have beens' nag more fiercely than if you've been knocked over by an unplayable delivery, and the fact that this was the second time in eight days that I'd been run out made my disappointment even more palpable than usual.

The one standout for us, once again, was Simon Katich, who toughed it out gallantly for 88 from 171 balls. This knock meant that he had scored at least one fifty in each of his past eight Tests, and there was still more to come. For the past two years, Kato has been in total control of his game, and the way he's playing at the moment, based on what he's done against all Test-match attacks in recent times, I reckon he stacks up really well against the other top Test opening bats in world cricket, such as Virender Sehwag, Graeme Smith, Gautam Gambhir and Andrew Strauss. On this day, after he was dismissed, we lost our last five wickets for 32 runs. The pitch was awkward, but hardly that difficult, and while Doug Bollinger was able to get one through Tim McIntosh in his first over it ended up being New Zealand's day.

Day Two

The main story of the second day was Ross Taylor's explosive century. He made 138 from 104 balls, out of an innings total of

VETTORI'S CENTURY

The Test is No. 100 for Daniel Vettori. He becomes the 50th man and second New Zealander (after Stephen Fleming) to reach what I consider to be one of the game's most important individual milestones. It takes genuine mental and physical toughness to play 100 Tests, and when you look down the list of those who have made it, there are no mugs among them.

Of the 50 men with 100 Tests, Dan is the 13th to have taken 125 or more Test wickets. Of these 13, only four are spinners: Shane Warne, Muttiah Muralitharan, Anil Kumble and Dan, the one left-hander in a celebrated quartet.

He made his debut back in 1997, as an 18-year-old, and has established himself as one of the best spinners in the game. The thing with Dan is that he mightn't make the ball fizz like a Warne or a Murali, but I can't ever recall him having a really bad day. That consistency, his ability to get something out of tracks that aren't doing much and his tenacity even when his team has been struggling have been his trademarks. Equally impressive is the way he has evolved into a genuine all-rounder, scorer of five Test centuries; he is currently entrenched in the Kiwi top six. He's been a very effective 50-over player, isn't out of place in T20, and he's a good captain, too, though he hasn't had a lot of luck in this series. I think the way he's got the New Zealand ODI team performing, winning well over 50 per cent of the games they play, is the best example of his leadership ability.

264, having reached his century from just 81 deliveries. By stumps, though, we were 0–35 in our second dig, a lead of two runs with all 10 second-innings wickets in hand, so — despite the fact most of us had batted poorly, we'd dropped catches and, Mitchell Johnson apart, had bowled only reasonably — we felt things were going to be okay.

HEADS AGAIN

I had a pretty weird run with the toss in Test matches last year, winning six straight against South Africa but then getting the call right only once in five Ashes Tests in England. This summer, however, I've been on fire, winning two of three tosses against the West Indies, all three against Pakistan and both times over here.

I also called correctly five times out of five in the Chappell-Hadlee series. It's been 'heads' every time when I've made the call, and when we've won the toss in the Tests I've batted first without fail.

The climax to Taylor's innings came after he'd reached his hundred. He was on 106, as Nathan Hauritz began his 13th over; at this point, Horrie's bowling figures were 0–43. Six balls later, those numbers had blown out to 0–68, as he became the second Australian bowler in a week more than 12 months to concede an Aussie Test record 25 runs in a single over. Last March, in Cape Town, AB De Villiers and Albie Morkel went 6, 6, 6, 6, 1, out against Andrew McDonald at Cape Town; this time, the sequence was 0, 4 (no-ball), 1, 1, 6, 6, 6, with the second single being scored by Taylor's partner, Jeetan Patel.

And it could have been even worse ... or better. That first single, off the delivery after the no-ball, came from a big swing to deep mid-wicket, where Shane Watson took a terrific catch but in the process stumbled over the boundary rope. Knowing he was about to put a foot over the line and consequently the catch wouldn't count, Watto threw the ball back onto the field, so he wouldn't concede anything more than one run. So it could have been out or six. The record for the most runs hit from one over in a Test match is 28, by Brian Lara off South Africa's Robin Peterson at Johannesburg in December 2003.

Days Three and Four

It felt like we'd been given a second chance after our ordinary first-innings effort, and I wanted us to take full advantage by grinding the New Zealanders right out of the game. This we did, with a disciplined effort that was built around another major contribution from the ever-reliable Simon Katich. He was very slow at times, taking 138 balls to hit his first boundary and 177 balls to reach his fifty, and the contrast with Taylor's thunderbolt of a century from the previous day was complete. But in the context of the game, Kat's knock was more important.

At stumps on the third day we were 4–333, a lead of exactly 300, and we batted on to lunch on day four, when I set the home team an unlikely 479 to win. The wicket seemed to be getting better all the time, but I had faith in our blokes to get the job done. Mitch had talked with bowling coach Troy Cooley about being more aggressive, and though the wicket had little life in it he still found something, and by the close of play he had three more wickets to go with the four he took on the second day.

ICC WORLD TWENTY20 SQUAD

During this second Test, the selectors named Australia's line-up for the ICC World Twenty20, which will be played in the West Indies from April 30 to May 16. Brett Lee has been chosen in a group that features a blend of Test and ODI regulars and a few guys – such as Dave Warner, Shaun Tait and Dirk Nannes – who have enjoyed some success wearing the green and gold in recent T20 internationals.

The team is: Michael Clarke (captain), Cameron White (vice-captain), Daniel Christian, Brad Haddin, Nathan Hauritz, David Hussey, Mike Hussey, Mitchell Johnson, Brett Lee, Dirk Nannes, Tim Paine, Steven Smith, Shaun Tait, David Warner and Shane Watson.

New Zealand were 5–185. Mitch's first wicket of the second innings — Tim McIntosh, bowled between bat and pad by a very quick in-dipper — was his 150th in Tests.

Day Five

Typically, New Zealand didn't lie down and we had to send down nearly 30 overs to get the last five wickets, yet I was pleased with the way we stuck at it. The wicket was very dead, which made Mitch's 10 wickets for the match all the more impressive. I can't help thinking back to how he was below his best form for much of the 2009 Ashes series, and that if he is at his very best next summer it's going to give us a huge advantage over England. If they think the Mitch they saw at Cardiff and Lord's last year is the same bloke they are going to face in 2010–11, they are in for a very rude shock.

LUCK'S A FORTUNE

I didn't realise it at the time, but when I was given out caught off the helmet for a first-ball duck in the final game of the Chappell-Hadlee series it was the start of a very unlucky mini-run for me. I'd hit the ball pretty well throughout the one-dayers without getting a big score, and was looking forward to the Tests, but it seemed like my fate was out of my hands.

I thought I was going pretty well at Wellington until Kato and I got involved in a mix-up and I was run out. Here in Hamilton, I made a mistake taking on Daniel Vettori's arm in the first innings and then in the second I'd only just started when I flicked a ball off my pads and BJ Watling grabbed an unlikely catch at short leg. One journo called it a 'one-in-a-million chance' but I was still out. All I could do was slam my bat into an unfortunately positioned plastic chair as I walked into the dressing room, and then sit back and watch the rest of batting order make up for my failure.

Claiming the man-of-the-match award for his 10–122 in a game in which Simon Katich scored 88 and 106 and Ross Taylor slammed the fastest ever century by a New Zealander in a Test was quite a good trick.

The Ashes was on many people's minds as we pondered all we've achieved since August, and my view is that we can't be much better placed than how we are going at the moment. With Marcus North having returned to form no one is worried about where his next run or wicket is coming from, and there's certainly no one in this current Test squad who I wouldn't want wearing a baggy green against England, and that includes the young guns, Steve Smith and Phillip Hughes. But I also know that guys like Ben Hilfenhaus and Peter Siddle should have recovered from their injuries by next November, so we'll have plenty of talent to choose from. We have two Tests to play against Pakistan in England in July, games in India in October, and then all eyes will be on the summer of '10–11. With the confidence in this group being so high at present, and the memory of our loss in England still burning in the back of my mind, I can hardly wait.

So now it was goodbye New Zealand and soon it will be hello Augusta, a process that began soon after the last wicket fell. When I learned we were booked on a 6am flight out of Auckland yesterday I initially thought it was an April Fool's joke, but it was for real. So at 2.30am we stumbled onto a bus for the drive north to the airport and a few hours later we were over the Tasman, bound for Sydney. The 2009–10 season was over.

AUGUSTA DREAMING

The idea of going to the US Masters was in my head from not long after it was confirmed I wouldn't be playing for the Knight Riders in the IPL. I thought to myself, *I'm going to have a long break after the upcoming New Zealand tour, no IPL, no ICC World Twenty20; what's on that I might be able to get to.* I didn't even have to look up the calendar; the answer was obvious: the Masters. Going to Augusta is something I've always wanted to do and when I suggested it to Rianna she was excited, too, as long as there was a family holiday at the end of it. So within a few days of getting back to Australia after the New Zealand tour, we flew as a big group to Los Angeles and then five of us — me, Dad, Callum Ferguson, Greg Blewett and a mate of Blewey's from Adelaide, Brett Crosby — continued on to Atlanta and then Augusta, where we rented a house just five minutes from the course.

There are few blokes in the world who love golf more than my father. I've told stories many times of how he can't miss the Saturday competition at Mowbray Golf Club, not even for a Hobart Test match, but he outdid himself here. During the third round, on the Saturday, a day described on the official PGA Tour website as 'one of the most memorable days ever at Augusta National', with champions such as Phil Mickelson and Tiger moving into contention, Dad suddenly turned to me and said flatly, 'I've just missed a game of golf on Saturday at home, haven't I?'

'Yeah, you would have,' I replied, trying not to look too stunned. I really thought he would have been preoccupied with what was going on right in front of him. 'It'd be Sunday morning back home.'

That night, when we got back to the house, the first thing he made me do was get on the internet, to check out who'd won the Saturday comp at Mowbray.

The thing about Augusta that stands out for me is just how superbly pristine the course is. There is not a piece of grass out of place. I reckon, at the end of each day, that all the pine needles around the trees are raked back into the same place they were at the start of play, so that when the golfers turn up the next day the course is *exactly* as it was the day before. I've been watching the Masters since the early '80s, and I've been told many times by people who've been there that it's much hillier than what you imagine from the telecast, but I was still stunned by just how severe the undulations are. The best example is the 10th, where the drop from tee to green must be all of 40 metres. The green on the par-three sixth has a pronounced rise in the centre of it that would be three metres high (I'd call it a 'hump' but you're not allowed to use terms like that to describe this course). This makes putting a little tricky, especially when they put the pin right at the peak of the rise, which is what they did for the second round. The famous 12th, a short par three, looks awkward on television, but I've always thought the explanation for great players coming to grief there on the Sunday was because of the pressure, and of course that does play a part. But the green is tiny from front to back, so I now realise that if there is any wind at all it can be a nightmare trying to keep your ball on the putting surface.

Everything about the week was fantastic. I spent some time with Marc Leishman, the young Aussie golfer playing his first Masters, and also scored an invite to a TaylorMade party on the Tuesday night, where Dad was introduced to Sergio Garcia, which made his night. On the dramatic final day, when Mickelson charged past England's Lee Westwood to win by three strokes, we set ourselves up halfway down the 13th fairway, from where we could watch the approach shots into that hole and the 14th as well, which runs back up the hill. The first group through was Chad Campbell, who'd been in the three-way play-off won by Angel Cabrera the year before, and Australia's Nathan Green, who promptly eagled 13 for our benefit. Soon after, there was plenty of commotion over at No. 16, the par three, where the green is not far from the 14th tee, and we knew something big had happened. Quickly, we learned that Nathan had made a hole in one. It set the scene for the day — as a series of cheers and roars signalled that something else fantastic had happened, and then the word buzzed around about the latest development.

At one point we ran into George Gregan, the former Wallaby captain, who had caddied for the 2005 US Open champion Michael Campbell in the par-three tournament that precedes the main event. George got to putt at the last hole of Michael's round, something many of the caddies do, and he sunk a long one, which he told us was one of the best experiences he'd ever had in sport. Considering George has played in World Cup finals and captained his country that was a big statement, but it does reflect just what an extraordinary event the Masters is, how you get totally involved in every aspect of it, how you feel special just being there. Just being able to see close up how this great golfing tradition continues ... I hope one day I'll be able to do it again.

CHAPTER TWELVE
ANOTHER ASHES QUEST FOR THE BAGGY GREENS

ENGLAND IN AUSTRALIA 2010-11:
A PREVIEW

I REMEMBER WHEN STEVE Waugh's treasured baggy green started fraying at the edges during the 2002–03 Ashes series, we all wondered what he was going to do. It's not like you can just put your cap at the back of a cupboard, or even put it on display somewhere — the cap has been with you on so many journeys, so many good times, that you start seeing it as part security blanket, part good-luck charm and part best mate. Sending it back to the manufacturer for repairs is a gamble, because no matter what the reassurances you're not quite sure it will make it back in one piece. But eventually Steve's baggy green reached the point of no return, and so, during the Australian summer just gone, did mine. Still, I hung on to it a little longer, using the tight schedule as a reason for delaying the surgery, but eventually — immediately after the Sydney Test and with the next game in Hobart eight days away — I handed the cap to a representative from Albion, who make the baggy greens for Cricket Australia. All I could do after that was wait … and wait …

There have been a number of Australian cricketers over the years who *always* wore their baggy green in the field, and I am one of those. It would feel very, very weird for me to be fielding in a Test match without it. I'm not a sentimentalist, and while I have tremendous respect for the great players of the past, it's not a case of me paying some sort of tribute to them — that because they wore a baggy green, I should too. But when I was first picked for Australia, I was so excited to be handed *my* very own baggy green. I modelled it in front of a mirror, thought about wearing it to sleep and couldn't wait to take it out onto the field

THE ASHES SCHEDULE 2010–11

Test	Date	Venue
First Test	November 25–29, 2010	The Gabba, Brisbane
Second Test	December 3–7, 2010	Adelaide Oval
Third Test	December 16–20, 2010	WACA Ground, Perth
Fourth Test	December 26–30, 2010	Melbourne Cricket Ground
Fifth Test	January 3–7, 2011	Sydney Cricket Ground

with me for my first day as a Test cricketer. I'm not sure I am quite into the 'mystique' and 'aura' of the cap like Steve is, but whereas the rest of my clothes and gear tended to change from series to series, my baggy green stayed with me, and became a constant in my climb up the international cricket ladder. Sure, I could have got a new one from time to time, but the new one wouldn't know what I'd been through, wouldn't quite feel right.

I remember feeling very despondent when I lost the baggy green I wore in my debut Test. That happened in 1999, when it was stolen in Sri Lanka, during our tour of that country and Zimbabwe. I'd had an excellent series with the old cap against the Sri Lankans, scoring 96 and 51 in the first Test and 105 not out in the third and final game of the series, but after making 31 in the one-off Test in Harare I then made three Test ducks in a row, including a pair at Bellerive Oval. I wondered if losing the cap had ruined my career, but fortunately I then made three hundreds in four Tests and my faith in the replacement baggy green was restored. We've been together ever since, through more than 100 Tests, including five Ashes series. Thanks to an outstanding restoration job, it'll be with me again this November, when all things going well I'll be playing in my eighth Test series against England.

I first spoke to Albion about fixing the cap when we were in Perth for the third Test against the West Indies. The fabric on the peak was wearing thin, which meant the plastic in the peak was forcing its way through, to the point that sooner or later it was going to become unwearable. It was looking too ratty, hardly fitting for an Australian cricketer, so I knew we had to repair it or place it gently in the archives. I was assured that while they couldn't (and wouldn't) make it look as good as new, they could fix it up so that it would make it through to the end of my career, whenever that might be. The job they did was fantastic — no new material was involved but the brim now feels and looks a lot stronger — and I couldn't be happier. Whatever cricket adventures lie ahead of me, my old baggy green is certainly coming along for the ride. But, as I explained to Malcolm Conn from the *Australian* before the Hobart Test, 'It's not up to my baggy green to score some runs. It's up to me and my bat to do all that stuff.'

There's no doubt the baggy green carries a sense of history. And this feeling is accentuated whenever we fight for the Ashes, simply because the story of Australia–England Tests goes back further and has more tradition than any other cricket battle. When I was a kid reading briefly about the history of the game and the giants of the past, so many of the great Australian players were playing England and wearing their Australian caps. In that

AUSTRALIA V ENGLAND TESTS RESULTS (1877 TO 2009)

Venue	Tests	Won by Australia	Won by England	Drawn	Abandoned
In Australia	166	85	54	26	1
In England	158	47	45	64	2
Total	324	132	99	90	3

famous photo of Victor Trumper 'jumping out to drive', he's wearing his Aussie cap. When Stan McCabe took on bodyline, when The Don was bowled for a duck in his last innings, when Dougie hit Bob Willis for six off the last ball of the day to bring up a century in a session, they were wearing their baggy greens. When the Australian team runs out onto the field at the Gabba in November for the start of the 2010–11 Ashes series, every single player will be wearing his baggy green.

It's a symbol of our unity, that we're proud of where we come from and we're all committed to the same cause. I wouldn't want it any other way ...

I SAT DOWN TO begin writing this Ashes Preview section of the book on May 17, the morning after England had beaten Michael Clarke's Aussie team in the final of the World Twenty20 in the West Indies. The boys had enjoyed a pretty sensational tournament to this point, the highlight being their dramatic win in the semi-final against Pakistan — when Mike Hussey smashed 23 from the first five balls of the final over to rescue a game that looked lost. Until the final, they were definitely the best team in the Windies, and I couldn't help thinking afterwards that it might be better if a big T20 competition like the World Twenty20 is decided by a best-of-three final series, rather than just one match.

Of course, you always want to win it all, but there was still a lot to like about the Aussie effort: Pup's captaincy was consistently terrific, the boys' fielding was brilliant and, while T20 will always be a batter's game, some of our bowling was really high class. Dirk Nannes was the tournament's leading wicket-taker, with 14 (no one else took more than 11), while four of the top nine wicket-takers were Aussies: Nannes, Steve Smith (11), Mitchell Johnson (10) and Shaun Tait (nine).

In this photo section are images of the 26 men with whom I played international cricket (Tests or ODI) from the 2009 ICC Champions Trophy to our Tests against Pakistan in July 2010, starting with James Hopes (above left) and Peter Siddle (above right), at the Champions Trophy.

Shane Watson (feet on ground) with James Hopes after hitting a six to reach his hundred and our target in the ICC Champions Trophy final against New Zealand.

With Mike Hussey (centre) and Callum Ferguson (right) at the
ICC Champions Trophy presentation.

Left: The ODI at Vadodara was Brett Lee's final international of the season.
Right: Moises Henriques at Delhi, after taking his first ODI wicket.

Shaun Marsh (left, after reaching his hundred) and Adam Voges (right, embracing bowler Clint McKay after taking the catch that dismissed MS Dhoni) during our great victory at Hyderabad.

Left: Keeper Graham Manou after running out Praveen Kumar, the final wicket at Hyderabad. *Right:* Ben Hilfenhaus during his man-of-the-match performance against the West Indies at the Gabba.

Clint McKay at the WACA after taking his first Test wicket.

Left: Nathan Hauritz (centre) with Peter Siddle (left) and Mike Hussey after dismissing Pakistan's Misbah-ul-Haq on the dramatic final day in Sydney.
Right: Simon Katich in Hobart, after scoring his ninth Test century.

Michael Clarke has just reached his century on the first day at Bellerive.

Doug Bollinger on the fly against the West Indies at the MCG.

Left: Ryan Harris on Australia Day, after marking his return to the Australian ODI team with a five-for against Pakistan. *Right:* Brad Haddin during his superb century in game three of the Chappell–Hadlee series.

Mitchell Johnson copped plenty from the fans in Auckland, so it was no surprise he was excited when he took us to the brink of victory by knocking over Shane Bond.

Left: Marcus North during his fighting century in the first Trans-Tasman Test at Wellington. *Right:* Phillip Hughes avoids a riser during his blazing unbeaten 86 in our second innings of the same game.

Josh Hazlewood (without cap), Australia's youngest ever ODI cricketer — at 19 years and 165 days — has just taken his first international wicket.

Left: Cameron White at Cardiff, scoring 86 not out in game two of the NatWest series. *Right:* Shaun Tait's return to our ODI line-up was one of the big positives to come out of our tour of the UK and Ireland.

Tim Paine (left) and Steve Smith were the first Aussie cricketers to make their Test debuts at Lord's since 1977.

All four of this quartet had tournament bowling averages of less than 15, but none could beat David Hussey's bowling average of 7.83 (6–47 from eight overs). Of the batters, Mike Hussey was the standout, averaging 94 and slamming his runs at a strike-rate of 175.70, while Cameron White (who hit 12 sixes, more than any other batter), Shane Watson and David Hussey all had their moments.

It was an interesting experience watching the T20 guys playing in the West Indies from the comfort of my own lounge. The toughest time was when they won their semi, to see them celebrate so proudly and spontaneously; I've always loved those moments, and when Huss said afterwards it was up there with any win he'd been involved in I couldn't help thinking, *I wish I'd been part of that*. The other times I have found it difficult and awkward being out of the T20 team have been when an ODI or Test tour comes straight after a T20 game or series, when I've felt like a bit of an intruder walking into someone else's party. It's only for a day or two, but the T20 boys might still be buzzing from their recent experiences and I've been doing something else. That certainly happened in New Zealand recently, when a few of us were in Napier waiting for the Chappell–Hadlee series to begin while the second T20 game — a thriller that went to 'extra time' — was being fought out in Christchurch. When the T20 guys finally joined us, it felt a little like they'd been out to a fantastic party the previous night, while the rest of us had gone to bed early.

At the same time, in the months since I decided to give the T20 away I've come to really appreciate the time off, and I'm sure it's helping my cricket. I feel like I'm in a really good place at the moment — and while it's impossible to say if my decision will extend my career, I'm sure it won't shorten it.

Staying with the 'workload' theme, a key for us in the weeks before the opening Ashes encounter will be how we manage our

ICC WORLD TWENTY20 IN THE WEST INDIES, APRIL 3–MAY 16, 2010

Game 6 (Group A), Australia v Pakistan, at Gros Islet (May 2): Australia 191 (20 overs: SR Watson 81, DJ Hussey 53; Mohammad Aamer 3–23) defeated **Pakistan** 157 (20 overs: Misbah-ul-Haq 41, Shahid Afridi 33; DP Nannes 3–41, SW Tait 3–20) by 24 runs

Game 11 (Group A), Australia v Bangladesh, at Bridgetown (May 5): Australia 7–141 (MEK Hussey 47*) defeated **Bangladesh** 114 (18.4 overs: DP Nannes 4–18) by 27 runs

Game 15 (Group F), Australia v India, at Bridgetown (May 7): Australia 5–184 (20 overs: SR Watson 54, DA Warner 72, DJ Hussey 35) defeated **India** 135 (17.4 overs: RG Sharma 79; DP Nannes 3–25, SW Tait 3–21) by 49 runs

Game 20 (Group F), Australia v Sri Lanka, at Bridgetown (May 9): Australia 5–168 (20 overs: CL White 85*, MEK Hussey 39*; S Randiv 3–20) defeated **Sri Lanka** 87 (16.2 overs: MG Johnson 3–15) by 81 runs

Game 24 (Group F), Australia v West Indies, at Gros Islet (May 11): West Indies 105 (19 overs: SPD Smith 3–20) lost to **Australia** 4–109 (16.2 overs: BJ Haddin 42) by six wickets

Second Semi Final, Australia v Pakistan, at Gros Islet (May 14): Pakistan 6–191 (20 overs: Kamran Akmal 50, Umar Akmal 56) lost to **Australia** 7–197 (19.5 overs: CL White 43, MEK Hussey 60*; Mohammad Aamer 3–35) by three wickets

Final, Australia v England, at Bridgetown (May 16): Australia 6–147 (20 overs: DJ Hussey 59, CL White 30) lost to **England** 3–148 (17 overs: C Kieswetter 63, KP Pietersen 47) by seven wickets

> **May 15** Great win by the boys overnight. No surprise to see Michael Hussey and Cameron White bat the team to victory. Huss loves those situations and he delivered again. The final will be a beauty on Monday morning.

guys' time on and off the field. We will be in India in October, playing Tests and ODIs, and then, in the first week of November, we will play three ODIs at home against Sri Lanka. The third of these games is scheduled for Sunday, November 7, 18 days before the start of the Test series against England. My preference would be for the guys who will be facing England to play two Sheffield Shield games in the three weeks before the first Test, rather than three one-dayers and one Shield game. Of course, long gone are the days when teams had lengthy preparations before a specific Test series; the key now is getting the balance right, and hopefully we'll achieve that. An irony here is that in 2009 we couldn't have been in any better shape going into Cardiff for the first Test, but that, on its own, didn't get us the result we were after.

In 2006–07, we had an ultra-experienced side, one that had by and large been together for a number of years. This time, we are a younger group, but we will be more battle-hardened for this series than they were for the Ashes in England in 2009. Our team for the first Test of that series had played a total of 308 Tests and I'd played 131 of those; every member of that XI will most likely be available for the '10–11 series, and our overall Test-match experience has been boosted by the many games we've played together since June '09. England is pretty much in the same boat — the only man from their XI at Cardiff who has since retired is Andrew Flintoff — meaning this upcoming Ashes series should be played between two teams on the rise.

In the lead-up to November 25, I want to set an example in everything I do, so that come the toss at the Gabba I will be as well-organised and well-prepared as I can possibly be. I've always tried to do that, but this time I'm pushing the bar even higher. I expect the other guys in the squad to see what I'm doing and join me on the journey. I'm looking at this Ashes series as being potentially the biggest series that I'll ever play, so I want to

TEST RESULTS: ASHES SERIES IN AUSTRALIA
1998–99 TO 2006–07

2006–07

Test	Venue	Toss	Bat First	Result	Pace	Spin
First	Gabba	Aust	Aust	Aust by 277 runs	25	5
Second	Adelaide	Eng	Eng	Aust by 6 wickets	21	7
Third	WACA	Aust	Aust	Aust by 206 runs	21	13
Fourth	MCG	Eng	Eng	Aust by innings & 99 runs	23	7
Fifth	SCG	Aust	Aust	Aust by 10 wickets	24	4

2002–03

Test	Venue	Toss	Bat First	Result	Pace	Spin
First	Gabba	Eng	Aust	Aust by 384 runs	24	10
Second	Adelaide	Eng	Eng	Aust by innings & 51 runs	20	9
Third	WACA	Eng	Eng	Aust by innings & 48 runs	21	3
Fourth	MCG	Aust	Aust	Aust by 5 wickets	22	9
Fifth	SCG	Eng	Eng	Eng by 225 runs	32	6

1998–99

Test	Venue	Toss	Bat First	Result	Pace	Spin
First	Gabba	Aust	Aust	Drawn	21	8
Second	WACA	Aust	Eng	Aust by 7 wickets	30	3
Third	Adelaide	Aust	Aust	Aust by 205 runs	23	12
Fourth	MCG	Aust	Eng	Eng by 12 runs	33	7
Fifth	SCG	Aust	Aust	Aust by 98 runs	20	20

Notes
- 'Pace' indicates wickets to fall to pace bowling; 'Spin' indicates wickets to fall to spinners.
- Ricky Ponting has appeared in 13 Ashes Tests in Australia (three in 1998–99, all five in 2002–03 and 2006–07), scoring 1040 runs at 54.74, with four hundreds and three fifties, and a highest score of 196. His only loss in an Ashes Test in Australia was the fifth Test of 2002–03; the only draw was his first Ashes Test in Australia – the first Test of 1998–99.

make sure I'm fitter and fresher than I've ever been in the past. That's the commitment I'm making to myself. If things don't work out for me, there will be no excuses.

I GUESS ENGLAND WILL take something from their World Twenty20 victory — you can never get damaged by a win — but the truth is, of course, that T20 is far removed from Test cricket, a fact reflected by the reality that of the 22 guys who played in the final in Bridgetown only nine or 10 will be playing in the opening Test of the 2010–11 Ashes series.

What happened in the two most recent Ashes series, on the other hand, does have plenty of significance in my opinion. So, in a way, does the 2005 series, in the sense that we can take some encouragement from the fact that we came back from our defeat in '05 to win five out of five in Australia 18 months later. But I think England would also have learned a lot from that experience — they felt a certain loyalty to the guys who did so well in that famous '05 series and stuck with them even though they were out of form. I think they also underestimated just how suffocating the sense of expectation their win in '05 would bring, and when things didn't start well that became a real stumbling block for them. I'll never forget how a few of their blokes — captain Andrew Flintoff, Steve Harmison and Jimmy Anderson among them — stayed for hours in our dressing room after they lost in Adelaide, rather than go back to their own room. It was as if they wanted to avoid the gloom bad defeats bring and didn't have the energy to look forward to the next Test, a game they had to win.

We, of course, were buzzing. They say 'winning is contagious' and I reckon the way the Aussie team has gone over the previous five years is proof of that. We were so successful for so long, not losing a series from the Ashes in England in 2001 to the end of the

Australian summer of 2004–05, that when we got behind the eight ball in England in 2005 we suddenly discovered that we'd forgotten that fighting back isn't easy. We got back to our winning ways soon enough, but then when a group of great players (Warne, McGrath, Langer, Gilchrist, et al) retired pretty much all at once the guys that replaced them, talented as they are, just didn't have the experience of winning that these past champions had. Things that the old guys used to do instinctively their replacements had to learn, and it's also a hell of a lot easier to 'back yourself' in tough situations when you've scored 5000 Test runs or taken 300 wickets than if you're new to the international game, much easier to have faith in your team-mates if they've 'been there and done that'. It wasn't until this season just gone, when we won just about every game we played, that we started to truly get that winning feeling back; I think the Australian side that takes the field in the Gabba Test of 2010–11 will be a much more confident group than the XI that ran out at Cardiff in 2009.

I have thought long and hard about that Cardiff Test, especially about how we could have done things better after we had them five down before lunch on the last day, then seven down with 38 overs to go. The more I think about it, that's where we lost the Ashes. If we'd won there I think we would have been in a better state of mind going into Lord's; I'm not saying we would have run away with the series, but because the two sides were fairly evenly matched it was imperative we took that chance to take an early series lead. Through the remainder of the series we battled inconsistency, the trait that eventually brought us undone — in part because we hadn't given ourselves a buffer zone by winning the first Test.

At that stage in this Australian cricket team's evolution it was probably unfair to expect a high level of consistency in our play. We'd showed before that series, by winning in South Africa, that

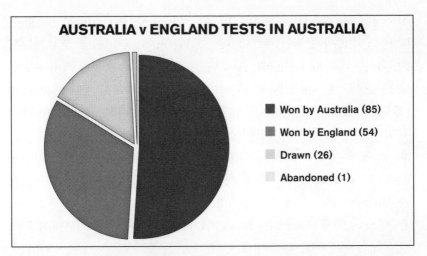

AUSTRALIA v ENGLAND TESTS IN AUSTRALIA

- ■ Won by Australia (85)
- ■ Won by England (54)
- ▨ Drawn (26)
- ▨ Abandoned (1)

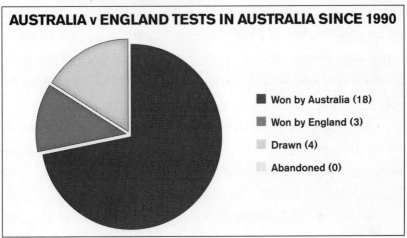

AUSTRALIA v ENGLAND TESTS IN AUSTRALIA SINCE 1990

- ■ Won by Australia (18)
- ■ Won by England (3)
- ▨ Drawn (4)
- ▨ Abandoned (0)

we were capable of playing to a very high standard — and we reproduced that form when we dominated the Test at Headingley — but we were still learning the art of fighting through the hard times, when conditions are tough, the opposition is on top, and you've got to have faith in your ability and, just as important, the ability of your team-mates. Instead, when it really mattered, we capitulated, suffering though two or three of the worst sessions of Test cricket (from an Australian perspective) I've been involved in.

When I compare our defeats in 2005 and 2009, I see more differences than similarities (though, of course, the very big constant is that we lost the Ashes both times). With all respect to the '09 guys, we were a better team on paper in '05, when we had Justin Langer, Matthew Hayden, Adam Gilchrist, Shane Warne and Glenn McGrath (though Glenn did miss two Tests), but I've no doubt our attitude was sharper the second time around. We dropped too many catches and bowled too many no-balls in 2005, but perhaps our most significant failing was our inability to build major partnerships with either the bat or the ball. It was as if we didn't fancy going that extra metre, the one that separates the good from the genuinely great. In 2009, our batters had a number of very big stands and our bowlers were fantastic as a unit when we won the fourth Test by an innings, but at other times we pretty much fell apart — especially during the first two days at Lord's and then, crucially, for one dreadful session at the Oval. That cost us the series.

The challenge I set the team after the 2005 Ashes series was to get our preparation for Tests right. We'd gone away from that, lost that intensity that had set us apart. As I wrote in 2006:

'We just weren't getting the type of practice we needed. In the nets, we weren't preparing with our opponents in mind. This was especially true of the batsmen — in the nets, it was too much about just getting the feel of bat on ball, or about getting your feet moving, rather than deliberately rehearsing for what we would be facing in the middle. Our practices weren't competitive enough; it was as if we wanted to avoid rather than recreate the intensity of game day ...

I have always been an advocate of training competitively, so with hindsight I'm dirty as the captain that I allowed us to slip away from that philosophy when

we were in the UK in 2005. As an example, I have also
always said that all the fielding practice we do in
preparation for a game should be done in a group, as a
team, but that stopped happening consistently. I always
wanted to be the finest fielder in my group, and as a
young member of the Australian team that meant my aim
was to be the best fielder in the world. At training, I
always sought to be better than Mark Waugh, who in my
eyes was the best we had. I think the more that you
challenge yourself in a group, with other eyes and other
pressures on you, the better you will be. Further, the
energy that comes with the competition lifts the whole
team.

I knew we had to get our training back to that level,
but it was all very well for me to say that — unless
everyone in the squad made the same commitment and
had the same belief in the value of competitive practice as
I did, it wasn't going to work ...

In fact, it worked brilliantly. The bowlers started charging in
during net sessions and the batters stood up to them. In 2005–
06, we won 11 Tests out of 12 and then in 2006–07 we earned
our Ashes clean sweep and then went on to win the World Cup
— results that demonstrated just how unconditionally everyone
responded and how good our training became. During the 2006–
07 Ashes series, we really only had one bad spell, and that was
more because Paul Collingwood and Kevin Pietersen batted
superbly (in Adelaide) than because we were ordinary. We were
relentless the rest of the time, and I loved it!

In 2009, when I contemplated our defeat at the Oval, I
didn't see anything too wrong with what we were doing off the
field. But I did think we needed to get tougher on it. We were too

ASHES HOLDERS (1882 TO 2009)

Holder	Years Held	Approximate Span
Australia	1882 to 1882–83	Six months
England	1882–83 to 1891–92	Nine years
Australia	1891–92 to 1893	18 months
England	1893 to 1897–98	Four and a half years
Australia	1897–98 to 1903–04	Six years
England	1903–04 to 1907–08	Four years
Australia	1907–08 to 1911–12	Four years
England	1911–12 to 1920–21	Nine years
Australia	1920–21 to 1926	Five and a half years
England	1926 to 1930	Four years
Australia	1930 to 1932–33	Two and a half years
England	1932–33 to 1934	18 months
Australia	1934 to 1953	19 years
England	1953 to 1958–59	Five and a half years
Australia	1958–59 to 1970–71	12 years
England	1970–71 to 1974–75	Four years
Australia	1974–75 to 1977	Two and a half years
England	1977 to 1982–83	Five and a half years
Australia	1982–83 to 1985	Two and a half years
England	1985 to 1989	Four years
Australia	1989 to 2005	16 years
England	2005 to 2006–07	18 months
Australia	2006–07 to 2009	Two and a half years
England	2009 to present	

Note

Had the Ashes existed from the first Australia–England Test (played in March 1877), Australia would have held the Ashes from 1877 to 1880 (two and a half years); England from 1880 to 1881–82 (one and a half years); and Australia from 1881–82 to 1882–83 (one year).

inconsistent, had been for a while. We couldn't accept being good some of the time, even most of the time. I don't want guys going 'missing' when a game or series is on the line.

In short, we had to rediscover the art of winning. And here we got a bit lucky, in that the authorities had scheduled a seven-game ODI series for straight after the Ashes Tests. I think most people consider that putting on that long a one-day series was overkill, but for us it worked out well because we came out and won the first six games, which kicked off a run of excellent ODI performances that included the Champions Trophy and a 4–2 triumph in India. That latter win, because we managed to overcome any number of injuries, was doubly significant; suddenly, there was a real belief in that group, a feeling that eventually transcended into the Test squad. I know I was exhilarated by our success, and I got a real kick out of seeing blokes like Nathan Hauritz, Doug Bollinger and Shane Watson grow as players and men.

I think Watto's the best example — he is still, in a way, a 'work in progress', but it's hard not to be impressed by the way he has evolved as a Test-match cricketer in the past 12 months, from fledgling opening bat to now being among the most dangerous batters in the game. The fact he can also get us important wickets is just a terrific bonus. With Horrie, the key was to get him to be more aggressive in Test matches, to bowl that line that could get people out and to be prepared to concede a four or two in the quest for wickets. Like so many things about cricket, it was a question of balance, and Horrie got it right last summer against Pakistan, keeping the pressure on and bowling for wickets. Twice in the space of eight days, he spun us to victory.

The thing I liked best about our Test form in Australia and New Zealand last season was that we were, in the main, consistently good. We won seven Tests out of eight, and four of the last five decisively — with a famous comeback thrown into the mix. As the team got used to winning, you could see how much the senior guys, like Simon Katich, Mike Hussey and Brad Haddin, were enjoying it; all three of those blokes had tremendous seasons in 2009–10.

Maybe it's because he took so long to cement a place in the team, or maybe it's because he's hardly an elegant player, but I still don't think Kat has being recognised for the fantastic batter he is. His Test record over the past two years — eight hundreds and 14 fifties in 27 matches — is first-class, and I think you have to rank him on the same tier as two other left-handed Aussie opening bats of recent years: Mark Taylor and Justin Langer. Huss and Hadds struggled a little during the '09 Ashes, but they returned to their best in all forms of the game back home, and I'll be surprised if they're not key players against England when we meet again in November.

However, the bloke I really want to see going full speed at Andrew Strauss's team is Mitchell Johnson. By his own measure, Mitch had a disappointing start to the Ashes series in 2009. I thought he might be the difference between the two teams, but as we all know he struggled with his line and length in the first two Tests and it was only in the fourth game of the series, at Headingley, where he took 5–69 in their second innings, that he truly displayed the form that won him the ICC's player-of-the-year award for 2008–09. Eighteen months on, he's a veteran of more than 30 Tests and one of the few left-arm quicks in Test history to have taken more than 150 Test wickets. There were a few reasons why he didn't get off to the flying start in England, but once we moved him to first change he improved sharply and again became a leading part of our bowling attack. This time, we're going to have a real smorgasbord of quicks to choose from

THE CROWD GOES WILD

If the crowd support for us in this summer's Ashes series is as strong as it was four years ago, I'll be very happy. That first morning, when England's Steve Harmison started with a wide to second slip and then Matthew Hayden and Justin Langer got us off to a flying start, the Gabba faithful were right behind us and that backing stayed with us for the entire series. Of course, that crowd support won't be there when we're working hard in the weeks and months before the first Test – our drive then must come from within – but if we can get on a bit of a roll once the cricket starts it can only help us. In England last year there were plenty of times, from about day three of the Lord's Test, when sections of the crowd there were into me, booing me loudly at every opportunity, and I don't think the Aussie fans will forget that.

As an aside, it's funny when I think back to that experience of some fans heckling me – I'm not 100 per cent sure when it really started. I think a lot of people assume it goes back to the last day at Cardiff, when England sent their 12th man out onto the ground near the end, to try to buy a few seconds, and I didn't like it. Their media tried to make something out of that, but I didn't cop or feel any negativity from the crowd on the first day of the following Test at Lord's. It wasn't until day three, I reckon, that the booing started.

That was when I dropped Ravi Bopara and they replayed it on the big screen about 20 times, and then soon after Bopara hit what we thought was a fair catch to Nathan Hauritz at mid-on. Before anyone could do anything, Kevin Pietersen, the batter at the non-striker's end, was in the umpire's ear, claiming it hadn't carried, and then I had a discussion with the ump about not listening to what Kevin had to say. It looked like I was arguing with the umpire, and from then until the end of the series I was barracked by some spectators every time I walked to the wicket.

as his supporting cast — it could be any two of Doug Bollinger, Ryan Harris, Ben Hilfenhaus, Clint McKay and Peter Siddle, blokes who to a man have done good things for us in the past 12 months. So Mitch won't feel as if it all depends on him and that, I'm sure, will be a good thing for us.

THERE IS SO MUCH to look forward to. For example, some of the match-ups will be terrific. I think everyone who played in the 2009 series would love to see those two teams go at it again, and while there will inevitably be a few changes I can't really see too many. This upcoming series will make a few reputations, I'm sure of that, and it wouldn't surprise me if, years from now there are cricketers who look back on the 2010–11 Ashes summer as the most important series in which they've played.

My focus right at the moment, a few months out from the first delivery, is to get myself as fit as I can possibly be. This will be my last Ashes series in Australia and I want to give myself every chance of doing well. I also believe that if my team-mates see how committed I am to being ready, then they will do the same. One thing I can assure all Australian fans about is their team will be very well prepared come November 25. And there are a few other things they might want to look out for …

The Toss

I think the fact I was only able to win one out of five tosses in England in 2009 did have a bearing on the final result, but over the past three Ashes series in Australia, the toss hasn't proved to be a major factor. It's no secret that I much prefer to bat first if the coin lands my way, but that doesn't mean I'm automatically going to say, 'We'll have a bat, thanks.' And my memory of Adelaide in 2006–07 is still massive, when England made 6–551 declared after batting first but we still won, so I'll never be one to say that we can't win just because we're bowling first on a flat deck.

The team winning the toss won three of the five Tests in 2006–07, two of the five in 2002–03 and three of the five in 1998–99 (with one draw). There have been three instances of a captain sending a team in — England captain Nasser Hussain did so but Australia won comfortably in Brisbane in 2002–03; Australia's Mark Taylor sent England in twice in 1998–99, for a win in Perth and a narrow defeat in Melbourne. The team batting first won nine of the 15 Tests over these three series.

When I first came into Test cricket in the mid '90s, it wasn't unusual for a Test captain to send the opposition in, but it's a lot rarer now. I think there are two reasons for this. One, back in the early '90s, in the days before Shane Warne demonstrated that a spinner did still have a place in big-time cricket, it was generally considered that fast bowlers were the guys most likely to take wickets — so there was a lot of logic in letting them bowl on the first morning. And two, these days the pitches just don't seem to have the same life in them that they had in the old days, so there is less incentive to bowl first.

The First Hour in Brisbane

I've said many times now that the Tests at the Gabba and the MCG are my two favourite Test matches of the Australian summer. I'll never forget how Brisbane was buzzing before the first Ashes Test of 2006–07 — the talk in the hotel foyer, the traffic hold-ups on the way to the ground, the way so many seats were occupied an hour and more before the start, the manner in which the crowd belted out *Advance Australia Fair*.

I felt we handled the hype really well, while the England players seemed nervous — none more so than opening bowler Steve Harmison, who infamously speared the first ball of the series to second slip. This time, at least half of the England team that runs out at the Gabba will be playing their first Ashes Test in Australia, so it will be interesting to watch their body language, to see if any of them 'do a Harmison'.

The first hour at the Gabba can be awkward, but the pitch usually settles down into a nice batting track, as demonstrated by what's occurred at the start of the two most recent Ashes Tests at the ground. In 2002–03, Nasser Hussain sent us in but we reached 2–364 by stumps. Four years later, Justin Langer batted beautifully from the jump and we were 0–57 at the opening drinks break, 1–109 at lunch and 3–346 at the end of the day. Both times, a firm platform was established that led to a big Australian victory. If those two games are anything to go by, in 2010–11 I imagine England will be very, very keen to bat first if the coin rolls their way.

The biggest thing in determining how the Gabba might play is what the conditions are like overhead — there's usually some grass on the wicket, so if you bat first and there is a little moisture in the deck and some decent cloud cover, then it can be hard work for most of the opening day. But if it's a nice sunny day, like most November days in Brisbane, and you survive the first hour, then it's a terrific place to bat for the rest of the opening day and the following two days as well. That's what happened four years ago, when Lang and Haydos got us off to a fantastic start. I was in after about 90 minutes of play, survived until lunch, and from then until well into day two I felt I was 'in control' in a way I've rarely been when batting in a Test match.

The Value of a Quality All-Rounder

I've said many times that one of the keys to having a good cricket team is finding the balance a good fifth bowler provides. I'm not keen to put the tag of 'key player' on anyone before the series, but

I will say that I think we're a much better side if we've got a bloke in our top six who can keep the pressure on while the bowling specialists are resting. Shane Watson fills that role perfectly.

It was back in September 2006 that I wrote of Watto: 'One day he might even open the batting for Australia in a Test match. He's got the talent to do that.' I've always thought of him as a batter who bowls rather than the other way round, and his success since we brought him into the team during the Ashes series in 2009 hasn't surprised me at all. He's established himself as a genuine star of the game in the 12 months since the selectors picked him to bat at the top of our order, and he'll go into the first Test at the Gabba just as talented a player as he was in '09, but feeling right at home as a Test-match cricketer and looking to have a major impact on the series, rather than just retain his place in the side.

The Absence of Andrew Flintoff

England got one outstanding Test match out of 'Freddie' Flintoff in the 2009 Ashes series, and it was enough to get them a crucial victory at Lord's. Aside from that, though, his impact was pretty meagre — though he did run me out in our second innings at the Oval, for which I'll never be able to forgive him.

I guess the guy the Englishmen will be looking for to fill Flintoff's boots as the bowling all-rounder will be Stuart Broad. I'm not sure Broad will ever be as good a batter as Flintoff, but he looked like a pretty fair bowler when we faced him in England, especially when he went through our top order in the first innings of the final Test. In my experience, there have been a few English quicks over the years who have struggled in Australian conditions, but some others — such as Darren Gough, Dean Headley, Andrew Caddick and Matthew Hoggard — have had their moments. What might make it hard for Broad is if they need him to make plenty of runs as well. It'll be interesting to see which way he goes.

The Video Referral System

If there is going to be an ongoing controversy during the Ashes series this summer, my bet is that it will concern the video referrals. Which would be a real pity because, having played with the system in Tests last season, I've come to the conclusion that it can be a really good thing for international cricket ... if it's used the right way.

The key, I think, as I've written earlier in this book, is that we can't expect the video umpire to solve *every* problem. The aim has to be to reduce the number of mistakes, and to eliminate the howlers that look terrible on television, when the slow-motion replays prove that the on-field umpire got it wrong.

For me, what happened at the end of the Test against the West Indies in Perth last season showed how the system should work. Kemar Roach got a faint but clear edge through to Brad Haddin, we appealed, the umpire gave it out and Roach asked for a referral. All good. The video couldn't confirm that Roach had hit it but that wasn't relevant; what did matter was that there was nothing in the replay to change the on-field umpire's decision, so the batter was still out. I know there is something slightly incongruous with the fact that if the ump had said not out and we'd 'gone upstairs', then the batter would have stayed not out, but I'm okay with all that. It's a close call, the on-field umpire makes a tough decision, and the system backs him up. Surely, if we use the video this way we're not undermining the umps' authority; we're helping him out.

If the players, critics and commentators look at the video referral system in this light, I'm sure it will be a good thing for this Ashes series. I know that once or twice I'll probably look a little cranky on the field when a decision doesn't go our way, but that's just because I can get pretty passionate out there. I hope you can understand that.

OF COURSE, THERE'LL BE a sense of nostalgia for me about this series: my last Ashes series in Australia. I know there is some conjecture about me going to England in 2013 and the truth is that right at the moment I'm not sure how much longer I'll keep playing. But I can assure you I won't be still wearing the baggy green in 2014–15.

On the presumption I make it to the Gabba, this will be the eighth Ashes series I've played in, going back to 1997 in England. My co-author reckons that will make me just the sixth Australian player since World War II — after Neil Harvey, Rod Marsh, Allan Border, Steve Waugh and Shane Warne — to play in at least eight Test series against England.

Looking back, there's been a bit of everything in these personal experiences:

- A century on my Ashes debut, in the fourth Test of 1997, at Leeds, after I was left out of the team for the first three Tests.
- Dropped after three Tests in my first home series, in 1998–99. I'd scored 47 runs in four digs, so I could hardly complain.
- Another century at Leeds, in 2001, which might have saved my spot. I'd been promoted to No. 3 at the start of the series, but didn't have a lot of luck in the first three Tests, all of which we won. That was the first time a five-Test Ashes series had been decided in three Tests since 1950–51.
- I scored a hundred in each of the first two Tests of 2002–03, as we again retained the Ashes at the earliest opportunity.
- In 2005, I played one of my most important knocks against England, a fifth-day 156 that helped save the

AUSTRALIAN CAPTAINS TO LOSE AND
THEN REGAIN THE ASHES

Captain	Lost Ashes	Regained Ashes
Monty Noble	1903–04	1907–08
Bill Woodfull	1932–33	1934
Greg Chappell	1977	1982–83
Allan Border	1985	1989
Ricky Ponting	2005	2006–07

Third Test, but that mattered for very little when we lost the Ashes.

- The redemption — a 5–0 triumph in 2006–07 that will always be among my sweetest cricket memories.
- And then the 2009 campaign, which for me started with a big hundred but ended with a painful run out at The Oval, when for the second time in four years I had to watch the locals celebrate an Ashes triumph.

This time, all I'm after is a series win. If, after the fifth Test, I can walk around the SCG wearing my old baggy green and with the Ashes Trophy in my hands then I'll be a very happy cricketer. We've certainly got the players to do that, and if we can build on the spirit we developed through 2009–10 I know we'll be hard to beat. If we win as decisively as we did four years ago, that'll be a bonus.

As we arrive at each of the Ashes venues this summer, I'll be doing my best to think about what is in front of us, but I know recollections of past battles will come back to me, especially images from our big wins in 2006–07.

Here is a guide to some of the great moments I might be thinking about, and a few things from each of the five grounds that we'll need to look out for …

THE GABBA

AUSTRALIA V ENGLAND TESTS AT THE GABBA

Matches	Played	Australia	England	Drawn
Tests	18*	10	4	4
Tests since 1970	10	6	2	2

RICKY PONTING IN ASHES TESTS AT THE GABBA

Tests	Won	Lost	Drawn	Inn	NO	HS	Runs	Avge	100s	50s	Ct
3	2	–	1	5	1	196	403	100.75	2	1	6

Note
- The first Ashes Test of 1928–29 was played at the Brisbane Exhibition Ground in 1928–29, England winning by 675 runs; otherwise, all Australia–England Tests in Australia have been played at the venues to be used in 2010–11.

My memories of Ashes Tests at the Gabba are almost universally good — not surprising given Australia has won four of the past five Ashes Tests played in Brisbane. I didn't get many runs there the first time I was actively involved in a Test against England, in 1998–99, but it's still a game I remember fondly, not least because of the way the fans at the Gabba responded to seeing one of their own, Ian Healy, make a big hundred. Four years later, I got a ton of my own — my first Ashes century in Australia — and I was able to get to three figures again in 2006–07, which means I'll be trying for a pretty rare trifecta when the first Test comes around this November.

I guess I'm one of those guys who goes all right 'first up from a spell'. I've managed to score a century in the opening Test of a series 11 times during my career, including six times in the past five years. I've also done so in three of the past four Ashes series (2002–03, 2006–07 and 2009), so it's little wonder I can

Stumps on day one at the Gabba, November 23, 2006.

hardly wait for the upcoming battle to commence. I take great pride in being 100-per-cent ready for a series opener, and relish the fact I'm one of a small group who have scored a hundred in the first Test of an Ashes series three or more times.

I've always thought that, once you are 'in', the Gabba is one of the best places to bat anywhere in the world, mostly because the pace and bounce is so consistent. Sure, it can get a little bit 'up and down' late in the game, but that's true of most wickets in the world. I've never thought of it as a spinner's deck, mainly because it doesn't turn very much, but I'm sure Warney had more success in Tests in Brisbane than anywhere else in Australia, and as recently as last November Nathan Hauritz had match figures of 5–57 in the Test against the West Indies.

THE ADELAIDE OVAL

AUSTRALIA V ENGLAND TESTS AT THE ADELAIDE OVAL

Matches	Played	Australia	England	Drawn
Tests	29	16	8	5
Tests since 1970	10	5	2	3

RICKY PONTING IN ASHES TESTS AT THE ADELAIDE OVAL

Tests	Won	Lost	Drawn	Inn	NO	HS	Runs	Avge	100s	50s	Ct
3	2	–	1	5	–	154	360	72.00	2	–	2

Adelaide was the scene of my best and worst memories in Ashes Tests in Australia. The worst was in December 1998, when after the game I was dropped for the Boxing Day Test. My scores in the series to that point, batting at No. 6, were 21, 11, 5 and 10, and the selectors brought Darren Lehmann into to the team for Melbourne. I didn't get back into the side until halfway through Australia's next series, in the West Indies.

When I first started playing first-class cricket, the Adelaide wicket had a tendency to break up on the fourth and fifth days. Late in the game, the pitch would spin, keep low, reverse, and it was hard to score runs. In more recent times, it has held together better, yet it is still a track that usually gets results — even if a draw has looked the most likely outcome at the halfway point of the game (I've played 14 Tests at the Adelaide Oval and while they've all featured plenty of runs, 11 of them have ended in a result, 10 of them Aussie wins.). Why is that? You still get cracks in the pitch, though not as pronounced, and the ball might be spinning or reversing and if a wicket falls it can be hard for the new guy to settle in, especially if he needs to keep the score moving.

With Mike Hussey after beating England at the Adelaide Oval, December 5, 2006.

Suddenly, a collapse is happening, and once momentum builds for one team or the other, it can be hard to stop. That's what happened four years ago, when England collapsed on the final morning.

There's so much about the game in 2006–07 that I remember well, but three things really stand out. First, there was me saying to the boys before the start of play on day three that I was sick and tired of hearing about how badly we'd played for the opening two days of the Test, that if we produced three days of perfect cricket we could still win. That's what we promptly did. Two, was how negative England were on the last day and a half. They were in an excellent position to win the Test, but rather than going for the victory they decided to make sure of the draw, which gave Shane Warne, Glenn McGrath and Brett Lee an opening. And three, there was our elation at the end of the game. We all felt that if we could win that Test from where we did, then we could win from anywhere. It's nice to feel impregnable. From that moment, the Ashes clean sweep was on.

THE WACA GROUND

AUSTRALIA V ENGLAND TESTS AT THE WACA

Matches	Played	Australia	England	Drawn
Tests	11	7	1	3
Tests since 1970	11	7	1	3

RICKY PONTING IN ASHES TESTS AT THE WACA

Tests	Won	Lost	Drawn	Inn	NO	HS	Runs	Avge	100s	50s	Ct
3	3	–	–	4	–	75	156	39.00	–	2	2

I've got myself into trouble in the past for criticising the pitch in Perth, but I'll never back away from my concerns that in recent seasons the WACA has not been as quick and bouncy as it has been in the past. Ashes stats help tell that story: in the Test at the WACA in 1998–99, 30 wickets fell to pace and just three to spinners; in 2002–03, it was 21 to pace and three to spinners; in 2006–07, 21 wickets fell to the quicks and 13 to the spinners, including eight to Monty Panesar.

Over the past few seasons I've often wished that they'd somehow find a way to transplant the practice wickets out to the middle. Those decks are like lightning. If you're facing your own quicks and you manage to hit a few balls in the middle of the bat during net practice in Perth, then I reckon that makes you a batting genius, especially when the boys are ignoring the no-ball rule and using brand new balls. They reckon in the old days some bowlers would come to a Test at the WACA and see how much the pitch was bouncing and as a consequence bowl too short. Well, you should see what happens when our boys see the WACA practice wickets — every delivery seems to land in their half of

The home dressing room at the WACA after we regained the Ashes, December 18, 2006.

the wicket. There have been times in the past few years, though, when we'd get out in the middle and the pitch was much more placid. However, last season, in what I thought was a good sign, the pitch was closer to the old days — something I learnt the hard way when Kemar Roach crashed a short one into my elbow.

Australia's record in Tests against England at the WACA is excellent; the only time they have won there was in 1978–79, the series that coincided with World Series Cricket and we had to use a much-weakened line-up. The last time England even got a draw in an Ashes Test in Perth was 24 years ago, and I think part of the reason we've gone so well there has been that quicks such as Craig McDermott, Merv Hughes, Glenn McGrath, Damien Fleming and Jason Gillespie knew the right line and length to bowl when the ball was jumping.

Three of the past four Ashes series in Australia have been decided in Perth, and we retained the Ashes there in 2002–03 and regained them there in 2006–07. It wouldn't surprise me at all if once again it becomes a key game of the summer.

THE MELBOURNE CRICKET GROUND

AUSTRALIA V ENGLAND TESTS AT THE MCG

Matches	Played	Australia	England	Drawn
Tests	53	27	19	7
Tests since 1970	13	7	4	2

RICKY PONTING IN ASHES TESTS AT THE MCG

Tests	Won	Lost	Drawn	Inn	NO	HS	Runs	Avge	100s	50s	Ct
2	2	–	–	3	–	30	58	19.33	–	–	3

I've stated many times that Brisbane and Melbourne are my two favourite Tests matches of the Australian summer. I've also said that an Ashes Test is just slightly more special than any other game for an Australian cricketer — a product of the history, the tradition and the hype; the fact that as kids when we dreamed about wearing a baggy green cap that dream usually involved a match against England. So it stands to reason that for me a Boxing Day Ashes Test is just about as big as it gets.

To date, I've only played two Tests against England in Melbourne, but I have plenty of fantastic memories. I'll never forget how, on Boxing Day in 2002–03, Matty Hayden tried to hook the first ball that he faced but top-edged a catch to deep fine leg, and as our No. 3, I was on my feet, ready to head out to the middle for my first Test innings in an Ashes Test at the MCG. But then I saw Steve Harmison run in too far and the ball looped over his head and bounced away for four. I sat down and Haydos and Justin Langer went on to add 195 for the first wicket. Four years later, Haydos made another century, but this time what I recall most is how excited he was when Andrew Symonds

Shane Warne's 700th Test wicket, Andrew Strauss bowled, MCG,
Boxing Day, 2006.

reached *his* hundred. Of course, Symmo was very excited, too,
and the emotion they showed captured perfectly the spirit in our
side during that magical summer. That was also the Test in
which Shane Warne took his 700th Test wicket, on Boxing Day,
in front of his hometown fans — another famous day.

There hasn't been a drawn Ashes Test at the MCG since the
third Test of 1974–75, when Australia finished at 8–238 chasing
246 to win. The past 12 Tests in Melbourne have all ended in a
result, too, so if the Ashes are still on the line at Christmas this
game should be a beauty. My guess is that if there is a chance we
can regain the Ashes at the MCG we might, on Boxing Day, break
the record for the biggest Test crowd for a day's play in Australia.
If that happens, I really hope I win the toss, we bat first, and
during the day I can finally make a big score against England in
Melbourne. I've never got past 30 in an Ashes Test at the MCG,
and that's one deficiency in my resume I'd like to set straight.

THE SYDNEY CRICKET GROUND

AUSTRALIA V ENGLAND TESTS AT THE SCG

Matches	Played	Australia	England	Drawn
Tests	53	25	21	7
Tests since 1970	14	5	5	4

RICKY PONTING IN ASHES TESTS AT THE SCG

Tests	Won	Lost	Drawn	Inn	NO	HS	Runs	Avge	100s	50s	Ct
2	1	1	–	3	–	45	63	21.00	–	–	1

When I was watching cricket on TV as a boy, the SCG was absolutely a spinners' wicket. I can remember when Bob Holland and Murray Bennett beat the West Indies one year and then Peter Taylor took six-for on his Test debut, the same game in which Peter Sleep's leg-breaks spun Australia to an Ashes victory. In the '90s, Shane Warne and Stuart MacGill had big Tests in Sydney, never more so than in 1998–99 when Stuey took 12–107 to wreck England's hopes of squaring the series.

But that was then; in my two Ashes Tests in Sydney, 2002–03 and 2006–07, the spinners have snared only 10 wickets, while the quicks have taken 56. Last season, against Pakistan, Nathan Hauritz did take 5–53 on the last day but that was only after quicks took 19 of the first 20 wickets to fall in the Test.

We've seen a few different wickets in Sydney in recent seasons — from last summer, when we were bowled out for 127, to 2003–04, when India made more than 700, so it's a bit hard to predict exactly how the SCG will play from year to year. The weather leading up to the Test last season was atrocious, which meant there was plenty of moisture in the deck, and that plus the

Australia take the field at the SCG before the fifth Ashes Test, January 2, 2007.

cloud cover for the first day and a half turned the conditions in the pace bowlers' favour, but to tell you the truth I reckon the pitch was actually close to being a 'belter'. However, there have been a few wickets for ODIs in Sydney recently where it *has* been difficult to bat against the new ball. One certainty about the SCG is that towards the end of the Test it will turn; that's the nature of the soil on which the square is built. It might not buzz about as much as it did in the '80s, but it will spin, which could make for an exciting end to the series.

Another certainty is that it'll take something very special to beat the Sydney Test from 2006–07 — when Justin Langer, Shane Warne, Glenn McGrath and John Buchanan retired; when the English players gave Lang a guard of honour onto the field in our second innings; when Haydos reluctantly hit the winning runs with his little mate at the other end; how all of us were wearing our sunnies at the presentation after the game because we didn't want the public to see the tears in our eyes. These are irreplaceable memories, things I'll never forget.

EPILOGUE

SIX WEEKS BEHIND ENEMY LINES

THE AUSTRALIANS' WINTER TOUR 2010

Monday, July 26

NATWEST ODI SERIES, AUSTRALIA V ENGLAND, JUNE 22–JULY 3, 2010

Game 1, at Southampton (June 22): Australia 7–267 (50 overs: MJ Clarke 87*) lost to **England** 6–268) 46 overs: EJG Morgan 103*; RJ Harris 3–42) by four wickets

Game 2, at Cardiff (June 24): Australia 7–239 (50 overs: SR Watson 57, CL White 86*, SPD Smith 41; SCJ Broad 4–44) lost to **England** 6–243 (45.2 overs: AJ Strauss 51, PD Collingwood 48, EJG Morgan 52; DE Bollinger 3–46) by four wickets

Game 3, at Manchester (June 27): Australia 212 (46 overs: SR Watson 61, TD Paine 44, JM Anderson 3–22, GP Swann 4–37) lost to **England** 9–214 (49.1 overs: AJ Strauss 87, PD Collingwood 40; SW Tait 3–28, DE Bollinger 3–20) by one wicket

Game 4, at The Oval (June 30): Australia 5–290 (50 overs: SR Watson 31, RT Ponting 92, MJ Clarke 99*) defeated **England** 212 (42.4 overs: EJG Morgan 47, MH Yardy 57; RJ Harris 5–32) by 78 runs

Game 5, at Lord's (July 3): Australia 7–277 (50 overs: TD Paine 54, SE Marsh 59, MEK Hussey 79; SCJ Broad 4–64, GP Swann 3–32) defeated **England** 235 (46.3 overs: PD Collingwood 95; SW Tait 4–48) by 42 runs

It's been interesting being in England with the Australian team for an extended period so close to the start of an Ashes series in Australia. We arrived in Britain back on June 12, and in the six weeks since I have sensed the mood here when it comes to the upcoming series is one of careful optimism; there is some hope that blokes who haven't played a Test in Australia before, such as Stuart Broad and Graeme Swann, can make a real impact this time. At the same time, though, I think in part because of what occurred in 2006–07 and also after the way the England team struggled at the football World Cup, there is a worry things could go badly wrong for them again. To tell you the truth, I don't think that will happen — as they've showed in recent times, including in the just-completed one-dayers, they are a good and competitive side and I think they will have learned from past mistakes. I've been impressed with the way Andy Flower has worked with the England team since he became their coach in April 2009, so I'll be surprised if they are not primed for a real battle when the first ball is bowled at the Gabba on November 25.

This was a point I conceded to the *Daily Mail*'s Paul Newman when I spoke to him after England had taken a 3–0 lead in the five-game NatWest one-day series we played before two Tests against Pakistan. 'You can tell England are making progress because they haven't kept on changing their side like they have done in the past, and you have to give Andrew Strauss and Andy Flower the credit,' I said. 'I've watched Flower pretty closely over the last couple of weeks and he seems an active guy who is out and about, talking a lot.'

Not that this praise received much attention. Of much more interest to the media was this comment:

> *I'd probably be looking for a new job if we lose again.*
> *It's as simple as that.*

It wasn't my intention, but that generated a headline or two. The first sentence is absolutely right — it's a reality of my

---

June 19 Long day today – flight to London from Dublin, an open media session and then training. The boys are looking forward to playing against Adam Gilchrist tomorrow when he captains Middlesex against us.

EVERYONE DESERVES A FAIR GO

One of the best things I did during my time off between the end of the New Zealand Test series and the start of our winter tour was to attend an Australian Captains Dinner held at Star City in Sydney on May 17. The ambition was to raise money and awareness for the fight against youth cancer, and I'm sure the function did that. For me, it was a tremendous honour to be in the same room as men like Socceroos captain Lucas Neill (who was just a few days away from flying out for the football World Cup in South Africa), current Wallabies skipper Rocky Elsom and former captain John Eales, plus a number of other notable figures from the worlds of sport, entertainment, media and politics.

One line from Lucas' speech really struck a chord with me – how he said it is up to our country's current leaders to ensure that every teenage Australian has a chance to be one of our next Aussie captains. The then Prime Minister Kevin Rudd emphasised the same point when he said, 'All Australians believe in the idea of a fair go, it's a part of our national identity. Currently, our young people with cancer don't get a fair go and together government, business and the community will do what has to be done to change this.'

During the night Rianna and I announced that the Ponting Foundation will join with the Sony Foundation's 'You Can Campaign' to help build youth cancer centres for Australian teens. To date, we have been mainly focusing on helping kids with cancer, but the more we've become involved the more we've come to realise that Aussie teenagers fighting cancer face their own challenges. As I explained on the night, our aim is to 'assist in ensuring that every young Australian receives the most appropriate treatment in the most appropriate facility to give them the best possible chance of survival'.

position right now, having led the team to two Ashes defeats, that if we lose again there *probably* will be a change of leader. But, of course, it's not quite that simple (so I shouldn't have added the second line), in that I guess there could be scenarios where it would be in the best interests of the team for me to stay in charge. And that really is the bottom line: if I have a say in my future, whether we win or lose, what I believe is best for the team will be the overriding factor when I make my decision one way or the other. That and if I continue to enjoy my cricket and can keep improving as a batter and captain. For me, it's not so much about leaving on a high note or after a big win — the day I feel I'm treading water or going downhill, which means I won't be helping the team ... that will be the day I know it's time to go.

CAMÁN AND SLIOTAR

Our first couple of days in Dublin, before we played a ODI against Ireland, had a real Irish sporting flavour, as we went to Croke Park on June 13 to watch a game of Gaelic football between Dublin and Wexford, and the following day we were back at the famous stadium to meet hurling legend DJ Carey, who showed us a few of the finer points of handling the camán (can I call it a 'bat'?) and sliotar (ball).

It was an interesting day. DJ told us he did like one-day cricket, but Test matches are a little long for his liking, while we also learned that one of the big grandstands at Croke Park is the 'Cusack Stand', named after Michael Cusack, a founder of the Gaelic Athletic Association, who also happened to be a good cricketer back in the late 1800s. At one point we had a 'longest drive' competition, which I think Cameron White won, though Merv Hughes (who is the selector travelling with the team at present) refused to give up until he was landing shots in the seats of the faraway Davin Stand.

> **July 1** Nice to wake up the day after a win – especially at the Oval! I'm very proud of the boys and the way we played yesterday. Confidence is such an important factor in sport and yesterday will give us great faith to repeat the performance at Lord's on Saturday. Enjoyed my own knock and partnership with Pup. Family has arrived so looking forward to a relaxed morning ahead of a sponsor commitment this afternoon.

For now, though, I'm totally focused on the cricket we'll be playing up to the end of the 2011 World Cup, a process that started with the games we've just played over here in the UK.

'I've got the biggest eight months of my career coming up,' I explained to Paul. 'We are playing India, then England and then the World Cup. It doesn't get any bigger than that and everything I do between now and April will be geared at getting the most out of myself and, most importantly, the group. If I'm able to do that I think there are some pretty special things on the horizon for this team.'

AT ONE POINT, I think it was after game four of the NatWest series, I quipped that it would be handy one day if, as captain, I didn't have to worry about injuries. It wasn't quite as brutal as what happened in India last October, but what happened before and during this tour was still maddening. The bad run began in the first week of May when Phillip Hughes dislocated his shoulder while training, which ruled him out for the entire winter. Then, not long before we were due to depart, Brad Haddin and Mitchell Johnson also withdrew.

I knew Hadds had been struggling with an elbow injury in New Zealand, and apparently things got worse for him during the

World T20 in the Caribbean. Originally, he was only going to miss the one-dayers here in Ireland and England but eventually it was decided a longer break would do the elbow good so Tim Paine was called into our Test and one-day teams. Mitch would be back for the Pakistan Test matches, but his spot for the 50-over games went to 19-year-old NSW quick Josh Hazlewood, who became Australia's youngest ever ODI cricketer when he made his debut in the first NatWest game, at Southampton. Another newcomer for the backend of the one-day series and the Tests was the Blues' rookie left-arm spinner Steve O'Keefe, who came into the squad a few days after Shaun Tait was drafted in, when Nathan Hauritz hurt his foot and then Ryan Harris damaged a knee. Steve had taken a seven-for for Australia A against Sri Lanka in a game that was played in Brisbane just as the NatWest series was getting underway, and with Jason Krejza and Jon Holland unavailable because of ... you guessed it ... injuries, he was the logical selection. With Huey out, his exciting NSW team-mate, Usman Khawaja, was brought into our squad for the Tests.

Also into the Test squad came a more familiar face in Ben Hilfenhaus, who had proved he had recovered from his knee tendonitis by bowling strongly for Australia A. As it turned out, Ryno's knee injury was bad enough for him to be ruled out of the matches against Pakistan, which ensured that Hilfy played in

> **July 6** Hectic last few days. Excellent win by the boys at Lord's on Saturday. I then played in a charity T20 game at Windsor Castle on Sunday before flying to Edinburgh where I played a charity round of golf on the Dukes course yesterday. All great fun. Came back to London last night and am now getting ready to drive to Notts today ahead of our 2-day tour game against Derby.

TOUR GAMES

ODI, Australia v Ireland, at Dublin (June 17): Australia 9–231 (50 overs: TD Paine 81, CL White 42; KJ O'Brien 3–43) defeated **Ireland** 192 (42 overs: JR Hopes 5–14) by 39 runs

50-over game, Australians v Middlesex, at Lord's (June 19): Middlesex 5–273 (50 overs: OA Shah 92, NJ Dexter 45, SA Newman 55; DE Bollinger 3–24) lost to the **Australians** 5–277 (47.5 overs: CL White 106, MEK Hussey 72*; TJ Murtagh 3–43) by five wickets

First T20I, at Birmingham (July 5): Pakistan 8–167 (20 overs: Umar Akmal 64) defeated **Australia** 144 (18.4 overs: DA Warner 41, DJ Hussey 34; Mohammad Aamer 3–27, Saeed Ajmal 3–26) by 23 runs

Second T20I, at Birmingham (July 6): Pakistan 9–162 (20 overs: Salman Butt 31, Kamran Akmal 33; DP Nannes 3–30, SNJ O'Keefe 3–29) defeated **Australia** 151 (19.4 overs: MJ Clarke 30, JR Hopes 30, DJ Hussey 33; Mohammad Aamer 3–27) by 11 runs

Two-day game, Australians v Derbyshire, at Derby (July 8–9): Australians 436 (89.3 overs: RT Ponting 116, MEK Hussey 132, TD Paine 52*, SPD Smith 48) drew with **Derbyshire** 5–235 (79 overs: CJL Rogers 93, WL Madsen 58, GT Park 43)

the first Test, seven months after his man-of-the-match effort against the West Indies at the Gabba. Peter George was called into our squad as the fourth paceman. Finally, when Hilfy bruised a shoulder in the first Test, Clint McKay was brought back into the Test squad, in case we suffered another injury before the second Test.

THE TWO MONTHS I had off in April-May was the longest stretch I've had without actively being involved in cricket for as long as I can remember. For the first part of it, in America and when we got home, I just tried to enjoy the rest as much as I could, but from about the start of May I began doing a bit of physical work to make sure my body would be up for the two tour games, six ODIs and two Test matches we'd be playing from mid June to the end of July.

One thing I did do during my time off was keep an eye on the short Test series between England and Bangladesh, noting especially the impressive debut of young quick Steven Finn and also the fact they rested two of the established players, Stuart

MURALI'S FAREWELL

A few weeks ago, when I chose my international team of the decade, an obvious selection was Muttiah Muralitharan, because he has stood apart as the best spinner we Australians have faced over the past 15 years. Little did I know then that Murali was about to announce his retirement from Tests. His farewell game was the just completed match against India in Galle, and he finished in style by inspiring Sri Lanka to a decisive victory. In the process, he took the eight wickets he needed to reach 800 Test wickets – a phenomenal achievement.

I think of him as a player who had a mighty impact on the world game and especially in Sri Lanka, where he stands as their greatest ever cricketer as clearly as Sir Donald Bradman does for Australia and Sir Richard Hadlee for New Zealand. Coming so soon after Shane Warne arrived on the scene, Murali confirmed that top-flight spinners can be match-winners in all forms of the game, and the slow bowlers of today owe him plenty for that.

I'll also remember how he played cricket with a smile, even though he was constantly fighting, competing, trying his utmost to win. They're the blokes we Australian cricketers admire the most – the ones who are up for the contest – and Murali was always that.

Broad and Paul Collingwood. Then they decided to keep Finn out of the NatWest series, presumably because they didn't want us to have a good look at him. I'm not sure if this means Finn will be in Australia in November, but I guess it has to be a possibility. Clearly, the England selectors had half an eye on the Ashes, even though there was six months' worth of cricket to be played before they set off for Australia.

Their first chance to have a look at us came in Ireland, who we played in a one-dayer on June 17, but I doubt they discovered anything too revealing, because we were more than a little rusty, to the point that there was a stage during the game when it looked like we might get beaten. Our total of 9–231 was par at best, and the Irish reached 3–137 in the 25th over before James Hopes grabbed five wickets for six runs in 34 balls. 'Hopes was outstanding and I thought Nathan Hauritz (who took 2–40) was very good as well,' I said afterwards. 'Once we took the pace off the ball it was very hard to score.'

SOME COMMENTS BY ENGLAND veteran Paul Collingwood in the days before the NatWest series also got some attention in the UK papers. Paul was reminiscing about a T20 game that was played before the 2005 Ashes series, when England played aggressively and won the game.

'That was a bit of a benchmark as to how we wanted to attack Australia,' he said. 'You've got to go hard at them. We've learnt that over the last five or six years. If you go hard at them and it comes off, it puts them under a lot of pressure. The 2005 series was a prime example because we had a lot of skill but also went hard at them and we'll continue to do that.'

Of course, I was quickly asked for a reaction, and I was happy to admit that his remarks didn't worry me.

'Isn't playing hard what international cricket is all about?' I said. 'I would expect that they would come out aggressive in every match that they play. I can't see why they would want to come out aggressive in one match and not in another game.'

ENGLAND DESERVED THEIR VICTORY in the one-dayers. They outplayed us in the first two matches and probably should have won game three more easily than they eventually did. But maybe we were short of a gallop, and I was pleased by the way we fought back to win the final two games comfortably. Most of our guys played some good cricket at various points in the series, and I was especially pleased with the efforts of our young blokes, like Tim Paine, Steve Smith, Ryan Harris and Shaun Marsh. Most notable of all, in my view, was the comeback to one-day internationals of Shaun Tait, who was quick and dangerous in the last three games, to the point that after he took four wickets at Lord's the idea was

> **July 11** Had a great time at our Foundation net session this afternoon. Great bunch of kids, parents and adults there for a bit of fun and hope they'll remember it for a long time to come. Huge thanks to Justin Langer for helping me out. How about Mark Webber! Sensational win today and I am thrilled for him. He deserves all the success in the world.

floated that he might even be a factor in the Ashes Tests. But Shaun explained he is happy to concentrate on ODI and T20 cricket.

In the end, England must have been happy that they won the series and we were pleased with the way we recovered, but as a guide to how the Ashes might turn out I think it proved very little. At different times, guys like Broad, Swann, Anderson, Strauss, Pietersen and Collingwood performed very well, but we know what they can do. Perhaps their best player through the five games, certainly at the start of the series, was the Irishman

A MOVE UP THE ORDER

It was only a few weeks ago, when I was choosing my team of the decade, that I was writing about the value of having right-handers and left-handers intermittent in the batting order. We've had that in our Test team in recent times with the right-handed Shane Watson and left-handed Simon Katich opening, then me (a right-hander) at No. 3 followed by a left-hander (Mike Hussey), right-hander (Michael Clarke), left-hander (Marcus North), right-hander (Brad Haddin) and left-hander (Mitchell Johnson). But as we approached this tour, I couldn't help thinking that now was the time for Pup to move up the order, to reflect his leadership role and status in the game. The counter argument was that left-hand/right-hand combination and also that because we have been winning we should leave things as they are, but I've never been convinced by the 'if it ain't broke, don't fix it' argument. Even when you're winning, if you see a chance to improve things, you're obliged to grab it.

I spoke to Huss and Pup before our warm-up game at Derby and went through the reasons behind the move and why I think it's best for the team. Pup is keen, Huss saw the positives in the move straight away, and if everything goes to plan we'll be sticking with this new order right through to the Ashes Tests.

Eion Morgan, who scored a clever century in game one and was also impressive in games two and four. But Morgan is no certainty to play in the Tests in Australia, with the strong possibility that batters like Ian Bell and Jonathan Trott will be picked ahead of him.

To tell you the truth, I didn't think we played that badly in the first three games, but you don't need to be that far away from your best to be shown up in international cricket. I simply reminded the team before game four that we have to keep backing our instincts and talents; whenever we do that, soon enough the good form and positive results will come. My own batting was pretty ordinary until we got to London for the last two games of the series. I managed to make 92 at the Oval and enjoyed another long stand with Michael Clarke, who finished unbeaten but one short of his hundred, and I also thought I was batting well at Lord's until Stuart Broad surprised me with a quicker ball that I tried to hook but only gloved through to the wicketkeeper. Broad bowled a number of short ones to us through the series, and it will be interesting to see if he tries the same tactic in Australia. In game five, things were pretty evenly balanced until Mike Hussey and Shaun Marsh led a charge that saw us score no less than 130 runs in the final 11 overs of our innings, and then Taity ripped into their top order. One delivery in his first over was measured at 161kmph, which is more than 100mph on the old scale.

July 12 Two big Tests against Pakistan ahead for us over the next two weeks here in England. We only have four Tests to play between now and the Ashes starting on 25 November. Every session of every Test we play is an important part of our preparation for the Ashes.

MCC SPIRIT OF CRICKET TEST SERIES, AUSTRALIA V PAKISTAN, JULY 2010

First Test, at Lord's (July 13–16): Australia 253 (76.5 overs: SM Katich 80, MEK Hussey 56*; Mohammad Aamer 4–72) and 334 (91 overs: SM Katich 83, BW Hilfenhaus 56*; Umar Gul 4–61) defeated **Pakistan** 148 (40.5 overs: Salman Butt 63; SR Watson 5–40) and 289 (91.1 overs: Salman Butt 92; MJ North 6–55) by 150 runs

Second Test, at Leeds (July 21–24): Australia 88 (33.1 overs) and 349 (95.3 overs: RT Ponting 66, MJ Clarke 77, SPD Smith 77; Mohammad Aamer 4–86) lost to **Pakistan** 258 (64.5 overs: SR Watson 6–33) and 7–180 (50.4 overs: Imran Farhat 67, Azhar Ali 51) by three wickets

OUR OPENING TEST MATCH against Pakistan was notable for the fact that it was the first time three Tasmanians wore the baggy green for Australia in the same Test. Ben Hilfenhaus, Tim Paine and I have played together in ODIs before, but with Tim (along with Steve Smith) making his Test debut, this was an even bigger occasion than those matches last year in England and India — for us as a trio and for our state too. On the third day, when my two mates put on a ninth-wicket partnership of 74, they became, as far as I can work out, only the third pair of Tasmanians to bat together in a Test match, after Shaun Young and me at the Oval in 1997, and Colin Miller and me in Sri Lanka and the West Indies in 1999. I never got to bat with David Boon in a Test, something I really wish had happened.

The game itself turned out to be a pretty good one for all of us in the Australian set-up. These days in Test cricket, a captain needs a compelling reason to send the opposition in, and for this match at Lord's the juicy combination of a green deck and low cloud cover meant that whoever won the toss was going to bowl first. In Mohammad Asif, Mohammad Aamer and Umar Gul, Pakistan have just the right pace bowlers to make life very difficult in such conditions, so we did really well to get to 2–171 on the opening day. Simon Katich was sensational, a trick he would repeat in our second innings. Unfortunately, Mike Hussey aside, our batting late on the first day was disappointing, but then Hilfy cut through their top order and Shane Watson did the rest, completing his first Test five-for, to give us a first-innings lead of 105.

As can sometimes happen when batting conditions are very difficult through the first day of a Test, things got easier from about halfway through day three. The sun came out late in our second innings, as we added 126 for the last two wickets, so we expected it would be a battle to chisel them out. The key moment came when they were 2–186 after 55 overs, when I brought Marcus North on to bowl and he immediately had Salman Butt stumped by Tim Paine so clearly and brilliantly (a ball from an off-spinner sliding down the leg-side behind a left-handed batter is always a hard one for the keeper to take) that umpire Rudi Koertzen didn't need to go upstairs for a second opinion. Half an hour later, last over before lunch, Northy conned Umar Akmal into playing a cut shot that wasn't quite on and Michael Clarke took the catch at slip. There were two left-handers batting when I brought Northy, an off-spinner, on to bowl and I liked the idea of him turning the ball away from the bat, but I didn't really expect this bowling change to turn out as beautifully as it did.

A game that started with the ball swinging and seaming all

over the place ended with our spin attack of North and Smith taking all but one of Pakistan's second-innings wickets. Northy finished with 6–55, which after Watto's effort on day two means that of the current top six in our batting order only Huss and I haven't taken five wickets in a Test innings. I've always said I like going into a game with a 'balanced' side, and having four quicks (two of them left-handed), four spinners (a right-hand leggie and offie, left-arm finger-spin and left-arm wrist spin) and Mitchell Johnson (scorer of a Test century) batting at nine has to be just about the ultimate example of that. Our winning margin was 150 runs — impressive, I reckon, given that we lost the toss.

The only downside for me was on a personal level, in that for the fourth time I was unable to make a big score in a Test at Lord's. I guess everyone has to have a 'bogey' ground, and it's just

PERSONAL SPACE

I was involved in a minor incident on the opening day of the first Test, after Pakistan's young left-arm quick Mohammad Aamer and I came together immediately after I was dismissed for 26. If Aamer was guilty of anything it was getting over-excited after he got me out, and this was essentially what match referee Chris Broad ruled when he looked at the matter at the end of the day's play.

Some of the English papers tried to make a meal of what happened, suggesting I'd raised my elbow in a provocative way, but that was nonsense. I played my shot, went to see where the ball was going, the fielder at short leg caught it and suddenly, when I turned back around to look up the wicket, there was someone right in front of my nose, in what I think anyone would consider to be my space. As a reflex, I went to protect myself, then both of us realised what was happening and we went our separate ways, me to the pavilion, the bowler to where he should have gone in the first place – to celebrate with his team-mates.

A CHANGE OF CAPTAIN

Taking down the opposition captain was something the great West Indies sides of the 1980s always set out to do, and something we've tried to achieve for as long as I've been in the Australian side. But I must confess that we didn't expect to see the back of new Pakistan Test captain Shahid Afridi as quickly as we did.

Afridi has been a terrific one-day cricketer for a number of years, and T20 cricket seems made for him, but we were a bit surprised he was named Test skipper. Still, there was some logic to it, in that the younger players in their squad clearly look up to him and he is a dangerous player who can change a game. The Test started well for him when he won the toss, but his 15-ball cameo for 31 when wickets were falling in their first innings was not what they needed, and then he played a poor slog in their second dig and was out for two. Straight after the Test, he decided he was retiring and soon after it was announced that Salman Butt would be in charge for the Test at Headingley.

a pity mine has to be the Home of cricket, but at least I'm not alone as none of Brian Lara, Sachin Tendulkar and Jacques Kallis has made a decent score in a Test there either. I do feel I was a little unlucky this time. In the first innings, for the second Test in a row, I clipped a ball firmly in the middle of the bat but was caught brilliantly at bat-pad, and then the next day I was given out lbw in one of those decisions that could have gone either way. It's funny, since I got lucky in Hobart (when Mohammad Aamer

July 19 Had a really good bat at training today. Boys trained well and there was a really positive buzz around the place. Lighter day tomorrow ahead of the start of play on Wednesday.

dropped that sitter at fine leg and I went on to make a double hundred) I've hardly had one stroke of good fortune go my way.

I suppose some people might point to the first ball I received in our second innings of the second Test as a case of me being fortunate, but I don't see it that way. We'd been bowled out on the first day for just 88, after I'd won the toss and opted to bat (more of that in a moment), and Pakistan earned a first-innings lead of 170. I came out to bat after Kato had been bowled by Mohammad Aamer, and straightaway I padded up to a ball that swung back in. Out in the middle, I was sure it was missing off stump, but I still looked up a bit nervously to see if Rudi Koertzen agreed with me. After that, I thought I batted pretty well to get to 61 by stumps on day two, and I had visions of going on to make a really big score, but then I played a dreadful shot the next morning, maybe my most disappointing moment of the entire cricket year covered in this book.

Before the game, we talked about bowling first in this Test, and if I'd known the pitch would seam around as much as it did, I probably would have sent Pakistan in. I knew their bowlers would swing it around with the clouds low at the start of the day, but I was expecting the sun to come out much sooner than it did, and we also believed the wicket would deteriorate as the game went on, to the point that batting on day five might be very tricky (of course, that became irrelevant after our first-innings batting effort). I've scored plenty of runs in Tests at Headingley, and to me the pitch looked pretty similar to those past wickets, where the pace and bounce for the first three days was good, so I was very surprised just how hard batting was in the Test, especially on the first day. And there is one thing we shouldn't forget — as I've said and written before, when the ball is swinging and seaming this Pakistan pace attack is very impressive.

WINNING FORM

The bloke who said 'winning form is good form' knew what he was talking about, and I certainly hope we do very well in our Tests against India this October, to further boost our confidence going into the Ashes series, but if recent history is anything to go by it won't matter much at all if we head into the first Test against England without a last-start win under our belt. Australia dominated the Ashes from 1989 to 2002–03, but only once in that time (2002–03) did we win the Test we played immediately before the start of an Ashes series …

Series	Ashes result	Australia's Result in Test Prior to Ashes
1989	Australia won 4–0	Drew fifth Test versus West Indies
1990–91	Australia won 3–0	Lost one-off Test versus New Zealand
1993	Australia won 4–1	Lost third Test versus New Zealand
1994–95	Australia won 3–1	Drew third Test versus Pakistan
1997	Australia won 3–2	Lost third Test versus South Africa
1998–99	Australia won 3–1	Drew third Test versus Pakistan
2001	Australia won 4–1	Lost third Test versus India
2002–03	Australia won 4–1	Won third Test versus Pakistan
2005	England won 2–1	Won third Test versus New Zealand
2006–07	Australia won 5–0	Won second Test versus Bangladesh
2009	England won 2–1	Lost third Test versus South Africa

I noticed how the critics were quick to go back to Edgbaston in 2005 — when I sent England in and they made 400 on the first day — to suggest that because that decision went awry I'm now not game to send anyone in, whatever the circumstances. But that's not true; I would have bowled first at Lord's last week if I'd called correctly. In fact, the right analogy with Edgbaston is that both times we played very poorly on the opening day after I won the toss. We also fought back pretty well on both occasions, and at the end we weren't too far away from winning the game.

It was just 12 months ago that Andrew Strauss batted first at Leeds after winning the toss, and we knocked them over for 102; then, like now, it was a combination of bad batting and excellent bowling that led to the meagre first-innings total.

It was a bit eerie how this Test almost mimicked the game in Sydney from seven months ago, in that I won the toss, batted first in difficult conditions, we were bowled out for a very low score, the Pakistan top-order batted well, we faced a first-innings deficit or around 200, and then we batted all right until our lower order did excellently to set Pakistan an awkward target — 176 at the SCG; 180 at Leeds. In the Sydney Test, we took their fourth wicket when their total was 77, and after that the pressure got too much for them. This time, we didn't get them four down until they reached 146, and though we fought all the way to the end they snuck home with three wickets to spare. When a game is won and lost by such a narrow margin, there are usually good performances from players on both sides, and in our case I was pleased with the way Watto bowled for us, taking 6–33 this time to follow up his five-for at Lord's, and with how Pup batted in our second dig, vindicating his move up to No. 4. There was also plenty to like about the way Smithy batted on the third day, when he slammed 77 from 100 balls, while Tim Paine's keeping was again very smooth. My understanding is that by completing 12 dismissals in this series, Painey equalled the Aussie record for most dismissals by a keeper in his first two Tests.

For all this, though, in the same way I can argue that because we won in Sydney my decision at the toss then was right; at Leeds, because we lost, I have to accept that I made a mistake in batting first. It's my responsibility, no one else's, to get those sorts of decisions right and unfortunately I blew the call here. I would love to have made it nine wins from 10 Tests since the 2009

Ashes series and sustained our unbeaten record against Pakistan that went back to 1995, but it wasn't to be.

'Late November is a long way away yet,' I said immediately afterwards. 'A loss quite often just highlights some of the things you're not doing well. That's all this week will do for us. We know we've got to continue to work hard and not take anything for granted. I don't think it will do too much to dent our confidence.

'You want to win every game that you play, there's no doubt about that. And we haven't been at our best in this game, there's no doubt about that.'

All we can do now is shift our attention to our next assignment — India in October. In one sense, given how different subcontinent conditions can be to what we experience at home, playing two Tests and three one-dayers in India would not be my first choice for where I want to be playing cricket a month out from an Ashes series. But on the other hand, playing against such a good and competitive side will be good for us and most likely will give us a reasonable indication of how we are travelling. If, as I strongly suspect, this last Test was just a hiccup, and the last 10 months are a true guide to how we are improving as a group, then I think you'll find the games in India will show we're heading in the right direction.

After that, the fight for the Ashes will be a beauty. And unless something totally unexpected happens, I can assure you of one thing: we'll be ready for it.

July 25 Not the end of the series I was hoping for but we were always up against it after being bowled out for 88 on the first day. We have had a really good talk about the game and our performance so I know we will take some positives and, importantly, some key lessons learned back home with us.

STATISTICS
SCORES AND AVERAGES

IN JULY 2010, in the first Test against Pakistan at Lord's, Ricky Ponting became the second highest run-scorer in Test history, going past Brian Lara. Only Sachin Tendulkar is ahead of him. Nine days later, at Headingley, Ricky scored his 12,000th Test run, and he ended the Pakistan series having scored 12,021 runs in Test matches, at 54.66. Twenty years ago, no Australian batsman had scored even 9000 Test runs, and only Bradman had scored even 2000 Test runs and also averaged more than 54.00.

I know Ricky is proud of these achievements but I know, too, that he is sincere when he says that such records will mean much more to him when he is retired from big-time cricket and has time to reflect on his fantastic career. For the moment, what matters most to the Australian captain is that he and his team are always seeking to improve, to be consistent and to be working as a unit. He has spent months thinking about and preparing for the upcoming Ashes series, but in that time he has never stopped to think what records might be on the horizon. What matters for him is playing to the best of his ability, and finding a way to win.

So the temptation here in this statistics section is to just list the scores and averages from the past 10 months, and leave it at that. But inevitably, given the length of Ricky's career, there are a number of milestones awaiting him in the upcoming Ashes series, so to complement his Ashes Preview I will list a few of them here:

- To date, Ricky has played in 19 Australian wins in Tests against England, level with Syd Gregory, Clem Hill and Monty Noble. Ahead of him are Steve Waugh (28 wins), Shane Warne (24), Warwick Armstrong and

Glenn McGrath (22), and Ian Healy and Mark Taylor (both 20). The Englishman with the most wins in Tests against Australia is the left-arm spinner Johnny Briggs (1884–1899), who played in 17 wins, followed by Ian Botham with 16.

- He needs 137 more runs to become the sixth Australian (after Don Bradman, Allan Border, Steve Waugh, Clem Hill and Greg Chappell) to score 2500 runs in Ashes Tests.
- He needs to play in all five Tests in 2010–11 to become the ninth Australian to appear in 30 or more consecutive Tests against England — after Allan Border 44, Victor Trumper 40, Monty Noble 39, Neil Harvey 37, Syd Gregory 36, Jim Kelly 33, Ian Healy 33 and Mark Taylor 33. His current sequence of 25 straight Ashes Tests dates back to the start of the 2001 series.
- If he captains Australia throughout the 2010–11 Ashes series, he will become the third man — after Australia's Allan Border (29) and England's Archie MacLaren (22) — to captain his country in 20 or more Australia-England Tests.

Ricky will also be chasing a little history in the first Test in Brisbane, given that he has scored a hundred in the opening game of the last two Ashes series in Australia, both times at the Gabba. Only four men have scored hundreds in each of three or more consecutive Ashes Tests at the same ground: England's Jack Hobbs, who did it at Melbourne (1911–12 to 1920–21) and Adelaide (1911–12 to 1924–25); Wally Hammond, four in a row at Sydney (1928–29 to 1936–37); Herbert Sutcliffe at Melbourne (1924–25 to 1928–29); and Australia's Don Bradman, five in a row at Melbourne (1928–29 to 1936–37) and four in a row at Leeds (1930 to 1948).

ONE SHORT OF A HUNDRED

England needs one more Ashes Test victory for 100 wins in Australia-England Test cricket (Australia have won 132 Tests). England won the most recent Ashes Test, at the Oval in 2009. They have not won two Ashes Tests in a row since 1986, when they won the first Test of the 1986–87 series in Australia, having won the last two Ashes Tests of 1985. Since 1986–87, Australia have won two Ashes Tests in a row on 21 occasions.

The only batsman to have scored a century in the opening Test of an Ashes series four times is Don Bradman, who did so in 1930, 1938, 1946–47 and 1948 (he also scored a hundred in the second Test of the bodyline series in 1932–33, after missing the first Test of that series). Ricky is currently one of five to have scored a hundred in the opening Test of an Ashes series three times (2002–03, 2006–07 and 2009), along with England's Archie McLaren (1897–98, 1901–02, 1905) and Australia's Lindsay Hassett (1946–47, 1948, 1953), Mark Taylor (1989, 1993, 1997) and Steve Waugh (1989, 1998–99, 2001).

In 2010–11, Ricky will also be in a position to become only the second Australian captain, after Bill Woodfull, to regain the Ashes twice. Woodfull did so in 1930, his first series as leader, and 1934, after England won in 1932–33. Ricky will also be aiming to move further up the list of captains with most wins in Australia-England Tests. Allan Border, with 13, has won the most Ashes Tests as captain, followed by Don Bradman and Mike Brearley with 11; Mark Taylor with nine; WG Grace, Monty Noble, Warwick Armstrong and Steve Waugh with eight; and Ian Chappell and Ricky with seven.

Beyond Ashes Tests, Ricky needs 210 more runs to become the first man to score 7000 runs in Tests in Australia. And he

MAKING HISTORY AT THE MCG

You'd think Ashes history would be full of stories of the urn changing hands at the Melbourne Cricket Ground but that's not actually the case. The last time the fate of the Ashes was decided in Melbourne was in 1986–87, when England retained the Ashes by winning the fourth Test of that series. Since then, the Ashes were retained or regained in Sydney (1990–91), Sydney (1994–95), Adelaide (1998–99), Perth (2002–03) and Perth (2006–07).

The last time Australia retained the Ashes at the MCG was in 1965–66, when the fifth Test ended in a draw. The last time the Ashes changed hands in Melbourne was way back in 1911–12, when England went 3–1 up by winning the fourth Test of a five-game series. The last time Australia regained the Ashes in Melbourne was in 1907–08, more than a century ago.

needs to appear in one more Test in Australia to become the third player (after Allan Border and Steve Waugh) to appear in 80 Tests at home.

By now, though, I can hear Ricky saying, 'Enough of this!' None of these numbers will matter to him at all if he and his team cannot come up with an Ashes series victory. On the following pages are a summary of the Australians' 2009–10 cricket year, then the scorecards for the 10 Tests and 32 ODIs the teams played, then the Aussies' averages for the Champions Trophy and each Test and ODI series, and finally a brief analysis of just how successful, compared with previous years, Ricky's men have been since the end of last year's Ashes tour.

That analysis suggests that the Australians' Ashes preparation is going all right. While the captain might not be a stats aficionado, he has to be pleased with numbers like that.

AUSTRALIA'S MATCHES
SEPTEMBER 26, 2009–JULY 25, 2010

Date	Match	Opponent	Venue	Result
Sep 26	Champions Trophy	West Indies	Johannesburg	won by 50 runs
Sep 28	Champions Trophy	India	Centurion	no result
Sep 30	Champions Trophy	Pakistan	Centurion	won by 2 wickets
Oct 2	Champions Trophy semi	England	Centurion	won by 9 wickets
Oct 5	Champions Trophy final	New Zealand	Centurion	won by 6 wickets
Oct 25	first ODI	India	Vadodara	won by 4 runs
Oct 28	second ODI	India	Nagpur	lost by 99 runs
Oct 31	third ODI	India	Delhi	lost by 6 wickets
Nov 2	fourth ODI	India	Mohali	won by 24 runs
Nov 5	fifth ODI	India	Hyderabad	won by 3 runs
Nov 8	sixth ODI	India	Guwahati	won by 6 wickets
Nov 11	seventh ODI	India	Mumbai	abandoned
Nov 26–28	first Test	West Indies	Brisbane	won by inns & 65 runs
Dec 4–8	second Test	West Indies	Adelaide	drawn
Dec 16–20	third Test	West Indies	Perth	won by 35 runs
Dec 26–30	first Test	Pakistan	Melbourne	won by 170 runs
Jan 3–6	second Test	Pakistan	Sydney	won by 36 runs
Jan 14–18	third Test	Pakistan	Hobart	won by 231 runs
Jan 22	first ODI	Pakistan	Brisbane	won by 5 wickets
Jan 24	second ODI	Pakistan	Sydney	won by 140 runs
Jan 26	third ODI	Pakistan	Adelaide	won by 40 runs
Jan 29	fourth ODI	Pakistan	Perth	won by 135 runs
Jan 31	fifth ODI	Pakistan	Perth	won by 2 wickets
Feb 5	T20I	Pakistan	Melbourne	won by 2 runs
Feb 7	first ODI	West Indies	Melbourne	won by 113 runs
Feb 9	second ODI	West Indies	Adelaide	won by 8 wickets
Feb 12	third ODI	West Indies	Sydney	no result
Feb 14	fourth ODI	West Indies	Brisbane	won by 50 runs
Feb 19	fifth ODI	West Indies	Melbourne	won by 125 runs
Feb 21	first T20I	West Indies	Hobart	won by 38 runs
Feb 23	second T20I	West Indies	Sydney	won by 8 wickets
Feb 26	first T20I	New Zealand	Wellington	won by 6 wickets
Feb 28	second T20I	New Zealand	Christchurch	lost in extra overs
Mar 3	first ODI	New Zealand	Napier	lost by 2 wickets
Mar 6	second ODI	New Zealand	Auckland	won by 12 runs
Mar 9	third ODI	New Zealand	Hamilton	won by 6 wickets
Mar 11	fourth ODI	New Zealand	Auckland	won by 6 wickets
Mar 13	fifth ODI	New Zealand	Wellington	lost by 51 runs
Mar 19–23	first Test	New Zealand	Wellington	won by 10 wickets
Mar 27–31	second Test	New Zealand	Hamilton	won by 176 runs
May 2	World T20	Pakistan	Gros Islet	won by 34 runs
May 5	World T20	Bangladesh	Bridgetown	won by 27 runs
May 7	World T20	India	Bridgetown	won by 49 runs
May 9	World T20	Sri Lanka	Bridgetown	won by 81 runs

Date	Match	Opponent	Venue	Result
May 11	World T20	West Indies	Gros Islet	won by 6 wickets
May 14	World T20 semi	Pakistan	Gros Islet	won by 3 wickets
May 16	World T20 final	England	Bridgetown	lost by 7 wickets
Jun 17	ODI	Ireland	Dublin	won by 39 runs
June 19	50-over game	Middlesex	Lord's	won by 5 wickets
Jun 22	first ODI	England	Southampton	lost by 4 wickets
Jun 24	second ODI	England	Cardiff	lost by 4 wickets
Jun 27	third ODI	England	Manchester	lost by 1 wicket
Jun 30	fourth ODI	England	The Oval	won by 78 runs
Jul 3	fifth ODI	England	Lord's	won by 42 runs
Jul 5	first T20I	Pakistan	Birmingham	lost by 23 runs
Jul 6	second T20I	Pakistan	Birmingham	lost by 11 runs
Jul 8–9	two-day game	Derbyshire	Derby	drawn
July 13–16	first Test	Pakistan	Lord's	won by 150 runs
Jul 21–25	second Test	Pakistan	Leeds	lost by 3 wickets

SUMMARY

Tests

Opponent	Tests	Won	Lost	Drawn
West Indies	3	2	–	1
Pakistan	3	3	–	–
New Zealand	2	2	–	–
Pakistan	2	1	1	–
Total	10	8	1	1

One-Day Internationals

Opponent	ODIs	Won	Lost	No Result
West Indies	6	5	–	1
India	7	4	2	1
Pakistan	6	6	–	–
England	6	3	3	–
New Zealand	6	4	2	–
Ireland	1	1	–	–
Total	32	23	7	2

Twenty20 Internationals

Opponent	T20Is	Won	Lost	No Result
Pakistan	5	3	2	–
West Indies	3	3	–	–
New Zealand	2	1	1	–
Bangladesh	1	1	–	–
India	1	1	–	–
Sri Lanka	1	1	–	–
England	1	–	1	–
Total	14	10	4	–

First Test, Australia v West Indies at Brisbane

November 26–28, 2009 • Toss: Australia
Umpires: Asad Rauf (Pakistan) and IJ Gould (England) • TV umpire: MR Benson (England)
Match referee: BC Broad (England)
Player of the match: BW Hilfenhaus (Australia)

Australia first innings

SR Watson	lbw Taylor	0
SM Katich	c Ramdin b Bravo	92
RT Ponting	c Ramdin b Roach	55
MEK Hussey	c&b Benn	66
MJ Clarke	c Gayle b Bravo	41
MJ North	c Ramdin b Bravo	79
BJ Haddin	c Ramdin b Rampaul	38
MG Johnson	c Ramdin b Benn	7
NM Hauritz	not out	50
PM Siddle	not out	20
Extras	(b 2, lb 9, w 1, nb 20)	32
Total	(8 wickets dec; 135 overs)	480

Did not bat: BW Hilfenhaus

Fall of wickets: 1–0 (Watson, 2.1 overs), 2–126 (Ponting, 27.5 overs), 3–200 (Katich, 48.1 overs), 4–253 (Hussey, 64.6 overs), 5–287 (Clarke, 79.3 overs), 6–371 (Haddin, 104.5 overs), 7–386 (Johnson, 111.2 overs), 8–444 (North, 124.5 overs)

Bowling: JE Taylor 9–2–43–1; KAJ Roach 25–4–76–1; R Rampaul 26–4–110–1; DJ Bravo 32–4–118–3; SJ Benn 34–5–86–2; CH Gayle 9–0–36–0

West Indies first innings

CH Gayle	lbw Hilfenhaus	31
AB Barath	c Watson b Johnson	15
TM Dowlin	c Watson b Hauritz	62
S Chanderpaul	lbw Siddle	2
DJ Bravo	c Watson b Johnson	0
BP Nash	c Haddin b Watson	18
D Ramdin	c North b Johnson	54
SJ Benn	c Siddle b Hilfenhaus	28
JE Taylor	c Katich b Hauritz	8
KAJ Roach	c Clarke b Hauritz	0
R Rampaul	not out	1
Extras	(b 1, lb 3, nb 5)	9
Total	(all out; 63 overs)	228

Fall of wickets: 1–49 (Gayle, 12.3 overs), 2–49 (Barath, 13.5 overs), 3–58 (Chanderpaul, 16.5 overs), 4–63 (Bravo, 17.3 overs), 5–96 (Nash, 29.2 overs), 6–174 (Ramdin, 46.6 overs), 7–212 (Benn, 57.5 overs), 8–221 (Taylor, 60.5 overs), 9–221 (Roach, 60.6 overs), 10–228 (Dowlin, 62.6 overs)

Bowling: BW Hilfenhaus 16–6–50–2; PM Siddle 13–4–51–1; MG Johnson 19–4–75–3; SR Watson 9–0–31–1; NM Hauritz 6–3–17–3

West Indies second innings (following on)

CH Gayle	lbw Hilfenhaus	1
AB Barath	lbw Watson	104
TM Dowlin	b Hilfenhaus	4
S Chanderpaul	c Katich b Hilfenhaus	2
DJ Bravo	c Hilfenhaus b Hussey	23
BP Nash	lbw Hauritz	7
D Ramdin	c Haddin b Hauritz	16
JE Taylor	c Hilfenhaus b Watson	0
SJ Benn	not out	15
KAJ Roach	c Hussey b Siddle	5
R Rampaul	c Haddin b Johnson	0
Extras	(lb 4, nb 6)	10
Total	(all out; 52.1 overs)	187

Fall of wickets: 1–6 (Gayle, 2.1 overs), 2–18 (Dowlin, 6.1 overs), 3–39 (Chanderpaul, 10.2 overs), 4–105 (Bravo, 27.2 overs), 5–141 (Nash, 38.6 overs), 6–154 (Barath, 41.6 overs), 7–158 (Taylor, 43.1 overs), 8–170 (Ramdin, 46.5 overs), 9–187 (Roach, 51.6 overs), 10–187 (Rampaul, 52.1 overs)

Bowling: BW Hilfenhaus 7–3–20–3; PM Siddle 10–3–41–1; MG Johnson 9.1–1–35–1; SR Watson 10–0–44–2; NM Hauritz 14–1–40–2; MEK Hussey 2–0–3–1

Stumps scores

Day 1: Australia first innings 5–322 (North 42, Haddin 9; 90 overs)
Day 2: West Indies first innings 5–134 (Dowlin 40, Ramdin 22; 39 overs)

Australia won by an innings and 65 runs

Second Test, Australia v West Indies at Adelaide

December 4–8, 2009 • **Toss:** West Indies
Umpires: MR Benson (England) and IJ Gould (England) • **TV umpire:** Asad Rauf (Pakistan)
Match referee: BC Broad (England)
Player of the match: CH Gayle (West Indies)

West Indies first innings

CH Gayle	c Haddin b Bollinger	26
AB Barath	c Hussey b Bollinger	3
RR Sarwan	c Clarke b Johnson	28
S Chanderpaul	c Haddin b Watson	62
BP Nash	b Johnson	92
DJ Bravo	b Hauritz	104
D Ramdin	b Watson	4
DJG Sammy	lbw Siddle	44
SJ Benn	lbw Hauritz	17
KAJ Roach	c Haddin b Johnson	2
R Rampaul	not out	40
Extras	(b 5, lb 14, w 5, nb 5)	29
Total	(all out; 124.1 overs)	451

Fall of wickets: 1–26 (Barath, 4.3 overs), 2–39 (Gayle, 8.4 overs), 3–84 (Sarwan, 18.1 overs), 3–119 (Nash, retired hurt, 24.6 overs), 4–235 (Chanderpaul, 62.3 overs), 5–239 (Ramdin, 62.6 overs), 6–273 (Bravo, 73.2 overs), 7–336 (Sammy, 85.1 overs), 8–380 (Benn, 103.1 overs), 9–383 (Roach, 104.3 overs), 10–451 (Nash, 124.1 overs)

Bowling: DE Bollinger 25–3–67–2; PM Siddle 25–6–92–1; MG Johnson 26.1–3–105–3; NM Hauritz 36–5–111–2; SR Watson 12–2–57–2

West Indies second innings

CH Gayle	not out	165
AB Barath	run out (Hauritz)	17
RR Sarwan	c Haddin b Johnson	7
S Chanderpaul	lbw Bollinger	27
BP Nash	b Watson	24
DJ Bravo	c Hauritz b Johnson	22
D Ramdin	b Johnson	0
DJG Sammy	c Ponting b Bollinger	10
SJ Benn	c Siddle b Johnson	5
R Rampaul	b Johnson	14
KAJ Roach	c Ponting b Bollinger	8
Extras	(b 8, lb 3, w 1, nb 6)	18
Total	(all out; 99.5 overs)	317

Fall of wickets: 1–45 (Barath, 11.5 overs), 2–61 (Sarwan, 14.5 overs), 3–133 (Chanderpaul, 45.5 overs), 4–194 (Nash, 67.4 overs), 5–251 (Bravo, 84.2 overs), 6–251 (Ramdin, 84.4 overs), 7–277 (Sammy, 89.3 overs), 8–284 (Benn, 92.2 overs), 9–302 (Rampaul, 96.6 overs), 10–317 (Roach, 99.5 overs)

Bowling: MG Johnson 22–1–103–5; DE Bollinger 17.5–3–50–3; NM Hauritz 27–4–68–0; PM Siddle 8–2–28–0; MJ North 14–2–42–0; SR Watson 11–5–15–1

Australia first innings

SR Watson	b Benn	96
SM Katich	c Barath b Benn	80
RT Ponting	c Bravo b Roach	36
MEK Hussey	c Ramdin b Roach	41
MJ Clarke	c Sarwan b Benn	71
MJ North	c Bravo b Benn	16
BJ Haddin	not out	55
MG Johnson	c Gayle b Sammy	7
NM Hauritz	c Ramdin b Roach	17
PM Siddle	c Bravo b Benn	0
DE Bollinger	run out (Benn/Roach)	0
Extras	(lb 2, nb 18)	20
Total	(all out; 131.1 overs)	439

Fall of wickets: 1–174 (Watson, 48.2 overs), 2–193 (Katich, 56.2 overs), 3–233 (Ponting, 71.6 overs), 4–312 (Hussey, 97.5 overs), 5–353 (North, 108.2 overs), 6–370 (Clarke, 114.4 overs), 7–377 (Johnson, 117.6 overs), 8–418 (Hauritz, 125.6 overs), 9–419 (Siddle, 126.6 overs), 10–439 (Bollinger, 131.1 overs)

Bowling: KAJ Roach 25.1–3–93–3; R Rampaul 14–1–52–0; DJ Bravo 12–1–43–0; DJG Sammy 18–2–79–1; SJ Benn 53–8–155–5; CH Gayle 9–1–15–0

Australia second innings

SR Watson	c Bravo b Sammy	48
SM Katich	c Barath b Bravo	21
RT Ponting	b Rampaul	20
MEK Hussey	c Ramdin b Bravo	29
MJ Clarke	not out	61
MJ North	c Sarwan b Bravo	2
BJ Haddin	not out	21
Extras	(b 1, lb 2, nb 7)	10
Total	(5 wickets; 76 overs)	212

Fall of wickets: 1–33 (Katich, 8.1 overs), 2–68 (Ponting, 22.5 overs), 3–114 (Watson, 41.1 overs), 4–133 (Hussey, 47.4 overs), 5–139 (North, 55.3 overs)

Bowling: KAJ Roach 16–3–66–0; R Rampaul 9–2–22–1; SJ Benn 27–10–51–0; DJ Bravo 15–4–37–3; CH Gayle 3–1–8–0; DJG Sammy 5–0–21–1; AB Barath 1–0–4–0

Stumps scores
Day 1: West Indies first innings 6–336 (Nash 44, Sammy 44; 85 overs)
Day 2: Australia first innings 0–174 (Watson 96, Katich 71; 48 overs)
Day 3: West Indies second innings 0–23 (Gayle 12, Barath 10; 4 overs)
Day 4: West Indies second innings 8–284 (Gayle 155, Rampaul 0; 93 overs)

Match drawn
Australia retained The Frank Worrell Trophy

Third Test, Australia v West Indies at Perth

December 16–20, 2009 • **Toss:** Australia
Umpires: BF Bowden (New Zealand) and IJ Gould (England)
TV umpire: Asad Rauf (Pakistan) • **Match referee:** BC Broad (England)
Player of the match: CH Gayle (West Indies) • **Player of the series:** CH Gayle (West Indies)

Australia first innings

SR Watson	c Ramdin b Roach	89
SM Katich	c Roach b Benn	99
RT Ponting	retired hurt	23
MEK Hussey	c Ramdin b Rampaul	82
MJ Clarke	c Gayle b Deonarine	11
MJ North	c&b Deonarine	68
BJ Haddin	c Ramdin b Roach	88
MG Johnson	c Benn b Bravo	35
NM Hauritz	not out	2
Extras	(b 4, lb 2, w 1, nb 16)	23
Total	(7 wickets dec; 130.4 overs)	520

Did not bat: DE Bollinger, CJ McKay

Fall of wickets: 1–132 (Watson, 35.2 overs), 1–175 (Ponting, retired hurt), 2–260 (Katich, 67.2 overs), 3–277 (Clarke, 72.3 overs), 4–355 (Hussey, 95.5 overs), 5–444 (North, 112.4 overs), 6–510 (Haddin, 125.4 overs), 7–520 (Johnson, 130.4 overs)

Bowling: KAJ Roach 22–2–104–2; R Rampaul 22–6–85–1; GC Tonge 18–1–85–0; DJ Bravo 17.4–1–79–1; SJ Benn 28–4–87–1; N Deonarine 23–4–74–2

West Indies first innings

CH Gayle	c Watson b Bollinger	102
TM Dowlin	c Hussey b Johnson	55
RR Sarwan	c Hussey b Bollinger	42
N Deonarine	c Watson b Johnson	18
BP Nash	c Clarke b Hauritz	44
DJ Bravo	c Haddin b Bollinger	26
D Ramdin	b Bollinger	8
SJ Benn	c Haddin b Hauritz	3
R Rampaul	c Haddin b Hauritz	0
KAJ Roach	not out	0
GC Tonge	c Haddin b Bollinger	2
Extras	(lb 5, w 1, nb 6)	12
Total	(all out; 81 overs)	312

Fall of wickets: 1–136 (Gayle, 24.1 overs), 2–175 (Dowlin, 33.5 overs), 3–214 (Sarwan, 46.2 overs), 4–239 (Deonarine, 56.4 overs), 5–285 (Bravo, 72.6 overs), 6–295 (Nash, 75.4 overs), 7–310 (Benn, 79.3 overs), 8–310 (Rampaul, 79.5 overs), 9–310 (Ramdin, 80.2 overs), 10–312 (Tonge, 80.6 overs)

Bowling: DE Bollinger 20–3–70–5; MG Johnson 18–3–92–2; CJ McKay 14–3–45–0; NM Hauritz 17–1–66–3; SR Watson 12–3–34–0

Australia second innings

SR Watson	lbw Tonge	30
SM Katich	b Rampaul	10
MJ Clarke	c Ramdin b Bravo	25
MEK Hussey	c Dowlin b Benn	17
MJ North	c Ramdin b Bravo	1
BJ Haddin	c Bravo b Benn	23
MG Johnson	c Nash b Bravo	5
NM Hauritz	c Sarwan b Bravo	11
RT Ponting	c Dowlin b Roach	2
CJ McKay	c Deonarine b Benn	10
DE Bollinger	not out	2
Extras	(b 9, lb 2, w 1, nb 2)	14
Total	(all out; 51.3 overs)	150

Fall of wickets: 1–15 (Katich, 3.2 overs), 2–66 (Watson, 16.4 overs), 3–81 (Clarke, 23.6 overs), 4–89 (Hussey, 28.2 overs), 5–109 (North, 33.5 overs), 6–117 (Haddin, 36.2 overs), 7–125 (Johnson, 41.6 overs), 8–134 (Ponting, 44.5 overs), 9–146 (McKay, 48.4 overs), 10–150 (Hauritz, 51.3 overs)

Bowling: KAJ Roach 6–0–18–1; R Rampaul 6–1–21–1; GC Tonge 10–2–28–1; N Deonarine 1–0–1–0; DJ Bravo 17.3–6–42–4; SJ Benn 11–2–29–3

West Indies second innings

CH Gayle	c Haddin b Watson	21
TM Dowlin	c Clarke b Bollinger	22
RR Sarwan	c Haddin b Hauritz	11
N Deonarine	b Watson	82
BP Nash	b Bollinger	65
DJ Bravo	c Hussey b Johnson	1
D Ramdin	b McKay	14
SJ Benn	c sub (TP Doropoulos) b Johnson	33
R Rampaul	c McKay b Johnson	10
KAJ Roach	c Haddin b Bollinger	17
GC Tonge	not out	23
Extras	(b 9, lb 9, w 1, nb 5)	24
Total	(all out; 94.3 overs)	323

Fall of wickets: 1–35 (Dowlin, 8.4 overs), 2–52 (Gayle, 14.1 overs), 3–68 (Sarwan, 17.6 overs), 4–196 (Deonarine, 66.1 overs), 5–197 (Bravo, 67.5 overs), 6–231 (Ramdin, 75.5 overs), 7–245 (Nash, 80.6 overs), 8–279 (Benn, 85.4 overs), 9–279 (Rampaul, 85.6 overs), 10–323 (Roach, 94.3 overs)

Bowling: DE Bollinger 20.3–3–71–3; MG Johnson 16–5–67–3; CJ McKay 14–2–56–1; SR Watson 14–5–30–2; NM Hauritz 23–7–61–1; MJ North 7–1–20–0

Stumps scores
Day 1: Australia first innings 3–339 (Hussey 81, North 23; 90 overs)
Day 2: West Indies first innings 2–214 (Sarwan 42, Deonarine 10; 46 overs)
Day 3: Australia second innings 8–137 (Hauritz 11, McKay 1; 47 overs)
Day 4: West Indies second innings 9–308 (Roach 13, Tonge 12; 91 overs)

Australia won by 35 runs
Australia won the series 2–0

First Test, Australia v Pakistan at Melbourne

December 26–30, 2009 • **Toss:** Australia
Umpires: BR Doctrove (West Indies) and RE Koertzen (South Africa)
TV umpire: EAR de Silva (Sri Lanka) • **Match referee:** RS Madugalle (Sri Lanka)
Player of the match: SR Watson (Australia)

Australia first innings

SR Watson	run out (Salman Butt/Imran Farhat)	93
SM Katich	c Salman Butt b Mohammad Asif	98
RT Ponting	c Misbah-ul-Haq b Mohammad Asif	57
MEK Hussey	lbw Saeed Ajmal	82
NM Hauritz	lbw Abdur Rauf	75
MJ Clarke	not out	28
Extras	(b 2, lb 12, nb 7)	21
Total	(5 wickets dec; 128 overs)	454

Did not bat: MJ North, BJ Haddin, MG Johnson, DE Bollinger, PM Siddle

Fall of wickets: 1–182 (Watson, 60.1 overs), 2–233 (Katich, 74.3 overs), 3–291 (Ponting, 83.2 overs), 4–382 (Hussey, 112.5 overs), 5–454 (Hauritz, 127.6 overs)

Bowling: Mohammad Asif 27–5–86–2; Mohammad Aamer 27–7–101–0; Abdur Rauf 23–4–86–1; Saeed Ajmal 46–3–150–1; Imran Farhat 5–0–17–0

Pakistan first innings

Imran Farhat	lbw Johnson	9
Salman Butt	lbw Watson	45
Faisal Iqbal	c Clarke b Hauritz	15
Mohammad Yousuf	c Haddin b Siddle	22
Umar Akmal	c Ponting b Johnson	51
Mohammad Aamer	c North b Bollinger	15
Misbah-ul-Haq	not out	65
Kamran Akmal	c Haddin b Bollinger	12
Abdur Rauf	c North b Bollinger	3
Mohammad Asif	c Watson b Siddle	0
Saeed Ajmal	b Johnson	4
Extras	(b 4, lb 3, w 1, nb 9)	17
Total	(all out; 99 overs)	258

Fall of wickets: 1–26 (Imran Farhat, 12.2 overs), 2–59 (Faisal Iqbal, 31.2 overs), 3–84 (Salman Butt, 39.3 overs), 4–109 (Mohammad Yousuf, 48.5 overs), 5–159 (Umar Akmal, 60.6 overs), 6–203 (Mohammad Aamer, 80.3 overs), 7–215 (Kamran Akmal, 82.5 overs), 8–219 (Abdur Rauf, 86.6 overs), 9–220 (Mohammad Asif, 87.6 overs), 10–258 (Saeed Ajmal, 98.6 overs)

Bowling: DE Bollinger 20–6–50–3; PM Siddle 24–7–77–2; NM Hauritz 20–3–58–1; MG Johnson 22–10–36–3; SR Watson 13–3–30–1

Australia second innings

SR Watson	not out	120
SM Katich	c Kamran Akmal b Mohammad Asif	2
RT Ponting	c Salman Butt b Mohammad Aamer	12
MEK Hussey	lbw Mohammad Aamer	4
MJ Clarke	c Kamran Akmal b Mohammad Aamer	37
MJ North	b Mohammad Aamer	8
BJ Haddin	c Kamran Akmal b Mohammad Aamer	0
MG Johnson	run out (Mohammad Asif/ Saeed Ajmal)	22
NM Hauritz	st Kamran Akmal b Saeed Ajmal	8
Extras	(lb 2, w 3, nb 7)	12
Total	(8 wickets dec; 73.1 overs)	225

Fall of wickets: 1–15 (Katich, 6.3 overs), 2–32 (Ponting, 9.4 overs), 3–40 (Hussey, 11.1 overs), 4–143 (Clarke, 40.6 overs), 5–161 (North, 46.1 overs), 6–161 (Haddin, 46.3 overs), 7–198 (Johnson, 63.2 overs), 8–225 (Hauritz, 73.1 overs)

Bowling: Mohammad Asif 16–3–38–1; Mohammad Aamer 24–6–79–5; Saeed Ajmal 23.1–1–73–1; Abdur Rauf 10–3–33–0

Pakistan second innings

Imran Farhat	lbw Bollinger	12
Salman Butt	lbw Johnson	33
Faisal Iqbal	b Hauritz	48
Mohammad Yousuf	c Katich b Hauritz	61
Umar Akmal	c Haddin b Johnson	27
Misbah-ul-Haq	c Haddin b Johnson	0
Kamran Akmal	st Haddin b Hauritz	30
Mohammad Aamer	c Katich b Hauritz	0
Abdur Rauf	b Bollinger	5
Saeed Ajmal	c Watson b Hauritz	10
Mohammad Asif	not out	1
Extras	(b 13, lb 4, w 2, nb 5)	24
Total	(all out; 72 overs)	251

Fall of wickets: 1–18 (Imran Farhat, 6.3 overs), 2–80 (Salman Butt, 22.2 overs), 3–116 (Faisal Iqbal, 31.3 overs), 4–171 (Umar Akmal, 45.4 overs), 5–171 (Misbah-ul-Haq, 45.5 overs), 6–214 (Kamran Akmal, 61.2 overs), 7–214 (Mohammad Aamer, 61.3 overs), 8–221 (Abdur Rauf, 62.6 overs), 9–250 (Mohammad Yousuf, 71.1 overs), 10–251 (Saeed Ajmal, 71.6 overs)

Bowling: DE Bollinger 15–5–42–2; PM Siddle 13–5–32–0; NM Hauritz 24–4–101–5; MG Johnson 18–6–46–3; SM Katich 2–0–13–0

Stumps scores
Day 1: Australia first innings 3–305 (Hussey 37, Hauritz 5; 90 overs)
Day 2: Pakistan first innings 4–109 (Umar Akmal 10, Mohammad Aamer 0; 49 overs)
Day 3: Australia second innings 3–111 (Watson 64, Clarke 21; 34 overs)
Day 4: Pakistan second innings 3–170 (Mohammad Yousuf 45, Umar Akmal 27; 45 overs)

Australia won by 170 runs

Second Test, Australia v Pakistan at Sydney

January 3–6, 2010 • **Toss:** Australia
Umpires: EAR de Silva (Sri Lanka) and BR Doctrove (West Indies)
TV umpire: RE Koertzen (South Africa) • **Match referee:** Ranjan Madugalle (Sri Lanka)
Player of the match: MEK Hussey (Australia)

Australia first innings

SR Watson	c Kamran Akmal b Mohammad Sami	6
PJ Hughes	c Faisal Iqbal b Mohammad Sami	0
RT Ponting	c Umar Gul b Mohammad Sami	0
MEK Hussey	c Misbah-ul-Haq b Mohammad Asif	28
MJ Clarke	b Mohammad Asif	3
MJ North	c Kamran Akmal b Mohammad Asif	10
BJ Haddin	c Mohammad Yousuf b Mohammad Asif	6
MG Johnson	c Imran Farhat b Mohammad Asif	38
NM Hauritz	b Mohammad Asif	21
PM Siddle	not out	1
DE Bollinger	b Umar Gul	9
Extras	(b 1, lb 2, w 1, nb 1)	5
Total	(all out; 44.2 overs)	**127**

Fall of wickets: 1–2 (Hughes, 3.4 overs), 2–2 (Ponting, 3.5 overs), 3–10 (Watson, 7.6 overs), 4–36 (Clarke, 17.2 overs), 5–51 (Hussey, 21.5 overs), 6–51 (North, 21.6 overs), 7–62 (Haddin, 25.1 overs), 8–106 (Hauritz, 37.4 overs), 9–117 (Johnson, 39.5 overs), 10–127 (Bollinger, 44.2 overs)

Bowling: Mohammad Asif 20–6–41–6; Mohammad Sami 12–4–27–3; Umar Gul 10.2–0–38–1; Danish Kaneria 2–0–18–0

Pakistan first innings

Imran Farhat	c Haddin b Hauritz	53
Salman Butt	c Haddin b Johnson	71
Faisal Iqbal	c Watson b Siddle	27
Mohammad Yousuf	c Haddin b Johnson	46
Umar Akmal	lbw Bollinger	49
Misbah-ul-Haq	c Haddin b Bollinger	11
Kamran Akmal	c Watson b Bollinger	14
Mohammad Sami	c Haddin b Watson	13
Umar Gul	c Bollinger b Watson	12
Danish Kaneria	c Hussey b Bollinger	4
Mohammad Asif	not out	0
Extras	(b 2, lb 16, w 5, nb 10)	33
Total	(all out; 96.5 overs)	**333**

Fall of wickets: 1–109 (Imran Farhat, 42.3 overs), 2–144 (Salman Butt, 56.6 overs), 3–205 (Faisal Iqbal, 70.5 overs), 4–237 (Mohammad Yousuf, 74.6 overs), 5–277 (Umar Akmal, 84.3 overs), 6–286 (Misbah-ul-Haq, 86.1 overs), 7–295 (Kamran Akmal, 88.1 overs), 8–323 (Umar Gul, 93.5 overs), 9–331 (Mohammad Sami, 95.2 overs), 10–333 (Danish Kaneria, 96.5 overs)

Bowling: DE Bollinger 21.5–5–72–4; PM Siddle 22–4–62–1; MG Johnson 20–2–64–2; SR Watson 17–4–40–2; NM Hauritz 16–3–77–1

Australia second innings

SR Watson	c Faisal Iqbal b Umar Gul	97
PJ Hughes	c&b Danish Kaneria	37
RT Ponting	c Faisal Iqbal b Umar Gul	11
MEK Hussey	not out	134
MJ Clarke	lbw Mohammad Asif	21
MJ North	c Faisal Iqbal b Danish Kaneria	2
BJ Haddin	lbw Danish Kaneria	15
MG Johnson	b Danish Kaneria	3
NM Hauritz	c Misbah-ul-Haq b Umar Gul	4
PM Siddle	c Misbah-ul-Haq b Mohammad Asif	38
DE Bollinger	b Danish Kaneria	0
Extras	(b 6, lb 5, w 3, nb 5)	19
Total	(all out; 125.4 overs)	**381**

Fall of wickets: 1–105 (Hughes, 31.6 overs), 2–144 (Ponting, 41.2 overs), 3–159 (Watson, 45.5 overs), 4–217 (Clarke, 61.5 overs), 5–226 (North, 66.1 overs), 6–246 (Haddin, 74.6 overs), 7–252 (Johnson, 76.3 overs), 8–257 (Hauritz, 79.2 overs), 9–380 (Siddle, 124.6 overs), 10–381 (Bollinger, 125.4 overs)

Bowling: Mohammad Asif 27–8–53–2; Mohammad Sami 19.5–4–74–0; Umar Gul 28–4–83–3; Danish Kaneria 47.5–3–151–5; Imran Farhat 3–0–9–0

Pakistan second innings

Imran Farhat	c Johnson b Bollinger	22
Salman Butt	c Haddin b Johnson	21
Faisal Iqbal	c Haddin b Johnson	7
Mohammad Yousuf	c&b Hauritz	19
Umar Akmal	c Johnson b Bollinger	49
Misbah-ul-Haq	c Hussey b Hauritz	0
Kamran Akmal	c Haddin b Johnson	11
Mohammad Sami	c Haddin b Hauritz	2
Umar Gul	c Siddle b Hauritz	6
Danish Kaneria	c Watson b Hauritz	0
Mohammad Asif	not out	0
Extras	(w 1, nb 1)	2
Total	(all out; 38 overs)	**139**

Fall of wickets: 1–34 (Imran Farhat, 6.6 overs), 2–50 (Faisal Iqbal, 10.4 overs), 3–51 (Salman Butt, 10.6 overs), 4–77 (Mohammad Yousuf, 19.3 overs), 5–77 (Misbah-ul-Haq, 19.5 overs), 6–103 (Kamran Akmal, 26.4 overs), 7–133 (Mohammad Sami, 33.5 overs), 8–133 (Umar Akmal, 34.5 overs), 9–135 (Danish Kaneria, 37.4 overs), 10–139 (Umar Gul, 37.6 overs)

Bowling: DE Bollinger 12–3–32–2; PM Siddle 4–1–27–0; NM Hauritz 12–1–53–5; MG Johnson 10–2–27–3

Stumps scores

Day 1: Pakistan first innings 0–14 (Imran Farhat 9, Salman Butt 3; 4.1 overs)
Day 2: Pakistan first innings 9–331 (Danish Kaneria 2, Mohammad Asif 0; 96 overs)
Day 3: Australia second innings 8–286 (Hussey 73, Siddle 10; 87 overs)

Australia won by 36 runs

Third Test, Australia v Pakistan at Hobart

January 14–18, 2010 • **Toss:** Australia
Umpires: EAR de Silva (Sri Lanka) and RE Koertzen (South Africa)
TV umpire: BR Doctrove (West Indies) • **Match referee:** RS Madugalle (Sri Lanka)
Player of the match: RT Ponting (Australia) • **Player of the series:** SR Watson (Australia)

Australia first innings

SR Watson	c Imran Farhat b Umar Gul	29
SM Katich	lbw Mohammad Asif	11
RT Ponting	c Mohammad Yousuf b Mohammad Aamer	209
MEK Hussey	c Sarfraz Ahmed b Mohammad Aamer	6
MJ Clarke	b Danish Kaneria	166
MJ North	c Sarfraz Ahmed b Mohammad Asif	21
BJ Haddin	c Umar Gul b Danish Kaneria	41
MG Johnson	c Sarfraz Ahmed b Danish Kaneria	8
NM Hauritz	not out	12
Extras	(b 1, lb 3, w 5, nb 7)	16
Total	**(8 wickets dec; 142.5 overs)**	**519**

Did not bat: PM Siddle, DE Bollinger

Fall of wickets: 1–28 (Katich, 6.6 overs), 2–52 (Watson, 15.6 overs), 3–71 (Hussey, 20.2 overs), 4–423 (Clarke, 122.6 overs), 5–443 (Ponting, 129.1 overs), 6–498 (Haddin, 138.3 overs), 7–499 (North, 139.1 overs), 8–519 (Johnson, 142.5 overs)

Bowling: Mohammad Asif 36–8–104–2; Mohammad Aamer 31–7–97–2; Umar Gul 25–4–98–1; Danish Kaneria 42.5–2–189–3; Shoaib Malik 8–0–27–0

Pakistan first innings

Imran Farhat	c Haddin b Siddle	38
Salman Butt	c Clarke b Katich	102
Khurram Manzoor	c Ponting b Siddle	0
Mohammad Yousuf	run out (Johnson/Haddin)	7
Umar Akmal	run out (Hussey/Haddin)	8
Shoaib Malik	c Bollinger b Hauritz	58
Sarfraz Ahmed	c Clarke b Katich	1
Mohammad Aamer	c Watson b Katich	4
Umar Gul	not out	38
Danish Kaneria	c Ponting b Hauritz	8
Mohammad Asif	c Hussey b Hauritz	29
Extras	(b 2, lb 2, w 2, nb 2)	8
Total	**(all out; 105.4 overs)**	**301**

Fall of wickets: 1–63 (Imran Farhat, 22.2 overs), 2–63 (Khurram Manzoor, 22.6 overs), 3–74 (Mohammad Yousuf, 28.6 overs), 4–84 (Umar Akmal, 33.3 overs), 5–213 (Salman Butt, 78.3 overs), 6–215 (Sarfraz Ahmed, 80.5 overs), 7–219 (Shoaib Malik, 81.6 overs), 8–227 (Mohammad Aamer, 86.6 overs), 9–248 (Danish Kaneria, 91.2 overs), 10–301 (Mohammad Asif, 105.4 overs)

Bowling: DE Bollinger 15–6–35–0; PM Siddle 20–8–39–2; MG Johnson 20–2–76–0; NM Hauritz 33.4–9–96–3; SR Watson 7–2–17–0; SM Katich 10–3–34–3

Australia second innings

SR Watson	c Mohammad Yousuf b Mohammad Aamer	1
SM Katich	c Shoaib Malik b Danish Kaneria	100
RT Ponting	c Sarfraz Ahmed b Shoaib Malik	89
MEK Hussey	not out	13
BJ Haddin	run out (Mohammad Aamer)	8
MG Johnson	c Imran Farhat b Shoaib Malik	0
Extras	(b 4, lb 4)	8
Total	**(5 wickets dec; 48.4 overs)**	**219**

Fall of wickets: 1–1 (Watson, 1.2 overs), 2–192 (Katich, 43.1 overs), 3–202 (Ponting, 46.4 overs), 4–213 (Haddin, 47.4 overs), 5–219 (Johnson, 48.4 overs)

Bowling: Mohammad Asif 9–0–48–0; Mohammad Aamer 12–2–46–1; Umar Gul 10–0–45–0; Danish Kaneria 14–2–56–1; Shoaib Malik 3.4–0–16–2

Pakistan second innings

Imran Farhat	c Haddin b Siddle	14
Salman Butt	b Bollinger	8
Khurram Manzoor	c Haddin b Hauritz	77
Mohammad Yousuf	lbw Watson	23
Umar Akmal	lbw Watson	15
Shoaib Malik	c Haddin b Siddle	19
Sarfraz Ahmed	c Clarke b Hauritz	5
Mohammad Aamer	not out	30
Umar Gul	c Clarke b Hauritz	0
Mohammad Asif	b Johnson	0
Danish Kaneria	b Siddle	1
Extras	(b 10, lb 3, nb 1)	14
Total	**(all out; 86.2 overs)**	**206**

Fall of wickets: 1–11 (Salman Butt, 4.6 overs), 2–29 (Imran Farhat, 9.6 overs), 3–61 (Mohammad Yousuf, 19.1 overs), 4–83 (Umar Akmal, 25.2 overs), 5–104 (Shoaib Malik, 36.1 overs), 6–123 (Sarfraz Ahmed, 47.1 overs), 7–189 (Khurram Manzoor, 78.5 overs), 8–191 (Umar Gul, 80.4 overs), 9–192 (Mohammad Asif, 81.4 overs), 10–206 (Danish Kaneria, 86.2 overs)

Bowling: DE Bollinger 13–4–31–1; PM Siddle 15.2–7–25–3; MG Johnson 21–4–59–1; SR Watson 17–4–38–2; NM Hauritz 17–6–30–3; SM Katich 3–1–10–0

Stumps scores

Day 1: Australia first innings 3–302 (Ponting 137, Clarke 111; 90 overs)
Day 2: Pakistan first innings 4–94 (Salman Butt 34, Shoaib Malik 4; 36 overs)
Day 3: Australia second innings 1–59 (Katich 33, Ponting 25; 18 overs)
Day 4: Pakistan second innings 4–103 (Khurram Manzoor 23, Shoaib Malik 18; 34.2 overs)

Australia won by 231 runs
Australia won the series 3–0

First Test, New Zealand v Australia at Wellington

March 19–23, 2010 • **Toss:** Australia
Umpires: Asad Rauf (Pakistan) and IJ Gould (England)
TV umpire: Aleem Dar (Pakistan) • **Match referee:** J Srinath (India)
Player of the match: MJ Clarke (Australia)

Australia first innings

PJ Hughes	c Taylor b Arnel	20
SM Katich	lbw Arnel	79
RT Ponting	run out (Watling)	41
MEK Hussey	c Watling b Martin	4
MJ Clarke	st McCullum b Vettori	168
MJ North	not out	112
BJ Haddin	not out	11
Extras	(b 2, lb 15, w 2, nb 5)	24
Total	(5 wickets dec; 131 overs)	**459**

Did not bat: MG Johnson, NM Hauritz, DE Bollinger, RJ Harris

Fall of wickets: 1–25 (Hughes, 5.5 overs), 2–104 (Ponting, 35.1 overs), 3–115 (Hussey, 38.5 overs), 4–176 (Katich, 61.5 overs), 5–429 (Clarke, 123.3 overs)

Bowling: CS Martin 30–3–115–1; TG Southee 19–4–68–0; BJ Arnel 26–4–89–2; DR Tuffey 22–7–49–0; DL Vettori 33–5–111–1; MJ Guptill 1–0–10–0

New Zealand first innings

TG McIntosh	c Hussey b Harris	9
BJ Watling	lbw Bollinger	0
PJ Ingram	run out (Johnson)	5
LRPL Taylor	c North b Bollinger	21
MJ Guptill	c Haddin b Bollinger	30
DL Vettori	c Ponting b Harris	46
BB McCullum	c Harris b Bollinger	24
DR Tuffey	run out (Hauritz)	0
TG Southee	c Haddin b Johnson	5
BJ Arnel	c Ponting b Bollinger	0
CS Martin	not out	0
Extras	(lb 4, w 2, nb 11)	17
Total	(all out; 59.1 overs)	**157**

Fall of wickets: 1–3 (Watling, 0.5 overs), 2–14 (Ingram, 12.6 overs), 3–31 (McIntosh, 17.4 overs), 4–43 (Taylor, 26.1 overs), 5–112 (Vettori, 47.5 overs), 6–148 (McCullum, 56.1 overs), 7–148 (Guptill, 56.3 overs), 8–154 (Tuffey, 58.3 overs), 9–156 (Arnel, 58.4 overs), 10–157 (Southee, 59.1 overs)

Bowling: DE Bollinger 13–4–28–5; RJ Harris 17–4–42–2; MG Johnson 11.1–5–38–1; NM Hauritz 14–4–39–0; MJ North 4–1–6–0

New Zealand second innings (following on)

BJ Watling	lbw Bollinger	33
TG McIntosh	c Katich b Hauritz	83
PJ Ingram	c Haddin b Bollinger	1
LRPL Taylor	lbw Hauritz	25
MJ Guptill	c North b Harris	6
DL Vettori	b Hauritz	77
BB McCullum	c Clarke b Harris	104
DR Tuffey	not out	47
TG Southee	c Clarke b Harris	0
BJ Arnel	lbw Harris	3
CS Martin	b Johnson	1
Extras	(b 1, lb 14, w 1, nb 11)	27
Total	(all out; 134.5 overs)	**407**

Fall of wickets: 1–70 (Watling, 34.2 overs), 2–78 (Ingram, 38.3 overs), 3–115 (Taylor, 47.3 overs), 4–136 (Guptill, 58.6 overs), 5–183 (McIntosh, 69.5 overs), 6–309 (Vettori, 105.6 overs), 7–388 (McCullum, 127.5 overs), 8–392 (Southee, 129.1 overs), 9–396 (Arnel, 131.6 overs), 10–407 (Martin, 134.5 overs)

Bowling: DE Bollinger 27–3–80–2; RJ Harris 24–3–77–4; MG Johnson 29.5–7–107–1; NM Hauritz 49–16–119–3; MJ North 5–2–9–0

Australia second innings

PJ Hughes	not out	86
SM Katich	not out	18
Extras	(nb 2)	2
Total	(0 wickets; 23 overs)	**106**

Bowling: CS Martin 6–0–43–0; BJ Arnel 10–2–31–0; DL Vettori 7–1–32–0

Stumps scores
Day 1: Australia first innings 4–316 (Clarke 100, North 52; 90 overs)
Day 2: New Zealand first innings 4–108 (Guptill 19, Vettori 42; 47 overs)
Day 3: New Zealand second innings 5–187 (Vettori 18, McCullum 4; 72 overs)
Day 4: New Zealand second innings 6–369 (McCullum 94, Tuffey 23; 124 overs)

Australia won by 10 wickets
Australia retained the Trans-Tasman Trophy

Second Test, New Zealand v Australia at Hamilton

March 27–31, 2010 • **Toss:** Australia
Umpires: Aleem Dar (Pakistan) and Asad Rauf (Pakistan)
TV umpire: IJ Gould (England) • **Match referee:** J Srinath (India)
Player of the match: MG Johnson (Australia)

Australia first innings

SR Watson	c Arnel b Southee	12
SM Katich	c Watling b Vettori	88
RT Ponting	run out (Vettori)	22
MEK Hussey	c McCullum b Southee	22
MJ Clarke	c Southee b Patel	28
MJ North	lbw Southee	9
BJ Haddin	c&b Southee	12
MG Johnson	c McIntosh b Vettori	0
NM Hauritz	not out	12
RJ Harris	lbw Vettori	10
DE Bollinger	b Vettori	4
Extras	(b 4, lb 6, nb 2)	12
Total	(all out; 74.3 overs)	**231**

Fall of wickets: 1–25 (Watson, 7.4 overs), 2–63 (Ponting, 23.3 overs), 3–129 (Hussey, 39.2 overs), 4–172 (Clarke, 49.3 overs), 5–180 (Katich, 56.4 overs), 6–199 (Haddin, 65.6 overs), 7–200 (Johnson, 66.6 overs), 8–200 (North, 67.1 overs), 9–217 (Harris, 72.2 overs), 10–231 (Bollinger, 74.3 overs)

Bowling: CS Martin 12–3–42–0; TG Southee 19–3–61–4; BJ Arnel 12–2–53–0; DL Vettori 19.3–5–36–4; JS Patel 12–2–29–1

New Zealand first innings

TG McIntosh	b Bollinger	4
BJ Watling	b Bollinger	46
MS Sinclair	b Johnson	11
LRPL Taylor	c Haddin b Bollinger	138
MJ Guptill	c Ponting b Harris	4
DL Vettori	c Haddin b Harris	15
BB McCullum	c Ponting b Johnson	5
JS Patel	c Ponting b Johnson	7
TG Southee	not out	22
BJ Arnel	c Haddin b Johnson	7
CS Martin	b Harris	0
Extras	(w 1, nb 4)	5
Total	(all out; 63.3 overs)	**264**

Fall of wickets: 1–4 (McIntosh, 0.6 overs), 2–30 (Sinclair, 18.5 overs), 3–114 (Watling, 32.1 overs), 4–143 (Guptill, 38.4 overs), 5–167 (Vettori, 42.2 overs), 6–193 (McCullum, 50.3 overs), 7–234 (Patel, 56.6 overs), 8–236 (Taylor, 57.6 overs), 9–263 (Arnel, 62.6 overs), 10–264 (Martin, 63.3 overs)

Bowling: DE Bollinger 14–3–57–3; RJ Harris 15.3–3–50–3; MG Johnson 16–2–59–4; NM Hauritz 13–1–68–0; SR Watson 5–1–30–0

Australia second innings

SR Watson	c Watling b Southee	65
SM Katich	c McCullum b Arnel	106
RT Ponting	c Watling b Southee	6
MEK Hussey	c McCullum b Arnel	67
MJ Clarke	lbw Arnel	63
MJ North	c McCullum b Vettori	90
BJ Haddin	b Patel	48
MG Johnson	c Patel b Vettori	0
NM Hauritz	not out	41
RJ Harris	not out	18
Extras	(b 2, lb 1, nb 4)	7
Total	(8 wickets dec; 153 overs)	**511**

Fall of wickets: 1–85 (Watson, 32.4 overs), 2–91 (Ponting, 34.2 overs), 3–246 (Hussey, 89.3 overs), 4–247 (Katich, 91.6 overs), 5–389 (Clarke, 127.6 overs), 6–443 (North, 136.1 overs), 7–443 (Johnson, 136.2 overs), 8–453 (Haddin, 141.1 overs)

Bowling: CS Martin 14–1–60–0; TG Southee 23–4–89–2; BJ Arnel 26–6–77–3; DL Vettori 48–10–140–2; JS Patel 39–8–141–1; MS Sinclair 3–2–1–0

New Zealand second innings

BJ Watling	c Haddin b Johnson	24
TG McIntosh	b Johnson	19
MS Sinclair	lbw Clarke	29
LRPL Taylor	c Haddin b Johnson	22
MJ Guptill	c Ponting b Johnson	58
DL Vettori	lbw Hauritz	22
BB McCullum	c Hussey b Bollinger	51
JS Patel	c North b Bollinger	3
TG Southee	c Clarke b Johnson	45
BJ Arnel	c Haddin b Johnson	0
CS Martin	not out	5
Extras	(b 12, lb 10, nb 2)	24
Total	(all out; 91.1 overs)	**302**

Fall of wickets: 1–40 (McIntosh, 13.2 overs), 2–53 (Watling, 17.5 overs), 3–107 (Taylor, 33.6 overs), 4–119 (Sinclair, 38.3 overs), 5–152 (Vettori, 47.5 overs), 6–239 (McCullum, 80.3 overs), 7–249 (Patel, 84.1 overs), 8–273 (Guptill, 87.5 overs), 9–295 (Arnel, 89.3 overs), 10–302 (Southee, 91.1 overs)

Bowling: DE Bollinger 16–2–87–2; RJ Harris 14–3–38–0; SR Watson 6–2–18–0; MG Johnson 20.1–6–73–6; MJ Clarke 16–4–27–1; NM Hauritz 17–5–37–1; MJ North 2–2–0–0

Stumps scores
Day 1: New Zealand first innings 1–19 (Watling 6, Sinclair 8; 13 overs)
Day 2: Australia second innings 0–35 (Watson 28, Katich 6; 14 overs)
Day 3: Australia second innings 4–333 (Clarke 42, North 42; 114 overs)
Day 4: New Zealand second innings 5–185 (Guptill 29, McCullum 19; 62 overs)

Australia won by 176 runs
Australia won series 2–0

First Test, Pakistan v Australia, at Lord's

July 13–16, 2010 • **Toss:** Pakistan
Umpires: RE Koertzen (South Africa) and IJ Gould (England)
TV umpire: Ahsan Raza (Pakistan) • **Match referee:** BC Broad (England)
Players of the match: SM Katich (Australia) and Salman Butt (Pakistan

Australia first innings

SR Watson	b Mohammad Aamer	4
SM Katich	c Kamran Akmal b Mohammad Asif	80
RT Ponting	c Umar Amin b Mohammad Aamer	26
MJ Clarke	lbw Mohammad Asif	47
MEK Hussey	not out	56
MJ North	b Mohammad Aamer	0
TD Paine	c Kamran Akmal b Umar Gul	7
SPD Smith	lbw Danish Kaneria	1
MG Johnson	b Danish Kaneria	3
BW Hilfenhaus	b Mohammad Aamer	1
DE Bollinger	b Mohammad Aamer	4
Extras	(b 10, lb 2, w 2, nb 10)	24
Total	(all out; 76.5 overs)	253

Fall of wickets: 1–8 (Watson, 4.4 overs), 2–51 (Ponting, 16.6 overs), 3–171 (Clarke, 42.6 overs), 4–174 (Katich, 44.3 overs), 5–174 (North, 44.6 overs), 6–206 (Paine, 58.1 overs), 7–208 (Smith, 59.1 overs), 8–213 (Johnson, 61.6 overs), 9–222 (Hilfenhaus, 64.6 overs), 10–253 (Bollinger, 76.5 overs)

Bowling: Mohammad Aamer 19.5–2–72–4; Mohammad Asif 19–5–63–3; Umar Gul 17–3–32–1; Shahid Afridi 3–0–25–0; Danish Kaneria 18–7–49–2

Australia second innings

SR Watson	c Imran Farhat b Mohammad Asif	31
SM Katich	c Kamran Akmal b Umar Gul	83
RT Ponting	lbw Mohammad Asif	0
MJ Clarke	b Umar Gul	12
MEK Hussey	c Imran Farhat b Umar Gul	0
MG Johnson	b Umar Gul	30
MJ North	c Kamran Akmal b Mohammad Asif	20
TD Paine	b Shahid Afridi	47
SPD Smith	lbw Danish Kaneria	12
BW Hilfenhaus	not out	56
DE Bollinger	b Danish Kaneria	21
Extras	(b 6, lb 5, w 2, nb 9)	22
Total	(all out; 91 overs)	334

Fall of wickets: 1–61 (Watson, 16.3 overs), 2–73 (Ponting, 18.3 overs), 3–97 (Clarke, 26.3 overs), 4–97 (Hussey, 26.4 overs), 5–149 (Johnson, 42.6 overs), 6–188 (Katich, 54.5 overs), 7–188 (North, 55.1 overs), 8–208 (Smith, 61.2 overs), 9–282 (Paine, 79.4 overs), 10–334 (Bollinger, 90.6 overs)

Bowling: Mohammad Aamer 18–3–67–0; Mohammad Asif 21–3–77–3; Umar Gul 21–5–61–4; Danish Kaneria 17–2–74–2; Shahid Afridi 14–0–44–1

Pakistan first innings

Imran Farhat	c Paine b Hilfenhaus	4
Salman Butt	b Watson	63
Azhar Ali	c Paine b Hilfenhaus	16
Umar Amin	c Paine b Johnson	1
Umar Akmal	lbw Watson	5
Kamran Akmal	lbw Watson	0
Shahid Afridi	c Johnson b Watson	31
Mohammad Aamer	c Paine b Bollinger	0
Umar Gul	c Watson b Bollinger	7
Danish Kaneria	c Smith b Watson	14
Mohammad Asif	not out	4
Extras	(lb 2, nb 1)	3
Total	(all out; 40.5 overs)	148

Fall of wickets: 1–11 (Imran Farhat, 6.1 overs), 2–45 (Azhar Ali, 16.6 overs), 3–54 (Umar Amin, 19.2 overs), 4–75 (Umar Akmal, 26.4 overs), 5–83 (Kamran Akmal, 28.1 overs), 6–117 (Shahid Afridi, 30.6 overs), 7–117 (Mohammad Aamer, 31.2 overs), 8–129 (Umar Gul, 35.4 overs), 9–133 (Salman Butt, 36.6 overs), 10–148 (Danish Kaneria, 40.5 overs)

Bowling: DE Bollinger 11–3–38–2; BW Hilfenhaus 12–2–37–2; MG Johnson 10–2–31–1; SR Watson 7.5–1–40–5

Pakistan second innings

Imran Farhat	c Watson b Smith	24
Salman Butt	st Paine b North	92
Azhar Ali	c Paine b Hilfenhaus	42
Umar Amin	c Katich b North	33
Umar Akmal	c Clarke b North	22
Kamran Akmal	b Smith	46
Shahid Afridi	c Hussey b North	2
Mohammad Aamer	c Hussey b North	19
Umar Gul	c Ponting b Smith	1
Danish Kaneria	c Ponting b North	2
Mohammad Asif	not out	1
Extras	(b 2, lb 1, nb 2)	5
Total	(all out; 91.1 overs)	289

Fall of wickets: 1–50 (Imran Farhat, 15.1 overs), 2–152 (Azhar Ali, 46.6 overs), 3–186 (Salman Butt, 55.1 overs), 4–216 (Umar Akmal, 63.3 overs), 5–227 (Umar Amin, 67.1 overs), 6–229 (Shahid Afridi, 67.5 overs), 7–283 (Kamran Akmal, 86.5 overs), 8–285 (Mohammad Aamer, 87.4 overs), 9–287 (Umar Gul, 90.1 overs), 10–289 (Danish Kaneria, 91.1 overs)

Bowling: DE Bollinger 12–4–43–0; BW Hilfenhaus 16–8–37–1; MG Johnson 18–5–74–0; SPD Smith 21–5–51–3; SR Watson 6–0–26–0; MJ North 18.1–1–55–6

Stumps scores

Day 1: Australia first innings 9–229 (Hussey 39, Bollinger 0; 70 overs)
Day 2: Australia second innings 4–100 (Katich 49, Johnson 2; 29.3 overs)
Day 3: Pakistan second innings 1–114 (Salman Butt 58, Azhar Ali 28; 37 overs)

Australia won by 150 runs

Second Test, Pakistan v Australia, at Leeds

July 21–24, 2010 • Toss: Pakistan
Umpires: RE Koertzen (South Africa) and IJ Gould (England)
TV umpire: Nadeem Ghauri (Pakistan) • Match referee: BC Broad (England)
Players of the match: SR Watson (Australia) and Mohammad Aamer (Pakistan

Australia first innings

SR Watson	lbw Mohammad Asif	5
SM Katich	lbw Mohammad Aamer	13
RT Ponting	lbw Mohammad Asif	6
MJ Clarke	b Umar Gul	3
MEK Hussey	lbw Umar Gul	5
MJ North	c Kamran Akmal b Umar Amin	16
TD Paine	c Kamran Akmal b Mohammad Asif	17
SPD Smith	b Mohammad Aamer	10
MG Johnson	b Mohammad Aamer	0
BW Hilfenhaus	run out (Umar Amin/Kamran Akmal)	3
DE Bollinger	not out	2
Extras	(lb 6, nb 2)	8
Total	(all out; 33.1 overs)	88

Fall of wickets: 1–20 (Katich, 6.1 overs), 2–20 (Watson, 7.2 overs), 3–27 (Clarke, 12.3 overs), 4–29 (Ponting, 13.5 overs), 5–41 (Hussey, 16.5 overs), 6–60 (North, 22.5 overs), 7–73 (Smith, 25.1 overs), 8–73 (Johnson, 25.2 overs), 9–86 (Hilfenhaus, 32.4 overs), 10–88 (Paine, 33.1 overs)

Bowling: Mohammad Aamer 11–4–20–3; Mohammad Asif 10.1–1–30–3; Umar Gul 9–3–16–2; Umar Amin 2–0–7–1; Danish Kaneria 1–0–9–0

Australia second innings

SR Watson	b Umar Amin	24
SM Katich	b Mohammad Aamer	11
RT Ponting	c Kamran Akmal b Mohammad Aamer	66
MJ Clarke	c Kamran Akmal b Mohammad Asif	77
MEK Hussey	c Umar Akmal b Mohammad Aamer	8
MJ North	b Mohammad Aamer	0
TD Paine	c Azhar Ali b Danish Kaneria	33
SPD Smith	b Umar Gul	77
MG Johnson	lbw Mohammad Asif	12
BW Hilfenhaus	c Umar Akmal b Danish Kaneria	17
DE Bollinger	not out	0
Extras	(b 4, lb 10, w 2, nb 8)	24
Total	(all out; 95.3 overs)	349

Fall of wickets: 1–15 (Katich, 4.3 overs), 2–55 (Watson, 15.5 overs), 3–144 (Ponting, 43.4 overs), 4–158 (Hussey, 47.2 overs), 5–164 (North, 49.1 overs), 6–217 (Clarke, 66.1 overs), 7–246 (Paine, 75.3 overs), 8–283 (Johnson, 84.3 overs), 9–320 (Hilfenhaus, 89.5 overs), 10–349 (Smith, 95.3 overs)

Bowling: Mohammad Aamer 27–6–86–4; Mohammad Asif 26–4–83–2; Umar Gul 15.3–1–80–1; Umar Amin 6–1–12–1; Danish Kaneria 21–2–74–2

Pakistan first innings

Imran Farhat	lbw Watson	43
Salman Butt	b Hilfenhaus	45
Azhar Ali	c Paine b Watson	30
Umar Amin	c North b Hilfenhaus	25
Umar Akmal	c Paine b Johnson	21
Shoaib Malik	c Paine b Watson	26
Kamran Akmal	c North b Watson	15
Mohammad Aamer	lbw Watson	0
Umar Gul	b Watson	0
Danish Kaneria	run out (Smith)	15
Mohammad Asif	not out	9
Extras	(b 11, lb 9, nb 9)	29
Total	(all out; 64.5 overs)	258

Fall of wickets: 1–80 (Salman Butt, 19.4 overs), 2–133 (Imran Farhat, 33.3 overs), 3–140 (Azhar Ali, 37.2 overs), 4–171 (Umar Akmal, 43.4 overs), 5–195 (Umar Amin, 50.3 overs), 6–222 (Kamran Akmal, 56.5 overs), 7–222 (Mohammad Aamer, 56.6 overs), 8–224 (Umar Gul, 58.6 overs), 9–234 (Shoaib Malik, 60.5 overs), 10–258 (Danish Kaneria, 64.5 overs)

Bowling: DE Bollinger 17–4–50–0; BW Hilfenhaus 20.5–3–77–2; SR Watson 11–3–33–6; MG Johnson 15–0–71–1; SPD Smith 1–0–7–0

Pakistan second innings

Imran Farhat	b Bollinger	67
Salman Butt	c Clarke b Hilfenhaus	13
Azhar Ali	c Paine b Bollinger	51
Umar Amin	c Paine b Bollinger	0
Umar Akmal	c Paine b Hilfenhaus	8
Shoaib Malik	c North b Hilfenhaus	10
Kamran Akmal	c Hussey b Johnson	13
Mohammad Aamer	not out	5
Umar Gul	not out	1
Extras	(lb 7, nb 5)	12
Total	(7 wickets; 50.4 overs)	180

Fall of wickets: 1–27 (Salman Butt, 5.1 overs), 2–137 (Imran Farhat, 32.6 overs), 3–137 (Umar Amin, 34.6 overs), 4–146 (Azhar Ali, 38.4 overs), 5–150 (Umar Akmal, 41.4 overs), 6–161 (Shoaib Malik, 45.4 overs), 7–179 (Kamran Akmal, 50.3 overs)

Bowling: DE Bollinger 13–2–51–3; BW Hilfenhaus 13–2–39–3; MG Johnson 10.4–1–41–1; SR Watson 5–1–18–0; SPD Smith 9–2–24–0

Stumps scores
Day 1: Pakistan first innings 3–148 (Umar Amin 1, Umar Akmal 8; 39 overs)
Day 2: Australia second innings 2–136 (Ponting 61, Clarke 32; 41 overs)
Day 3: Pakistan second innings 3–140 (Azhar Ali 47, Umar Akmal 2; 37 overs)

Pakistan won by three wickets
Series tied 1–1

ICC Champions Trophy, Game Five

Australia v West Indies at Johannesburg (Group A)
September 26, 2009 • **Toss:** West Indies
Umpires: Asad Rauf (Pakistan) and AL Hill (New Zealand)
TV umpire: BF Bowden (New Zealand)
Match referee: JJ Crowe (New Zealand)
Player of the match: MG Johnson (Australia)

Australia innings

SR Watson	b Roach	0
TD Paine	c Walton b Bernard	33
RT Ponting	st Walton b Miller	79
MEK Hussey	c Fletcher b Bernard	6
CJ Ferguson	b Roach	20
CL White	b Miller	4
JR Hopes	c Walton b Sammy	5
MG Johnson	not out	73
B Lee	run out (Walton/Sammy)	25
NM Hauritz	not out	7
Extras	(lb 7, w 9, nb 7)	23
Total	**(8 wickets; 50 overs)**	**275**

Did not bat: PM Siddle

Fall of wickets: 1–0 (Watson, 0.1 overs), 2–85 (Paine, 19.1 overs), 3–120 (Hussey, 25.2 overs), 4–148 (Ponting, 30.3 overs), 5–162 (White, 34.5 overs), 6–164 (Ferguson, 35.3 overs), 7–171 (Hopes, 39.2 overs), 8–241 (Lee, 47.6 overs)

Bowling: KAJ Roach 10–0–73–2; GC Tonge 10–1–55–0; DJG Sammy 10–0–53–1; DE Bernard 10–0–63–2; NO Miller 10–1–24–2

West Indies innings

DS Smith	c Paine b Siddle	17
ADS Fletcher	run out (Johnson)	54
TM Dowlin	c Paine b Lee	55
CAK Walton	b Hopes	0
FL Reifer	c Hauritz b Watson	28
DE Bernard	b Siddle	8
DJG Sammy	c Hussey b Watson	20
NO Miller	c Ponting b Hauritz	4
KAJ Roach	c Johnson b Hauritz	3
GC Tonge	not out	0
DM Richards	absent hurt	–
Extras	(b 1, lb 18, w 16, nb 1)	36
Total	**(all out; 46.5 overs)**	**225**

Fall of wickets: 1–38 (Smith, 5.4 overs), 2–124 (Fletcher, 24.3 overs), 3–128 (Walton, 25.2 overs), 4–170 (Dowlin, 36.4 overs), 5–187 (Bernard, 39.1 overs), 6–215 (Sammy, 44.1 overs), 7–219 (Reifer, 44.5 overs), 8–225 (Miller, 46.4 overs), 9–225 (Roach, 46.5 overs)

Bowling: B Lee 8–0–41–1; PM Siddle 8–1–37–2; MG Johnson 10–0–44–0; SR Watson 7–0–34–2; NM Hauritz 7.5–0–23–2; JR Hopes 6–1–27–1

Australia won by 50 runs

ICC Champions Trophy, Game Nine

Australia v India at Centurion (Group A)
September 28, 2009 • **Toss:** Australia
Umpires: BF Bowden (New Zealand) and IJ Gould (England)
TV umpire: Asad Rauf (Pakistan)
Match referee: JJ Crowe (New Zealand)

Australia innings

SR Watson	c Harbhajan Singh b Nehra	0
TD Paine	c Harbhajan Singh b Mishra	56
RT Ponting	run out (Gambhir)	65
MEK Hussey	c Tendulkar b Sharma	67
CL White	not out	35
CJ Ferguson	not out	2
Extras	(b 1, lb 1, w 7)	9
Total	**(4 wickets; 42.3 overs)**	**234**

Did not bat: JR Hopes, MG Johnson, B Lee, NM Hauritz, PM Siddle

Fall of wickets: 1–3 (Watson, 2.2 overs), 2–87 (Paine, 16.4 overs), 3–175 (Ponting, 32.5 overs), 4–227 (Hussey, 40.1 overs)

Bowling: A Nehra 8–1–38–1; P Kumar 8–0–34–0; I Sharma 7.3–0–53–1; A Mishra 9–0–45–1; Harbhajan Singh 9–0–54–0; SK Raina 1–0–8–0

India: G Gambhir, SR Tendulkar, R Dravid, SK Raina, MS Dhoni, V Kohli, A Mishra, Harbhajan Singh, A Nehra, I Sharma, P Kumar

No result

ICC Champions Trophy, Game 11

Australia v Pakistan at Centurion (Group A)
September 30, 2009 • **Toss:** Australia
Umpires: BF Bowden (New Zealand) and
AL Hill (New Zealand)
TV umpire: IJ Gould (England)
Match referee: J Srinath (India)
Player of the match: MEK Hussey (Australia)

Pakistan innings

Kamran Akmal	b Watson	44
Shahid Afridi	c Hopes b Johnson	15
Younis Khan	c Johnson b Hopes	18
Shoaib Malik	c Ponting b Johnson	27
Mohammad Yousuf	c White b Lee	45
Misbah-ul-Haq	hit wicket b Watson	41
Umar Akmal	not out	2
Naved-ul-Hasan	not out	7
Extras	(w 6)	6
Total	**(6 wickets; 50 overs)**	**205**

Did not bat: Umar Gul, Mohammad Asif, Saeed Ajmal

Fall of wickets: 1–30 (Shahid Afridi, 7.1 overs), 2–75 (Kamran Akmal, 18.3 overs), 3–89 (Younis Khan, 23.4 overs), 4–123 (Shoaib Malik, 31.5 overs), 5–186 (Mohammad Yousuf, 46.2 overs), 6–198 (Misbah-ul-Haq, 49.3 overs)

Bowling: B Lee 10–0–30–1; PM Siddle 5–0–24–0; MG Johnson 10–0–45–2; SR Watson 8–0–32–2; JR Hopes 10–0–50–1; NM Hauritz 7–1–24–0

Australia innings

SR Watson	c Kamran Akmal b Umar Gul	24
TD Paine	lbw Shahid Afridi	29
RT Ponting	c Umar Gul b Shoaib Malik	32
MEK Hussey	b Naved-ul-Hasan	64
CJ Ferguson	b Saeed Ajmal	7
CL White	b Mohammad Asif	5
JR Hopes	c Younis Khan b Mohammad Asif	1
MG Johnson	b Saeed Ajmal	9
B Lee	not out	12
NM Hauritz	not out	9
Extras	(b 1, w 12, nb 1)	14
Total	**(8 wickets; 50 overs)**	**206**

Did not bat: PM Siddle

Fall of wickets: 1–44 (Watson, 8.4 overs), 2–59 (Paine, 11.3 overs), 3–140 (Ponting, 31.2 overs), 4–157 (Ferguson, 36.4 overs), 5–174 (Hussey, 40.5 overs), 6–175 (Hopes, 41.2 overs), 7–176 (White, 41.5 overs), 8–187 (Johnson, 45.5 overs)

Bowling: Umar Gul 9–1–38–1; Mohammad Asif 8–0–34–2; Shahid Afridi 10–0–47–1; Naved-ul-Hasan 9–2–39–1; Saeed Ajmal 10–1–31–2; Shoaib Malik 4–0–16–1

Australia won by two wickets

ICC Champions Trophy, First Semi-Final

Australia v England at Centurion
October 2, 2009 • **Toss:** England
Umpires: Aleem Dar (Pakistan) and
BF Bowden (New Zealand)
TV umpire: AL Hill (New Zealand)
Match referee: JJ Crowe (New Zealand)
Player of the match: SR Watson (Australia)

England innings

AJ Strauss	c Hopes b Siddle	14
JL Denly	c Paine b Siddle	36
OA Shah	c Paine b Lee	0
PD Collingwood	c Paine b Johnson	34
EJG Morgan	c Paine b Watson	9
SM Davies	b Watson	5
LJ Wright	c Paine b Siddle	48
TT Bresnan	b Lee	80
GP Swann	run out (Hauritz/Paine)	18
JM Anderson	not out	5
G Onions	run out (Ferguson/Paine)	1
Extras	(w 6, nb 1)	7
Total	**(all out; 47.4 overs)**	**257**

Fall of wickets: 1–15 (Strauss, 1.6 overs), 2–16 (Shah, 2.4 overs), 3–71 (Collingwood, 11.2 overs), 4–91 (Denly, 17.2 overs), 5–100 (Davies, 18.5 overs), 6–101 (Morgan, 20.2 overs), 7–208 (Wright, 39.6 overs), 8–245 (Swann, 45.1 overs), 9–251 (Bresnan, 46.2 overs), 10–257 (Onions, 47.4 overs)

Bowling: B Lee 9–0–46–2; PM Siddle 10–0–55–3; JR Hopes 4–0–28–0; MG Johnson 10–1–61–1; SR Watson 8.4–1–35–2; NM Hauritz 6–0–32–0

Australia innings

SR Watson	not out	136
TD Paine	c Davies b Onions	4
RT Ponting	not out	111
Extras	(lb 2, w 5)	7
Total	**(1 wicket; 41.5 overs)**	**258**

Did not bat: MEK Hussey, CL White, CJ Ferguson, JR Hopes, MG Johnson, B Lee, NM Hauritz, PM Siddle

Fall of wicket: 1–6 (Paine, 1.3 overs)

Bowling: JM Anderson 8.5–0–48–0; G Onions 8–0–47–1; TT Bresnan 8–0–51–0; PD Collingwood 8–0–50–0; GP Swann 5–0–31–0; LJ Wright 3–0–18–0; OA Shah 1–0–11–0

Australia won by nine wickets

ICC Champions Trophy, Final

Australia v New Zealand at Centurion
October 5, 2009 • Toss: New Zealand
Umpires: Aleem Dar (Pakistan) and IJ Gould (England) • TV
umpire: Asad Rauf (Pakistan)
Match referee: RS Mahanama (Sri Lanka)
Player of the match: SR Watson (Australia)
Player of the series: RT Ponting (Australia)

New Zealand innings

BB McCullum	c Paine b Siddle	0
AJ Redmond	st Paine b Hauritz	26
MJ Guptill	c&b Hauritz	40
LRPL Taylor	c Hussey b Johnson	6
GD Elliott	lbw Lee	9
NT Broom	run out (Hussey/Watson)	37
JEC Franklin	b Lee	33
KD Mills	run out (Ponting)	12
IG Butler	lbw Hauritz	6
JS Patel	not out	16
SE Bond	not out	3
Extras	(b 1, lb 2, w 9)	12
Total	(9 wickets; 50 overs)	200

Fall of wickets: 1–5 (McCullum, 3.2 overs), 2–66 (Redmond, 18.3 overs), 3–77 (Guptill, 22.2 overs), 4–81 (Taylor, 23.1 overs), 5–94 (Elliott, 26.4 overs), 6–159 (Broom, 40.5 overs), 7–166 (Franklin, 41.6 overs), 8–174 (Butler, 43.4 overs), 9–187 (Mills, 46.4 overs)

Bowling: B Lee 10–1–45–2; PM Siddle 10–1–30–1; MG Johnson 10–1–35–1; SR Watson 10–0–50–0; NM Hauritz 10–0–37–3

Australia innings

SR Watson	not out	105
TD Paine	c Taylor b Bond	1
RT Ponting	lbw Mills	1
CL White	b Mills	62
MEK Hussey	c Patel b Mills	11
JR Hopes	not out	22
Extras	(lb 3, w 1)	4
Total	(4 wickets; 45.2 overs)	206

Did not bat: CJ Ferguson, MG Johnson, B Lee, NM Hauritz, PM Siddle

Fall of wickets: 1–2 (Paine, 1.2 overs), 2–6 (Ponting, 2.2 overs), 3–134 (White, 34.5 overs), 4–156 (Hussey, 38.3 overs)

Bowling: KD Mills 10–2–27–3; SE Bond 10–2–34–1; IG Butler 9–0–50–0; JEC Franklin 9–0–42–0; JS Patel 6.2–0–44–0; GD Elliott 1–0–6–0

Australia won by six wickets
Australia won the ICC Champions Trophy

First ODI, Australia v India at Vadodara

October 25, 2009 • Toss: Australia
Umpires: AM Saheba (India) and SK Tarapore (India)
TV umpire: S Asnani (India)
Match referee: BC Broad (England)
Player of the match: MEK Hussey (Australia)

Australia innings

SR Watson	lbw Nehra	5
TD Paine	c Dhoni b Sharma	50
RT Ponting	lbw Jadeja	74
CL White	c Raina b Nehra	51
MEK Hussey	c Kohli b Sharma	73
AC Voges	c Gambhir b Harbhajan Singh	3
JR Hopes	run out (Sehwag/Nehra)	14
MG Johnson	not out	14
B Lee	b Sharma	0
Extras	(lb 2, w 4, nb 2)	8
Total	(8 wickets; 50 overs)	292

Did not bat: NM Hauritz, PM Siddle

Fall of wickets: 1–5 (Watson, 1.2 overs), 2–102 (Paine, 18.6 overs), 3–151 (Ponting, 29.3 overs), 4–227 (White, 42.2 overs), 5–233 (Voges, 43.5 overs), 6–256 (Hopes, 46.3 overs), 7–291 (Hussey, 49.1 overs), 8–292 (Lee, 49.6 overs)

Bowling: P Kumar 10–0–77–0; A Nehra 10–0–58–2; I Sharma 10–0–50–3; Harbhajan Singh 10–0–57–1; RA Jadeja 9–0–39–1; SK Raina 1–0–9–0

India innings

V Sehwag	c Paine b Lee	13
SR Tendulkar	c Ponting b Watson	14
G Gambhir	lbw Johnson	68
V Kohli	c Watson b Voges	30
MS Dhoni	c Lee b Watson	34
SK Raina	c&b Johnson	9
RA Jadeja	lbw Hauritz	5
Harbhajan Singh	b Siddle	49
P Kumar	not out	40
A Nehra	not out	2
Extras	(lb 10, w 14)	24
Total	(8 wickets; 50 overs)	288

Did not bat: I Sharma

Fall of wickets: 1–25 (Sehwag, 4.2 overs), 2–45 (Tendulkar, 8.1 overs), 3–103 (Kohli, 20.4 overs), 4–167 (Gambhir, 34.1 overs), 5–183 (Raina, 36.3 overs), 6–186 (Dhoni, 37.2 overs), 7–201 (Jadeja, 39.5 overs), 8–285 (Harbhajan Singh, 49.2 overs)

Bowling: B Lee 6–0–28–1; PM Siddle 9–0–55–1; SR Watson 10–0–70–2; MG Johnson 10–0–59–2; JR Hopes 2–0–10–0; AC Voges 4–0–22–1; NM Hauritz 9–1–34–1

Australia won by four runs

Second ODI, Australia v India at Nagpur

October 28, 2009 • **Toss:** Australia
Umpires: AM Saheba (India) and SK Tarapore (India)
TV umpire: SS Hazare (India)
Match referee: BC Broad (England)
Player of the match: MS Dhoni (India)

India innings

V Sehwag	c Hilfenhaus b Johnson	40
SR Tendulkar	c White b Siddle	4
G Gambhir	run out (Hauritz)	76
Yuvraj Singh	c&b Hilfenhaus	23
MS Dhoni	c Paine b Johnson	124
SK Raina	c Paine b Johnson	62
Harbhajan Singh	not out	1
P Kumar	run out (Siddle/Paine)	1
Extras	(b 1, lb 6, w 14, nb 2)	23
Total	(7 wickets; 50 overs)	354

Did not bat: RA Jadeja, A Nehra, I Sharma

Fall of wickets: 1–21 (Tendulkar, 3.3 overs), 2–67 (Sehwag, 10.1 overs), 3–97 (Yuvraj Singh, 15.1 overs), 4–216 (Gambhir, 33.6 overs), 5–352 (Dhoni, 49.3 overs), 6–353 (Raina, 49.5 overs), 7–354 (Kumar, 49.6 overs)

Bowling: BW Hilfenhaus 10–0–83–1; PM Siddle 10–0–55–1; MG Johnson 10–0–75–3; NM Hauritz 10–0–54–0; AC Voges 5–0–33–0; SR Watson 5–0–47–0

Australia innings

SR Watson	c Tendulkar b Sharma	19
TD Paine	b Kumar	8
RT Ponting	lbw Kumar	12
CL White	c Raina b Harbhajan Singh	23
MEK Hussey	b Jadeja	53
AC Voges	b Jadeja	36
SE Marsh	st Dhoni b Jadeja	21
MG Johnson	b Nehra	21
NM Hauritz	not out	30
PM Siddle	c Dhoni b Sharma	3
BW Hilfenhaus	run out (Yuvraj Singh/Dhoni)	16
Extras	(lb 5, w 8)	13
Total	(all out; 48.3 overs)	255

Fall of wickets: 1–20 (Paine, 4.6 overs), 2–41 (Watson, 9.1 overs), 3–45 (Ponting, 10.1 overs), 4–93 (White, 20.6 overs), 5–140 (Hussey, 30.3 overs), 6–180 (Marsh, 36.5 overs), 7–194 (Voges, 38.3 overs), 8–223 (Johnson, 43.3 overs), 9–230 (Siddle, 44.4 overs), 10–255 (Hilfenhaus, 48.3 overs)

Bowling: P Kumar 8–1–37–2; A Nehra 7–0–40–1; I Sharma 8–0–34–2; Harbhajan Singh 10–0–62–1; Yuvraj Singh 8–0–39–0; RA Jadeja 6.3–0–35–3; SK Raina 1–0–3–0

India won by 99 runs

Third ODI, Australia v India at Delhi

October 31, 2009 • **Toss:** Australia
Umpires: SS Hazare (India) and AM Saheba (India)
TV umpire: SK Tarapore (India)
Match referee: BC Broad (England)
Player of the match: Yuvraj Singh (India)

Australia innings

SR Watson	st Dhoni b Yuvraj Singh	41
RT Ponting	lbw Jadeja	59
MEK Hussey	not out	81
CL White	c Dhoni b Raina	0
AC Voges	c Kumar b Harbhajan Singh	17
MC Henriques	b Jadeja	12
MG Johnson	not out	9
Extras	(b 4, lb 3, w 3)	10
Total	(5 wickets; 50 overs)	229

Did not bat: GA Manou, NM Hauritz, PM Siddle, DE Bollinger

Fall of wickets: 1–72 (Watson, 16.2 overs), 2–128 (Ponting, 31.1 overs), 3–129 (White, 32.4 overs), 4–172 (Voges, 41.5 overs), 5–200 (Henriques, 46.3 overs)

Bowling: P Kumar 5–1–16–0; A Nehra 9–0–51–0; I Sharma 5–0–24–0; RA Jadeja 9–1–41–2; Harbhajan Singh 10–0–37–1; Yuvraj Singh 8–0–30–1; SK Raina 4–0–23–1

India innings

V Sehwag	b Johnson	11
SR Tendulkar	run out (Johnson)	32
G Gambhir	b Hauritz	6
Yuvraj Singh	lbw Henriques	78
MS Dhoni	not out	71
SK Raina	not out	9
Extras	(b 4, lb 4, w 14, nb 1)	23
Total	(4 wickets; 48.2 overs)	230

Did not bat: RA Jadeja, Harbhajan Singh, A Nehra, P Kumar, I Sharma

Fall of wickets: 1–37 (Sehwag, 8.5 overs), 2–51 (Tendulkar, 13.3 overs), 3–53 (Gambhir, 15.2 overs), 4–201 (Yuvraj Singh, 43.6 overs)

Bowling: MG Johnson 9.2–2–43–1; PM Siddle 10–0–41–0; DE Bollinger 10–0–26–0; MC Henriques 8–0–51–1; NM Hauritz 10–0–48–1; AC Voges 1–0–13–0

India won by six wickets

Fourth ODI, Australia v India at Mohali

November 2, 2009 • **Toss:** India
Umpires: EAR de Silva (Sri Lanka) and AM Saheba (India)
TV umpire: SS Hazare (India)
Match referee: BC Broad (England)
Player of the match: SR Watson (Australia)

Australia innings

SR Watson	c Dhoni b Harbhajan Singh	49
SE Marsh	lbw Nehra	5
RT Ponting	run out (Jadeja)	52
CL White	run out (Nehra)	62
MEK Hussey	c Sharma b Yuvraj Singh	40
MC Henriques	st Dhoni b Harbhajan Singh	6
MG Johnson	b Nehra	8
GA Manou	run out (Kumar)	7
NM Hauritz	not out	9
PM Siddle	c Jadeja b Nehra	1
DE Bollinger	run out (Yuvraj Singh/Kumar)	0
Extras	(lb 1, w 9, nb 1)	11
Total	(all out; 49.2 overs)	250

Fall of wickets: 1–24 (Marsh, 7.4 overs), 2–88 (Watson, 18.1 overs), 3–123 (Ponting, 26.5 overs), 4–196 (Hussey, 38.1 overs), 5–217 (Henriques, 42.4 overs), 6–226 (White, 44.5 overs), 7–236 (Johnson, 46.1 overs), 8–241 (Manou, 47.1 overs), 9–247 (Siddle, 48.4 overs), 10–250 (Bollinger, 49.2 overs)

Bowling: P Kumar 9.2–0–41–0; A Nehra 8–0–37–3; I Sharma 5–0–42–0; RA Jadeja 7–0–27–0; Harbhajan Singh 10–0–48–2; Yuvraj Singh 10–0–54–1

India innings

V Sehwag	c Watson b Bollinger	30
SR Tendulkar	lbw Hauritz	40
V Kohli	c Manou b Bollinger	10
Yuvraj Singh	run out (Ponting)	12
MS Dhoni	c Manou b Bollinger	26
SK Raina	b Hauritz	17
RA Jadeja	run out (Ponting/Manou)	7
Harbhajan Singh	c&b Watson	31
P Kumar	c Manou b Watson	16
A Nehra	c Hauritz b Watson	7
I Sharma	not out	3
Extras	(b 1, lb 5, w 20, nb 1)	27
Total	(all out; 46.4 overs)	226

Fall of wickets: 1–40 (Sehwag, 6.5 overs), 2–78 (Kohli, 14.3 overs), 3–94 (Tendulkar, 18.5 overs), 4–113 (Yuvraj Singh, 23.2 overs), 5–145 (Dhoni, 31.2 overs), 6–156 (Raina, 34.2 overs), 7–177 (Jadeja, 38.4 overs), 8–204 (Harbhajan Singh, 42.1 overs), 9–217 (Kumar, 44.4 overs), 10–226 (Nehra, 46.4 overs)

Bowling: MG Johnson 9–0–74–0; PM Siddle 5–2–15–0; DE Bollinger 9–2–38–3; MC Henriques 7–0–33–0; NM Hauritz 9–1–31–2; SR Watson 7.4–1–29–3

Australia won by 24 runs

Fifth ODI, Australia in India at Hyderabad

November 5, 2009 • **Toss:** Australia
Umpires: EAR de Silva (Sri Lanka) and SK Tarapore (India)
TV umpire: SS Hazare (India)
Match referee: BC Broad (England)
Player of the match: SR Tendulkar (India)

Australia innings

SR Watson	c Jadeja b Harbhajan Singh	93
SE Marsh	c Gambhir b Nehra	112
RT Ponting	b Kumar	45
CL White	c Tendulkar b Kumar	57
MEK Hussey	not out	31
Extras	(lb 6, w 5, nb 1)	12
Total	(4 wickets; 50 overs)	350

Did not bat: AC Voges, GA Manou, NM Hauritz, DE Bollinger, BW Hilfenhaus, CJ McKay

Fall of wickets: 1–145 (Watson, 25.2 overs), 2–236 (Ponting, 38.5 overs), 3–270 (Marsh, 42.5 overs), 4–350 (White, 49.6 overs)

Bowling: P Kumar 9–0–68–2; A Nehra 10–0–79–1; MM Patel 9–0–73–0; RA Jadeja 5–0–44–0; Harbhajan Singh 10–0–44–1; Yuvraj Singh 7–0–36–0

India innings

V Sehwag	c Bollinger b Hilfenhaus	38
SR Tendulkar	c Hauritz b McKay	175
G Gambhir	c Hilfenhaus b McKay	8
Yuvraj Singh	c&b Watson	9
MS Dhoni	c Voges b McKay	6
SK Raina	c Manou b Watson	59
Harbhajan Singh	c Manou b Watson	0
RA Jadeja	run out (White/McKay)	23
P Kumar	run out (Hauritz/Manou)	9
A Nehra	c Hussey b Bollinger	1
MM Patel	not out	2
Extras	(b 1, lb 5, w 8, nb 3)	17
Total	(all out; 49.4 overs)	347

Fall of wickets: 1–66 (Sehwag, 8.5 overs), 2–92 (Gambhir, 13.3 overs), 3–126 (Yuvraj Singh, 18.3 overs), 4–162 (Dhoni, 23.3 overs), 5–299 (Raina, 42.3 overs), 6–300 (Harbhajan Singh, 42.6 overs), 7–332 (Tendulkar, 47.1 overs), 8–333 (Jadeja, 47.4 overs), 9–335 (Nehra, 48.1 overs), 10–347 (Kumar, 49.4 overs)

Bowling: BW Hilfenhaus 10–0–72–1; DE Bollinger 10–0–75–1; CJ McKay 10–0–59–3; SR Watson 8.4–0–47–3; NM Hauritz 5–0–43–0; AC Voges 3–0–19–0; MEK Hussey 3–0–26–0

Australia won by three runs

Sixth ODI, Australia v India at Guwahati

November 8, 2009 • **Toss:** India
Umpires: EAR de Silva (Sri Lanka) and SK Tarapore (India)
TV umpire: SS Hazare (India)
Match referee: BC Broad (England)
Player of the match: DE Bollinger (Australia)

India innings

V Sehwag	b Johnson	6
SR Tendulkar	c&b Bollinger	10
G Gambhir	b Johnson	0
Yuvraj Singh	b Bollinger	6
MS Dhoni	lbw Bollinger	24
SK Raina	c Hauritz b Johnson	0
RA Jadeja	c White b Bollinger	57
Harbhajan Singh	b Bollinger	0
P Kumar	not out	54
A Nehra	b Watson	4
MM Patel	b Watson	0
Extras	(b 1, lb 1, w 4, nb 3)	9
Total	(all out; 48 overs)	170

Fall of wickets: 1–7 (Sehwag, 0.4 overs), 2–7 (Gambhir, 0.6 overs), 3–23 (Tendulkar, 5.1 overs), 4–24 (Yuvraj Singh, 7.6 overs), 5–27 (Raina, 8.6 overs), 6–75 (Dhoni, 30.1 overs), 7–75 (Harbhajan Singh, 30.3 overs), 8–149 (Jadeja, 44.1 overs), 9–170 (Nehra, 47.4 overs), 10–170 (Patel, 47.6 overs)

Bowling: MG Johnson 9–1–39–3; DE Bollinger 10–4–35–5; CJ McKay 10–1–44–0; NM Hauritz 9–2–19–0; SR Watson 8–0–27–2; AC Voges 2–0–4–0

Australia innings

SR Watson	c Sehwag b Harbhajan Singh	49
SE Marsh	lbw Patel	6
RT Ponting	c Raina b Harbhajan Singh	25
CL White	lbw Raina	25
MEK Hussey	not out	35
AC Voges	not out	23
Extras	(b 6, lb 2, w 1)	9
Total	(4 wickets; 41.5 overs)	172

Did not bat: MG Johnson, GA Manou, NM Hauritz, DE Bollinger, CJ McKay

Fall of wickets: 1–24 (Marsh, 4.3 overs), 2–85 (Watson, 18.6 overs), 3–90 (Ponting, 20.4 overs), 4–143 (White, 36.3 overs)

Bowling: P Kumar 2–0–10–0; A Nehra 3–0–21–0; MM Patel 4–1–13–1; RA Jadeja 10–1–36–0; Harbhajan Singh 10–1–23–2; Yuvraj Singh 7–1–29–0; SK Raina 3–0–13–1; V Sehwag 2–0–8–0; SR Tendulkar 0.5–0–11–0

Australia won by six wickets

Game Seven of the series, scheduled for Mumbai on November 11, was abandoned without a ball being bowled. Australia won the series 4–2. SR Watson was named player of the series.

First ODI, Australia v Pakistan at Brisbane

January 22, 2010 • **Toss:** Pakistan
Umpires: EAR de Silva (Sri Lanka) and RJ Tucker (Australia)
TV umpire: PR Reiffel (Australia)
Match referee: RS Madugalle (Sri Lanka)
Player of the match: CL White (Australia)

Pakistan innings

Salman Butt	c Haddin b Bollinger	72
Kamran Akmal	c Clarke b Watson	34
Younis Khan	c Marsh b McKay	46
Mohammad Yousuf	b Bollinger	2
Umar Akmal	c Haddin b McKay	23
Shoaib Malik	c Haddin b Watson	28
Shahid Afridi	c Hussey b Watson	48
Mohammad Aamer	c Haddin b McKay	0
Naved-ul-Hasan	not out	8
Saeed Ajmal	c Clarke b Watson	2
Mohammad Asif	run out (Ponting)	0
Extras	(lb 4, w 5, nb 2)	11
Total	(all out; 49.4 overs)	274

Fall of wickets: 1–62 (Kamran Akmal, 12.5 overs), 2–117 (Salman Butt, 22.2 overs), 3–123 (Mohammad Yousuf, 24.4 overs), 4–156 (Umar Akmal, 30.2 overs), 5–205 (Shoaib Malik, 40.1 overs), 6–221 (Younis Khan, 43.1 overs), 7–227 (Mohammad Aamer, 43.4 overs), 8–269 (Shahid Afridi, 46.6 overs), 9–274 (Saeed Ajmal, 48.6 overs), 10–274 (Mohammad Asif, 49.4 overs)

Bowling: DE Bollinger 9.4–0–37–2; PM Siddle 8–1–48–0; CJ McKay 9–0–61–3; SR Watson 10–0–36–4; NM Hauritz 9–0–68–0; MJ Clarke 2–0–8–0; MEK Hussey 2–0–12–0

Australia innings

SR Watson	c Saeed Ajmal b Mohammad Aamer	5
SE Marsh	c Naved-ul-Hasan b Mohammad Asif	15
RT Ponting	c sub (Khalid Latif) b Shahid Afridi	27
MJ Clarke	run out (Naved-ul-Hasan)	58
CL White	b Naved-ul-Hasan	105
MEK Hussey	not out	35
BJ Haddin	not out	7
Extras	(b 4, lb 10, w 9)	23
Total	(5 wickets; 48.3 overs)	275

Did not bat: NM Hauritz, CJ McKay, PM Siddle, DE Bollinger

Fall of wickets: 1–16 (Watson, 3.3 overs), 2–37 (Marsh, 8.4 overs), 3–84 (Ponting, 17.6 overs), 4–186 (Clarke, 36.3 overs), 5–260 (White, 46.2 overs)

Bowling: Mohammad Asif 10–1–44–1; Mohammad Aamer 9–0–29–1; Naved-ul-Hasan 10–0–61–1; Shahid Afridi 10–0–66–1; Saeed Ajmal 9.3–0–61–0

Australia won by five wickets

Second ODI, Australia v Pakistan at Sydney

January 24, 2010 • Toss: Pakistan
Umpires: EAR de Silva (Sri Lanka) and RJ Tucker (Australia)
TV umpire: PR Reiffel (Australia)
Match referee: RS Madugalle (Sri Lanka)
Player of the match: SR Watson (Australia)

Australia innings

SR Watson	c Shoaib Malik b Shahid Afridi	69
SE Marsh	c Umar Gul b Shahid Afridi	41
RT Ponting	c Mohammad Yousuf	
	b Mohammad Aamer	13
MJ Clarke	c Shahid Afridi b Umar Gul	25
CL White	c Mohammad Yousuf	
	b Mohammad Aamer	55
MEK Hussey	c Shoaib Malik	
	b Mohammad Aamer	29
BJ Haddin	not out	27
NM Hauritz	not out	1
Extras	(b 1, lb 3, w 2, nb 1)	7
Total	(6 wickets; 50 overs)	267

Did not bat: CJ McKay, PM Siddle, DE Bollinger

Fall of wickets: 1–100 (Watson, 19.5 overs), 2–114 (Marsh, 23.3 overs), 3–138 (Ponting, 29.4 overs), 4–166 (Clarke, 35.4 overs), 5–221 (Hussey, 45.2 overs), 6–261 (White, 49.3 overs)

Bowling: Mohammad Aamer 9–0–53–3; Umar Gul 10–0–70–1; Naved-ul-Hasan 7–0–47–0; Shahid Afridi 10–0–35–2; Saeed Ajmal 10–1–41–0; Shoaib Malik 4–0–17–0

Pakistan innings

Salman Butt	c White b Bollinger	2
Kamran Akmal	run out (McKay)	16
Younis Khan	c White b Bollinger	0
Mohammad Yousuf	c Hauritz b McKay	58
Umar Akmal	b Siddle	0
Shoaib Malik	c Ponting b McKay	2
Shahid Afridi	c&b Watson	9
Mohammad Aamer	c&b Hauritz	4
Naved-ul-Hasan	st Haddin b Hauritz	27
Umar Gul	not out	1
Saeed Ajmal	c Haddin b McKay	3
Extras	(lb 1, w 4)	5
Total	(all out; 37.3 overs)	127

Fall of wickets: 1–7 (Salman Butt, 4.3 overs), 2–7 (Younis Khan, 4.6 overs), 3–32 (Kamran Akmal, 10.6 overs), 4–32 (Umar Akmal, 11.2 overs), 5–42 (Shoaib Malik, 16.6 overs), 6–58 (Shahid Afridi, 21.4 overs), 7–71 (Mohammad Aamer, 24.6 overs), 8–117 (Naved-ul-Hasan, 32.6 overs), 9–123 (Mohammad Yousuf, 35.2 overs), 10–127 (Saeed Ajmal, 37.3 overs)

Bowling: DE Bollinger 9–1–19–2; PM Siddle 8–1–23–1; CJ McKay 7.3–0–15–3; SR Watson 3–0–10–1; NM Hauritz 7–0–45–2; MJ Clarke 3–0–14–0

Australia won by 140 runs

Third ODI, Australia v Pakistan at Adelaide

January 26, 2010 • Toss: Australia
Umpires: EAR de Silva (Sri Lanka) and SJA Taufel (Australia)
TV umpire: RJ Tucker (Australia)
Match referee: RS Madugalle (Sri Lanka)
Player of the match: RJ Harris (Australia)

Australia innings

SR Watson	b Mohammad Asif	33
SE Marsh	st Kamran Akmal b Saeed Ajmal	83
RT Ponting	lbw Naved-ul-Hasan	0
MJ Clarke	b Umar Gul	80
CL White	c Kamran Akmal b Naved-ul-Hasan	28
MEK Hussey	c Younis Khan b Umar Gul	49
BJ Haddin	not out	1
NM Hauritz	not out	0
Extras	(b 1, lb 1, w 5, nb 5)	12
Total	(6 wickets; 50 overs)	286

Did not bat: CJ McKay, RJ Harris, DE Bollinger

Fall of wickets: 1–63 (Watson, 12.6 overs), 2–64 (Ponting, 13.5 overs), 3–149 (Marsh, 31.6 overs), 4–204 (White, 42.4 overs), 5–284 (Hussey, 49.3 overs), 6–284 (Clarke, 49.4 overs)

Bowling: Mohammad Asif 10–0–51–1; Umar Gul 10–1–80–2; Naved-ul-Hasan 10–0–57–2; Shahid Afridi 10–0–55–0; Saeed Ajmal 10–0–41–1

Pakistan innings

Salman Butt	lbw McKay	34
Kamran Akmal	lbw Harris	1
Younis Khan	c Haddin b McKay	12
Mohammad Yousuf	b Watson	11
Umar Akmal	c Haddin b Harris	59
Fawad Alam	b McKay	33
Shahid Afridi	b Harris	40
Naved-ul-Hasan	c White b Harris	33
Umar Gul	c Haddin b Harris	0
Saeed Ajmal	not out	8
Mohammad Asif	c Haddin b Hauritz	1
Extras	(lb 11, w 3)	14
Total	(all out; 47.4 overs)	246

Fall of wickets: 1–14 (Kamran Akmal, 1.6 overs), 2–47 (Salman Butt, 11.3 overs), 3–58 (Mohammad Yousuf, 12.5 overs), 4–60 (Younis Khan, 13.3 overs), 5–145 (Umar Akmal, 32.2 overs), 6–168 (Fawad Alam, 36.4 overs), 7–226 (Shahid Afridi, 43.2 overs), 8–226 (Umar Gul, 43.4 overs), 9–238 (Naved-ul-Hasan, 45.1 overs), 10–246 (Mohammad Asif, 47.4 overs)

Bowling: DE Bollinger 9–0–35–0; RJ Harris 10–0–43–5; SR Watson 9–0–66–1; CJ McKay 10–1–48–3; NM Hauritz 7.4–0–37–1; MJ Clarke–2–0–6–0

Australia won by 40 runs

Fourth ODI, Australia v Pakistan at Perth

January 29, 2010 • **Toss:** Australia
Umpires: EAR de Silva (Sri Lanka) and RJ Tucker (Australia)
TV umpire: PR Reiffel (Australia)
Match referee: RS Madugalle (Sri Lanka)
Player of the match: RJ Harris (Australia)

Australia innings

SE Marsh	c Kamran Akmal b Mohammad Asif	12
BJ Haddin	b Naved-ul-Hasan	32
RT Ponting	c Kamran Akmal b Shahid Afridi	30
MJ Clarke	run out (Fawad Alam)	10
CL White	c Mohammad Asif b Saeed Ajmal	44
MEK Hussey	c Mohammad Yousuf b Saeed Ajmal	67
JR Hopes	b Mohammad Asif	16
NM Hauritz	not out	53
RJ Harris	c Shahid Afridi b Mohammad Asif	4
CJ McKay	not out	0
Extras	(lb 2, w 6, nb 1)	9
Total	(8 wickets; 50 overs)	277

Did not bat: PM Siddle

Fall of wickets: 1–30 (Marsh, 6.5 overs), 2–55 (Haddin, 11.3 overs), 3–77 (Clarke, 14.5 overs), 4–110 (Ponting, 21.4 overs), 5–159 (White, 34.5 overs), 6–190 (Hopes, 39.4 overs), 7–270 (Hussey, 48.6 overs), 8–275 (Harris, 49.4 overs)

Bowling: Mohammad Asif 10–1–42–3; Naved-ul-Hasan 10–0–70–1; Iftikhar Anjum 10–0–64–0; Shahid Afridi 10–1–44–1; Saeed Ajmal–10–0–55–2

Pakistan innings

Salman Butt	c White b Harris	0
Kamran Akmal	c Haddin b Siddle	17
Younis Khan	c Haddin b Harris	6
Mohammad Yousuf	c Haddin b Siddle	10
Umar Akmal	b Harris	38
Fawad Alam	run out (Hauritz)	21
Shahid Afridi	c Hauritz b McKay	29
Naved-ul-Hasan	c Haddin b Harris	0
Iftikhar Anjum	c Haddin b Harris	5
Saeed Ajmal	b Hauritz	7
Mohammad Asif	not out	0
Extras	(lb 5, w 3, nb 1)	9
Total	(all out; 37.5 overs)	142

Fall of wickets: 1–2 (Salman Butt, 0.4 overs), 2–14 (Younis Khan, 4.1 overs), 3–38 (Kamran Akmal, 9.3 overs), 4–39 (Mohammad Yousuf, 9.5 overs), 5–99 (Fawad Alam, 27.1 overs), 6–125 (Umar Akmal, 29.2 overs), 7–125 (Naved-ul-Hasan, 29.3 overs), 8–131 (Shahid Afridi, 30.6 overs), 9–140 (Saeed Ajmal, 34.4 overs), 10–142 (Iftikhar Anjum, 37.5 overs)

Bowling: RJ Harris 9.5–3–19–5; PM Siddle 6–0–31–2; CJ McKay 7–2–16–1; JR Hopes 7–0–23–0; NM Hauritz 8–0–48–1

Australia won by 135 runs

Fifth ODI, Australia v Pakistan at Perth

January 31, 2010 • **Toss:** Pakistan
Umpires: EAR de Silva (Sri Lanka) and PR Reiffel (Australia)
TV umpire: RJ Tucker (Australia)
Match referee: RS Madugalle (Sri Lanka)
Player of the match: CJ McKay (Australia)
Player of the series: RJ Harris (Australia)

Pakistan innings

Salman Butt	c Haddin b Harris	0
Khalid Latif	c&b Johnson	0
Younis Khan	c Haddin b McKay	3
Shoaib Malik	run out (Johnson)	36
Umar Akmal	b McKay	67
Fawad Alam	c Hauritz b McKay	63
Shahid Afridi	c Hauritz b Harris	1
Sarfraz Ahmed	c White b Johnson	6
Naved-ul-Hasan	b Harris	8
Iftikhar Anjum	c Ponting b McKay	16
Mohammad Asif	not out	0
Extras	(b 5, lb 3, w 4)	12
Total	(all out; 49.3 overs)	212

Fall of wickets: 1–0 (Salman Butt, 0.5 overs), 2–0 (Khalid Latif, 1.5 overs), 3–16 (Younis Khan, 8.5 overs), 4–76 (Shoaib Malik, 24.3 overs), 5–158 (Umar Akmal, 40.4 overs), 6–162 (Shahid Afridi, 41.4 overs), 7–180 (Sarfraz Ahmed, 45.5 overs), 8–189 (Naved-ul-Hasan, 46.6 overs), 9–212 (Iftikhar Anjum, 49.2 overs), 10–212 (Fawad Alam, 49.3 overs)

Bowling: RJ Harris 10–1–44–3; MG Johnson 10–1–42–2; CJ McKay 9.3–3–35–4; JR Hopes 10–1–45–0; NM Hauritz 10–0–38–0

Australia innings

SE Marsh	c Fawad Alam b Mohammad Asif	25
BJ Haddin	c Shoaib Malik b Naved-ul-Hasan	7
RT Ponting	c Umar Akmal b Shoaib Malik	55
CL White	b Shahid Afridi	13
AC Voges	c Younis Khan b Shoaib Malik	24
MEK Hussey	not out	40
JR Hopes	c Younis Khan b Shahid Afridi	6
MG Johnson	c Sarfraz Ahmed b Naved-ul-Hasan	13
NM Hauritz	lbw Iftikhar Anjum	18
RJ Harris	not out	2
Extras	(w 9, nb 1)	10
Total	(8 wickets; 49.2 overs)	213

Did not bat: CJ McKay

Fall of wickets: 1–21 (Haddin, 5.1 overs), 2–54 (Marsh, 11.4 overs), 3–73 (White, 16.5 overs), 4–122 (Ponting, 31.3 overs), 5–139 (Voges, 35.1 overs), 6–150 (Hopes, 38.6 overs), 7–178 (Johnson, 44.3 overs), 8–210 (Hauritz, 49.1 overs)

Bowling: Mohammad Asif 10–0–40–1; Naved-ul-Hasan 10–0–55–2; Iftikhar Anjum 9.2–1–39–1; Shahid Afridi 10–0–31–2; Shoaib Malik 10–0–48–2

Australia won by two wickets
Australia won the series 5–0

First ODI, Australia v West Indies at Melbourne

February 7, 2010 • **Toss:** West Indies
Umpires: BF Bowden (New Zealand) and
BNJ Oxenford (Australia)
TV umpire: PR Reiffel (Australia)
Match referee: J Srinath (India)
Player of the match: SR Watson (Australia)

Australia innings

SR Watson	c Morton b Gayle	59
SE Marsh	c Ramdin b Smith	20
RT Ponting	b Pollard	49
MJ Clarke	c Ramdin b Pollard	18
CL White	c Ramdin b Roach	22
MEK Hussey	c Ramdin b Rampaul	28
BJ Haddin	c&b Pollard	8
MG Johnson	b Rampaul	21
NM Hauritz	not out	6
RJ Harris	not out	2
Extras	(b 4, lb 9, w 10)	23
Total	(8 wickets; 50 overs)	256

Did not bat: DE Bollinger

Fall of wickets: 1–50 (Marsh, 10.3 overs), 2–135 (Watson, 26.5 overs), 3–144 (Ponting, 29.1 overs), 4–179 (Clarke, 37.4 overs), 5–189 (White, 40.2 overs), 6–210 (Haddin, 43.5 overs), 7–241 (Hussey, 47.4 overs), 8–254 (Johnson, 49.5 overs)

Bowling: KAJ Roach 10–1–41–1; R Rampaul 8–0–43–2; DR Smith 8–0–42–1; NO Miller 8–0–40–0; CH Gayle 6–0–32–1; KA Pollard 10–0–45–3

West Indies innings

CH Gayle	c Johnson b Bollinger	7
RS Morton	c Haddin b Harris	3
TM Dowlin	c White b Bollinger	1
LMP Simmons	c Haddin b Watson	29
N Deonarine	c Ponting b Johnson	19
KA Pollard	c Johnson b Hauritz	31
D Ramdin	b Harris	17
DR Smith	c Watson b Hauritz	7
NO Miller	c Haddin b Harris	4
R Rampaul	c Marsh b Hauritz	3
KAJ Roach	not out	0
Extras	(b 4, lb 7, w 11)	22
Total	(all out; 34.2 overs)	143

Fall of wickets: 1–11 (Gayle, 2.1 overs), 2–12 (Morton, 3.4 overs), 3–12 (Dowlin, 4.2 overs), 4–44 (Deonarine, 12.5 overs), 5–108 (Pollard, 24.5 overs), 6–111 (Simmons, 25.3 overs), 7–135 (Smith, 30.4 overs), 8–136 (Ramdin, 31.1 overs), 9–143 (Miller, 33.6 overs), 10–143 (Rampaul, 34.2 overs)

Bowling: DE Bollinger 6–3–18–2; RJ Harris 9–1–24–3; MG Johnson 7–0–31–1; SR Watson 6–0–31–1; NM Hauritz 6.2–0–28–3

Australia won by 113 runs

Second ODI, Australia v West Indies at Adelaide

February 9, 2010 • **Toss:** West Indies
Umpires: BF Bowden (New Zealand) and
BNJ Oxenford (Australia)
TV umpire: PR Reiffel (Australia)
Match referee: J Srinath (India)
Player of the match: DE Bollinger (Australia)

West Indies innings

CH Gayle	lbw Bollinger	0
RS Morton	lbw Bollinger	4
TM Dowlin	c Haddin b McKay	2
LMP Simmons	c Haddin b Bollinger	1
N Deonarine	lbw Johnson	23
D Ramdin	c Haddin b Watson	30
KA Pollard	c Johnson b Bollinger	32
DR Smith	c Hussey b McKay	43
NO Miller	c Marsh b Hauritz	6
R Rampaul	run out (Ponting)	18
KAJ Roach	not out	0
Extras	(lb 4, w 4, nb 3)	11
Total	(all out; 39.4 overs)	170

Fall of wickets: 1–0 (Gayle, 0.1 overs), 2–11 (Dowlin, 3.6 overs), 3–11 (Morton, 4.3 overs), 4–16 (Simmons, 6.2 overs), 5–62 (Deonarine, 16.5 overs), 6–77 (Ramdin, 20.1 overs), 7–114 (Pollard, 28.6 overs), 8–125 (Miller, 31.3 overs), 9–170 (Rampaul, 39.3 overs), 10–170 (Smith, 39.4 overs)

Bowling: DE Bollinger 8–2–28–4; MG Johnson 8–0–36–1; CJ McKay 7.4–1–33–2; SR Watson 6–1–24–1; NM Hauritz 10–0–45–1

Australia innings

SR Watson	c Ramdin b Roach	53
SE Marsh	b Smith	27
RT Ponting	not out	57
MJ Clarke	not out	27
Extras	(w 6, nb 1)	7
Total	(2 wickets; 26.3 overs)	171

Did not bat: MEK Hussey, CL White, BJ Haddin, MG Johnson, NM Hauritz, DE Bollinger, CJ McKay

Fall of wickets: 1–51 (Marsh, 8.6 overs), 2–99 (Watson, 15.1 overs)

Bowling: KAJ Roach 6–0–44–1; R Rampaul 6–0–36–0; DR Smith 4–0–28–1; NO Miller 5–0–24–0; KA Pollard 4–0–28–0; N Deonarine 1.3–0–11–0

Australia won by eight wickets

Third ODI, Australia v West Indies at Sydney

February 12, 2010 • **Toss:** West Indies
Umpires: BF Bowden (New Zealand) and
BNJ Oxenford (Australia)
TV umpire: PR Reiffel (Australia)
Match referee: J Srinath (India)

Australia innings

TD Paine	b Rampaul	16
AC Voges	lbw Smith	8
RT Ponting	b Sammy	22
MJ Clarke	c Ramdin b Sammy	46
CL White	c Ramdin b Pollard	17
MEK Hussey	b Smith	44
JR Hopes	c Deonarine b Rampaul	30
MG Johnson	c Pollard b Smith	2
NM Hauritz	b Rampaul	2
RJ Harris	c Pollard b Rampaul	21
DE Bollinger	not out	0
Extras	(lb 5, w 12)	17
Total	(all out; 49.5 overs)	**225**

Fall of wickets: 1–28 (Paine, 6.6 overs), 2–30 (Voges, 7.4 overs), 3–78 (Ponting, 18.4 overs), 4–107 (White, 29.1 overs), 5–144 (Clarke, 37.1 overs), 6–194 (Hussey, 46.6 overs), 7–198 (Hopes, 47.2 overs), 8–202 (Hauritz, 47.6 overs), 9–206 (Johnson, 48.4 overs), 10–225 (Harris, 49.5 overs)

Bowling: R Rampaul 9.5–0–61–4; DR Smith 10–0–45–3; DJG Sammy 10–0–46–2; KA Pollard 9–2–26–1; NO Miller 10–0–35–0; CH Gayle 1–0–7–0

West Indies innings

CH Gayle	not out	0
TM Dowlin	not out	0
Extras	(b 4, w 2)	6
Total	(0 wickets; 1 overs)	**6**

Did not bat: LMP Simmons, N Deonarine, WW Hinds, KA Pollard, D Ramdin, DR Smith, DJG Sammy, NO Miller, R Rampaul

Bowling: DE Bollinger 1–0–2–0

No result

Fourth ODI, Australia v West Indies at Brisbane

February 14, 2010 • **Toss:** West Indies
Umpires: BF Bowden (New Zealand) and PR Reiffel
(Australia)
TV umpire: BNJ Oxenford (Australia)
Match referee: J Srinath (India)
Player of the match: RT Ponting (Australia)

Australia innings

SR Watson	c Hinds b Smith	26
TD Paine	c Pollard b Sammy	24
RT Ponting	c Rampaul b Smith	106
CL White	c Sammy b Miller	63
AC Voges	c Miller b Rampaul	16
MEK Hussey	b Pollard	23
JR Hopes	c Smith b Sammy	42
MG Johnson	not out	7
RJ Harris	not out	0
Extras	(lb 11, w 6)	17
Total	(7 wickets; 50 overs)	**324**

Did not bat: NM Hauritz, DE Bollinger

Fall of wickets: 1–43 (Watson, 6.1 overs), 2–95 (Paine, 15.3 overs), 3–226 (White, 39.5 overs), 4–252 (Voges, 42.5 overs), 5–252 (Ponting, 43.1 overs), 6–304 (Hussey, 48.2 overs), 7–318 (Hopes, 49.4 overs)

Bowling: DR Smith 8–0–59–2; R Rampaul 10–0–68–1; DJG Sammy 8–0–44–2; KA Pollard 7–0–45–1; NO Miller 10–0–55–1; CH Gayle 1–0–9–0; N Deonarine 6–0–33–0

West Indies innings

CH Gayle	c Paine b Bollinger	34
TM Dowlin	c Paine b Harris	8
LMP Simmons	c Hauritz b Hopes	1
N Deonarine	c Harris b Hauritz	53
WW Hinds	run out (Hopes)	20
D Ramdin	b Bollinger	15
KA Pollard	c Hussey b Johnson	62
DR Smith	not out	59
DJG Sammy	b Harris	0
NO Miller	not out	5
Extras	(b 2, lb 6, w 9)	17
Total	(8 wickets; 50 overs)	**274**

Did not bat: R Rampaul

Fall of wickets: 1–44 (Dowlin, 5.5 overs), 2–44 (Gayle, 6.2 overs), 3–55 (Simmons, 10.1 overs), 4–100 (Hinds, 20.6 overs), 5–127 (Deonarine, 27.3 overs), 6–146 (Ramdin, 30.4 overs), 7–248 (Pollard, 47.1 overs), 8–265 (Sammy, 48.6 overs)

Bowling: DE Bollinger 10–1–44–2; RJ Harris 10–0–64–2; JR Hopes 6–1–39–1; MG Johnson 10–0–55–1; NM Hauritz 10–1–47–1; AC Voges 4–0–17–0

Australia won by 50 runs

Fifth ODI, Australia v West Indies at Melbourne

February 19, 2010 • **Toss:** Australia
Umpires: BF Bowden (New Zealand) and
BNJ Oxenford (Australia)
TV umpire: PR Reiffel (Australia)
Match referee: J Srinath (India)
Player of the match: JR Hopes (Australia)
Player of the series: RT Ponting (Australia)

Australia innings

SR Watson	c Smith b Sammy	51
BJ Haddin	b Pollard	32
RT Ponting	c Ramdin b Pollard	61
MJ Clarke	c Deonarine b Rampaul	47
CL White	c Ramdin b Rampaul	22
AC Voges	not out	45
JR Hopes	not out	57
Extras	(lb 4, w 4, nb 1)	9
Total	(5 wickets; 50 overs)	324

Did not bat: SPD Smith, RJ Harris, CJ McKay, DE Bollinger

Fall of wickets: 1–81 (Watson, 13.3 overs), 2–88 (Haddin, 16.2 overs), 3–192 (Ponting, 33.1 overs), 4–206 (Clarke, 36.3 overs), 5–242 (White, 42.5 overs)

Bowling: R Rampaul 10–0–68–2; DR Smith 8–0–55–0; NO Miller 8–0–60–0; DJG Sammy 10–0–51–1; KA Pollard 9–0–59–2; CH Gayle 3–0–17–0; N Deonarine 2–0–10–0

West Indies innings

CH Gayle	c Clarke b Bollinger	14
TM Dowlin	lbw Bollinger	0
N Deonarine	b Harris	4
KA Pollard	c Smith b Hopes	45
WW Hinds	c Smith b Harris	5
LMP Simmons	c Clarke b Bollinger	29
DR Smith	run out (Clarke)	21
D Ramdin	lbw Smith	3
DJG Sammy	not out	47
NO Miller	c Clarke b McKay	22
R Rampaul	st Haddin b Smith	4
Extras	(w 5)	5
Total	(all out; 36.5 overs)	199

Fall of wickets: 1–1 (Dowlin, 0.2 overs), 2–17 (Gayle, 2.3 overs), 3–19 (Deonarine, 3.5 overs), 4–39 (Hinds, 9.4 overs), 5–80 (Pollard, 17.2 overs), 6–118 (Smith, 23.3 overs), 7–124 (Simmons, 25.1 overs), 8–135 (Ramdin, 26.5 overs), 9–190 (Miller, 35.1 overs), 10–199 (Rampaul, 36.5 overs)

Bowling: DE Bollinger 7–1–33–3; RJ Harris 7–2–26–2; CJ McKay 7–1–35–1; JR Hopes 6–0–27–1; SPD Smith 9.5–0–78–2

Australia won by 125 runs
Australia won the series 4–0

Chappell-Hadlee Trophy Series Game One Australia v New Zealand at Napier

March 3, 2010 • **Toss:** Australia
Umpires: AL Hill (New Zealand) and
RE Koertzen (South Africa)
TV umpire: CB Gaffaney (New Zealand)
Match referee: RS Madugalle (Sri Lanka)
Player of the match: LRPL Taylor (New Zealand)

Australia innings

SR Watson	c Ingram b Oram	45
BJ Haddin	b Bond	12
RT Ponting	c Guptill b Franklin	44
MJ Clarke	c McCullum b Tuffey	22
CL White	b Tuffey	33
MEK Hussey	b Bond	59
JR Hopes	b Southee	33
MG Johnson	not out	21
NM Hauritz	c sub (NL McCullum) b Tuffey	4
RJ Harris	not out	0
Extras	(b 1, w 1)	2
Total	(8 wickets; 50 overs)	275

Did not bat: DE Bollinger

Fall of wickets: 1–50 (Haddin, 5.6 overs), 2–58 (Watson, 8.3 overs), 3–100 (Clarke, 17.6 overs), 4–148 (Ponting, 26.1 overs), 5–172 (White, 34.1 overs), 6–244 (Hopes, 46.5 overs), 7–252 (Hussey, 47.5 overs), 8–268 (Hauritz, 49.3 overs)

Bowling: TG Southee 8–0–66–1; SE Bond 10–1–50–2; JDP Oram 7–0–29–1; DR Tuffey 10–0–58–3; JEC Franklin 9–0–44–1; SB Styris 6–0–27–0

New Zealand innings

BB McCullum	b Bollinger	45
PJ Ingram	c Hussey b Johnson	40
MJ Guptill	c Watson b Hopes	9
LRPL Taylor	c Hussey b Watson	70
JEC Franklin	c Haddin b Hauritz	12
NT Broom	b Bollinger	19
SB Styris	not out	49
DR Tuffey	b Harris	12
TG Southee	run out (White/Harris)	2
SE Bond	not out	11
Extras	(lb 10, w 2)	12
Total	(8 wickets; 49.2 overs)	281

Did not bat: JDP Oram

Fall of wickets: 1–75 (Ingram, 11.2 overs), 2–90 (McCullum, 14.6 overs), 3–106 (Guptill, 20.5 overs), 4–175 (Franklin, 33.2 overs), 5–204 (Taylor, 38.6 overs), 6–207 (Broom, 41.1 overs), 7–234 (Tuffey, 44.6 overs), 8–246 (Southee, 46.2 overs)

Bowling: RJ Harris 10–1–57–1; DE Bollinger 9.2–0–58–2; MG Johnson 10–1–46–1; JR Hopes 6–0–40–1; SR Watson 9–0–47–1; MJ Clarke 2–0–8–0; NM Hauritz 3–0–15–1

New Zealand won by two wickets

Chappell-Hadlee Trophy Series
Game Two
Australia v New Zealand at Auckland

March 6, 2010 • **Toss:** Australia
Umpires: BF Bowden (New Zealand) and
RE Koertzen (South Africa)
TV umpire: GAV Baxter (New Zealand)
Match referee: RS Madugalle (Sri Lanka)
Player of the match: DL Vettori (New Zealand)

Australia innings

SR Watson	c Guptill b Tuffey	47
BJ Haddin	c&b Vettori	53
RT Ponting	c McCullum b Vettori	1
MJ Clarke	c Guptill b Bond	11
CL White	c McCullum b Franklin	54
MEK Hussey	c sub (NL McCullum) b Bond	56
JR Hopes	run out (Hopkins/Tuffey)	29
MG Johnson	not out	16
Extras	(w 6)	6
Total	(7 wickets; 50 overs)	273

Did not bat: RJ Harris, NM Hauritz, DE Bollinger

Fall of wickets: 1–73 (Watson, 13.4 overs), 2–79 (Ponting, 14.5 overs), 3–114 (Haddin, 22.3 overs), 4–116 (Clarke, 23.4 overs), 5–217 (White, 42.3 overs), 6–238 (Hussey, 45.2 overs), 7–273 (Hopes, 49.6 overs)

Bowling: SE Bond 10–1–42–2; TG Southee 10–0–57–0; JEC Franklin 4.3–0–35–1; DR Tuffey 9–1–64–1; DL Vettori 10–0–43–2; SB Styris 6.3–0–32–0

New Zealand innings

BB McCullum	c Haddin b Johnson	24
PJ Ingram	lbw Harris	14
MJ Guptill	c Haddin b Watson	18
NT Broom	lbw Harris	0
JEC Franklin	c Haddin b Johnson	2
SB Styris	c Ponting b Hauritz	46
GJ Hopkins	c Bollinger b Watson	35
DL Vettori	b Harris	70
DR Tuffey	c White b Johnson	20
SE Bond	b Johnson	6
TG Southee	not out	4
Extras	(lb 2, w 11, nb 1)	14
Total	(all out; 43.2 overs)	253

Fall of wickets: 1–27 (McCullum, 4.5 overs), 2–43 (Ingram, 7.4 overs), 3–43 (Broom, 7.5 overs), 4–46 (Franklin, 10.1 overs), 5–89 (Guptill, 16.3 overs), 6–131 (Styris, 26.2 overs), 7–176 (Hopkins, 32.4 overs), 8–213 (Tuffey, 36.6 overs), 9–239 (Bond, 40.3 overs), 10–253 (Vettori, 43.2 overs)

Bowling: DE Bollinger 8–0–63–0; RJ Harris 8.2–0–34–3; MG Johnson 9–1–51–4; SR Watson 5–0–33–2; JR Hopes 6–0–29–0; NM Hauritz 7–0–41–1

Australia won by 12 runs (D/L method)

Chappell-Hadlee Trophy Series
Game Three
Australia v New Zealand at Hamilton

March 9, 2010 • **Toss:** Australia
Umpires: Asad Rauf (Pakistan) and
BF Bowden (New Zealand)
TV umpire: EA Watkin (New Zealand)
Match referee: RS Madugalle (Sri Lanka)
Player of the match: BJ Haddin (Australia)

New Zealand innings

BB McCullum	b Bollinger	23
PJ Ingram	c Haddin b Harris	5
MJ Guptill	c White b Johnson	21
LRPL Taylor	c Hussey b Watson	62
NT Broom	c Watson b Johnson	24
SB Styris	c Harris b Watson	41
GJ Hopkins	c Watson b Harris	45
DL Vettori	run out (Ponting)	0
SE Bond	c Haddin b Johnson	11
TG Southee	b Harris	1
MJ Mason	not out	2
Extras	(b 1, lb 1, w 6, nb 2)	10
Total	(all out; 46.2 overs)	245

Fall of wickets: 1–7 (Ingram, 0.6 overs), 2–45 (McCullum, 7.2 overs), 3–55 (Guptill, 10.4 overs), 4–126 (Broom, 22.6 overs), 5–146 (Taylor, 29.2 overs), 6–213 (Styris, 41.5 overs), 7–213 (Vettori, 42.2 overs), 8–240 (Hopkins, 45.1 overs), 9–243 (Southee, 45.5 overs), 10–245 (Bond, 46.2 overs)

Bowling: RJ Harris 7–0–48–3; DE Bollinger 8–1–39–1; MG Johnson 9.2–1–41–3; NM Hauritz 8–0–40–0; JR Hopes 8–0–49–0; SR Watson 6–0–26–2

Australia innings

SR Watson	run out (Hopkins)	15
BJ Haddin	st Hopkins b Vettori	110
RT Ponting	c Taylor b Mason	69
MEK Hussey	c Ingram b Southee	9
CL White	not out	25
AC Voges	not out	13
Extras	(lb 2, w 4, nb 1)	7
Total	(4 wickets; 47.2 overs)	248

Did not bat: RJ Harris, NM Hauritz, JR Hopes, MG Johnson, DE Bollinger

Fall of wickets: 1–25 (Watson, 7.1 overs), 2–176 (Ponting, 32.3 overs), 3–190 (Hussey, 35.3 overs), 4–230 (Haddin, 41.5 overs)

Bowling: SE Bond 8–1–43–0; TG Southee 10–0–43–1; MJ Mason 10–0–68–1; DL Vettori 10–0–36–1; SB Styris 7.2–0–43–0; MJ Guptill 2–0–13–0

Australia won by six wickets

Chappell-Hadlee Trophy Series
Game Four
Australia v New Zealand at Auckland

March 11, 2010 • Toss: Australia
Umpires: Asad Rauf (Pakistan) and
GAV Baxter (New Zealand)
TV umpire: CB Gaffaney (New Zealand)
Match referee: RS Madugalle (Sri Lanka)
Player of the match: CL White (Australia)

New Zealand innings

BB McCullum	c White b Hauritz	61
MJ Guptill	c Ponting b Watson	30
LRPL Taylor	c Hussey b Hopes	15
SL Stewart	c Watson b Hauritz	4
SB Styris	c&b Hopes	8
DL Vettori	lbw Johnson	12
GJ Hopkins	c Haddin b Watson	20
JEC Franklin	b Hauritz	10
DR Tuffey	c&b Harris	34
SE Bond	c Hauritz b Johnson	19
TG Southee	not out	1
Extras	(lb 9, w 13, nb 2)	24
Total	(all out; 44.1 overs)	238

Fall of wickets: 1–63 (Guptill, 7.4 overs), 2–120 (Taylor, 19.5 overs), 3–128 (Stewart, 22.2 overs), 4–130 (McCullum, 24.3 overs), 5–152 (Styris, 29.2 overs), 6–154 (Vettori, 30.4 overs), 7–177 (Franklin, 38.3 overs), 8–213 (Hopkins, 41.1 overs), 9–236 (Tuffey, 43.3 overs), 10–238 (Bond, 44.1 overs)

Bowling: RJ Harris 7–1–37–1; DE Bollinger 5–0–34–0; MG Johnson 8.1–0–40–2; SR Watson 6–1–34–2; JR Hopes 10–0–38–2; NM Hauritz 8–0–46–3

Australia innings

SR Watson	lbw Vettori	32
BJ Haddin	c Styris b Bond	0
RT Ponting	lbw Vettori	50
CL White	not out	50
AC Voges	c Vettori b Franklin	34
MEK Hussey	not out	28
Extras	(lb 6, w 2)	8
Total	(4 wickets; 31.1 overs)	202

Did not bat: JR Hopes, MG Johnson, NM Hauritz, RJ Harris, DE Bollinger

Fall of wickets: 1–2 (Haddin, 0.3 overs), 2–84 (Watson, 12.2 overs), 3–85 (Ponting, 14.1 overs), 4–150 (Voges, 25.4 overs)

Bowling: SE Bond 6–0–28–1; TG Southee 5.1–0–55–0; DR Tuffey 5–0–38–0; DL Vettori 7–1–29–2; SB Styris 5–0–20–0; JEC Franklin 3–0–26–1

Australia won by six wickets (D/L method)
Australia retained the Chappell-Hadlee Trophy

Chappell-Hadlee Trophy Series
Game Five
Australia v New Zealand
at Wellington

March 13, 2010 • Toss: Australia
Umpires: Asad Rauf (Pakistan) and
GAV Baxter (New Zealand)
TV umpire: EA Watkin (New Zealand)
Match referee: RS Madugalle (Sri Lanka)
Player of the match: TG Southee (New Zealand)

New Zealand innings

BB McCullum	c Ponting b McKay	1
MJ Guptill	run out (Hopes)	7
LRPL Taylor	c Bollinger b Watson	30
SL Stewart	c Haddin b Johnson	6
SB Styris	b Hopes	55
DL Vettori	b Bollinger	28
GJ Hopkins	c Haddin b Hauritz	26
NL McCullum	c&b Johnson	17
DR Tuffey	c Ponting b McKay	36
SE Bond	not out	6
Extras	(lb 3, w 19, nb 7)	29
Total	(9 wickets; 50 overs)	241

Did not bat: TG Southee

Fall of wickets: 1–21 (BB McCullum, 4.1 overs), 2–25 (Guptill, 4.6 overs), 3–32 (Stewart, 7.6 overs), 4–85 (Taylor, 19.1 overs), 5–153 (Styris, 31.3 overs), 6–155 (Vettori, 32.5 overs), 7–186 (Hopkins, 38.4 overs), 8–214 (NL McCullum, 44.5 overs), 9–241 (Tuffey, 49.6 overs)

Bowling: CJ McKay 10–1–57–2; DE Bollinger 9–2–37–1; MG Johnson 10–0–42–2; SR Watson 8–1–31–1; NM Hauritz 7–0–43–1; JR Hopes 6–0–28–1

Australia innings

SR Watson	c Taylor b NL McCullum	53
BJ Haddin	c Southee b Bond	17
RT Ponting	c Hopkins b Bond	0
CL White	c Vettori b Southee	6
AC Voges	c Hopkins b Southee	5
MEK Hussey	b Southee	46
JR Hopes	c Guptill b Vettori	40
MG Johnson	c sub (JEC Franklin) b Southee	6
NM Hauritz	c Styris b Bond	9
CJ McKay	c Southee b Bond	2
DE Bollinger	not out	1
Extras	(lb 1, w 4)	5
Total	(all out; 46.1 overs)	190

Fall of wickets: 1–27 (Haddin, 6.3 overs), 2–27 (Ponting, 6.4 overs), 3–46 (White, 12.6 overs), 4–72 (Voges, 19.6 overs), 5–96 (Watson, 26.1 overs), 6–146 (Hussey, 38.3 overs), 7–157 (Johnson, 40.2 overs), 8–186 (Hauritz, 44.4 overs), 9–186 (Hopes, 45.1 overs), 10–190 (McKay, 46.1 overs)

Bowling: SE Bond 9.1–1–26–4; DR Tuffey 8–0–41–0; DL Vettori 10–1–39–1; TG Southee 9–0–36–4; NL McCullum 8–0–31–1; SB Styris 2–0–16–0

New Zealand won by 51 runs
Australia won the series 3–2

ODI, Ireland v Australia at Dublin

June 17, 2010 • Toss: Australia
Umpires: RA Kettleborough (England) and NJ Llong (England)
Match referee: BC Broad (England)
Player of the match: JR Hopes (Australia)

Australia innings

SR Watson	c Wilson b Rankin	13
TD Paine	c NJ O'Brien b KJ O'Brien	81
RT Ponting	c White b Stirling	33
MJ Clarke	st Wilson b Cusack	0
CL White	c Porterfield b Stirling	42
MEK Hussey	c NJ O'Brien b KJ O'Brien	8
JR Hopes	b Rankin	12
NM Hauritz	c NJ O'Brien b KJ O'Brien	19
RJ Harris	c Mooney b Cusack	6
CJ McKay	not out	4
Extras	(lb 6, w 6, nb 1)	13
Total	(9 wickets; 50 overs)	231

Did not bat: DE Bollinger

Fall of wickets: 1–20 (Watson, 4.6 overs), 2–86 (Ponting, 21.4 overs), 3–86 (Clarke, 22.5 overs), 4–152 (White, 37.6 overs), 5–186 (Paine, 43.5 overs), 6–194 (Hussey, 45.2 overs), 7–218 (Hauritz, 47.4 overs), 8–222 (Hopes, 48.3 overs), 9–231 (Harris, 49.6 overs)

Bowling: WB Rankin 10–1–45–2; DT Johnston 5–1–21–0; KJ O'Brien 10–1–43–3; P Connell 5–0–37–0; AR Cusack 8–0–38–2; PR Stirling 10–0–34–2; AR White 2–0–7–0

Ireland innings

WTS Porterfield	b Hauritz	39
PR Stirling	b Harris	36
GC Wilson	lbw Harris	4
NJ O'Brien	c Paine b Hauritz	15
AR Cusack	lbw Hopes	30
KJ O'Brien	c Paine b Hopes	5
AR White	c Paine b Hopes	4
JF Mooney	c Ponting b Watson	38
DT Johnston	b Hopes	1
P Connell	lbw Hopes	0
WB Rankin	not out	3
Extras	(lb 3, w 11, nb 3)	17
Total	(all out; 42 overs)	192

Fall of wickets: 1–80 (Stirling, 10.6 overs), 2–86 (Wilson, 12.6 overs), 3–86 (Porterfield, 13.4 overs), 4–137 (Cusack, 24.2 overs), 5–139 (NJ O'Brien, 25.4 overs), 6–146 (White, 28.3 overs), 7–150 (KJ O'Brien, 30.6 overs), 8–156 (Johnston, 34.4 overs), 9–156 (Connell, 34.5 overs), 10–192 (Mooney, 41.6 overs)

Bowling: DE Bollinger 6–0–30–0; RJ Harris 7–0–40–2; CJ McKay 6–0–39–0; NM Hauritz 10–0–40–2; JR Hopes 9–1–14–5; SR Watson 4–0–26–1

Australia won by 39 runs

NatWest Series Game One England v Australia at Southampton

June 22, 2010 • Toss: Australia
Umpires: Aleem Dar (Pakistan) and IJ Gould (England)
TV umpire: RK Illingworth (England)
Match referee: J Srinath (India)
Player of the match: EJG Morgan (England)

Australia innings

SR Watson	c&b Broad	32
TD Paine	b Wright	26
RT Ponting	c Broad b Wright	21
MJ Clarke	not out	87
CL White	b Anderson	10
MEK Hussey	c Kieswetter b Yardy	28
JR Hopes	c Bresnan b Anderson	34
NM Hauritz	c Strauss b Broad	22
RJ Harris	not out	0
Extras	(lb 2, w 4, nb 1)	7
Total	(7 wickets; 50 overs)	267

Did not bat: JR Hazlewood, DE Bollinger

Fall of wickets: 1–52 (Watson, 8.5 overs), 2–66 (Paine, 13.2 overs), 3–86 (Ponting, 17.2 overs), 4–98 (White, 21.2 overs), 5–168 (Hussey, 34.1 overs), 6–225 (Hopes, 44.4 overs), 7–266 (Hauritz, 49.5 overs)

Bowling: JM Anderson 9–1–43–2; TT Bresnan 8–1–49–0; SCJ Broad 8–0–54–2; LJ Wright 7–1–34–2; MH Yardy 10–2–41–1; GP Swann 8–0–44–0

England innings

AJ Strauss	c Paine b Harris	10
C Kieswetter	b Hazlewood	38
KP Pietersen	c Ponting b Watson	29
PD Collingwood	c Hopes b Watson	11
EJG Morgan	not out	103
LJ Wright	lbw Harris	36
TT Bresnan	b Harris	27
MH Yardy	not out	1
Extras	(lb 8, w 4, nb 1)	13
Total	(6 wickets; 46 overs)	268

Did not bat: GP Swann, SCJ Broad, JM Anderson

Fall of wickets: 1–16 (Strauss, 3.1 overs), 2–75 (Pietersen, 13.5 overs), 3–81 (Kieswetter, 16.1 overs), 4–97 (Collingwood, 19.6 overs), 5–192 (Wright, 34.5 overs), 6–263 (Bresnan, 45.4 overs)

Bowling: DE Bollinger 9–0–48–0; RJ Harris 9–2–42–3; JR Hazlewood 7–0–41–1; SR Watson 8–1–55–2; JR Hopes 5–0–30–0; NM Hauritz 8–0–44–0

England won by four wickets

NatWest Series Game Two
England v Australia at Cardiff

June 24, 2010 • **Toss:** Australia
Umpires: Aleem Dar (Pakistan) and NJ Llong (England)
TV umpire: IJ Gould (England)
Match referee: J Srinath (India)
Player of the match: SCJ Broad (England)

Australia innings

SR Watson	c Kieswetter b Wright	57
TD Paine	c Kieswetter b Broad	16
RT Ponting	c Kieswetter b Broad	13
MJ Clarke	c Swann b Broad	1
CL White	not out	86
MEK Hussey	b Anderson	14
SPD Smith	c Collingwood b Broad	41
JR Hopes	run out (Bresnan)	8
NM Hauritz	not out	0
Extras	(w 2, nb 1)	3
Total	**(7 wickets; 50 overs)**	**239**

Did not bat: DE Bollinger, CJ McKay

Fall of wickets: 1–51 (Paine, 10.3 overs), 2–67 (Ponting, 14.4 overs), 3–77 (Clarke, 16.6 overs), 4–94 (Watson, 21.3 overs), 5–118 (Hussey, 29.1 overs), 6–202 (Smith, 45.5 overs), 7–238 (Hopes, 49.5 overs)

Bowling: JM Anderson 10–1–63–1; TT Bresnan 9–0–44–0; SCJ Broad 10–0–44–4; LJ Wright 9–0–38–1; MH Yardy 8–0–31–0; GP Swann 4–0–19–0

England innings

AJ Strauss	c&b Hauritz	51
C Kieswetter	c Paine b Bollinger	8
KP Pietersen	c Ponting b Smith	33
PD Collingwood	b Bollinger	48
EJG Morgan	c Paine b Bollinger	52
LJ Wright	b Hopes	10
TT Bresnan	not out	12
GP Swann	not out	19
Extras	(lb 2, w 3, nb 5)	10
Total	**(6 wickets; 45.2 overs)**	**243**

Did not bat: MH Yardy, SCJ Broad, JM Anderson

Fall of wickets: 1–23 (Kieswetter, 2.2 overs), 2–91 (Pietersen, 14.6 overs), 3–109 (Strauss, 19.3 overs), 4–192 (Collingwood, 36.2 overs), 5–211 (Wright, 39.4 overs), 6–211 (Morgan, 40.2 overs)

Bowling: DE Bollinger 10–2–46–3; CJ McKay 9.2–0–60–0; JR Hopes 5–0–30–1; NM Hauritz 10–0–56–1; SPD Smith 8–0–40–1; SR Watson 3–0–9–0

England won by four wickets

NatWest Series Game Three
England v Australia at Manchester

June 27, 2010 • **Toss:** England
Umpires: Aleem Dar (Pakistan) and IJ Gould (England)
TV umpire: RA Kettleborough (England)
Match referee: J Srinath (India)
Player of the match: GP Swann (England)

Australia innings

SR Watson	c Strauss b Swann	61
TD Paine	lbw Yardy	44
RT Ponting	st Kieswetter b Swann	3
MJ Clarke	c sub (IR Bell) b Swann	33
CL White	c Strauss b Swann	12
MEK Hussey	b Collingwood	21
SPD Smith	lbw Anderson	20
JR Hopes	b Anderson	7
RJ Harris	c Strauss b Broad	1
DE Bollinger	b Anderson	3
SW Tait	not out	1
Extras	(w 6)	6
Total	**(all out; 46 overs)**	**212**

Fall of wickets: 1–75 (Paine, 13.3 overs), 2–93 (Ponting, 18.1 overs), 3–130 (Watson, 26.6 overs), 4–154 (White, 34.1 overs), 5–169 (Clarke, 38.4 overs), 6–183 (Hussey, 40.2 overs), 7–202 (Hopes, 43.6 overs), 8–207 (Harris, 44.5 overs), 9–211 (Smith, 45.4 overs), 10–212 (Bollinger, 45.6 overs)

Bowling: JM Anderson 8–1–22–3; TT Bresnan 6–0–43–0; SCJ Broad 6–1–30–1; LJ Wright 1–0–14–0; MH Yardy 10–0–45–1; GP Swann 10–1–37–4; PD Collingwood 5–0–21–1

England innings

AJ Strauss	c Paine b Harris	87
C Kieswetter	b Tait	0
KP Pietersen	c&b Tait	25
PD Collingwood	b Bollinger	40
EJG Morgan	c Ponting b Smith	27
MH Yardy	c Paine b Tait	8
LJ Wright	c Hopes b Smith	0
TT Bresnan	not out	14
GP Swann	b Bollinger	1
SCJ Broad	b Bollinger	0
JM Anderson	not out	0
Extras	(b 1, lb 3, w 6, nb 2)	12
Total	**(9 wickets; 49.1 overs)**	**214**

Fall of wickets: 1–1 (Kieswetter, 0.4 overs), 2–52 (Pietersen, 12.5 overs), 3–128 (Collingwood, 30.1 overs), 4–185 (Morgan, 41.4 overs), 5–189 (Strauss, 42.5 overs), 6–190 (Wright, 43.3 overs), 7–197 (Yardy, 44.5 overs), 8–203 (Swann, 47.1 overs), 9–203 (Broad, 47.6 overs)

Bowling: SW Tait 10–1–28–3; DE Bollinger 10–3–20–3; RJ Harris 10–0–59–1; JR Hopes 6.1–0–44–0; MJ Clarke 4–0–25–0; SPD Smith 9–0–34–2

England won by one wicket

NatWest Series Game Four
England v Australia at The Oval

June 30, 2010 • **Toss:** England
Umpires: Aleem Dar (Pakistan) and
RA Kettleborough (England)
TV umpire: RK Illingworth (England)
Match referee: J Srinath (India)
Player of the match: RJ Harris (Australia)

Australia innings

SR Watson	c Morgan b Swann	41
TD Paine	c Morgan b Bresnan	8
RT Ponting	c Strauss b Anderson	92
MJ Clarke	not out	99
CL White	c Anderson b Broad	17
MEK Hussey	run out (Anderson/Strauss)	1
SPD Smith	not out	18
Extras	(b 3, lb 2, w 9)	14
Total	(5 wickets; 50 overs)	290

Did not bat: JR Hopes, RJ Harris, DE Bollinger, SW Tait

Fall of wickets: 1–33 (Paine, 9.1 overs), 2–73 (Watson, 16.3 overs), 3–228 (Ponting, 42.1 overs), 4–263 (White, 47.2 overs), 5–266 (Hussey, 48.2 overs)

Bowling: JM Anderson 10–1–66–1; TT Bresnan 9–1–52–1; SCJ Broad 10–0–46–1; MH Yardy 9–0–49–0; GP Swann 6–0–31–1; LJ Wright 3–0–14–0; PD Collingwood 3–0–27–0

England innings

AJ Strauss	c Paine b Tait	37
C Kieswetter	b Harris	12
KP Pietersen	lbw Harris	8
PD Collingwood	lbw Smith	15
EJG Morgan	c Paine b Harris	47
MH Yardy	c White b Bollinger	57
LJ Wright	b Smith	2
TT Bresnan	c Watson b Harris	22
GP Swann	c Paine b Bollinger	1
SCJ Broad	c Hussey b Harris	4
JM Anderson	not out	0
Extras	(b 1, lb 3, w 3)	7
Total	(all out; 42.4 overs)	212

Fall of wickets: 1–37 (Kieswetter, 8.4 overs), 2–53 (Pietersen, 10.3 overs), 3–61 (Strauss, 13.2 overs), 4–90 (Collingwood, 19.2 overs), 5–140 (Morgan, 28.2 overs), 6–151 (Wright, 31.4 overs), 7–199 (Bresnan, 40.2 overs), 8–207 (Swann, 41.2 overs), 9–208 (Yardy, 41.4 overs), 10–212 (Broad, 42.4 overs)

Bowling: SW Tait 7–2–23–1; DE Bollinger 8–0–38–2; RJ Harris 8.4–1–32–5; JR Hopes 10–0–56–0; SPD Smith 9–0–59–2

Australia won by 78 runs

NatWest Series Game Five
England v Australia at Lord's

July 3, 2010 • **Toss:** Australia
Umpires: Aleem Dar (Pakistan) and NJ Llong (England)
TV umpire: RA Kettleborough (England)
Match referee: J Srinath (India)
Player of the match: SW Tait (Australia)
Player of the series: EJG Morgan (England)

Australia innings

SR Watson	c Anderson b Broad	14
TD Paine	b Swann	54
RT Ponting	c Kieswetter b Broad	15
CL White	c Yardy b Swann	20
SE Marsh	c Morgan b Swann	59
MEK Hussey	c Anderson b Broad	79
SPD Smith	c Anderson b Broad	15
JR Hopes	not out	12
RJ Harris	not out	0
Extras	(lb 3, w 6)	9
Total	(7 wickets; 50 overs)	277

Did not bat: DE Bollinger, SW Tait

Fall of wickets: 1–27 (Watson, 8.5 overs), 2–55 (Ponting, 16.6 overs), 3–104 (White, 27.2 overs), 4–106 (Paine, 29.3 overs), 5–213 (Marsh, 44.5 overs), 6–263 (Smith, 49.1 overs), 7–265 (Hussey, 49.3 overs)

Bowling: JM Anderson 10–0–75–0; TT Bresnan 10–1–48–0; SCJ Broad 10–0–64–4; LJ Wright 6–0–32–0; MH Yardy 5–0–19–0; GP Swann 8–0–32–3; PD Collingwood 1–0–4–0

England innings

AJ Strauss	b Tait	6
C Kieswetter	c Hussey b Harris	11
MH Yardy	b Tait	0
PD Collingwood	b Tait	95
EJG Morgan	c Marsh b Hopes	9
KP Pietersen	b Smith	0
LJ Wright	c Marsh b Smith	21
TT Bresnan	run out (Ponting)	34
GP Swann	c Harris b Tait	33
SCJ Broad	c&b Bollinger	3
JM Anderson	not out	5
Extras	(b 4, lb 6, w 8)	18
Total	(all out; 46.3 overs)	235

Fall of wickets: 1–14 (Strauss, 4.3 overs), 2–19 (Yardy, 4.5 overs), 3–44 (Kieswetter, 7.5 overs), 4–72 (Morgan, 15.5 overs), 5–73 (Pietersen, 16.5 overs), 6–129 (Wright, 30.2 overs), 7–194 (Bresnan, 40.4 overs), 8–194 (Collingwood, 40.6 overs), 9–229 (Broad, 45.1 overs), 10–235 (Swann, 46.3 overs)

Bowling: SW Tait 8.3–0–48–4; DE Bollinger 8–0–26–1; RJ Harris 8–1–38–1; JR Hopes 10–1–42–1; SPD Smith 10–0–49–2; MEK Hussey 2–0–22–0

Australia won by 42 runs
England won the series 3–2

AUSTRALIA TEST SERIES AVERAGES, NOVEMBER 2009–JULY 2010

Australia v West Indies in Australia 2009–10

Batting & Fielding

Batsman	Tests	Inns	NO	Runs	HS	Avge	50s	100s	Ct	St
BJ Haddin	3	5	2	225	88	75.00	2	0	14	0
SM Katich	3	5	0	302	99	60.40	3	0	2	0
SR Watson	3	5	0	263	96	52.60	2	0	5	0
MJ Clarke	3	5	1	209	71	52.25	2	0	4	0
MEK Hussey	3	5	0	235	82	47.00	2	0	5	0
NM Hauritz	3	4	2	80	50*	40.00	1	0	1	0
RT Ponting	3	5	1	136	55	34.00	1	0	1	0
MJ North	3	5	0	166	79	33.20	2	0	2	0
PM Siddle	2	2	1	20	20*	20.00	0	0	2	0
MG Johnson	3	4	0	54	35	13.50	0	0	0	0
CJ McKay	1	1	0	10	10	10.00	0	0	1	0
DE Bollinger	2	2	1	2	2*	2.00	0	0	0	0
BW Hilfenhaus	1	0	0	0	–	–	0	0	2	0

Bowling

Bowler	O	M	R	W	Best	Avge	5w	10w	SR	ER
MEK Hussey	2	0	3	1	1–3	3.00	0	0	12.00	1.50
BW Hilfenhaus	23	9	70	5	3–20	14.00	0	0	27.60	3.04
DE Bollinger	83.2	12	258	13	5–70	19.85	1	0	38.46	3.10
SR Watson	72	16	211	8	2–30	26.38	0	0	54.00	2.93
MG Johnson	110.2	17	477	17	5–103	28.06	1	0	38.94	4.33
NM Hauritz	123	21	363	11	3–17	33.00	0	0	67.09	2.95
PM Siddle	56	15	212	3	1–41	70.67	0	0	112.00	3.79
CJ McKay	28	5	101	1	1–56	101.00	0	0	168.00	3.61
MJ North	21	3	62	0	–	–	0	0	–	2.95

Australia v Pakistan in Australia 2009–10

Batting & Fielding

Batsman	Tests	Inns	NO	Runs	HS	Avge	50s	100s	Ct	St
SR Watson	3	6	1	346	120*	69.20	2	1	6	0
MEK Hussey	3	6	2	267	134*	66.75	1	1	3	0
MJ Clarke	3	5	1	255	166	63.75	0	1	5	0
RT Ponting	3	6	0	378	209	63.00	2	1	3	0
SM Katich	2	4	0	211	100	52.75	1	1	2	0
PM Siddle	3	2	1	39	38	39.00	0	0	1	0
NM Hauritz	3	5	1	120	75	30.00	1	0	1	0
PJ Hughes	1	2	0	37	37	18.50	0	0	0	0
MG Johnson	3	5	0	71	38	14.20	0	0	2	0
BJ Haddin	3	5	0	70	41	14.00	0	0	17	1
MJ North	3	4	0	41	21	10.25	0	0	2	0
DE Bollinger	3	2	0	9	9	4.50	0	0	2	0

Bowling

Bowler	O	M	R	W	Best	Avge	5w	10w	SR	ER
SM Katich	15	4	57	3	3–34	19.00	0	0	30.00	3.80
DE Bollinger	96.5	29	262	12	4–72	21.83	0	0	48.42	2.72
NM Hauritz	122.4	26	415	18	5–53	23.06	2	0	40.89	3.39
SR Watson	54	13	125	5	2–38	25.00	0	0	64.80	2.31
MG Johnson	111	26	308	12	3–27	25.67	0	0	55.50	2.77
PM Siddle	98.2	32	262	8	3–25	32.75	0	0	73.75	2.67

Australia v New Zealand in New Zealand 2009–10

Batting & Fielding

Batsman	Tests	Inns	NO	Runs	HS	Avge	50s	100s	Ct	St
PJ Hughes	1	2	1	106	86*	106.00	1	0	0	0
MJ North	2	3	1	211	112*	105.50	1	1	3	0
SM Katich	2	4	1	291	106	97.00	2	1	1	0
MJ Clarke	2	3	0	259	168	86.33	1	1	3	0
SR Watson	1	2	0	77	65	38.50	1	0	0	0
BJ Haddin	2	3	1	71	48	35.50	0	0	9	0
MEK Hussey	2	3	0	93	67	31.00	1	0	2	0
RJ Harris	2	2	1	28	18*	28.00	0	0	1	0
RT Ponting	2	3	0	69	41	23.00	0	0	6	0
DE Bollinger	2	1	0	4	4	4.00	0	0	0	0
MG Johnson	2	2	0	0	0	0.00	0	0	0	0
NM Hauritz	2	2	2	53	41*	–	0	0	0	0

Bowling

Bowler	O	M	R	W	Best	Avge	5w	10w	SR	ER
DE Bollinger	70	12	252	12	5–28	21.00	1	0	35.00	3.60
RJ Harris	70.3	13	207	9	4–77	23.00	0	0	47.00	2.94
MG Johnson	77.1	20	277	12	6–73	23.08	1	1	38.58	3.59
MJ Clarke	16	4	27	1	1–27	27.00	0	0	96.00	1.69
NM Hauritz	93	26	263	4	3–119	65.75	0	0	139.50	2.83
MJ North	11	5	15	0	–	–	0	0	–	1.36
SR Watson	11	3	48	0	–	–	0	0	–	4.36

Australia v Pakistan in England 2010

Batting & Fielding

Batsman	Tests	Inns	NO	Runs	HS	Avge	50s	100s	Ct	St
SM Katich	2	4	0	187	83	46.75	2	0	1	0
MJ Clarke	2	4	0	139	77	34.75	1	0	2	0
TD Paine	2	4	0	104	47	26.00	0	0	11	1
BW Hilfenhaus	2	4	1	77	56*	25.67	1	0	0	0
SPD Smith	2	4	0	100	77	25.00	1	0	1	0
RT Ponting	2	4	0	98	66	24.50	1	0	2	0
MEK Hussey	2	4	1	69	56*	23.00	1	0	3	0
SR Watson	2	4	0	64	31	16.00	0	0	2	0
DE Bollinger	2	4	2	27	21	13.50	0	0	0	0
MG Johnson	2	4	0	45	30	11.25	0	0	1	0
MJ North	2	4	0	36	20	9.00	0	0	3	0

Bowling

Bowler	O	M	R	W	Best	Avge	5w	10w	SR	ER
MJ North	18.1	1	55	6	6–55	9.17	1	0	18.17	3.04
SR Watson	29.5	5	117	11	6–33	10.64	2	0	16.27	3.97
BW Hilfenhaus	61.5	15	190	8	3–39	23.75	0	0	46.38	3.09
SPD Smith	31	7	82	3	3–51	27.33	0	0	62.00	2.65
DE Bollinger	53	13	182	5	3–51	36.40	0	0	63.60	3.43
MG Johnson	53.4	8	217	3	1–31	72.33	0	0	107.33	4.06

AUSTRALIA ODI TOURNAMENT AND SERIES AVERAGES, SEPTEMBER 2009–JULY 2010

ICC Champions Trophy

Batting & Fielding

Batsman	ODIs	Inns	NO	Runs	HS	Avge	50s	100s	Ct	St
SR Watson	5	5	2	265	136*	88.33	0	2	0	0
MG Johnson	5	2	1	82	73*	82.00	1	0	2	0
RT Ponting	5	5	1	288	111*	72.00	2	1	2	0
B Lee	5	2	1	37	25	37.00	0	0	0	0
MEK Hussey	5	4	0	148	67	37.00	2	0	2	0
CL White	5	4	1	106	62	35.33	1	0	1	0
TD Paine	5	5	0	123	56	24.60	1	0	8	1
CJ Ferguson	5	3	1	29	20	14.50	0	0	0	0
JR Hopes	5	3	1	28	22*	14.00	0	0	2	0
NM Hauritz	5	2	2	16	9*	–	0	0	2	0
PM Siddle	5	0	0	0	–	–	0	0	0	0

Bowling

Bowler	O	M	R	W	Best	Avge	4w	SR	ER
NM Hauritz	30.5	1	116	5	3–37	23.20	0	37.00	3.80
PM Siddle	33	2	146	6	3–55	24.33	0	33.00	4.42
SR Watson	33.4	1	151	6	2–32	25.17	0	33.67	4.52
B Lee	37	1	162	6	2–45	27.00	0	37.00	4.38
MG Johnson	40	2	185	4	2–45	46.25	0	60.00	4.62
JR Hopes	20	1	105	2	1–27	52.50	0	60.00	5.25

Australia v India 2009

Batting & Fielding

Batsman	ODIs	Inns	NO	Runs	HS	Avge	50s	100s	Ct	St
MEK Hussey	6	6	3	313	81*	104.33	3	0	1	0
RT Ponting	6	6	0	267	74	44.50	3	0	1	0
SR Watson	6	6	0	256	93	42.67	1	0	4	0
CL White	6	6	0	218	62	36.33	3	0	2	0
SE Marsh	4	4	0	144	112	36.00	0	1	0	0
TD Paine	2	2	0	58	50	29.00	1	0	3	0
AC Voges	5	4	1	79	36	26.33	0	0	1	0
MG Johnson	5	4	2	52	21	26.00	0	0	1	0
BW Hilfenhaus	2	1	0	16	16	16.00	0	0	3	0
JR Hopes	1	1	0	14	14	14.00	0	0	0	0
MC Henriques	2	2	0	18	12	9.00	0	0	0	0
GA Manou	4	1	0	7	7	7.00	0	0	5	0
PM Siddle	4	2	0	4	3	2.00	0	0	0	0
DE Bollinger	4	1	0	0	0	0.00	0	0	2	0
B Lee	1	1	0	0	0	0.00	0	0	1	0
NM Hauritz	6	2	2	39	30*	–	0	0	3	0
CJ McKay	2	0	0	0	–	–	0	0	0	0

Bowling

Bowler	O	M	R	W	Best	Avge	4w	SR	ER
DE Bollinger	39	6	174	9	5–35	19.33	1	26.00	4.46
SR Watson	39.2	1	220	10	3–29	22.00	0	23.60	5.61
B Lee	6	0	28	1	1–28	28.00	0	36.00	4.67
MG Johnson	47.2	3	290	9	3–39	32.22	0	31.56	6.14
CJ McKay	20	1	103	3	3–59	34.33	0	40.00	5.15
NM Hauritz	52	4	229	4	2–31	57.25	0	78.00	4.40
BW Hilfenhaus	20	0	155	2	1–72	77.50	0	60.00	7.75
PM Siddle	34	2	166	2	1–55	83.00	0	102.00	4.88
MC Henriques	15	0	84	1	1–51	84.00	0	90.00	5.60
AC Voges	15	0	91	1	1–22	91.00	0	90.00	6.07
JR Hopes	2	0	10	0	–	–	0	–	5.00
MEK Hussey	3	0	26	0	–	–	0	–	8.66

Australia v Pakistan 2009–10

Batting & Fielding

Batsman	ODIs	Inns	NO	Runs	HS	Avge	50s	100s	Ct	St
MEK Hussey	5	5	2	220	67	73.33	1	0	1	0
NM Hauritz	5	4	3	72	53*	72.00	1	0	5	0
CL White	5	5	0	245	105	49.00	1	1	5	0
MJ Clarke	4	4	0	173	80	43.25	2	0	2	0
BJ Haddin	5	5	3	74	32	37.00	0	0	16	1
SR Watson	3	3	0	107	69	35.67	1	0	1	0
SE Marsh	5	5	0	176	83	35.20	1	0	1	0
RT Ponting	5	5	0	125	55	25.00	1	0	2	0
AC Voges	1	1	0	24	24	24.00	0	0	0	0
MG Johnson	1	1	0	13	13	13.00	0	0	1	0
JR Hopes	2	2	0	22	16	11.00	0	0	0	0
RJ Harris	3	2	1	6	4	6.00	0	0	0	0
CJ McKay	5	1	1	0	0*	–	0	0	0	0
DE Bollinger	3	0	0	0	–	–	0	0	0	0
PM Siddle	3	0	0	0	–	–	0	0	0	0

Bowling

Bowler	O	M	R	W	Best	Avge	4w	SR	ER
RJ Harris	29.5	4	106	13	5–19	8.15	2	13.77	3.59
CJ McKay	43	6	175	14	4–35	12.50	1	18.43	4.07
SR Watson	22	0	112	6	4–36	18.67	1	22.00	5.09
MG Johnson	10	1	42	2	2–42	21.00	0	30.00	4.20
DE Bollinger	27.4	1	91	4	2–19	22.75	0	41.50	3.32
PM Siddle	22	2	102	3	2–31	34.00	0	44.00	4.64
NM Hauritz	41.4	0	236	4	2–45	59.00	0	62.50	5.70
MJ Clarke	7	0	28	0	–	–	0	–	4.00
JR Hopes	17	1	68	0	–	–	0	–	4.00
MEK Hussey	2	0	12	0	–	–	0	–	6.00

Australia v West Indies 2009–10

Batting & Fielding

Batsman	ODIs	Inns	NO	Runs	HS	Avge	50s	100s	Ct	St
RT Ponting	5	5	1	295	106	73.75	2	1	1	0
JR Hopes	3	3	1	129	57*	64.50	1	0	0	0
SR Watson	4	4	0	189	59	47.25	3	0	1	0
MJ Clarke	4	4	1	138	47	46.00	0	0	3	0
AC Voges	3	3	1	69	45*	34.50	0	0	0	0
MEK Hussey	4	3	0	95	44	31.67	0	0	2	0
CL White	5	4	0	124	63	31.00	1	0	1	0
SE Marsh	2	2	0	47	27	23.50	0	0	2	0
RJ Harris	4	3	2	23	21	23.00	0	0	1	0
TD Paine	2	2	0	40	24	20.00	0	0	2	0
BJ Haddin	3	2	0	40	32	20.00	0	0	6	1
MG Johnson	4	3	1	30	21	15.00	0	0	3	0
NM Hauritz	4	2	1	8	6*	8.00	0	0	1	0
DE Bollinger	5	1	1	0	0*	–	0	0	0	0
CJ McKay	2	0	0	0	–	–	0	0	0	0
SPD Smith	1	0	0	0	–	–	0	0	2	0

Bowling

Bowler	O	M	R	W	Best	Avge	4w	SR	ER
DE Bollinger	32	7	125	11	4–28	11.36	1	17.45	3.91
RJ Harris	26	3	114	7	3–24	16.29	0	22.29	4.38
CJ McKay	14.4	2	68	3	2–33	22.67	0	29.33	4.72
NM Hauritz	26.2	1	120	5	3–28	24.00	0	31.60	4.58
SR Watson	12	1	55	2	1–24	27.50	0	36.00	4.58
JR Hopes	12	1	66	2	1–27	33.00	0	36.00	5.50
SPD Smith	9.5	0	78	2	2–78	39.00	0	29.50	8.21
MG Johnson	25	0	122	3	1–31	40.67	0	50.00	4.88
AC Voges	4	0	17	0	–	–	0	–	4.25

Chappell-Hadlee Trophy 2009–10

Batting & Fielding

Batsman	ODIs	Inns	NO	Runs	HS	Avge	50s	100s	Ct	St
CL White	5	5	2	168	54	56.00	2	0	3	0
MEK Hussey	5	5	1	198	59	49.50	2	0	4	0
MG Johnson	5	3	2	43	21*	43.00	0	0	1	0
BJ Haddin	5	5	0	192	110	38.40	1	1	9	0
SR Watson	5	5	0	192	53	38.40	1	0	4	0
JR Hopes	5	3	0	102	40	34.00	0	0	1	0
RT Ponting	5	5	0	164	69	32.80	2	0	4	0
AC Voges	3	3	1	52	34	26.00	0	0	0	0
MJ Clarke	2	2	0	33	22	16.50	0	0	0	0
NM Hauritz	5	2	0	13	9	6.50	0	0	1	0
CJ McKay	1	1	0	2	2	2.00	0	0	0	0
DE Bollinger	5	1	1	1	1*	–	0	0	2	0
RJ Harris	4	1	1	0	0*	–	0	0	2	0

Bowling

Bowler	O	M	R	W	Best	Avge	4w	SR	ER
MG Johnson	46.3	3	220	12	4–51	18.33	1	23.25	4.75
SR Watson	34	3	171	8	2–26	21.38	0	25.50	5.03
RJ Harris	32.2	2	176	8	3–34	22.00	0	24.25	5.47
CJ McKay	10	1	57	2	2–57	28.50	0	30.00	5.70
NM Hauritz	33	0	185	6	3–46	30.83	0	33.00	5.61
JR Hopes	36	0	184	4	2–38	46.00	0	54.00	5.11
DE Bollinger	39.2	3	231	4	2–58	57.75	0	59.00	5.89
MJ Clarke	2	0	8	0	–	–	0	–	4.00

NatWest Series 2010

Batting & Fielding

Batsman	ODIs	Inns	NO	Runs	HS	Avge	50s	100s	Ct	St
MJ Clarke	4	4	2	220	99*	110.00	2	0	0	0
SE Marsh	1	1	0	59	59	59.00	1	0	2	0
SR Watson	5	5	0	205	61	41.00	2	0	1	0
CL White	5	5	1	145	86*	36.25	1	0	1	0
SPD Smith	4	4	1	94	41	31.33	0	0	0	0
TD Paine	5	5	0	148	54	29.60	1	0	8	0
RT Ponting	5	5	0	144	92	28.80	1	0	3	0
MEK Hussey	5	5	0	143	79	28.60	1	0	2	0
NM Hauritz	2	2	1	22	22	22.00	0	0	1	0
JR Hopes	5	4	1	61	34	20.33	0	0	2	0
DE Bollinger	5	1	0	3	3	3.00	0	0	1	0
RJ Harris	4	3	2	1	1	1.00	0	0	1	0
CJ McKay	1	0	0	0	–	–	0	0	0	0
JR Hazlewood	1	0	0	0	–	–	0	0	0	0
SW Tait	3	1	1	1	1*	–	0	0	1	0

Bowling

Bowler	O	M	R	W	Best	Avge	4w	SR	ER
SW Tait	25.3	3	99	8	4–48	12.38	1	19.13	3.91
RJ Harris	35.4	4	171	10	5–32	17.10	1	21.40	4.83
DE Bollinger	45	5	178	9	3–20	19.78	0	30.00	3.96
SPD Smith	36	0	182	7	2–34	26.00	0	30.86	5.06
SR Watson	11	1	64	2	2–55	32.00	0	33.00	5.82
JR Hazlewood	7	0	41	1	1–41	41.00	0	42.00	5.86
NM Hauritz	18	0	100	1	1–56	100.00	0	108.00	5.56
JR Hopes	36.1	1	202	2	1–30	101.00	0	108.50	5.60
MJ Clarke	4	0	25	0	–	–	0	–	6.25
CJ McKay	9.2	0	60	0	–	–	0	–	6.52
MEK Hussey	2	0	22	0	–	–	0	–	11.00

A VERY GOOD YEAR

By any measure, the Australian cricket teams' 2009–10 campaigns were productive ones. The period described in this book comes to almost 12 months – from the ICC Champions Trophy that began in mid September to the Test series against Pakistan in England that concluded at the end of July – and in that time Ricky Ponting's Test and one-day international teams put together impressive runs, reviving memories of the great days of the early and mid 2000s.

That the Australians had one of their most successful seasons is borne out in the statistics. For the purpose of comparison, we shall consider the cricket year as running from September 1 to August 31 – a natural divide given that most northern hemisphere series end towards the end of August – with any series that crossed both August and September put completely in one year or the other, and on this basis there have been only four 'years' (out of 31) since the end of World Series Cricket in 1979 where Australia remained unbeaten in Test cricket. The end of WSC is used as a divide, because it was from then that bulk ODIs became part of the global cricket landscape. These unbeaten years were 1987–88, 1991–92 and 2006–07, when Australia played only five Test matches each year (the first Test of the series in Sri Lanka in August-September, which Australian won, being considered part of 1992–93), and the remarkable 2005–06 year, when a great Australian team with stars from top to tail won 11 of 12 Tests, with the other game drawn.

In 2009–10, the year described in this book, Australia played 10 Tests – against the West Indies, Pakistan and New Zealand – and won eight of them, with one loss and one draw. This win rate of 80 per cent for the year has been bettered only four times by Australia since WSC – in 1995–96, when the Aussies won five from six; in 2002–03, when they won 12 from 14; in 2005–06, when the Aussies won 11 of 12 Tests; and in 2006–07, when they won five from five – and equalled once.

In ODI cricket, the Australians won 29 of 39 matches (including two 'no results') from September 4 to July 3, the date of the final game in this year's one-day series in the UK. This tally includes the seven-game NatWest series that was played against England in early September 2009, which was won by Australia 6–1 at the end of last year's Ashes tour, but even if you omit those games that still gives the 2009–10 Australians a win-rate of 76.67 per cent, which compares very favourably with most years since WSC. Only five times since 1979 has Australia achieved a win-rate greater than that figure.

The Australian Test and ODI teams performances each year since WSC are summarised in the accompanying table.

AUSTRALIA'S WINNING PERCENTAGES IN TESTS AND ODIS 1979–2010

	Tests						ODIs					
Season	P	W	L	D	T	Win%	P	W	L	T	NR	Win%
1979–80	16	3	5	8	0	18.75	10	3	7	0	0	30.00
1980–81	12	4	4	4	0	33.33	17	11	5	0	1	68.75
1981–82	9	4	3	2	0	44.44	17	7	10	0	0	41.18
1982–83	9	3	4	2	0	33.33	26	9	14	0	3	39.13
1983–84	10	2	3	5	0	20.00	17	6	9	1	1	37.50
1984–85	11	2	6	3	0	18.18	26	12	12	0	2	50.00
1985–86	9	1	3	5	0	11.11	17	10	6	0	1	62.50
1986–87	8	1	2	4	1	12.50	22	7	14	0	1	33.33
1987–88	5	2	0	3	0	40.00	19	17	2	0	0	89.47
1988–89	14	5	4	5	0	35.71	15	7	7	1	0	46.67
1989–90	7	2	1	4	0	28.57	24	18	6	0	0	75.00
1990–91	10	4	2	4	0	40.00	15	13	2	0	0	86.67
1991–92	5	4	0	1	0	80.00	21	12	8	0	1	75.00
1992–93	17	7	4	6	0	41.18	18	11	6	1	0	60.00
1993–94	9	4	2	3	0	44.44	22	13	9	0	0	59.09
1994–95	12	5	3	4	0	41.67	22	13	9	0	0	59.09
1995–96	6	5	1	0	0	83.33	17	12	5	0	0	70.59
1996–97	15	8	6	1	0	53.33	27	9	18	0	0	33.33
1997–98	9	4	2	3	0	44.44	25	14	11	0	0	56.00
1998–99	12	6	3	3	0	50.00	38	26	10	2	0	68.42
1999–00	13	10	1	2	0	76.92	25	18	5	1	1	75.00
2000–01	13	10	3	0	0	76.92	22	18	4	0	0	81.81
2001–02	9	5	1	3	0	55.56	18	10	7	1	0	55.55
2002–03	14	12	2	0	0	85.71	39	33	5	0	1	86.84
2003–04	11	7	1	3	0	63.64	27	21	4	0	2	84.00
2004–05	17	10	3	4	0	58.82	29	20	6	1	2	74.07
2005–06	12	11	0	1	0	91.67	25	18	7	0	0	72.00
2006–07	5	5	0	0	0	100.00	34	25	8	0	1	75.76
2007–08	9	6	1	2	0	66.67	25	16	6	0	3	72.73
2008–09	17	6	7	4	0	35.29	24	12	11	0	1	52.17
2009–10	10	8	1	1	0	80.00	39	29	8	0	2	78.37
Totals	335	166	78	90	1	49.55	722	450	241	8	23	64.38

Notes

Each year is considered as being from September 1 to August 31 with the following exceptions (where a series or tournament ran over August-September):

- Sri Lanka Tests and ODIs in August-September 1992 are included in 1992–93
- The ODI tournament in Sri Lanka in August-September 1996 is included in 1996–97
- The Tri-Nations ODI tournament in Kenya in August-September 2002 is included in 2002–03
- The fifth Ashes Test of 2005, which was played in early September, is included in 2004–05
- The Bangladesh ODIs played in August-September 2008 are included in 2008–09

Test win-rate (win%) is calculated by dividing wins by games played; ODI win-rate (win%) is calculated by dividing wins by games played that ended in a result

PHOTOGRAPHS

The images that appear in the photo sections of *The Captain's Year* come from the libraries of Getty Images, AFP and Gallo Images. The photographers whose work appears in the book are Hamish Blair, Robert Cianflone, Mark Dadswell, Duif du Toit, Stu Forster, Gianluigi Guercia, Julian Herbert, Alexander Joe, Bradley Kanaris, Paul Kane, Mark Kolbe, Matthew Lewis, Marty Melville, Kenneth O'Halloran, Ryan Pierse, Robert Prezioso, Dibyangshu Sarkar, Tom Shaw, Prakash Singh, Cameron Spencer, Brendon Thorne and Phil Walter.

Getty Images: Section 1 – page 1 (bottom), page 2 (top), page 3 (both), page 4 (all), page 5 (all), page 6 (both), page 7 (both), page 8 (both); Section 2 – page 1 (both), page 2 (all), page 3 (both), page 4 (all), page 5 (both), page 6 (all), page 7 (both), page 8 (both); Section 3 – page 1 (all), page 2 (all), page 3 (top left & right, bottom right), page 4 (all), page 5 (both), page 6 (all), page 7 (all), page 8 (all); pages 290, 292, 294, 296, 298.
AFP/Getty Images: Section 1 – page 1 (top); Section 3 – page 3 (bottom left).
Gallo Images/Getty Images: Section 1 – page 2 (bottom)

Chapter Openers
Page 1: The Australians at the presentation after winning the ICC Champions Trophy at Centurion, October 5, 2009 (AFP/Getty Images).
Page 23: Ricky Ponting during India's innings in the third ODI at Delhi, October 31, 2009 (AFP/Getty Images).
Page 45: Ponting and Shane Watson celebrate after India's Yuvraj Singh is dismissed in the fifth ODI at Hyderabad, November 5, 2009 (AFP/Getty Images).
Page 65: Marcus North (left), bowler Mike Hussey (centre) and Ponting celebrate the dismissal of the West Indies' Dwayne Bravo during the first Test at the Gabba, November 28, 2009 (Getty Images).
Page 103: Ponting leaves the WACA with team physio Alex Kountouris after retiring hurt during the first day of the third Test against the West Indies, December 16, 2009 (Getty Images).
Page 121: Ponting tries to hook during Australia's second innings of the first Test against Pakistan at the MCG, December 28, 2009 (Getty Images).
Page 143: TV commentator Mark Nicholas (far left), Ponting, Pakistan captain Mohammad Yousuf and match referee Ranjan Madugalle at the toss before the second Test at Sydney, January 3, 2010 (Getty Images).
Page 163: Ponting reaches his century at Hobart during the first day's play of the third Test against Pakistan, January 14, 2010 (Getty Images).
Page 181: Sachin Tendulkar after scoring a century in the fifth ODI against Australia at Hyderabad, November 5, 2009 (Getty Images).
Page 191: Ponting during his innings of 57 not out in the second ODI against the West Indies at Adelaide, February 9, 2010 (Getty Images).
Page 217: The Australians walk off Eden Park after winning game two of the Chappell-Hadlee series, March 6, 2010 (Getty Images).
Page 263: Ponting with a replica Ashes urn after Australia regained the Ashes in Perth, December 18, 2006 (Getty Images).
Page 299: Ponting congratulates Steve Smith after Smith dismissed Pakistan's Umar Gul at Lord's, with Tim Paine running in, July 16, 2010 (Getty Images).
Page 321: Ponting at the WACA with the Frank Worrell Trophy, December 20, 2009 (Getty Images)

Thank you for reading *The Captain's Year*. I hope you have enjoyed it and gained a few insights into what goes on in the Australian cricket team, and I particularly hope you enjoyed reading my Ashes Preview. It's certainly going to be a huge Ashes summer for all of us and I am looking at it as the most important series I'll ever play in.

Throughout the Tests, I am going to continue to dedicate every run that I score to the challenge of helping children with cancer and their families. The Ponting Foundation successfully launched the RUN RICKY RUN fundraising program in time for the 2009 Ashes series in England and since then we have had literally thousands of people from all over the world sponsoring me for an amount of money for every run that I score.

RUN RICKY RUN will be even bigger and better for the 2010–11 Ashes, with a number of great Australian companies joining up with so many individual sponsors and donors, plus State Governments from around Australia to help the Ponting Foundation make a significant difference to the cancer journey of Australian children and their families. Every dollar raised this summer will be distributed back into your home state to support various childhood cancer projects. So it's up to me to score as many runs as I can – to achieve the best possible result on and off the field.

I'd be honoured to have you join me out in the middle every time I bat this summer. Donations can be as small as 20 cents-per-run, or you might prefer to make a set donation.

Thanks

All the information you need is available at our Foundation website www.pontingfoundation.com.au or you can donate direct at:

www.runrickyrun.org